Negotiating with the Chinese Communists:
The United States Experience, 1953-1967

Negotiating with the Chinese Communists: The United States Experience, 1953-1967

KENNETH T. YOUNG

A VOLUME IN THE SERIES
"THE UNITED STATES AND CHINA IN WORLD AFFAIRS"

PUBLISHED FOR THE COUNCIL ON FOREIGN RELATIONS BY THE

McGRAW-HILL BOOK COMPANY

New York · Toronto · London · Sydney

The Council on Foreign Relations is a nonprofit institution devoted to the study of political, economic, and strategic problems as related to American foreign policy. It takes no stand, expressed or implied, on American policy.

The authors of books published under the auspices of the Council are responsible for their statements of fact and expressions of opinion. The Council is responsible only for determining that they should be presented to the public.

NEGOTIATING WITH THE CHINESE COMMUNISTS:
THE UNITED STATES EXPERIENCE, 1953–1967

Copyright © 1968 by Council on Foreign Relations, Inc. All Rights Reserved. Printed in the United States of America. This book, or parts thereof, may not be reproduced in any form without permission of the publishers.

Library of Congress Catalog Card Number: 67-28088

First Edition   72330

To the patience of one family
and the profession of all diplomacy

Foreword

This is the seventh volume in the series on The United States and China in World Affairs, which is being sponsored by the Council on Foreign Relations through a generous grant from the Ford Foundation. In supporting this research program, the Council seeks to encourage more active and better informed considerations of one of the most important areas of foreign policy for the United States.

The Council program was under the able direction of Robert Blum until his untimely death, and it was he who envisaged the total project, arranged for the authors of the separate studies, and counseled them during the formative stages of their work. The appearance now of the completed studies constitutes appropriate memorials to his deep concern for a more enlightened public understanding of Asia.

This project, which has been guided by a Steering Committee under the chairmanship of Allen W. Dulles, has not sought to produce any single set of conclusions on a subject as complex as that of America's relations with China. Each study in the series, therefore, constitutes a separate and self-contained inquiry written on the responsibility of the author, who has reached his own judgments and conclusions regarding the subject of his investigations and its implications for United States policy. The list of authors includes persons with a variety of backgrounds in Chinese affairs and foreign policy. Some have had long personal experience in China. Others have studied China and Far Eastern problems during recent years or dealt with them as officials and administrators. In each case, they have been able to consult with a group of qualified persons invited by the Council on Foreign Relations to meet periodically with them.

The charge has often been made that a great chasm has come to separate Communist China and the United States and that regardless of Chinese attitudes the United States should be doing more to establish bridges of communications. It is said that we should not contribute to the isolation of the largest country in the world and that we should recognize the reality of Communist China and seek a dialogue with the rulers of Peking.

Others have sought to answer these charges against American policy by citing the record of our protracted negotiations and talks with the Chinese first at Panmunjom and Geneva and now at Warsaw. As a result of over 130 sessions of ambassadorial talks, the United States government has had more contacts with the Peking rulers than any other non-Communist government in the world. And it is further argued that the privacy of these talks may provide a more conducive environment for working toward constructive and accurate communication than the more dramatic and publicized approaches suggested by impatient champions of "doing something" for better understanding.

In planning the China Project, the Steering Committee felt that it might be useful to sponsor a study, based entirely on the public record, to see what might be done to make this channel of communication more useful in the years ahead. In seeking someone qualified to take on this assignment, which would require disciplined speculation and the careful marshalling of limited facts, we were fortunate to interest Ambassador Kenneth T. Young, who is currently President of the Asia Society and outside of government but who was personally involved in negotiating with the Chinese at both Panmunjom and Geneva.

Many readers may be disappointed with the story of our contacts with the Chinese Communists, for they may feel that little or nothing has come out of all these meetings, which have become to a degree stylized and bound by their own rituals. Yet, as Ambassador Young suggests, the talks have been worthwhile even if the direct results seem to be so meager. And since some day in the future they may perhaps play a more critical role in our relations with China, it would be well for all Americans concerned with China policy to know as much as possible about the history, style, and machinery of what are now referred to as the Ambassadorial Talks. In providing us with the first book on this subject, Ambassador Young has done a great public service.

LUCIAN W. PYE, *Director*
The United States and China
in World Affairs

Preface

This book is the story of United States negotiations and contacts with the People's Republic of China since the Korean armistice of July 1953. The full story has never been told before and is difficult to tell now, for the official record of most of these negotiations and contacts is still secret. The United States government cannot make it available for publication or study by writers and scholars.

In the research and composition of this book, my sources have been public or published material—primarily statements of American and Chinese Communist officials, newspaper and magazine articles, and references in a number of books dealing with the Chinese question or issues between the United States and the People's Republic of China. I have attempted to piece together the information in all these secondary sources to give at least an initial version of the circumstances, procedures, and substance of these negotiations and contacts. Naturally, there are gaps and perhaps inaccuracies in my treatment. Only the eventual publication of the diplomatic record and access to the documents and primary sources will eliminate these.

Under such circumstances, one might ask whether it is worthwhile trying to tell the story at all until the official record is declassified. My answer is that I have found, after considerable effort, sufficient material to provide a fairly reliable, generalized account of the negotiations and contacts. Although the exact details and the specific content of each secret meeting and undisclosed negotiation are not apparent from the public sources, the scope and nature of the negotiations and contacts do appear in broad outline.

To follow the drift and significance of this story, I have also drawn upon my recollections of my own participation in several aspects of these negotiations as an official of the Department of State until late 1963. In addition, I have informally consulted some of my former colleagues who have participated in the process of negotiating with the People's Republic of China, and they have assisted me greatly by calling attention to public citations and published interpretations of many aspects of Washington's dealings with Peking since 1953.

In preparing this study, I was assisted by a study group which the Council on Foreign Relations organized for me. Robert Murphy was its chairman, and its members included Robert Blum, Arthur Dean, Dr. John M. H. Lindbeck, John J. McCloy, Professor Philip E. Mosely, Joseph E. Slater, and Professor C. Martin Wilbur. Ralph Clough, who was an American participant in these negotiations, gave me the benefit of his personal opinions while he was at the Center for International Studies at Harvard during 1965–66. Before his unfortunate and untimely death, Robert Blum, the first director of the Council's project on The United States and China in World Affairs, was particularly helpful in reading over the first draft of my chapters and in advising me on many occasions. His successor, Professor Lucian Pye, of the Massachusetts Institute of Technology, has also helped me very much.

I could not have continued the complex and arduous task of finding and correlating the minutiae of public sources if it had not been for the constant encouragement of Allen Dulles, chairman of the Steering Committee for the Council's project, and Hamilton Fish Armstrong, of the Council on Foreign Relations.

I am also indebted to David Albright for his able help in gathering material for me, and to Mrs. Sylvia Sinanian and Robert Valkenier for skillful and painstaking editing of the manuscript. This study could never have been completed if it had not been for the cheerful and invaluable cooperation first of Miss Florence Thompson, who spent many evenings and weekends typing and proofreading the early drafts of this manuscript, and then Miss Gerry Crosland who finished them.

A word of explanation about the terminology employed in this book is needed. In general, I have referred to the "People's Republic of China (P.R.C.)" or "Chinese People's Republic (C.P.R.)" because these are the designations which have been used in the official negotiations at Panmunjom, Geneva, and Warsaw. But from time to time, I have used the phrase "Chinese Communists" for variation and simplicity. In addition, I have used the words "Peking" and "Washington" to mean the governments of the respective countries in order to save space and not to be limited to one designation.

There is also the question of what to call the relationship which has existed between Washington and Peking since 1953. Is it a talk, conversation, contact, negotiation, or relation in any diplomatic sense? This study concerns all these, but primarily in the specific context of what the United States government and the government of the People's Republic of China commonly refer to as the "Ambassadorial Talks." In fact, most of the book attempts to tell the story of more than a decade of these Talks.

I should explain, in addition, that the telling of this story is complicated not only by the unavailability of the actual record of American negotiations and conversations with the Chinese Communists but also by the intermingling of many different subjects over the course of the years. A number of these topics have remained active issues for more than ten years, and others have not. As a result, chronological treatment of every subject for a year or so in each chapter would fragment the story far too much; on the other hand, narrating the development of each major theme separately, chapter by chapter, would cover the same time span repetitiously and lose the total atmosphere of the negotiations as well as the interrelationship of the subjects themselves. Hence, I have compromised between the chronological and topical treatment.

Chapters 1 and 2 summarize the whole story of the origins and development of the negotiations and contacts. Chapter 3 concentrates on the only agreement concluded between Washington and Peking—the nonfulfillment of which has been a source of American complaint at almost every meeting with the Chinese Communists since 1955. Chapters 4 and 5 describe the proposals which Peking and, to some extent, Washington made in 1956 and 1957. Chapters 6 through 8 analyze the role of the Ambassadorial Talks in the critical Taiwan crisis of 1958. Chapters 9 and 10 cover exchanges of views between Washington and Peking from 1959 to 1966—exchanges which are not generally known to the public. Chapter 11 is a brief summary of official and private American efforts during 1959–66 to break the barriers to travel and personal contacts which exist between the United States and Communist China. The last chapters contain analytical assessments and evaluations.

KENNETH T. YOUNG

New York, N.Y.
June 1967

Contents

APPENDICES

"What a business this has been in China! So far we have got on by being honest and naive. I do not clearly see where we are to come the delayed cropper."

John Hay to Henry Adams
November 2, 1900.

"In the Empire at the Center of the World, the matter of what the West may think is of no concern to anyone."

Jules Roy, *Journey Through China* (1966).

PART I

The Setting

CHAPTER ONE

The Eagle and the Dragon: Contact and Impasse

If the most powerful country and the most populous country in the world could not have a normal diplomatic relationship, they would have to invent a substitute. And they have. For twelve years the United States and the Chinese People's Republic have dealt directly with each other by means of their special, if obscure, arrangement known as the Ambassadorial Talks, held at irregular intervals more than 130 times since 1955, first in Geneva and then in Warsaw. The two countries have had only two points of direct contact for dealing with each other—the Seventh Fleet in Asia and the Ambassadorial Talks in Europe—an odd but logical combination. Although by mutual understanding the official record of the Talks is kept secret, it is possible to write about their dealings. Official statements in Washington and Peking together with news reports in both countries provide material for describing the "longest established permanent floating diplomatic game" in modern history. Because the United States had no bilateral discussions with Peking during three international conferences also attended by the Chinese People's Republic, the principal American dealings with Peking have taken place in the Ambassadorial Talks. It is time to narrate and appraise these important and unusual dealings.*

The Talks are a distinctive paradox, virtually empty of results but full of consequences. They have provided Washington with more continuous diplomatic contact and diversified dialogue with the government in Peking than any of the non-Communist Western

---

* The source material and citations for the descriptions, inferences, and interpretations of the Talks contained in this summary chapter are not enumerated here but appear in later chapters.

governments with embassies there. Yet, despite the long duration and voluminous exchange, the net result has been one agreement in twelve years. In fact, nineteen specific proposals known to have been submitted by one or the other have been publicly rejected. Nevertheless, this forum has proved to be of some lasting value. It is better than a final split—diplomatic or military. Washington and Peking can at least meet across the conference table rather than the bomb line, to find shock-absorbers for adjusting the total antithesis existing between them.

This diplomatic arrangement has become a workable and essential channel for reducing miscalculations, clarifying intentions, and explaining proposals. The President of the United States has a dependable and rapid "switchboard" immediately available to talk with the Politburo in Peking about Vietnam, nuclear disarmament, improving relations, or anything else. The responsible leaders in Peking have the same facility in reverse when they choose to use it. The Ambassadorial Talks have indeed provided each government with an essential "diplomatic radar" to pick up the key emphasis and slight nuances in official expressions passed across the tables in the privacy of the conference room. Consequently, the cumulative experience of the American and Communist Chinese Ambassadors has established some credibility for both sides, indispensable to any form of diplomatic intercourse, and perfected a connection vital for international stability.

It is both paradoxical and implausible that professional diplomats should meet periodically during twelve years for serious discussions, while their leaders scorn and attack each other in public. Peking has regarded the United States as its "arch-enemy," aimed a ceaseless barrage of violent epithets on the Americans and particularly on President Kennedy, rallied Peking's sympathizers everywhere to win victory over "American imperialism—the most vicious enemy of the peoples of the world," and strained relations with the Soviet Union partly over the issue of correct Communist strategy for dealing with the United States. Washington, in turn, has treated Peking as an aggressor and outlaw, refused it diplomatic recognition, blocked its membership in the United Nations, prevented its taking over Taiwan, encouraged its "passing away," isolated it diplomatically and economically, confronted it with overwhelming force, and undertaken military operations along China's coast and near China's southern flank. Washington once sought the collapse of the Chinese People's Republic, while Peking has called for expulsion of the United States from Asia. Under these circumstances, two such vehement antagonists could open and maintain this singular contact only because there was some real advantage to their national interests.

Americans have dealt with the Chinese Communists on numerous subjects, and more often than most of the governments which recognize the Chinese People's Republic. Covering a broad range of issues and a dozen principal subjects, the Talks have involved the use of power, clash of interests, and manipulation of confrontations between the two parties to advance the interests of one side or to avoid military collision between both. Some subjects were treated intensely for a while and then dropped, while others were spasmodically or continuously treated over the past twelve years.

Character and Tone of the Talks

Despite the diversity of subjects and range of considerations, the Ambassadorial Talks have been more a meeting of men than of minds. Only six individuals—four Americans and two Chinese—have served their governments as the ambassadorial representatives at the Talks throughout these twelve years.*

Three career diplomats represented the United States in succession: U. Alexis Johnson, who was Ambassador in Prague, for the first 73 meetings until December 12, 1957; then our Ambassador in Warsaw, Jacob Beam, for 33 meetings from September 15, 1958, until November 29, 1961; and Ambassador John Moors Cabot for 21 meetings until September 15, 1965, when former Postmaster General John Gronouski took over at the next meeting on December 15, 1965. For Peking, the envoy of the Chinese People's Republic to Poland, Ambassador Wang Ping-nan, somehow survived nearly nine years and a total of 120 meetings with the Americans until April 1964! The second representative of Peking has the same family name as his predecessor, which helps to confuse the history of the Talks. Ambassador Wang Kuo-chuan attended his first meeting on July 29, 1964. Obviously the background and personalities of these diplomats varied greatly. In particular, the first Wang was a tough and skillful Party member, with long revolutionary experience and

* See Appendix A for a brief sketch of the principal persons involved in the Talks.

direct access to the handful of men who command the People's Republic of China. Although he had previously had considerable exposure to Americans, some of it unfortunate, he was amenable and flexible on personal and social contacts with the American Ambassadors, while adhering completely and convincingly to his instructions. The second Wang, also a Party member, has seemed to be inflexible, doctrinaire, and uninterested in personal contacts with the American representatives, probably reflecting Peking's lowered expectations and therefore deliberate downgrading of the Talks in the 1960s. On the other side of the table, the American Ambassadors have had long experience in the diplomatic profession. They too have carried out instructions and defended American policies and proposals and have taken a great deal of initiative in creating new proposals and formulating their final instructions. The Americans have usually sought to make the Talks easier to conduct by adding informal, personal touches here and there.

In addition to some 130 regular meetings, the two Ambassadors have from time to time met on unofficial occasions, such as "tea meetings," until the last few years when tensions increased and the second Wang came to Warsaw. Near the beginning of the Talks, Ambassador Johnson arranged a private, informal and secret dinner with Ambassador Wang Ping-nan on approval from President Eisenhower and Secretary Dulles. Ambassador Wang later reciprocated. On these occasions it was easier to converse at some length with adequate give-and-take of views and probing for possible openings. Both Ambassadors were able to explain their government's position and inquire into the attitudes of the other much better than at the formal, pre-arranged sessions. In flying from their respective posts to Geneva, the two ambassadors during the first years often were able to speak together in a normal manner at the airport, on the same plane, or in their hotel. However, the number of social and private contacts have declined in subsequent years, although private meetings between the Ambassadors or embassy officials can be easily arranged when required.

In any case, during the formative period of argument over many difficult issues, the Ambassadors of the United States of America and the Chinese People's Republic came to know each other officially and socially. When he finally left in 1964 after his diplomatic marathon in both Geneva and Warsaw, Ambassador Wang Ping-nan is reported to have made an unusually polite and friendly farewell. Such conduct among professionals is the hallmark of effective diplomacy. Moreover, the staff members of each delegation, particularly the interpreters, have had considerable dealings with each other on an informal basis in working out difficulties in translations and other technical problems. Thus, Peking and Washington have developed the practice, procedures, and machinery for regular and ready access to each other.

The Talks opened in Geneva in August 1955 and were conducted there until December 1957 when Ambassador Johnson was transferred to Thailand. Seventy-three numbered Talks took place in Geneva, which gave them the name "Geneva Talks." The Ambassadors met in a conference room provided by the Secretary-General of the United Nations at the Palais des Nations where the United Nations has its headquarters in Europe. Both governments shared the rent: $1.15 per month. The two parties, or sides, as they customarily call themselves, sat opposite each other at an oval table with a map of the world carved in inlaid Swedish wood between them. Each Ambassador brought three or four of his own aides, but no one else attended. They conducted the Talks in a correct and proper diplomatic manner, with the amenities and civilities being recognized even though the presentation was often vigorous and the official language usually firm and sometimes harsh. Ritualistic repetition and ambassadorial stamina soon came to characterize the Talks at Geneva. After the fifty-third meeting in 1956, *The New York Times* correspondent in Geneva remarked, "For sheer endurance there has been no United States diplomatic performance comparable to Mr. Johnson's since Benjamin Franklin's efforts to get financial help from the French monarchy for the American Revolution." [1]

After Ambassador Johnson's departure and the lapse of some nine months, the location of the Talks shifted in the fall of 1958 to Warsaw, Poland, where a new American Ambassador was taking up his duties and where Ambassador Wang Ping-nan was already in residence. One reason for choosing Warsaw was to reduce the burden on the Ambassadors of leaving their posts and traveling often to another country. In Warsaw they resumed the regular sessions. The Polish government provided the eighteenth-century Myslewicki Palace where the Talks have since been held. Fifty-eight were held in Warsaw during 1958–66, and they came to be referred to as the "Warsaw Talks."

According to press accounts, the Talks have now reached a well-understood and mutually-accepted style and method of operation. The two Ambassadors with their three or four aides arrive separately at the Palace. They enter the conference room by different doors on either side of green-covered tables which are placed parallel to each other with a space between them. Usually the Peking delegation is already at the table when the Americans enter. After the Americans have come to their chairs, each side nods slightly to the other and all sit down. There is a "ritual" of procedure. Each side takes turns, automatically opening every other meeting so there is never any question of deciding—or arguing—as to who speaks first; the side which does not make the closing statement of the day then proposes the adjournment of that session and the date for the next meeting. The Ambassadors cannot leave the table until that date has been agreed to. The whole exchange is oral; only sound waves cross the space between the Ambassadors. They avoid any official physical contact, apparently to symbolize the immense divide and total separation between the two governments and peoples. The Ambassadors apparently do not hand documents across the tables to each other. The representatives nod to one another, but they do not mix much. Fortunately, however, the diplomatic aides of both sides in each embassy now frequently consult each other by phone—in Chinese, not English—regarding difficulties in translation and various procedural matters. Similarly, copies of papers and documents are handed back and forth in this informal contact.

To judge from journalists' accounts, the secret proceedings follow a pattern of alternating oral statements. The format imitates the particular style developed at Panmunjom, which set a somewhat new and peculiar pattern in diplomatic practice.* The Ambassador opening the meeting customarily starts with a standard introduction in somewhat the following terms: "I am deeply disappointed to note that your side has continued since our last meeting to pursue the same unreasonable policies and that, in fact, your aggressive policy has not changed in any respect." This opening statement then proceeds to expound whatever subject that side prefers to begin with, such as the renunciation of force or bilateral contacts in the case of the Americans, or the withdrawal from Taiwan or Vietnam in the case of the Chinese Communists. There are usually few interruptions for questions or comments from across the table. When the opening side has concluded its opening statement, the other Ambas-

* See Chapter 2.

sador takes his turn to make his first statement which leads off with a variation of the following: "I am saddened to have to note that your side has completely misconstrued our policy and purpose. Everything that we do is strictly defensive and made necessary only by the aggressive policy of your side." [2]

The opening statements are always read from a prepared text—a position paper—with immediate sentence-by-sentence translation into Chinese or English by an interpreter for the speaking side. This is a slow, tedious process but it permits each side to make a reasonably accurate and complete stenographic record of that statement as well as to prepare for the rebuttal. After the first side has finished its initial statement, the other side either responds directly on that subject by reading from an already-prepared rebuttal or presents a prepared statement concerning some other matter. Since this initial round covers fairly predictable items, both sides come with written statements prepared for a long list of grievances. It apparently is just a question of taking the appropriate paper out of the briefcase to read into the record. This opening round usually takes about an hour.

Then the second phase of several alternating statements and rebuttals follow, again based on previously prepared positions. When both sides have finished that process, one or the other may then make extemporaneous remarks on what has occurred. This exchange is somewhat more spontaneous than the formal "readings," but it is not a dialogue or exploration. These oral replies are denials, rebuttals, accusations, explanations, and repetitions. This volley goes back and forth until neither Ambassador has anything more to add. There comes a pause; one Ambassador then proceeds to announce that he has nothing more to say; the other responds with the same words; a date is mutually agreed upon for the next session; all present pick up their papers, stand, nod, and leave separately.

An authentic up-to-date description of how the Ambassadorial Talks are actually conducted came from Ambassador Gronouski in the summer of 1966 when he spoke about them in a public interview:

The discussions are conducted without an agenda. In fact, there is only one rule of procedure followed: If it is my turn to open the discussion, then, at the end of the meeting, it is his turn to suggest the time of the next meeting. . . . We each, in effect, establish the agenda by introducing in our opening remarks those issues and questions which we want to raise and discuss. Each side presents a relatively brief opening statement.

Well over half the time of the last meeting—and I think this may be typical—was spent in give-and-take discussion of the issues. I think this is important, because we are able then to get not only a statement of position and a statement of argument, but we are also able to explore the nuances of the argument. We can raise questions on both sides and get answers to questions. . . .

We express—and sometimes rather forcefully—our points of view on issues, but it doesn't become a shouting match. It's done in a fairly relaxed tone in terms of attitude and mannerism; the positions are pretty clearly and directly expressed.

There are some polemics—it is impossible to avoid them—but essentially it's a discussion of the issues which both sides regard as important at that point in time. . . .

When we come in, I make it a point to exchange greetings, informally, before I sit down. And before we leave we chat briefly about extraneous matters.

I think it important that we develop some kind of personal rapport, which I hope will enable us better to understand each other and contribute to the progress of the talks. . . .

So far, it hasn't developed that way, but I'd be very susceptible to having a drink with my counterpart afterward.[3]

The most important feature of this whole ritual, it should be repeated, is the fixing of the date for the next session. A meeting cannot adjourn until that is assured, even if little new of substance is said and no agreement expected. If the date later turns out to be inconvenient for either Ambassador or one of the two governments, the embassies agree on another by phone. Occasionally a meeting can be called on short notice for some particular purpose. Both governments first have to be consulted and approve in advance a change of schedule or a special meeting. But it can be done and has proved useful at times.

The substance and the transcript of each meeting are secret. Both parties agreed at the beginning in Geneva, as a result of an American suggestion, that the Ambassadorial Talks would remain confidential. They still are. Neither side is supposed to release the subjects listed or discussed at a meeting until and unless the other party has been informed ahead of time. Accordingly, both parties have kept their separate and official records of each Talk classified. The only official notice of each meeting is usually a joint announcement put out by each party, stating that a meeting was held and specifying when the next one will take place. The American press sometimes prints this, but Peking has scrupulously publicized the little announcement, as a rule without comment. However, the agreement on the restricted nature of the sessions has been more honored in the breach than in the practice. Most of the substance of many of these Ambassadorial Talks has eventually become public knowledge in one way or another. Without giving prior notification, the Chinese in the early years of the Talks often announced in advance the subjects to be discussed or described the substance exchanged across the table in a manner favorable to them and prejudicial to the Americans. The Americans have usually been reticent about the record of each Talk unless forced to show their hand following a Chinese revelation. Peking's spokesmen have often resorted to press statements or long public announcements, quite contrary to mutual agreement, presumably to put pressure on the Americans or to embarrass them. In turn, Washington has revealed its position in the best light possible and "corrected" Peking's distortions.

In the early years, the Talks frequently suffered not only from unexpected disclosures, but also from charges and countercharges of indefinite stalling or of termination. While these "atmospheric pressures" have worn off with time and routine, they did hurt the Talks during the first five years. Peking often claimed that, while it was striving for agreement, the United States was deliberately "dragging out" the Ambassadorial Talks. Just a few days after their start in August 1955 with a world-wide aura of hopeful euphoria, Peking began accusing Washington of retarding or threatening the negotiations. Washington on occasion has blamed Peking for trying to "extract political concessions" and taunted Peking for refusing to make agreements. During 1960–66, both governments have acted very much as though their unusual diplomatic establishment were here to stay.

A Narrative of the Talks

Many efforts and numerous pressures joined in bringing the Americans and the Chinese Communists face to face with each other across a table in the same room at Geneva in 1955. These were the principal factors: a war in Korea, which left American prisoners in China, a fiasco for the West over Indochina, the political conferences in Panmunjom and Geneva where American and Chinese diplomats sat under the same roof, a crisis in the Taiwan Straits threatening nuclear holocaust, several Big Four meetings raising the question of Chinese Communist attendance, the anxieties of Allied and Asian statesmen over the specter of Sino-American war, and the brokerage function of British diplomats. These factors brought two bitter and implacable adversaries to the conference table and helped hold them there without a detailed agenda, in order to facilitate the "discussion and settlement" of disputes between them. They started the Talks with a two-item agenda, the first concerning the explicit repatriation of particular civilians in each country and the second referring vaguely to "certain other practical matters now at issue between both sides." That was a clear reflection of their opposed wishes. Neither wanted to discuss the items of the other but each insisted on itemizing his own subjects. For example, Peking wanted Washington to settle the issue of Taiwan, while Washington desired Peking to pledge not to use force. An agreement was quickly reached on the first item of the agenda, but the Talks have stalled on the second for over ten years. That is to say, there is no precise agenda now. Each side may take up any matter which it wishes, but Washington has always avoided any subject which would prejudice the rights or position of the Chinese government on Taiwan.

During twelve years, the Ambassadors negotiated only on three formal written draft agreements: the repatriation of civilians, the renunciation of force, and the exchange of newsmen. They concluded only one formal agreement when, in 1955, they put into effect an agreement on repatriation.

That single agreement came at the outset of the Ambassadorial Talks, and required fourteen successive meetings of a difficult give-and-take from August 1 to September 10, 1955. This negotiation constituted the only successful and full-fledged bargaining—that is, trading of commitments and concessions, indicating adjustments and maintaining demands, manipulating warnings and "sweetening" the atmosphere, and finally arguing over terminology and drafts in two non-equivalent languages. Since each desired some outcome rather than stalemate or failure, the divergent interests of Peking and Washington intersected in this one coordinated transaction to produce the unique result of the Talks. It provides a useful but limited case study of contrasting styles and methods of negotiating.

The next phase of 59 meetings lasted twenty-seven months, from September 1955 to December 1957. The negotiators dealt primarily first with a joint renunciation of force and then with some exchange of correspondents.* Despite some real negotiating, adjustment of proposals, and exchange of draft agreements, together with active maneuvering at the Talks and in public, doubtful contact in impasse was all that resulted for both sides. But during this 1955–57 phase each party also introduced or focused on other subjects. The Americans, on the defensive, hammered constantly for Peking's fulfillment of the Agreement on repatriation. The Chinese Communists, having the initiative, pressed Washington continually for a bilateral Foreign Ministers' conference, trade, and cultural relations.

After the first full year, and by the 60th meeting in mid-1956, the Talks had fallen into a kind of rhythmic ritual and alternating encounter of well-understood rules. Every six weeks or two months Peking would probe another flank with a new proposition. Invariably Ambassador Johnson would counter with the same two retorts: the return of all Americans and the renunciation of force. Then after a while, the Chinese would try another tack. This continued until Ambassador Johnson's last meeting in mid-December of 1957, when the Chinese even proposed an agreement on the highly technical subject of judicial assistance in the courts of each country in cases involving nationals of the other.

Then came a lapse of nine months during most of 1958. This interruption caused the only serious threat of termination of the Talks. It upset Peking considerably—much more than Washington, where no surprise or regret was evident when the contacts ceased indefinitely after the 73rd meeting on December 12, 1957. Ambassador Johnson was transferred to Thailand as Ambassador and no successor was immediately named to replace him. Secretary Dulles apparently was uncertain as to whether they should be continued at all. During this long lapse, the State Department explained that the frequent trips to Geneva from Prague for the Ambassadorial Talks had proved "sterile," been "burdensome" on United States diplomats, and would be downgraded to a lower diplomatic level. But the government of the Chinese People's Republic showed real concern, anger, and distress over what appeared to it to be Washington's *de facto* and indefinite suspension of the Talks. Months later, having already decided to continue the Talks while Peking impatiently waited, Washington finally announced in late July 1958 that Ambassador Beam in Warsaw had been named to resume the Ambassadorial Talks and suggested the meetings be held in Warsaw. Peking

* See Chapters 4 and 5.

remained silent, completely ignoring the American announcement for more than a month.

Then, as a result of the Taiwan crisis and the diplomatic initiative of Dulles, the Talks resumed dramatically in Warsaw with the 74th meeting on September 15, 1958. Never had the Talks been so much in the world spotlight or enjoyed such high-level attention from Eisenhower, Mao, Khrushchev, as well as Dulles and Chou. The Talks played a useful part in controlling and calming this crisis. In early September of 1958, Peking had brought the Taiwan crisis to the most dangerous point yet experienced. Under intense pressure from all sides, Secretary Dulles suggested a return to negotiations. He also made it utterly plain that the United States would fight to defend Quemoy—with nuclear weapons if necessary. Prime Minister Chou En-lai instantly responded that the two Ambassadors should meet in Warsaw to "settle" the crisis. Moscow publicly backed Peking's claims and China's security against any American attack—but only *after* the recourse to negotiation was underway. President Eisenhower and Secretary Dulles promptly facilitated the resumption of the Ambassadorial Talks in Warsaw. Ambassador Beam and Ambassador Wang held several long, tense, and difficult sessions during the latter part of September and early October. The Americans put forward numerous, even far-reaching, proposals, but Peking refused to negotiate the crisis. Interesting and positive changes in Sino-American relations might have ensued had Peking responded in 1958. However, the Chinese Communist bombardment of the offshore islands escalated the hostilities between the Chinese Communists and Chinese Nationalists until the United States Navy helped to break the blockade.* When that breach became effective, Peking undertook a *de facto* cease-fire apart from the Warsaw Talks. The severe military crisis abated, and the danger of an international war whether by miscalculation or by intention receded. Since Chou En-lai had not responded to earlier diplomatic soundings, Dulles decided to conduct the Talks at a slower pace.

The Americans did not then realize it, but Sino-Soviet publications have subsequently revealed that the Taiwan crisis, including the role played by the Talks, deepened the wedge in Sino-Soviet relations. The Talks contributed to diplomatic and military humiliation for Peking, gave Washington a negotiating advantage to probe and bargain for a substantial change in military and political rela-

* See Chapter 6.

tions in the Taiwan area, and offered an opportunity to Moscow to declare its support of Peking with lessened risk of having the commitment called. Peking learned from the crisis that Moscow would limit its intervention where the Americans were involved, and would exclude Taiwan altogether from any military or nuclear confrontation. The triangular relationship has not been the same since the Taiwan crisis of 1958.

Since then the Ambassadorial Talks have become a platform for exchanging polemics and notifications rather than a forum for negotiation. During 1959–60 the Americans shifted to the initiative on several issues, notably in seeking the exchange of newsmen, on which they modified their position so substantially that it became virtually identical with the original Peking proposal of 1956. For twenty sessions in this phase Ambassador Beam put forward variations on this and other proposals. In 1960 Senator John F. Kennedy indicated in his electoral campaign that the window at Warsaw could be opened wider if he won. However, Peking parried and then blocked negotiations altogether.

The first Warsaw meeting during President Kennedy's administration took place in March 1961. At that session Ambassador Beam vigorously urged an exchange of newsmen and a renunciation of force, proposals which were met by instant rejection from the Chinese. The vehemence of the Chinese Communist rebuttal and the finality of their rejection of the new administration's proposals shocked and dismayed the Americans. Perhaps Peking feared that Kennedy's appeal might be dangerous inside China. The new administration had publicly intimated and privately developed a renewed effort to ease tensions and lower barriers between the United States and the Chinese People's Republic—without, of course, lessening the American commitment to the Republic of China on Taiwan. Nevertheless, during the five years of 1961–66 under Presidents Kennedy and Johnson, Washington's persistent efforts to arrange many kinds of bilateral contacts have met nothing but unyielding insistence on prior agreement over Taiwan. Peking has consistently rebuffed every American initiative—on newsmen, trade, and private contacts—just as the Americans had for the first two years rejected Peking's proposals.

For some thirty meetings from mid-1961 to July 1967, Peking, focusing on Taiwan, constantly stalemated the Talks and frustrated Washington's persistent efforts to probe for new openings, initiate new agreements, and create a new climate. Perhaps the attempt was unrealistic because of various political factors. The six-year dealings consisted only in the deliberate elusion and tacit maneuvering of adversary negotiating rather than in reciprocal transaction. Nevertheless, the Talks did not lose all pretense of civility or opportunity for utility. They shifted in scope and character during these last years, and became a useful switchboard of communications for effectively relaying intentions and expounding views. Peking apparently used this channel in 1961 to convey its seriousness in seeking a neutral Laos when Washington had assumed otherwise. A year later Washington used Warsaw to convey its intention not to be involved in any military adventure against China's mainland. During 1963 and 1964 Washington tried unsuccessfully to develop a discussion and arrive at an understanding with Peking on the Test-Ban Treaty, nuclear arms control, and general disarmament. The Talks constituted the only official exchange undertaken by a non-Communist government with Peking concerning the nuclear problem. However, Peking evaded the American presentation and insisted on its unilateral propositions, but proposed a joint pledge not to use the bomb. In 1965–67 both governments, especially Washington, used the Talks to describe their views and define their positions on Vietnam, an issue which added acute tension to their relationships. Washington stressed assurances to Peking, and indirectly to Hanoi, and sought unsuccessfully through the Talks to set up negotiations. It is significant that Washington and Peking were in official and confidential communication regarding the dangerous issue of Vietnam and the limits of their confrontation there, but their disagreement remained profound.

During 1966–67 two new factors constrained United States dealings with Communist China. The internal convulsions of the so-called proletarian cultural revolution generally disrupted Peking's whole diplomatic conduct, including the Ambassadorial Talks, and probably accounted for Peking's blunt, adamant rejection of every American overture whether offered by the President or by professors. Secondly Moscow embroiled itself and the Sino-Soviet clash in Peking-Washington dealings by charging Peking with using the Ambassadorial Talks to make a "deal" on Vietnam. Moscow's motive evidently was to rebut Peking's similar charge of Moscow's "collusion" with Washington on Vietnam, disarmament, and other issues. Each charge seemed unfounded from the American viewpoint. Peking continued to defend its contact with the United States as well as its charge of collusion against the Soviet Union. However, these charges tended to complicate the triangular relationships and to interfere with the latitude of the Talks. Despite these pressures and meager results, Washington and Peking were each not so frustrated as to break up their single link.

Several features are noteworthy about the American experience in negotiating with the Chinese Communists since 1955. The sharp contrast between the initial three years of the Talks and the subsequent nine is the first. During 1955 to 1958 there was considerable substance, much activity, wide variety, and perhaps some small hope since both Peking and Washington in their different ways simultaneously and mutually devoted substantial efforts to negotiating on several proposals. This first period was uniquely characterized by the duel between two contrasting personalities: Prime Minister Chou En-lai—the Chinese Communist Party stalwart, revolutionary of the Long March, and Peking's authority in foreign affairs—and Secretary of State John Foster Dulles—the international negotiator, Republican statesman, and senior partner of a leading and eminent law firm on Wall Street, who died in the Spring of 1959. In this encounter, Chou En-lai showed himself to be an adroit, versatile challenger and bargainer, while Dulles demonstrated his unusual skills and resourcefulness in conducting a defensive game to deflect his adversary's initiatives. At first, Chou En-lai maneuvered imaginatively. Always seeking to enhance the status and power of the Chinese People's Republic, he used flexible tactics and various gambits to try to manipulate various agreements out of the Americans. Taking the defensive, Dulles had to parry and resist Chou's initiatives and ploys for three years. Then, for the last time, in 1958, Dulles and Chou faced each other in the dramatic, dangerous confrontation over Taiwan, staging their final duel in an intricate interplay of force and diplomacy and reversing their previous roles. Dulles took the offensive to bargain hard for various agreements and even hinted at a widening scope of discussions between himself and Chou. Now on the defensive, Chou En-lai had to parry and resist to avoid negotiations which he now did not desire.

The second feature of the twelve years of Talks has been the complete reversal of the attitudes and positions of each government. In 1955–58, Peking wanted to transact specific matters "comparatively easy to settle" while deferring its efforts to negotiate with

Washington on its principal object of getting the Americans out of Taiwan and obtaining full jurisdiction and control over it. On the other hand, the Americans refused to discuss Peking's several specific proposals until Peking accepted Washington's principles. Then, beginning in late 1958, the Americans shifted to the offensive just when Peking lost interest in negotiation and henceforth entirely dropped the initiative in the Talks. During 1960–67 Peking adamantly refused to negotiate any of Washington's proposals until Washington agreed to Peking's principle of total American withdrawal from Taiwan and the area of the Taiwan Straits. Conversely, the Americans for seven years flexibly deferred priority of negotiations on major issues of principle and vigorously sought to transact various agreements with Peking.

The third feature of a dozen years of exchanges has been the continual resort by both governments to "imagistic diplomacy." Using the medium of the Talks until early 1967 to convey the message of moderation in the face of deadlock and hostility, Peking and Washington each frequently projected the image of continuously dealing with the other, carefully maintaining the channel for negotiating, and sincerely seeking to improve relations and decrease tensions. From time to time, each has also portrayed the other as doing just the opposite. The Chinese once talked a lot about "sitting down" with the Americans to negotiate but described the Americans as "stonewalling" discussions. In recent years, the Americans have said that they wanted to "sit down" with the Chinese Communists but that they kept "hanging up the phone." These three features—the duel, the reversal, and the imagery—which are detailed in later chapters—did not narrow the wide gap between Peking and Washington, but contributed to a characteristic style of adversary negotiating used between these two governments.

Another, and curiously paradoxical feature of these negotiations, was the transposition of style within the reversal of approach. At first each government perhaps unwittingly tended to use the customary concept and style of negotiating of the other. Chou En-lai and Ambassador Wang Ping-nan in the initial period seem now to have somewhat followed the pragmatic and relative Western style of mutual bargaining in "good faith" for a commonly transacted result advantageous in varying degrees to both parties. In contrast, the Americans then seem to have negotiated more in the fashion of China's traditional style of absolutistic, unilateral insistence on the other party's acceptance of general principles and abstract criteria of an ethical or moral nature unobjectionable in and of themselves but far above the give and take process of litigating differences and transacting compromises. In the reversal since 1960 each government has reverted to its own customary style of negotiating which evolved into a composite style of adversary negotiations.

* * *

For twelve years the eagle and the dragon remained in contact bound by impasse. The beginning and the end of this period of unique paradoxical relationships are in sharp contrast. In 1955 the two governments demonstrated a sincere willingness to sit down together; in 1967 they were still in touch but there was no dialogue. It is fair to say that never was a stage reached when the two sides genuinely attempted to negotiate a substantial settlement. The intractable issue of Taiwan prevented accommodation on any important matter, reducing the range of maneuver for both Peking and Washington almost to zero. The best that might be said for the Talks and other contacts is that neither Washington nor Peking wanted to take the onus of breaking them off, and both recognized the value of the function they served in avoiding miscalculation. The worst that might be charged is that the whole experience has retarded, perhaps even immobilized rather than facilitated, the possibilities of a *modus vivendi* between the United States and China.

How have Washington and Peking in fact viewed the Talks? The emphasis for each has varied at different times and on different occasions. During the 1955–57 phase Secretary Dulles acknowledged that they had served a "useful purpose" and said he hoped for "positive results" but he also once called the Talks a "ritual of negotiations"; and at yet another time he viewed the Talks as a significant prelude to a definitive conference with Chou En-lai. President Kennedy at first described the Talks as "merely a matter of form and nothing of substance," but later considered them a useful instrument for exchanging views and notifying intentions. The Johnson administration has repeatedly endorsed open, direct diplomatic contacts. For their part, the Chinese Communists have demonstrated continued interest in maintaining some official link with the United States, as evidenced by their initiatives in the early phase of the Talks, their obvious distress over the interruption in 1958, Ambassador Wang Ping-nan's apparent effort to assure confirmation from the Americans for his successor's first meeting, and the several references to the Talks in 1964–66 by Chou En-lai and Chen Yi.

Their continuation over the years at least indicates their utility for both parties. If the Talks could settle and arrange nothing to either side's satisfaction, they at least prevented some things and explained others. In short, they became a well-grounded and institutionalized facility which Peking and Washington explicitly desired to preserve. The "subdiplomatic" system in Warsaw provided both Peking and Washington with an institutional framework and workable machinery for impersonal interchange in the form of: (1) direct communication instead of relay through third parties, (2) a dependable maildrop for delivering informational material, (3) an open switchboard for conveying and exploring views and proposals on any subject, and (4) a systematic forum always ready for confidential soundings or negotiations. The regular practice of Talks in Warsaw has evolved into an important "pseudo embassy" for Peking and Washington in a third country instead of in the two capitals.

In sum, what beneficial consequences have the Talks had for the United States?

They have facilitated the release of most of the Americans incarcerated in Chinese Communist jails.

They have eased critical tensions over Taiwan three times and lowered the danger of international nuclear conflict in that area.

They have signaled intentions, established limits, and prevented serious miscalculations in the dangerous Laotian and Vietnamese crises.

They have made possible the only serious exchange on record between Peking and any non-Communist government over the issue of arms control and nuclear proliferation.

They have served as a substitute for inclusion of Communist China in a "Big Five" conference several times.

They have assured the allies of the United States that it was not wholly "bellicose" toward Communist China or recalcitrant in dealing with Peking.

No American can presume to speculate on what the comparative consequences have been for the People's Republic of China. All we know is that Peking maintained this contact with Washington and often called it advantageous. No doubt the Talks put a strain on relations between Washington and Taipei, which served Peking's political objectives. Besides, certain of the benefits for Washington probably were of advantage to Peking, such as direct communication and reduced miscalculation. However, we should note that this systematic contact with the United States has probably complicated Peking's "fundamentalist" position in the world Communist movement, contributed to the Sino-Soviet antagonism and rupture, and contradicted the "devil image" and "hate cult" so assiduously propagated by Peking.

The Ambassadorial Talks can teach us much about dealing with the completely different style of Communist negotiators, a new and hard experience for an American. They are tough, able and persistent, shaped and guided by the techniques of adroit bargainers, the rigid orders of Party discipline, continuing determinants of Chinese history and nationalism, and the infallible dictates of Marxist-Maoist ideology. As Chinese and Maoists, they negotiate with a very different conception of time, showing endless patience and imperturbability. Operating in short time-spans, American negotiators can be put at an impossible disadvantage, for the traditional American style is to get a negotiation over with, not to prolong it. At their table, the Peking negotiators aim for total victory, with no attempt at accommodation of the opposing view. That is the predicament Americans have been faced with over the years.

Communist indoctrination and discipline bind them to the conviction of inevitable victory, the strategy of a military campaign. Peking-style negotiation aims at the capitulation, not the accommodation, of this "enemy" with whom there can be no lasting coexistence. Within this absolutist context, relatively limited negotiation for specific agreements with the United States are permissible and desirable as a matter of national interest and tactical expediency to ensure the fulfillment of the far-off ideological objective of total, inevitable defeat and destruction of "United States imperialism."

Despite their treatment of Americans as abominable enemies and their fanatic conviction of their own invincibility, the Chinese are extremely sensitive to any unequal treatment and insist on reciprocal arrangements. This does not, however, inhibit them from trying to maneuver the other side into the very unequal, nonreciprocal position they reject for themselves. They sometimes try to win the basic issue in dispute at the outset of a negotiation by the order and phrasing which they doggedly insist must be used to put the matter on an agreed agenda. In this vital battle of the agenda they try to predetermine the outcome of a negotiation by fixing its substance in advance. The Chinese Communist negotiators will then try to bargain one concession twice to gain double advantage. Unless rebuffed, their semantics and their style will dominate the negotiations. Whether, when, and what to concede without loss is the hardest test of nerves for the American negotiator.

As if these were not large enough hurdles, the American negotiator must also realize that he is operating in an atmosphere of high intensity of emotions and reciprocal images of suspicion, hostility, and fear, stemming from a bizarre syndrome of love-hate symptoms generated by over a century of Sino-American relations. Epitomizing several distorted symbols to his Chinese Communist counterpart, the man from Washington represents the epicenter of world power countervailing China's resurgence; he stands for the American vanguard in a world-wide, cosmopolitan, "revisionist" culture; and he personifies American "imperialism," the "arch-enemy," and the "foreign devil."

In this state of continuing "no war–no peace" between the Chinese People's Republic and the United States, the American negotiator, his government and public opinion should be prepared for an interminable "sit in" at this "permanent, floating, diplomatic game." American patience and sense of direction can do much to preserve and improve this important "subdiplomatic" machinery. Out of careful contacts, an objective, less emotional association might slowly and eventually incubate. In the meantime, however, it continues, as it began, in harsh, unpromising circumstances.

CHAPTER TWO

Origins of Contacts and Negotiations

The Korean Armistice, concluded in Panmunjom, started a long process which led to the Ambassadorial Talks. Translated from Korean, Panmunjom means "inn with wooden gate"—an apt description. In 1953 wooden gates and sentry boxes led into the international compound where a bazaar-like collection of men in varied uniforms and apparel wandered about the motley tents, quonset huts and flimsy plywood buildings. Panmunjom had brought together an unlikely assortment of blue-helmeted American guards, bearded Indian Sikhs, North Korean military policemen in dark, Russian-style uniforms and boots, Chinese soldiers in earth-colored baggy pants, and officers in smart dress uniforms from Sweden, Switzerland, Poland and Czechoslovakia. South Koreans in green fatigues made repairs, and newspapermen from all over the world looked for stories. The diplomats moved in and out of the compound, the Americans in business suits and the Communists in military-style tunics, never having any personal contact with one another.

The pressures and dangers felt throughout the world in the mid-1950s, born of the uneasy Korean truce, the critical Indochinese conflict, and the persisting clashes in the Taiwan area were the prime factors in bringing Washington and Peking to the negotiating table. The diplomatic maneuvers which these three military conflicts produced and which finally helped shape the form of the Ambassadorial Talks were long, difficult and often contradictory. Negotiations between the two hostile governments began in a windswept Korean village, but the tortuous path to the Talks included Chinese and American participation in the Geneva Conference of 1954; the 1955 Geneva Summit Conference of the "Big Four"; American opposition to any form of "Summitry" with Peking; unsuccessful involvement of the United Nations; moves for a cease-fire over the

23

offshore islands in the Taiwan area; the American government's responsibility for citizens mistreated abroad; and the availability of informal mediators between Peking and Washington.

Korea and the Panmunjom Talks

The Talks in Panmunjom were an exercise in the diplomacy of stalemate which has come to characterize much of the international politics of Asia since World War II. Article IV and Paragraph 60 of the Korean Armistice Agreement of 1953 recommended to "the governments concerned on both sides" that a Political Conference be held "to settle through negotiation the questions of the withdrawal of all foreign forces from Korea, the peaceful unification of Korea, etc." The "etc." was a Communist insertion designed to arrange an open-ended agenda, while both President Eisenhower and Secretary Dulles were determined to press for Korea's peaceful unification at the Conference.*

Panmunjom was the Americans' baptism of fire with the diplomatic representatives of the People's Republic of China, who had had some previous experience in dealing with Americans in China and who spoke English. After much difficult negotiation in the summer of 1953, the United Nations had designated the United States as its representative at Panmunjom in a meeting with the Chinese and Korean Communists to arrange the Political Conference. While these "talks on talks" were not diplomatic negotiations in the formal sense, the American representative, Arthur Dean, had the rank of special ambassador and was assisted by officials from the State Department,† while civilian Communist representatives spoke for their two governments in Peking and Pyongyang. In seven weeks nearly fifty meetings were held without reaching any agreement.

The diplomats first argued about an agenda and then about the arrangements for a Political Conference, until the Talks broke down when the United Nations representative walked out after enduring almost three hours of insulting charges against himself and the

---

* The text of the Armistice Agreement and the views of President Eisenhower and Secretary Dulles are contained in Department of State Publication 5150, August 1953.

† The author served as deputy representative and continued this meeting at Panmunjom along with Edwin Martin, also from the State Department, who later participated in many of the Ambassadorial Talks at Geneva with Ambassador Johnson.

United States government. Then, some lower-level conversations were held intermittently at Panmunjom for two months until the Communist side abruptly walked out of the meetings after the "Big Four" at Berlin had agreed on the arrangements for the conference which the Talks at Panmunjom had failed to establish. This failure, and the entire political experience at Panmunjom, would today be an obscure, almost irrelevant footnote to history if the form and character of Panmunjom's diplomacy had not set a pattern for the Ambassadorial Talks. The atmosphere of Panmunjom has haunted American dealings with Peking ever since.

Despite the truce in Korea, tension pervaded the neutral compound at Panmunjom when the civilian talks began in October 1953. They used the same military pattern of the previous armistice negotiations between the armed forces of both sides. No individual ever spoke personally to anyone on the other side. There was never an exchange of greetings or amenities on starting or ending a meeting. Nor was there any social intercourse or mixing outside. This was negotiation without contact, a contradiction in terms. It expressed the ruptured relations of the two sides and the bisected compound —two worlds apart, divided by a metal strip and mental segregation.

The quonset hut for the Talks, located in this demilitarized neutral zone, lay exactly at right angles athwart the military demarcation line whose metal bands bisected the zone and separated North and South Korea for some 150 miles from east to west. In turn, the negotiating table bisected the building from side to side. The straight crease along the middle of the table's green cover ran directly above the military demarcation line underneath. As a matter of practice, Communist officials never went into the United Nations half of the hut, and vice versa, although Communist policemen did wander around both ends. Each party in the political talks entered the hut only from its side of the zone and by opposite doors at each end of the hut. This total separation between the two sides was carried to such extremes that ash trays were always "stationed" on top of the crease when not in use so that they, too, were evenly bisected by the military demarcation line! Moreover, a divided ash tray was never used by opposite sides simultaneously! Smokers had to wait their turn while the ash tray alternated from one side of the crease to the other. The United Nations' side controlled the electric lights which the Communists could not turn off, while they controlled the stoves which the Americans could not turn up. The meetings took place every day but Sunday. They lasted about three hours, sometimes five, beginning promptly at 11:00. No one ever left the table. No lunch was ever served. Panmunjom institutionalized the diplomacy of stalemate.

At the opening meeting, contrary to advance agreement, the Communists read a long statement in front of the press and tried to put the Peking and Pyongyang flags beside the American for the photographers. They stole the propaganda march, as they did at Geneva nearly two years later. Then the Communist side tried to win a major concession by insisting on their procedure and order for enumerating the agenda. This was a clever negotiating tactic to force the concealed substance of the negotiations on a Political Conference to a showdown over what appeared to others to be only a trivial mechanical matter of the agenda. The Americans learned that the initial skirmish over the agenda with Communist negotiators can win or lose the first battle. The Communists manipulated a world spotlight to put the onus on the Americans for delaying the Talks over the mere order before they had even begun to negotiate the Political Conference. The Communist side wanted first to negotiate the composition of the Conference on Korea. The United Nations side insisted that the date, place and other matters—but not the composition or membership of the Conference—were the proper subjects for the Talks. The United Nations side held out on the agenda because the Korean Armistice Agreement had already determined the membership at a Political Conference on Korea. Yet, at these Talks, Peking and Pyongyang reopened a closed issue and made the matter of composition the blocking position for their strategy of delay. They insisted on re-negotiating what had already been negotiated; in other words, they tried to make the Americans and the United Nations pay twice for the same thing.

Eleven consecutive meetings at Panmunjom failed to settle the agenda. The Communists insisted on first settling the issue of composition of the Conference which meant inviting the neutrals, including the Soviet Union, which Peking appeared really to want. Ambassador Dean insisted that the first item should be the date and the place for convening a Political Conference. Finally, he proposed that the chief delegates turn the deadlock over to their deputies to discuss all questions of the agenda confidentially and simultaneously with more freedom of maneuver than the publicized and polemical meetings of the principals and with no disclosures to the press. The Communists at first denounced this proposal as "absolutely unacceptable" and then reversed themselves to accept it the next day. Six of these second-level meetings were held in secret without propaganda or provocation in pragmatic businesslike way with some give and take. Following his instructions, the United States Deputy Representative proposed a compromise for a new agenda combining the two issues of composition and date-place of the Conference, and providing for simultaneous discussion of them by the chief delegates in plenary sessions or in subcommittees. Again, the Communists instantly rejected that proposal outright. For several days they demanded unconditional acceptance of their order of priority. Then, while still denouncing the proposal of the United Nations side, the Communist deputies submitted their written version of a revised agenda in an effort to end the impasse. The two versions of the agenda were almost identical. The two sides had finally reached a compromise. The United States Deputy agreed to what in effect he had earlier proposed. The subcommittees recessed, the deputies reported to their principals, and the chief delegates accepted the formula of compromise on November 14. This was the first agreement of a diplomatic nature negotiated between Washington and Peking. The Talks on a Political Conference then spent the next four weeks of daily meetings in an attempt to reach agreement on the date, location, and composition of the Political Conference and other related matters. However, these preliminary talks failed.

Yet, before the deadlock of mid-December, the American and Chinese representatives produced some points of agreement, although only of historical interest now. They decided on a bilateral Political Conference with plenary authority. All member governments individually and both sides would be considered as "voting participants," but decisions would be reached collectively by both sides agreeing on a one-side plus one-side basis. If one side disagreed, no decision would be made. Individual governments on each side would add their affirmative votes and decide on casting a "yes" or "no" as a side. Neutral members could not vote but would be free to speak on agenda items. The two sides would set up a central secretariat and share expenses equally. However, the two sides at Panmunjom deadlocked on basic differences.

The main issue, and a heated one, was Peking's insistence on Moscow's "neutral" status at a Political Conference. In many tense and sharp exchanges, the United Nations representative rejected this contention. Yet the question of the Soviet status seemed to conceal Peking's opposition toward having a Political Conference on Korea at all—except on Peking's terms. That was the basic issue. Consequently, the two sides sparred over the location, date, and agenda; and argued over the rights of neutral participants and the role of the Secretariat of the United Nations. Various proposals on locations and dates alternated across the table without much discussion and without agreement. The Communists held out for Panmunjom, despite rejection by the other side, and finally suggested New Delhi which the United Nations had already proposed along with Geneva, Bandung, Colombo, Stockholm, or Vienna. As the Talks wore on, the proposed dates for convening a Political Conference on Korea receded one after another. However, the issue of the Soviet Union's status provided the fuel for a heated debate in the hut.

In the light of the subsequent Sino-Soviet split, it is now rather ironic to note the intense argument which continued for many days at Panmunjom on the role of the Soviet Union at a Political Conference. Peking incessantly portrayed Moscow as a "neutral" in the Korean War and strenuously insisted, sometimes too obviously, on keeping Moscow along the sidelines. The Chinese Communists vehemently rejected the proposal to have the Soviet Union attend as a full participant, responsible for and bound by the decisions of its side and of the Conference. Peking contended that the Soviet Union could only come as a "neutral," with no vote and unaccountable to the Conference for its past or future actions with regard to Korean matters. This might seem to have been a queer and uncharacteristic role for the Politburo in Moscow to take. Yet the Russians may well have insisted on this "neutral" position to conceal their real part in the Korean War.

The Americans at Panmunjom often speculated on the various possible motives behind Peking's demand. It would have excluded the Russians from the Chinese Communist side, and would have prevented them from officially taking part in the negotiations and decisions, if there were any, on the critical issues of the withdrawal of Chinese forces from North Korea, and on the crucial arrangements for unifying all Korea. Was this demand actually prompted by a desire to help Moscow conceal the Russian hand? Or did it also betray Peking's preference for keeping the Russians at arm's length, and out of a sensitive border area for China such as Korea? Were hints of divergence with Moscow hidden below this odd behavior? Probing for this at Panmunjom, the Americans taunted Peking with many scholarly or satirical definitions of "neutral," ridiculed this purported Soviet role, and twitted the Chinese for acting as Moscow's agent or "puppets." Comparing Moscow to the wolf in "Little Red Riding Hood" or to the "Great Northern Bear" in a Chinese play on words relieved the tension in the quonset hut but did not unravel the issue.

Urging the Chinese Communists to accept the United Nations program for a Conference at Geneva with the Soviet Union as a full participant in making and being bound by the decisions of the Conference, Ambassador Dean forcefully stated: "The mask of neutrality cannot begin to cover the naked and willful conspiracy of Soviet-inspired aggression here in Korea. Everyone knows who inspired, arranged, instigated and directed the Korean War. Every schoolboy knows it. You cannot escape the facts." [1] Nevertheless, the Chinese Communists never responded to Dean's brilliant, courtroom thrusts. Impassively and doggedly they adhered to their notion of Soviet neutral status. In this first encounter with the Chinese People's Republic the Americans at Panmunjom at least came away with the impression that something worth watching might be going on in Sino-Soviet relations.

The "talks on talks" could not cope with the Soviet question and headed toward stalemate or break-up. On November 30, 1953, the Communists tabled a 15-point proposal partly acceptable and partly unacceptable to the United Nations side, particularly the built-in veto. Then on December 8, Ambassador Dean tabled a "Draft Overall Agreement" of 16 points. The two drafts had much in common. However, the Communist side instantly rejected Ambassador Dean's oral presentation of the United Nations comprehensive proposal and left the document itself lying on the table across the crease. They attacked it out of hand for several days, and as the Talks wore on, the Communists increasingly hammered on their demand that the United Nations side "show sincerity" by forthwith accepting their proposal without change as final and unalterable, although they themselves often proceeded to vary and amend details when faced with measured but unyielding firmness. Finally, for reasons which remain obscure, the Chinese Communist representative at Panmunjom forced the Americans to a dramatic "talkdown." It may have been related superficially to the announcement in Washington of

December 10 that Ambassador Dean would return there for a few days of consultations before resuming his duties in Panmunjom.[2]

On December 11 and 12, Huang Hua, the Chinese Communist representative, carried out a calculated harangue against Ambassador Dean's authority, reliability, and sincerity. He read from prepared, typewritten texts. The Communists denigrated the trustworthiness of the United States government, accused it of "conniving" to violate agreements on prisoners of war, and charged it with "treacherous designs" and "perfidious actions." At about 2 o'clock on December 12, Ambassador Dean proposed an adjournment to clear the air and end the harangue because the Talks were virtually at the point of collapse. Ignoring him, Huang Hua intensified his barrage of increasingly hostile statements all afternoon every time it was his turn to speak. His attack mounted in rudeness and ferocity. He dared Ambassador Dean to walk out. He refused to clarify or answer any of the latter's questions regarding the two over-all draft proposals on the Political Conference. The Communist attacks were not only arrogant and deliberate: they became intolerable. The Communists had categorically rejected the United Nations proposals, left them lying on the table, refused even to acknowledge or refer to them, and peremptorily demanded time and again that the United Nations side submit to the Communist proposals unconditionally and without question. Then as the lengthening afternoon shadows began to fall across Panmunjom, the Communists branded the United States "perfidious" over and over again.

Ambassador Dean warned the Communist side that they were serving notice of an indefinite recess unless the charge of perfidy were instantly withdrawn. In the meantime, he informed the Communists of a significant new understanding which could have guaranteed the holding of a Conference. The representative of the Republic of Korea would agree to attend the Conference and abide by its decisions provided the Soviet Union would also attend as a full voting participant willing to carry out its solemn obligations with respect to the unification of Korea.[3] The Communist side ignored this statement, too. The tirade from across the divide continued. Ambassador Dean repeated his warnings.

Then, at about 5:00 o'clock, after nearly six hours of continuous sitting, Ambassador Dean suddenly picked up his papers, rose from the table and marched out of the hut. At first taken aback, Huang Hua called out after him "Come back," the first and only time he ever used English at the table. But Ambassador Dean strode out of the "inn with the wooden gate," never to return to Panmunjom. Having received general approval from the Department of State before his walk-out to return to Washington temporarily for consultations, Ambassador Dean told the stunned press outside the hut that he would wait only one week for the Communists to make a retraction of their accusations and withdraw the charge of perfidy. He interpreted the final tirade, he said, as a deliberate effort of the Communists to be so rude as to force the discontinuation of the Talks. However, the Communists not only refused to back down in any way; they publicly repeated their charges immediately over Radio Peking. It was all planned. Ambassador Dean left Korea soon after and turned over continuation of the negotiations to the United States Deputy Representative.[4]

Ambassador Dean's walkout represented a decision of his own taken at the table without anyone's foreknowledge. The Department of State had not been specifically consulted and so could not have authorized it. Even his colleagues sitting beside him at the table were caught by surprise as much as were the Communists. This was one of those unique moments when a single human being must serve history and make the crucial decision. Ambassador Dean's unrehearsed but deliberate exit upset Washington, frustrated Peking, but probably helped subsequent American dealings with Peking. The Chinese Communists no longer could take the American mettle for granted. A representative of the President and the American people had shown the gumption on his own to stand for no more abuse and mockery. Ambassador Dean's sudden exit drew the line on the limits of abuse and set a precedent for a future American option to walk out if necessary. That act may have served as some brake on Peking's language and behavior in subsequent negotiations.

Only a few weeks at Panmunjom passed in this intermission. In mid-January Peking suddenly acted to resume the Talks. The two chief Communist delegates at Panmunjom sent a brief note to the United States Deputy Representative proposing that a "liaison secretary" from each side meet immediately "to discuss the date for resumption of the discussions." [5] This note also enclosed a copy of the public statement of Prime Minister Chou En-lai urging resumption of the Talks and suggesting that the form of Soviet participation in the Political Conference be taken as a starting point for renewed discussions. After receiving approval from Washington, the United States Deputy wrote to the Communist representative that he agreed to a meeting of liaison secretaries on January 14 to discuss conditions for resuming conversations as well as for a date for their resumption. He indicated that while his side would not insist on a complete withdrawal of the charge of perfidy or an apology, something would have to be done to represent a retraction. If a new atmosphere for talks were "reasonable, constructive, and respectable," the plenary sessions could be resumed.[6] These letters were transmitted through the Secretariat of the Joint Military Armistice Commission of the two military sides at Panmunjom.

Then, the atmosphere in the international compound became explosive as January 22 neared, the date for the release or repatriation of Chinese, Korean, and American prisoners taken in custody from both sides by the Neutral Nations Repatriation Commission. Some people even feared a resumption of hostilities, not negotiations. Meanwhile, the two liaison secretaries met several times, discussed the problem of resuming the Talks, and, paradoxically, made a little headway. When 20,000 prisoners were released on January 22, nothing drastic happened. The Communists then seemed to become particularly interested again in arranging for the resumption of the Talks on the Political Conference.

The chief Communist representative suddenly wrote Ambassador Dean on January 26, proposing their immediate resumption and implying that the issue of the offensive remarks could be managed. Ambassador Dean replied affirmatively by letter, making several suggestions on the date, place, composition, the issue of the participation of the Soviet Union, and voting procedures. He said he was prepared to return to Panmunjom as soon as the liaison secretaries had worked out the necessary arrangement. The meetings continued spasmodically for several weeks, producing little result, while the Foreign Ministers of the Big Four meeting in Berlin secretly negotiated a formula for a Korean Conference. Again the Americans speculated that perhaps there was a hint of divergence between Peking and Moscow. Perhaps the leaders in Peking wanted to reactivate their talks with the Americans in Panmunjom in order not to be finessed by the Russians and the Big Four in Berlin regarding Asian problems. Or, turning the tables on its part, Peking might have thought of finessing the Russians by resuming the relevant discussions on Korea in Panmunjom in order to control the bidding.

In any case, against Berlin's prestigious backdrop, the liaison secretaries became a thin thread in negotiations between Washington and Peking. It was not surprising, therefore, when the thread snapped. The Communist secretaries suddenly, without warning or advance notice, rose from the table and walked out of the hut—as the Americans had done some two months before. Both sides departed Panmunjom without any official notice or leave-taking of each other, as separated and as disassociated as when they came. This initial American diplomatic contact with the Chinese People's Republic, culminating in a walk-out and rupture, left its mark on the pattern of future dealings between Washington and Peking.

The whole procedure was highly stereotyped and formalized between irreconcilable adversaries. Like the ashtrays on the table, the proposals and statements of both sides alternated mechanically from one representative to the other across the crease at Panmunjom. There was no dialogue then in the sense of exchanging views and asking questions for clarification. The method of delivery used at Panmunjom—followed in Geneva and Warsaw—was the "statement" by a "side." It could be long or short. It was delivered orally in the language of the "speaking" side, and translated orally paragraph by paragraph. The key rules of this procedure were, first, the monopoly of the "floor" for the speaking side until it relinquished that right with the remark "that is all" or "I have no more statements to make." Secondly, one side could not interrupt the other side's statement to ask for clarification, correct a point, or rebut a charge. That had to wait. Only when a statement was concluded could the other side take its turn for as long as it liked. Words became bullets in alternating sallies across the crease. Perhaps it was just as well that no person was permitted to cross it.

Meanwhile, during each statement, stenographers on both sides were busily making a verbatim account of everything spoken, but the written records of each side were never exchanged or compared. Since the Chinese applied themselves meticulously to these—as well as to all—negotiations, they always came well prepared. Their statements were written or typed out in Chinese in advance. They usually had a set of different items for each meeting. The United Nations side soon adopted the same practice of preparing a series of subjects and using them like different weapons for various targets. In fact, the Americans soon adopted the style characteristic to Communist negotiators who seldom miss a chance to put in adjectives and adverbs where they are unnecessary or tautological: for example, they may charge something to be "absolutely impermissible."

Not only did the tendentious style hinder these negotiations, but the reciprocal alternation of statements also made it difficult and awkward to probe, inquire, and explain. In fact, either side could ignore questions and probes of the other forever. The Panmunjom style and procedure prevented the Talks from coming to grips with an issue. The system protected more than it exposed a controversial matter. As a result, the only question open for discussion at Panmunjom was procedural: how to end each session and arrange for the next one. Neither side liked to be responsible for the day's adjournment, because there was some peculiar onus to calling it off. However, by tacit understanding and routine practice, a meeting would not adjourn until one side proposed a "recess" and both sides agreed on the date for the next session, usually the next day. Thereby, the contact remained unbroken. With this ritual completed, each side picked up its papers, ignored the other, and exited from opposite ends of the little building. So it is today in the Ambassadorial Talks, thirteen years later.

The Berlin Conference of Foreign Ministers

In 1954, the "fruitless talks" at Panmunjom, as President Eisenhower called them,[7] were left in limbo, never to resume or settle the arrangements for a Political Conference on Korea. Instead the scene shifted from the quonset hut in the cold and barren valley of Panmunjom to the large building in booming Berlin where the Foreign Ministers of the Big Four—France, the Soviet Union, the United Kingdom, and the United States—began a four-week conference on January 25. It was the second source of American negotiations and contacts with Peking, for it produced an agreement to hold an international conference on Korea and Indochina, including the People's Republic of China and the Democratic People's Republic of Korea. The Panmunjom talks were relegated to history. Yet, the Berlin meeting had not been called as a substitute for them, or even to discuss Asian matters, since its concern was Germany and Austria. The timing and consequence of the Berlin Conference were coincidental but expedient in the process of leading to American negotiations with Peking, as so often happens in diplomacy.

The situation in Indochina had deteriorated rapidly during the winter of 1953–54, when it came to dominate European diplomacy and East-West relations. Purely by chance, insofar as the Korean and Indochinese questions were concerned, the Big Four Conference on Germany happened to convene in Berlin at the end of January just as the Talks in Panmunjom had reached a stalemate and the French government appeared to face defeat over Vietnam. Pressures for American and Chinese Communist military intervention were rapidly increasing. In these circumstances, the Soviet Foreign Minister, Mr. Molotov, apparently decided that something had to be done. He proposed that the agenda for the Berlin Conference add the subject of "the convening of a 'five-power' conference including the Chinese People's Republic to seek measures for reducing tensions in international relations," in addition to the German and Austrian questions for which the Big Four had agreed to convene. In the previous November, Molotov had already made a "Big Five" conference the condition for any discussion of German or Austrian matters. Now in January he retreated by relating a "five-power" conference only to problems of Asia.

The British Foreign Minister, Sir Anthony Eden, later Lord Avon, capitalized on Molotov's proposal as the "chance we needed" to seek a negotiation for Far Eastern questions, particularly the increasingly critical and dangerous situation in Indochina. His handiwork led to the eventual negotiations of the United States with the Chinese People's Republic. Eden suggested to Prime Minister Winston Churchill that the Chinese People's Republic be included in a conference limited to Far Eastern questions. From Berlin, Eden informed Prime Minister Churchill and the British Cabinet that: "Mr. Dulles admits that non-recognition is no obstacle to meeting the Chinese and, in fact, the Americans are meeting them in Panmunjom." Eden observed that while Dulles remained firmly opposed to a five-power conference he was agreeable to discussing "appropriate questions" with the Chinese Communists, although he questioned whether Indochina could be appropriately so classified. But Eden thought there was a gleam of hope there.[8] After two weeks of hard bargaining, Eden's hope blossomed.

The four ministers neared agreement first on having themselves, the Chinese People's Republic, plus the two Korean governments meet in Geneva to discuss Korea and then possibly Indochina with other appropriate interested parties. However, the United States refused to have the Chinese People's Republic included as a "convening power" because that would have gone too far in according

Peking virtual diplomatic recognition as well as a status on a par with the United States, the Soviet Union, Great Britain, and France. For a while, Molotov stubbornly adhered to his negotiating tactic of refusing to concede anything and insisting on obtaining convening-power status and full parity for Peking with the Big Four. Eden, in the characteristically skilled diplomatic adroitness of the British, found the formula "to meet the bear without parting us from the eagle," [9] by simply dropping the distinction between the "con-veners" and the "convened." By then Moscow had won a place for Peking in the world's top councils for the first time in the short life of the Chinese People's Republic. The Big Four proceeded to call a conference on Korea for April 26 at Geneva, to which the United States would invite the governments on the United Nations side and the Soviet Union would invite the Chinese People's Republic and North Korea. As for Indochina, the Big Four agreed that they would decide to invite other states concerned with that problem.

The Geneva Conference of 1954

The Geneva Conference of 1954 on Korea and Indochina then brought the top representatives of the American and Chinese Com-munist governments together for the first time, along with the several other participants in the two-part meetings.* The Secretary of State of the United States, John Foster Dulles, and the Prime Minister of the Chinese People's Republic, Chou En-lai, sat in the same conference hall in the Palais des Nations, passed in the corri-dors, and stood not far from each other in the same diplomatic lounge taking refreshments from the same table. But they never met or exchanged a word or even a nod. Mr. Dulles refused to shake hands with Prime Minister Chou En-lai, a fact to which the Chinese leader bitterly alluded in a private conversation years later.[10] For some weeks no member of the American delegation, except for the author, had any contact with the Chinese Communist delegation. Occasionally during the intermissions of the conference the author exchanged brief and innocuous pleasantries in the delegates' lounge with Chou's special assistant and interpreter who also was both a Harvard graduate and a "veteran" of the civilian talks at Panmun-

---

* One group met on Korea; another on Indochina. The Chinese People's Republic, France, the United Kingdom, the U.S.S.R., and the United States participated in both sets.

jom. The human and diplomatic separation of Panmunjom continued at Geneva. As far as contacts at the Conference itself were concerned, the American and Chinese officials avoided each other, as was to be expected between the two governments without diplomatic relations. However, British officials—having diplomatic relations with Peking—saw a good deal of the Chinese who cultivated the men from London, although Eden later wrote that he had found Chou En-lai very difficult.[11] The British came to play the role of "go-between" which is indispensable in negotiating with Asians. At Geneva they helped to bring the Americans and the Chinese Communists together outside the Conference on the single issue which could have fused contacts between such rigid and hostile adversaries.

The magnet impelling such opposites as Dulles and Chou to allow their representatives to meet was the incarceration of some forty Americans in Communist China, and the presence of several thousand Chinese aliens in the United States. This was the "soldering" factor which eventually fused all the other elements into the Sino-American Ambassadorial Talks. But if it had not been for the war in Korea and the unfortunate imprisonment or detention of some Americans in China, it is doubtful that the mere presence of these representatives at the same conference would have led to further diplomatic contacts between the Americans and the Chinese Communists at that time.

The Chinese Communists apparently made the first overt move for talks with the Americans. Chinese representatives kept asking the British questions about the American delegation, and appeared to seek British help in establishing direct contacts with the Americans. This was appropriate and feasible because the British Chargé d'Affaires in Peking, Humphrey Trevelyan, had been charged with handling American matters, such as prisoners, for Washington and was a member of the British delegation in Geneva. The Chinese also indicated that they would not continue to discuss Americans held prisoner in China with anyone but an American representative at a high level. After secret, informal soundings the spokesman of the Chinese delegation, Huang Hua, who happened to have been the principal, if unapproachable, Chinese Communist representative at Panmunjom, hinted in a press conference of May 26 that his government would be willing to talk directly with the American delegation regarding the release of American prisoners in China and the return of some 5,000 alien Chinese in the United States to mainland China.[12]

At first the Americans reacted cautiously to this Chinese initiative as they subsequently did to many Chinese initiatives in these Talks. Washington announced that it was opposed "for the time being" to direct negotiations with Peking on Americans held in China and that there would be no major diplomatic concessions for freeing these prisoners.[13] At the same time the United States delegation in Geneva released a long statement reviewing the efforts of the United States government to find out what had happened to the Americans held by the Chinese Communists. The delegation also attempted to correct "the grave distortion of the facts" in the Chinese Communist statement to the effect that the United States was preventing some 5,000 Chinese students from returning home, that is, to mainland China. However, after careful assessment for a few days, and under considerable diplomatic pressure, the State Department decided to accept the situation and talk with the Chinese Communists. In view of the long-standing responsibilities of the American government and the vigorous feelings of the American people about unjust treatment and unlawful detention of Americans in foreign countries, it was mandatory for the State Department "to leave no stone unturned" and to respond to the Chinese offer for direct talks regarding Americans in China. Therefore, Washington instructed the American delegation at Geneva to respond to the Chinese feeler. Ambassador U. Alexis Johnson, the American envoy to Czechoslovakia and Coordinator for the American Delegation at the Geneva Conference, was designated to handle the matter. The British delegation informed the Chinese delegation, which immediately accepted.

On June 5, 1954, Ambassador Johnson attended the first meeting with the Chinese Communists. According to Washington, he had "accompanied" a member of the United Kingdom delegation, Humphrey Trevelyan. The State Department announcement explained:

The United States Government has made the decision to authorize informal United States participation in this meeting because of its obligation to protect the welfare of its citizens. It intends to leave no stone unturned in its endeavors to secure the release of American citizens whom the Chinese Communists hold.

At least 32 American civilians are known to be in prison and others have been unable to secure exit permits. There are also Air Force and other military personnel who are believed to be under detention.

United States participation in these conversations in no way implies United States accordance with any measure of diplomatic recognition to the Red Chinese regime.[14]

The Chinese delegation designated the Secretary-General of the Chinese delegation, Wang Ping-nan. Neither he nor Johnson at that time anticipated that they were to meet in a diplomatic marathon of nearly eighty formal meetings during the next three and one-half years, as well as on many informal occasions.

This first meeting at the ambassadorial level between representatives of the United States and the Chinese People's Republic took place in the European headquarters of the United Nations and lasted for about thirty minutes. While the only result of the first encounter was agreement to meet again, Ambassador Johnson has described his attempt to make this first encounter as informal as possible, and more like normal diplomatic exchange than Panmunjom's diplomacy of stalemate. He arranged the first meeting in a room without any table so that the participants could sit casually around in chairs with a few interpreters and aides, as is usually done. The meeting went smoothly if quickly. However, the second one returned to the rigid style of Panmunjom separation. Since it was up to Wang Ping-nan to arrange it, he had a large table put in the room so that he and his Chinese aides would sit on one side and Ambassador Johnson with his aides would be on the other side. This division and confrontation set the pattern for all future meetings of the Ambassadorial Talks. However, the second meeting did lead to arrangements for the American prisoners to send and receive mail.

Altogether there were five such meetings. At the fourth the Chinese reported on the people named on the list which Ambassador Johnson had previously submitted, while the Americans presented certain facts about the Chinese students in the United States. At these meetings in June and July the United States requested the release of Americans detained by the Chinese Communists, and the latter pressed for the return of Chinese students who were, in Peking's view, being forcibly prevented from leaving the United States. However, neither side agreed. These initial exchanges did not produce any immediate results with regard to the prisoners and the students, but they set the stage and created the pattern for the ambassadorial-level Talks in 1955. At least each side agreed to review the situation later. Meanwhile they set up arrangements for maintaining contact by designated staff officers of each delegation to exchange information on the results of these so-called reviews.

Before the Geneva Conference ended in late July, this contact by each delegation was shifted to consular representatives of both countries regularly stationed in Geneva. The State Department announced on August 11 that the United States was conducting these negotiations under the direction of Consul-General Franklin C. Gowan.[15] The consular representatives supplied the thin link which kept a semblance of diplomatic contact and a slight channel of communication open between Washington and Peking for about a year, after which they were replaced by a stronger link at a higher level. During these twelve months, the consular representatives held seventeen unsuccessful meetings regarding the matter of the prisoners. Peking would not agree to their release and return. The issue became exceedingly acute when Peking announced in November that thirteen additional American military prisoners had been convicted and sentenced to jail. Eleven were members of the Air Force and two were Army civilian employees. The United States protested strongly through Consul-General Gowan, as well as through the British in Peking. However, the consular contact did not succeed in releasing any of the Americans. The initial meetings in Geneva at the ambassadorial level in 1954 and the subsequent consular negotiations—like Panmunjom—became a blind alley.

Other Factors

Then the United Nations entered the sequence of events leading to the Talks. When some American prisoners of war were jailed in November 1954, the outcry in the United States was swift and vehement. Not only did Washington send protests to Geneva and Peking, but also to the United Nations General Assembly which then empowered the Secretary-General to seek the release of the Americans. In early 1955, Dag Hammarskjold went to Peking, held long discussions with Chou En-lai, but collided with immovable resistance. Despite skillful and persistent efforts, the Secretary-General was not able either then or later to bring about the release of any Americans. Yet, by exhausting the good offices of the United Nations, he indirectly helped to bring the Chinese and the Americans to the negotiating table. Upon returning from Peking, Hammarskjold reported on January 13, 1955, that his talks with Chou En-lai had been definitely useful and that the door which had been opened could be kept open. He intimated that discussions on other pertinent questions had led him to believe that Peking might release the eleven American airmen if tension between the United States and the Chinese People's Republic were lessened.

Meanwhile, in early 1955, an important factor entered the sequence. Tension mounted rapidly and alarmingly over Taiwan. Whether Peking manipulated this tension to force Dulles and the Americans to talk with them cannot yet be confirmed. In any case, Peking saw a Treaty of Mutual Defense being negotiated and ratified between Washington and Taipei in late 1954 and early 1955 which formalized the United States commitment to defend Taiwan and the offshore islands from armed attack. In January 1955, the Congress passed the famous "Formosa Resolution" by huge majorities which endorsed this commitment. Shortly thereafter, military build-up and exchange of fire between Chinese Communists and Nationalist forces took place in the Taiwan area. This menacing atmosphere created added pressures in the United Nations and in many foreign ministries, which, in turn, eventually helped bring about the establishment of Sino-American diplomatic discussions at the ambassadorial level in mid-1955. Substantial efforts by friendly governments finally persuaded the State Department to agree, however reluctantly. The Asian neutrals had much to do with activating the Ambassadorial Talks when it became evident that nothing could be worked out to relieve the tensions over Taiwan or to solve the issue of prisoners either under United Nations auspices, or at the consular level in Geneva.

At first, Mr. Dulles was not inclined to talk directly with Peking on any subject. He told a press conference on January 18 that the United States was not willing to resume bilateral negotiations at Geneva on the question of the American fliers and the Chinese students because the United States was letting the United Nations take responsibility in this matter.[16] But for the first time he discussed the possibility of a cease-fire in the Taiwan Straits with a pledge that the Nationalists would not attack the Chinese mainland if the Communists would forswear any armed assault on Taiwan. He thought that such a cease-fire would be in line with the broad objectives of the United States and the United Nations to seek peaceful solutions of controversial problems, even though it was easier to discuss such matters in principle than to work them out in practice. This was his first public reference to a proposal for the joint renunciation of force which, in a few months, became the principal contention at issue between himself and Chou through their intermediaries at Geneva.

In late January, New Zealand, with the support of the United States and Great Britain, asked the Secretary-General of the United Nations to deal with the hostilities and tensions in the Taiwan area between the Chinese Communists and the Chinese Nationalists over the small islands off the Chinese mainland. Peking could have taken part in the debate at the United Nations and the United States would not have opposed its participation to work out a cease-fire.[17] On January 31, the Security Council voted to invite Peking to send a representative to join in the debate on the fighting over the offshore islands. The United States Representative, Ambassador Henry Cabot Lodge, said:

We believe that in any effort to end an armed conflict to which the Chinese Communist regime is a party it is useful for this regime to be present. This was our attitude in 1953 concerning the Korean political conference. It is also the case here now.[18]

Peking immediately rejected the invitation, partly on the grounds that it would not accept until the Chinese Nationalists had been "driven out" from the Security Council and the People's Republic of China seated instead.

As if there were not enough complicating factors in the whole situation, another one was now added: a new Soviet proposal for an international conference including the People's Republic of China to deal with the Taiwan crisis. This was a Russian maneuver similar to the demand of 1954 at Berlin for including Peking as a convener in a "five-power" conference which had led to the Geneva Conference of 1954 with both the United States and the Chinese People's Republic as joint and equal participants. In a note of February 4 to Great Britain, the Soviet Union proposed a ten-power conference on the Taiwan situation which would not have included the Republic of China (the Chinese Nationalists) but would have been composed of the United States, the Soviet Union, Great Britain, France, the Chinese People's Republic and the five so-called Colombo powers in Asia—India, Burma, Indonesia, Pakistan, and Ceylon. It was partly the issue of the role of these Colombo powers in a conference on Korea which had led to the stalemate of political talks at

Panmunjom. Moscow's renewed pressure for another big conference with the Chinese People's Republic as a major participant also
helped induce the United States government to resume Ambassadorial Talks with Peking as the lesser evil to avoid another conference
like the one at Geneva in 1954. In early February the United States
government expressed its distaste for the idea of another conference
on the Geneva model to discuss a cease-fire in the Taiwan Straits
when a State Department spokesman said: "I find it difficult to
imagine that anyone who participated in that experience would wish
to repeat it." [19] However, the Department did not close the door
on possibilities for future negotiations in view of the fact that Moscow kept up its diplomatic pressures for a large conference including Peking.

With so many avenues blocked and tensions steadily mounting
over Taiwan, the next move in the sequence of events leading to the
Ambassadorial Talks came from the Asian neutral countries that
otherwise would have attended that conference. Prime Minister U
Nu of Burma played a leading role, initially as a self-appointed peace-
maker between Washington and Peking. This devout and sincere
man had cast himself in this role, as a practicing Buddhist leader
might quite naturally do, even if Washington or Peking considered
that this was an intrusion by an uninvited but respected friend.
Nevertheless, U Nu visited Peking in February 1955. He publicly
balanced the anti-American speeches of his hosts with some favorable comments about his American friends, and privately tried to
serve as the "go-between" in the customary Asian way of bringing
two contenders together. Peking made use of him in that capacity,
and he succeeded somewhat. When Dulles visited Rangoon in late
February 1955—the first visit of a high-ranking American statesman
to Burma—U Nu had some interesting news to convey to him.
With considerable intensity and seriousness, he privately related
Chou En-lai's willingness to negotiate the problem of American
airmen and other issues directly with Washington. According to U
Nu, Peking was agreeable to receiving an unofficial American mission for such discussion. U Nu benignly endorsed the proposal and
hoped that Dulles would follow it up.* The Secretary of State tact-
fully skirted the proposal but expressed his appreciation to U Nu
for his interest and effort in seeking to reduce unnecessary tensions.
U Nu immediately proceeded to announce Chou's offer publicly on

* The author was present during these talks in Rangoon.

February 28.[20] At the same time Peking was conveying similar word to certain delegations at the United Nations of its interest in bilateral talks with the Americans outside the United Nations.[21] However, the State Department opposed Chou's proposal transmitted by U Nu and the idea of bilateral talks, and did not follow up the conversations in Rangoon with enthusiasm or alacrity.

Later, at his news conference on April 5, Secretary Dulles was asked whether the recent American release of some Chinese students indicated a preference in Washington for peace rather than war over Taiwan. He answered: "In a broad sense you could say that it was indicative of our desire to keep our relations with the Chinese Communists on, you might call, a civilized peaceful basis." [22]

The Bandung Drama

The decisive move on the activation of the Ambassadorial Talks came suddenly and unexpectedly on April 23 in the colorful setting of Bandung, Java, where the Afro-Asian Conference was in progress at a time of severe tension over the Taiwan Straits. On this dramatic occasion, Chou En-lai abruptly launched a sensational initiative. It captured attention everywhere because it was utter in its surprise, precise in its timing, and total in its impact. At a luncheon given by the Prime Minister of Ceylon with the Prime Ministers of India, Burma, Pakistan, and Indonesia, the representative of Thailand (Prince Wan), and the representative from the Philippines (General Romulo) present, Prime Minister Chou En-lai issued the following announcement:

The Chinese people are friendly to the American people. The Chinese people do not want to have a war with the United States of America. The Chinese Government is willing to sit down and enter into negotiations with the United States Government to discuss the question of relaxing tension in the Far East and especially the question of relaxing tension in the Taiwan area.[23]

This brief and curt statement of 64 words caused a world-wide diplomatic explosion, and activated the series of final steps leading to the opening of the Ambassadorial Talks some ninety days later. It highlighted the posture of coexistence and display of affability which Chou effectively carried out at Bandung. Later, a Chinese spokesman reiterated this statement to the press and explained that the negotiations were intended to be bilateral, not multilateral, although the offer would not be transmitted directly to Washington. The next day, on April 24, 1955, Peking made the offer officially to a wide audience when Chou En-lai repeated his proposal for negotiations between Peking and Washington in his formal and final speech at the concluding session of the Asian-African conference in Bandung. Obviously he had come prepared well in advance to take this initiative.

Everyone in Bandung—and in most capitals of the world—immediately wondered how Washington would react. The initial American response was instant and negative, if somewhat confused. In a public statement never submitted to Dulles, who was not in Washington, the State Department, while welcoming any sincere efforts to bring peace to the world, noted that Chou's offer had not been submitted by official channels, insisted on the participation of the Republic of China in any discussions concerning the area, and called on Communist China "to give evidence before the world of its good intentions" by a cease-fire, release of the American airmen and others, and acceptance of the outstanding invitation of the United Nations Security Council.[24] However, Senator George, the highly respected Democratic spokesman on foreign policy, approved Chou's offer, declaring that it was "high time" for American officials to show a willingness to talk with Peking. On the other hand, the Republican leader, Senator Knowland, denounced Chou's offer as "another Munich."[25] The next day, Senator Lyndon Johnson declared that he hoped that Senator George's views would receive "careful consideration" from every American official at the policy level.[26] In the meantime, Chou amplified his announcement in hinting privately to the Pakistani Prime Minister that the American fliers would be freed if the United States agreed to negotiations on Taiwan. This was in keeping with an ancient Chinese custom of trading hostages for status and territory. Chou En-lai indicated that he considered the State Department's negative response more as an immediate rebuff than a final closure.[27]

The next move was up to John Foster Dulles, who returned to his office the following day. Public and diplomatic pressures focused on him. Chou had maneuvered Dulles into the position of either responding in some affirmative way or of defying favorable opinion around the world. But Dulles was always resourceful, particularly at times of crisis. In a press conference on April 26 he parried Chou's initiative and opened up room for maneuver. He softened the State

Department's initial reaction, eliminated the insistence on Chinese Nationalist participation, and cleared the way for "peaceful" negotiations with Peking under suitable circumstances. He recognized, as he put it, that "recent developments" might have seemed of "decisive importance" both in Europe and Asia, but whether Chou's proposal was sincere or merely a "propaganda game" remained to be ascertained. Willing to find out, Dulles opened the door to American negotiations with Peking:

> The first thing it seems to me that requires to be determined is whether we must prepare for war in that area or whether there is apt to be a cease-fire in the area. One cannot very well settle matters under the threat of a gun. So far there has been nothing but war threats in the area. . . . As I say, you do not negotiate—at least, the United States does not negotiate —with a pistol aimed at its head.
>
> The first thing is to find out whether there is a possibility of a cease-fire in the area. That is a matter which can be discussed perhaps bilaterally, or at the United Nations, or possibly under other circumstances.[28]

Whether the United States would actually sit down and talk with the Chinese Communists, depended, he pragmatically pointed out, "on what we talk about and whether there is evidence that such talks will be held in good faith on both sides." He made it perfectly clear as a precondition to any talks that the United States would not discuss the interests of the Republic of China behind its back nor negotiate the status of Taiwan and the offshore islands, for this, he suggested rather ambiguously, could only be done under United Nations auspices. However, subject to these qualifications, he specifically did not rule out bilateral Talks with Communist China which Chou had proposed at Bandung. Dulles did suggest that the freeing of the fliers would be an evidence of Peking's sincerity, though not a precondition to these Talks.

The next day President Eisenhower also modified the State Department's initial "chilly reaction." In a news conference, he backed Dulles' willingness to negotiate with the Chinese Communists without Chinese Nationalist participation. The President said the United States "would be ready to meet the Communists if there seemed to be an opportunity for us to further the easing of tensions, the advancement of world peace, and certainly getting back our prisoners." [29]

For the next few weeks Chou En-lai, with the initiative, kept his pressure on Dulles. In a report to the Standing Committee of the

National People's Congress on May 17 in Peking, Chou renewed his offer to "sit down and enter into negotiations" with the United States to ease tension in the Taiwan area. He went on to state that Peking was "willing to strive for the liberation of Taiwan by peaceful means so far as it is possible." However, he added the stipulation, which has since become such a common refrain, that "no negotiations should in the slightest degree affect the Chinese people's exercise of their own sovereign rights, their just demand and action, to liberate Taiwan." [30] On May 30, Peking announced that it was deporting four American airmen after having tried and found them guilty. In welcoming this act the State Department urged Peking to free the other Americans who were being held in Communist China.[31] On June 2, Chou repeated to Indonesian journalists his willingness to "sit down and negotiate" with the Americans, but rejected a cease-fire as unnecessary in view of the absence of any war between the United States and his country.[32]

The Diplomatic Brokers and the 1955 Summit Conference

In this thawing but still critical international atmosphere, a final round of secret diplomacy from several directions added the last push to starting the Ambassadorial Talks. Independent efforts of the Indian and British governments on the one hand, and the forthcoming Summit Conference of 1955 on the other, coincidentally produced the result. Prime Minister Nehru and his envoy, V.K. Krishna Menon, continuing from where Prime Minister U Nu had left off, followed up Chou En-lai's Bandung declaration. The intercession of these Indian officials put considerable pressure on the President and Secretary Dulles to agree to the Talks. Once Washington had made an affirmative decision, the Foreign Office in London helped Peking and Washington actually work out the mechanics for setting up the Talks. The efforts of Moscow and Peking to include the Chinese People's Republic in the Summit Conference of July 1955 also induced Washington to take the bypass of bilateral Talks as a detour around Peking's participation in any summit meeting.

As to the Indian role, Krishna Menon played the mediator with intense persistence. Acting on Nehru's strong desire to bring the Americans and the Chinese to the conference table, Krishna Menon assumed the task of finding a basis for negotiation and establishing communications between Peking and Washington so that they could "sit down" together. First, he went to Peking on a "volunteer mediation" trip in late May. He announced, upon returning to New Delhi on May 24, that four American airmen had been released and deported from China, implying that he had had some part in that release and that others would follow if negotiations were started.[33] He immediately proceeded on to Washington for long talks with President Eisenhower and Secretary Dulles in mid-June where he insistently and strenuously sought to persuade them that bilateral Talks could be and should be established in view of Peking's desire to negotiate.*

The President and Secretary Dulles were deeply concerned over the responsibilities and commitments of the United States to the Republic of China and the effect on its proper position if the United States did not carefully consider every aspect of any bilateral dealings with Peking. They were also uncertain about the validity of Peking's purported intentions toward such Talks, and the feasibility of outside mediation, however well-intentioned. In any event, the administration was not dead set against negotiations with Peking. In his news conference on June 28, Secretary Dulles reiterated that the United States was willing to enter into direct conversations with Communist China, but that any international discussion of a larger conference on Far Eastern subjects had reached an impasse because Communist China insisted on excluding Nationalist China.[34] That apparently ended the possibility in Washington's view of adding Peking to the Summit meeting or to some other multilateral conference. He said that the United States would be willing to talk about American prisoners and a cease-fire, but not on any matter concerning the Republic of China.

Nevertheless, in spite of lukewarm reactions by the President and Dulles, Prime Minister Nehru continued to seek their agreement. He exchanged a series of messages with President Eisenhower, discussing various considerations in opening bilateral talks.[35] By mid-July the two leaders had narrowed the matter down to Nehru's acceptance of Eisenhower's suggestion that American and Chinese diplomats discuss the problem in Geneva. If these initial contacts succeeded, then regular discussions could be established—perhaps between the two respective Ambassadors stationed in Berne, Swit-

---

* The author was involved in some of these discussions with Mr. Menon.

zerland.[36] This was the essence of the ultimate formula negotiated through the good offices of the British diplomats just before and during the Summit Conference at Geneva on July 18–23, 1955.

During this time Washington was actually working closely with London and Peking to negotiate arrangements for opening the Talks of the two Ambassadors. Before the Summit Conference opened later in July at Geneva, many but not all of the details had been settled by this diplomatic process. On July 11, Dulles decided to proceed with the completion of these arrangements in view of the forthcoming Summit. It was apparently felt that agreement on setting up the Ambassadorial Talks would circumvent pressure for including Peking in a "Big Five" at Geneva. Moreover, a Summit Conference would be a convenient occasion for the American and British leaders to settle the details of such Talks, or if necessary to contact the Russians regarding arrangements with Peking. Thus, the Summit Conference put the finishing touches on the actual establishment of American official contacts with Peking. Diplomatic exchanges on setting up the Talks also absorbed or diverted mounting anxiety in many capitals over another possible Taiwan crisis.

The situation in the area of Taiwan seriously affected the Summit. As Sir Anthony Eden has reported in his memoirs, he and the other three heads of government at the Summit Conference were deeply troubled and preoccupied by the situation in the Far East, especially the offshore islands of Quemoy and Matsu, and the private anxieties and informal conversations focused on the Far East, not on Europe. According to Eden, although the offshore islands were never mentioned at the conference table, they were in fact the world's "flashpoint" in the summer of 1955.[37] He was convinced that the Geneva Summit Conference could dampen their explosive force. Since the Far East situation was not a topic on which President Eisenhower could deal directly with the Russians,* Eden again served, as he had done in 1954, as a "broker" between the Americans who "knew that they had a bear by the tail" and the Soviet leaders who shared concern over the danger in the Taiwan area while persistently upholding Peking's position. The Russians insisted that it was difficult to discuss the issue while "the master of the house is

* In fact, the American delegation was determined not to take up any Far Eastern questions formally or informally at the Summit Conference, with the Russians at least, although the author participated in the Summit Conference as an advisor on Far Eastern matters and handled the mechanics for setting up the Ambassadorial Talks.

absent," an allusion to the Soviet desire to include Peking in a "Big Five" meeting. In any event, Eden's private discussions separately with President Eisenhower and then with Bulganin and Khrushchev convinced him that the two major world powers wished to avoid conflict in the area. He was able to convey to the Russians the American wish to calm things down in some way, and to convey to the Americans the notion that both the Russians and the Chinese were looking for a peaceful solution in bilateral negotiations between Washington and Peking. In summarizing the contribution of the Summit Conference to the "pacification" of the Taiwan crisis of 1955, Mr. Eden wrote:

Mr. Khrushchev said that traditionally the Chinese were a patient people. He believed that they would not take any rash action at the present time. It was to be hoped, however, that some fruitful result would come from the meetings which were to be held in Geneva between the two Ambassadors appointed by the United States and China. I said that these discussions should help. Though they would begin with such questions as release of prisoners, they might well broaden out to cover some of the more substantial issues.[38]

With Washington's green light already given in mid-July via British diplomatic channels to Peking for bilateral Talks in Geneva at a higher level and with a wider scope,[39] the finishing touches on the mechanics for opening the Ambassadorial Talks were made. Most of this was done during the Summit in a series of exchanges between Peking and Washington, again conveyed by British diplomatic channels. Messages were exchanged on the agenda, representation, location, date, and draft announcement for opening these Talks. Some of these details had to be reconciled in a series of three-way exchanges to get the concurrence of both the Americans and the Chinese.

An agenda for the Talks was the principal obstacle. As the Americans had learned at Panmunjom, it had to be prudently handled, lest it later prejudice the main issue. Peking apparently wanted an agenda predetermining the outcome of the Talks, and seems to have pressed for specifying such practical issues as a foreign ministers' conference, an end to the American embargo, withdrawal of American forces from Taiwan, and an exchange of newsmen and other cultural contacts. Washington insisted on specifying only the repatriation of Americans and an agreement on the renunciation of force. Such divergent positions threatened a deadlock again over the content and order of the agenda. Finally, the Americans came up with an ingenious formula to end the impasse by suggesting a simple two-point agenda to embrace both parties' positions: first, the return of citizens, and second, "other practical matters now at issue." That would cover everything and let each side present its case and discuss all these subjects simultaneously or not at all. After considerable exchange on this formula, both sides agreed. Only details remained to be reconciled. But these, too, proved to be exasperating for all concerned.

By way of illustrating these difficulties, the exchange of messages on the text of a simultaneous announcement of the opening of the Talks to be made during the Summit Conference almost bogged down over the political significance of spelling one word—the capital of the Chinese People's Republic—in two significantly different ways. The Chinese Communists insisted on "Peking"—which in Chinese means "northern capital"—while the Americans held out for "Peiping"—which in Chinese means "northern peace." The Chinese Nationalists and the Americans deliberately used that spelling for the use of "Peking" would have designated it as the capital of China, whereas they believed it to be Taipei, on the island of Taiwan. Toward the end of the Summit Conference all other details had been worked out but this single point of diplomatic nomenclature. The Summit Conference itself was about to wind up without having established talks between the Americans and Chinese. It was on the presumption that the Americans would be willing to enter such talks that pressure for including the Chinese had been dropped. Now President Eisenhower found himself faced with an embarrassing little decision on the mere spelling of a word, even though it made for a symbolic distinction, with an important difference for both Chinese parties. Unless quickly resolved, this would delay the agreement on the Ambassadorial Talks, prevent it from being made under the auspices of the Summit Conference, and possibly hold up the Conference, which had not produced significant results. The dispute was resolved when London suggested that both parties issue their own announcements with the particular spelling left to their own discretion! President Eisenhower was anxious to settle the matter and he and Secretary Dulles followed the British suggestion. Peking also sent its approval of the announcement with the full knowledge that Washington would use the word "Peiping" in its releases.

Consequently, on July 25, 1955, Washington and Peking issued the following joint communiqué to hold Ambassadorial Talks, beginning on August 1:

As a result of communication between the United States and the People's Republic of China through the diplomatic channels of the United Kingdom, it has been agreed that the talks held in the last year between consular representatives of both sides at Geneva should be conducted on the ambassadorial level in order to aid in settling the matter of repatriation of civilians who desire to return to their respective countries and to facilitate further discussions and settlement of certain other practical matters now at issue between both sides. The first meeting of ambassadorial representatives of both sides will take place on August 1, 1955, at Geneva.[40]

The State Department accompanied the communiqué with the explanation that Ambassador U. Alexis Johnson, who was stationed in Prague, Czechoslovakia, would again represent the United States and that several governments had suggested that such talks be held, after exploring the possibilities in "Peiping" and Washington, in the belief that the talks might produce agreement on the return of United States citizens in China and facilitate discussion of other matters.[41] The Department's announcement concluded with the same caveat of 1954 that these Talks would not involve diplomatic recognition of the Chinese People's Republic.

Opening Round in the Dulles-Chou Duel

At his news conference on July 26, Secretary Dulles explained his rationale for reversing himself in early July by responding affirmatively to Chou's move for direct bilateral discussions with the United States rather than continuing to seek United Nations-sponsored negotiations.[42] Dulles noted that several developments since Chou's proposal at Bandung had indicated the "possibility of obtaining beneficial results" from a continuation of the Talks at Geneva and their restoration to the original ambassadorial level. Four out of fifteen prisoners of war and some civilians had been released. Something of a *de facto* cease-fire had evolved in the Taiwan area. The former "belligerent Communist propaganda" about Taiwan and the United States had abated somewhat. And various governments having relations with the People's Republic of China had informed the United States government of their belief that Peking desired to pursue "a peaceful path." Dulles then outlined the "practical matters" which he wanted the Talks to cover:

1. Return of American civilians detained in Communist China. The United States was also prepared to discuss the status of "the few Chinese students" in the United States "who desire to return to Communist China and who the Chinese Communists claim are prevented from doing so."

2. Reinforcement of the efforts of the United Nations to secure the return of Americans who became prisoners of war under the United Nations command in Korea.

3. Precautions against a repetition of such incidents * as the shooting down of the Cathay airliner aircraft with a loss of American and other lives.

4. The determination of the basic point of whether a cease-fire in the Taiwan area could be arranged and the principle of the nonrecourse to force agreed to, or whether it was necessary to prepare for war in that area. The United States believed that differences which divide countries should not be settled by recourse to force where this would be apt to provoke international war.

Mr. Dulles concluded on a conciliatory note:

No doubt the Chinese Communists will have matters of their own to bring up. We shall listen to hear what they are, and if they directly involve the United States and Communist China we will be disposed to discuss them with a view to arriving at a peaceful settlement.

As President Eisenhower said last night, "The United States will go to any length consistent with our concepts of decency and justice and right to attain peace. For this purpose we will work cooperatively with the Soviets and any other people as long as there is sincerity of purpose and a genuine desire to go ahead."

That is the principle which will govern the continuation of our talks with the Chinese Communists at Geneva.[43]

The joint announcements and Dulles' explanations stirred up diplomatic excitement and general endorsement all over the world. Even Khrushchev voiced optimism when he remarked at a Swiss reception in Moscow that, if the United States wanted "positive results" as China did, the outcome could not be negative and the problems could be settled.[44] In the United States, even spokesmen for the government on Taiwan publicly assented, although it privately detested the very idea of Washington, its ally, talking alone with Peking, its mortal enemy.[45] The reaction of most senators and American editorial opinion were favorable, if not completely opti-

---

* This refers to the crash near Hainan island of a British unarmed civilian commercial plane in July 1954 when Chinese Communist fighter aircraft attacked it suddenly and shot it down in the sea. See *Department of State Bulletin*, August 2, 1954, p. 165, August 9, 1954, pp. 196–197, and August 16, 1954, pp. 241–242.

mistic. Senator George and some of his colleagues immediately called for a Foreign Ministers' meeting between Dulles and Chou and seemed to expect that such a meeting would soon take place.[46]

While Dulles did not exclude this possibility if the Chinese Communists showed sufficient good will, he also told his news conference on July 26 that he did not think a meeting of the two Foreign Ministers was a likely possibility and believed that the Ambassadorial Talks would suffice "for the time being and at the present stage." At his news conference, President Eisenhower seemed to go further with less hesitation in recognizing that the United States might eventually have to agree to a Foreign Ministers' meeting. He indicated that this would be "a logical development" which he would accept as a matter of course. However, he wanted the United States first to ascertain whether the Chinese Communists would accept a cease-fire.[47]

The government in Peking also appeared expansive, conciliatory and hopeful—in their terms. On July 28, Peking announced that Ambassador Wang Ping-nan, its envoy stationed in Warsaw, would again represent the People's Republic of China for Talks with the Americans at the ambassadorial level. Then, for his part, Chou followed up the joint communiqué of July 25 with a significant pronouncement in a long report on "The Present International Situation and China's Foreign Policy" which he presented to the National People's Congress on July 30.[48] After favorably reviewing the results of the Summit Conference at Geneva and a number of other situations in the world, he turned to the Far East. The most tense situation there, he said, was in the Taiwan area, caused by the United States' "occupation of China's territory, Taiwan, and United States' interference with the liberation of China's coastal islands." Defining this tension as "an international issue between China and the United States," Chou went on to declare the standard policy of the Peking government that the sovereign right to liberate Taiwan was a matter of China's internal affairs and that the two questions, namely, the actions of the United States and the Chinese liberation of Taiwan, should not be lumped together. He pointed out again that his government had already proposed that China and the United States sit down and enter into negotiations to discuss the question of easing and ultimately eliminating the tension in the Taiwan area. He then made the significant declaration: "There is no war between China and the United States; the peoples of China and the United States are friendly towards each other; the Chinese people want no war with the United States, so the question of cease-fire between China and the United States does not arise." He went on to note that, of the two possible ways for the Chinese People to liberate Taiwan, by war or by peaceful means, the Chinese people were ready to use the latter, "conditions permitting"—which meant that the United States should not interfere with such peaceful liberation. He offered to negotiate with "the responsible local authorities of Taiwan to map out concrete steps for its peaceful liberation" and proclaimed that the Chinese people were firmly opposed to any ideas or "plots" of the so-called "Two Chinas."

Noting that the Ambassadorial Talks would start in two days to settle the matter of repatriation of civilians of both sides and to facilitate further "discussion and settlement" of certain other practical matters at issue between them, Chou En-lai took a rather optimistic view of the outcome and canvassed quite a wide scope of subject matter for the Talks. He thought it possible to reach a "reasonable settlement" of the question of the return of civilians to their respective countries. Each could entrust a third party to look after its civilians in the other country and their return. He stressed that the situation of the Chinese students in the United States was "particularly inconsistent with humanitarian principles since they were obstructed from returning home while their relatives have no way to aid them financially." He went on to suggest that, if the United States were prepared to cooperate with China, the Ambassadorial Talks should be able to make preparations for negotiations between China and the United States for "relaxing and eliminating the tension in the Taiwan area," which would have meant a high-level conference with Dulles. Chou cited his "practical matters," which he implied should be taken up either at the Ambassadorial Talks or in his ministerial conference with Dulles. First, he suggested the removal of the "unjust blockade and embargo" so that peaceful trade between all countries would not be hindered. Second, he said that the Chinese people * would like to see the United States withdraw its armed forces from Taiwan and the Taiwan Straits. Third, he stated that the Chinese people demanded that foreign countries stop subversive activities against China. And, fourth, he mentioned that the Chinese people hoped for the conclusion of a "pact of collective

* In Peking parlance, "the Chinese people" means the Chinese government.

peace" by the countries of Asia and the Pacific region, including the United States, to replace "the antagonistic military blocs" now existing in that part of the world.

Chou En-lai finished his statement on what then sounded like a friendly, statesmanlike, and constructive tone.

We recognize that for the above wishes to be fulfilled, it is necessary first of all that China and the United States should display sincerity in negotiations, that the two sides establish contacts to increase mutual understanding and trust. Only by efforts of both sides and reciprocal demonstration of good will, can the tension in the Taiwan area be relaxed and ultimately eliminated.

China for her part, in accordance with its consistent stand of striving for the relaxation of tension, will endeavor to make the forthcoming Sino-American talks at the ambassadorial level pave the way for further negotiations between China and the United States.[48]

His diplomatic posture reflected the mood of 1955, expressed in the hopes of Bandung, the spirit of Geneva, and the vogue for "coexistence." His diplomatic strategy was to use this momentum to put himself on a par with Dulles. That was Peking's real aim.

Peking went to surprising and unusual lengths to create a favorable atmosphere for the opening of the Ambassadorial Talks on August 1. Not only did Chou En-lai appear reasonable and conciliatory, but Peking took a specific psychological initiative designed to please Washington and create a favorable impression on the eve of the Talks. On July 31, the day after Chou spoke and the day before the Talks opened, the Chinese government in Peking released the eleven American airmen who had been sentenced and imprisoned in November of 1954. Seizing the initiative and capturing the headlines, Ambassador Wang then opened the Ambassadorial Talks with this dramatic announcement before the official discussions began. He explained with unusual frankness that the release of the American prisoners was a deliberate move on the part of the Chinese government designed to produce "favorable" effects on the Talks. In other words, the motive was political. As to the Talks, he went on to put his government's "reasonable" attitude on the public and private record even before they had officially opened:

It is my sincere hope that our talks will contribute to the easing of tension between China and the United States, which will in turn contribute to the cause of safeguarding world peace and security. I am convinced that with our joint efforts it should be possible for our talks to realize this highly significant goal. . . .

In our present talks, so long as both of us adopt the attitude of negotiation and conciliation, there should not be any difficulty for us to reach a reasonable settlement of the question of the return of civilians of both sides to their respective countries.[49]

The American delegation at Geneva reserved comment and attended to the immediate business of formally agreeing on an agenda and launching the Talks.

But on August 2, in answering questions at his press conference regarding the previous day's opening of the Ambassadorial Talks, Secretary Dulles responded favorably to Chou's statement of July 30, which Washington considered promising and conciliatory.[50] As to the return of Chinese citizens from the United States to the mainland, he said that was a question that would be looked into as a result of the Geneva Talks. On the contradiction between himself and Chou as to whether a cease-fire was or was not a proper and valid matter for discussion between the United States and the Chinese People's Republic, Dulles explained that, whereas Chou En-lai was using the phrase "cease-fire" in a technical sense, he himself was thinking of the danger of possible fighting between the two countries and the desirability of obtaining assurances "that the Chinese Communists were not planning to use military force in order to achieve their ambitions in that area." Dulles thought the tone of Chou's statement in general indicated "his going further in the renunciation of force than anything he had said before." He was very glad to note that Chou En-lai had apparently approved his statement of July 26 to the effect that the difference which divided countries should not be resolved by the use of force. When Dulles was asked whether he was not seeking a cease-fire in terms of "a United Nations Charter declaration between the Chinese Communists and the United States," he replied: "That is correct." On the other hand, when he was asked if he envisaged a high-level talk since he did not expect "a broader no-shooting arrangement" to result from the Geneva Talks, he replied that would come about primarily as a result of a unilateral declaration of policy by the leaders of each government rather than through bilateral agreement between the two governments. And he thought that Chou En-lai, in his statement of July 30 had gone farther in that direction than at any other time.

Secretary Dulles reaffirmed his earlier statements, particularly of April 26, that the United States was not willing to negotiate with a pistol at its head, for that would make it impossible to negotiate the other "practical matters" which he did not define as concretely as Chou had done. But he indicated again that the situation now permitted an attempt to negotiate:

I pointed out last week that a number of things had happened which indicate that the pistol had been laid down and that it made it possible to try to clear up now some of these practical matters between us. But the important thing is that the pistol should be permanently discarded and we hope that the trend of events will be reassurance on that point.[50]

At the end of his news conference, Dulles was asked if there were not developing an easier relationship with Communist China, to which he replied:

The release of the fliers, the release of the civilians, if it comes about, such statements as are made by Chou En-lai, if I interpret them right and if they are sincere and permanent parts of policy, might mark the beginning of a new phase in Chinese Communist relations with the rest of the world. I pointed out some time ago that the Chinese Communists seem to be much more violent and fanatical, more addicted to the use of force than the Russians are or have become. Whether or not there is going to be a change in that respect I don't know. There are some auguries, but we always have to remember the adage that one swallow does not make a summer.[51]

The only serious resistance to opening the Talks had come from the government of the Republic of China on Taiwan and from the American Ambassador there, Karl Rankin. He has reported that the Chinese Nationalist government in Taipei regarded these Geneva Talks with grave misgivings because it feared that these contacts might lead to formal recognition of "Peiping." [52] It questioned whether most people would be able to differentiate between ambassadorial meetings and regular diplomatic relations. He reported that Taipei's alarm increased with indications that the United States would raise the question of a renunciation of the use of force, especially in the Taiwan area. According to Ambassador Rankin, our Chinese ally at first viewed the Ambassadorial Talks as a major change in American policy on the Chinese question. For these and other reasons, Ambassador Rankin opposed the Talks. Taipei has never felt comfortable with the Talks, although the opening rounds and the first years of the Talks did not prove to be alarming.

After Dulles and Chou had spoken so fully, it should have been clear at the outset what the Talks would cover and how they might progress. Actually, Washington wanted just two things: the quick release of the Americans and a simple renunciation of force in the Taiwan area. Peking sought the American evacuation of the Taiwan area and a new status in world affairs. All the other topics were secondary, or merely tactical. Thus, in reality, the encounter between Dulles and Chou began with irreconcilable matters. Yet it opened in an aura of euphoria and great expectations.

Despite the resistance of Taipei, the stipulations of Chou, and the reservations of Dulles, a propitious, optimistic aura surrounded the opening of these negotiations. Both parties spoke reasonably and stressed sincerity. World statesmen encouraged real negotiations and anticipated quick results. Tensions between China and the United States would be eased, the pistol dropped, force renounced, barriers lowered, citizens returned. Apparently the long and painstaking road of many efforts from Panmunjom, Berlin, Geneva, New York, Rangoon, Bandung, Washington, Peking, New Delhi, Moscow, London and back to Geneva culminated in such euphoric hope over the prospects for a Washington-Peking détente that it temporarily concealed the evident unbridgeable schism. Neither Dulles nor Chou publicly blurred or intentionally bypassed the non-negotiable issue of Taiwan in either strategic or political terms. Yet even the relatively technical question of repatriation of civilians ran into immediate hurdles. To this day it remains an unfinished and acrimonious issue.

PART II

Peking's Initiatives Rebuffed

CHAPTER THREE

The Single Agreement
on the
Repatriation of Civilians

It is curious and ironic that the United States and Communist China throughout their negotiations reached their only agreement over the issue of a relatively small group of human beings, a question of Americans in China and Chinese in the United States. Each government treated the matter of individuals and prisoners from opposite standpoints. This was a clash of long standing, one might even call it an ancestral divergence of two cultures: the concern for the individual, on the one hand, and his exploitation, on the other.

Americans put great value on the dignity of the individual and the duty of a government to protect individual citizens abroad. It has been a traditional requirement of American foreign policy to go to any lengths to protect the security and life of American individuals abroad, to assure that justice is accorded them, and that their imprisonment is validated by law. Undoubtedly the policy-makers in Peking were fully aware of the compulsion weighing upon the American authorities concerning American individuals in China, whether at liberty or in prison.

In contrast, Chinese imperial practice had used individuals and prisoners for political bargaining and as hostages. It was thus no break with China's historical method of dealing with "barbarian" nations for Peking to use the Americans in China as hostages in its diplomatic maneuvering with Washington. Peking used them to lead a reluctant United States government to the negotiating table. But even after the Agreement on the immediate repatriation of all Americans in China had been negotiated and concluded, the Chinese

63

Communist government kept the Americans in jail and only released them gradually over a number of years, presumably in order to gain the best advantage in subsequent negotiations with Washington. This attitude toward individuals and the practice of using them as hostages goes far to explain the willingness of Peking to agree to put this item on the agenda, to negotiate a clear and simple agreement, and then to frustrate and violate the implementation of what they had just agreed to do.

In addition, Communist philosophy and a totalitarian regime put little if any value on the life or dignity of the individual as such. The state is all important, while individuals are only instruments or resources to be used for achieving its goals. Evidently, Peking used the American prisoners as well as the alien Chinese in the United States to seek its foreign-policy objectives.

It is this clash in outlook of American philosophy and Chinese Communist ideology which accounts for the strange paradox of the United States negotiating with the People's Republic of China, concluding a formal agreement with a state which it did not recognize, and then arguing bitterly about its non-implementation for more than ten years. The single agreement, immediately violated by Peking from the American standpoint, became as much of a dispute between them as any of the other subjects taken up subsequently. Washington and Peking took only six weeks of hard but relatively normal negotiations to conclude this single agreement, but spent eleven years denouncing each other over it. The Americans sincerely believed that the agreement meant unconditionally that all the Americans in China, including those in jail (numbering less than one hundred), would be immediately released and returned to the United States in September 1955. However, there were still four Americans in Chinese jails in 1966. The Chinese Communists insisted that the agreement applied conditionally only to Americans who had not violated the laws of the People's Republic of China.

This experience is a useful lesson for negotiating with the Chinese Communists in the future, and therefore, this chapter details the experience and describes its aftermath. In the first place, the six weeks of negotiation demonstrated some of the problems and pitfalls which can be expected in negotiating with Peking, for this particular set of negotiations is the only concluded transaction which the Americans have had on a government-to-government basis with the Chinese Communists. In the second place, the aftermath passed through three difficult stages. In the first three months Peking's pledge was not fulfilled as the Americans expected it would be. Then came a bitter exchange of public charges and countercharges during 1956 and 1957. Meanwhile, the American prisoners were dribbled out of China until only ten were left in 1958. Finally, since then the matter has remained a ritual in the Ambassadorial Talks. The American Ambassador, according to public statements, has repeatedly called upon the Chinese to release the remaining Americans.

Looking back, it now seems rather strange that the fate of some forty Americans was the specific issue which brought the two sides together for diplomatic negotiations and helped keep them arguing for over a decade. In 1955 Washington could leave no stone unturned to secure the immediate release of some forty American civilians jailed in Communist China, after being arrested on a number of different charges and languishing unjustly in confinement, heartbroken or brainwashed, the unfortunate pawns in the conflict between Peking and Washington.

The Only Successful Negotiation *

The first session of the Ambassadorial Talks in Geneva to secure the release of the Americans in China began at 4:00 p.m. on August 1, 1955, in the favorable atmosphere of induced "coexistence" and under the spotlight of world attention. A large gathering of journalists had come to Geneva for the opening of the Talks and were writing speculative and descriptive stories for the news media all over the world. Attention was centered on the two diplomats when they met in the President's Room of the Palais des Nations where the armistice agreement for Indochina had been signed the year before. Ambassador U. Alexis Johnson was accompanied by three highly experienced assistants—Edwin Martin and Ralph Clough—both extremely capable Chinese-language officers of the United States Foreign Service—and Colonel Robert Ekvall, an ingenious and invaluable Chinese-language interpreter from the United States Army who had participated in the military and political negotiations at Panmunjom. For the Chinese People's Republic, Ambassador Wang Ping-nan came with three aides.

The Chinese had prepared a favorable atmosphere and seized the journalistic initiative at Geneva. Ambassador Wang echoed Chou

* The actual exchanges in the fourteen meetings are still secret. This reconstruction is based on later public official comments and Colonel Robert B. Ekvall's book, *The Faithful Echo*.

En-lai's optimism by publicly announcing on the eve of the Talks that the issue of prisoners could be easily settled and many other issues would then be raised by the Chinese government. He predicted that the Talks would progress quickly to a meeting of the Secretary of State of the United States and the Foreign Minister of the People's Republic of China.[1] At the opening of the Talks, Ambassador Wang then pre-empted the negotiating initiative. Taking the Americans somewhat by surprise, he led off with a prepared statement confirming the release of American airmen already announced in Peking. Ambassador Wang immediately made clear to the American side that the Chinese negotiators did not expect that matter to keep the Talks from proceeding directly to such basic questions as the establishment of diplomatic relations, the withdrawal of United States forces from Taiwan, development of trade and cultural relations, and United Nations membership for the People's Republic of China. Thus, at the outset of these "nondiplomatic" negotiations and in the very first meeting, Peking established the total range of issues which it sought to negotiate. Chou boldly challenged Dulles. The first meeting, however, was not even a warm-up, let alone a skirmish. It took only forty-five minutes of oral statements and translations. After procedural matters were settled, it was agreed that the return of civilians would constitute the first item for discussion.[2] The United States representatives had little to say, but concurred officially in the Ambassadorial Talks with Chou's proposal to take up the question of the return of civilians first and then move on to "other practical matters." Both sides also agreed to Johnson's proposal to keep the Talks private and confidential. Disagreements would not be publicly aired, and only agreements would be announced. Following this first meeting, the two Ambassadors issued a brief joint communiqué on the agenda, but no discussion of real substance took place. Ambassador Wang had stressed that both sides should be conciliatory and negotiate sincerely. He indicated that each side could raise questions involving both sides for a free exchange of views.

The second meeting, held the next day, August 2, lasted nearly an hour. Ambassador Wang proposed that the Americans in China and Chinese in the United States be repatriated and that two third parties be agreed upon to implement an agreement on such repatriation. Peking suggested India for checking on the Chinese in the United States. Not surprisingly, Prime Minister Nehru had already urged President Eisenhower to accept this arrangement in order to expedite the Talks. At their very outset the People's Republic of China was asking a third country to verify "the involuntary" inability or unwillingness of Chinese in America to return "home." Moreover, Peking was implying, if not explicitly charging, that the United States government was using force to prevent any Chinese individual from returning to mainland China. Peking's proposal immediately and seriously challenged the United States government. To agree would contravene the status and interests of its ally, the Republic of China, which in the American view had legal jurisdiction over Chinese nationals in the United States. The very reverse of forcible retention and nonrepatriation was the key issue which Washington wished to change by negotiation with Peking. Peking's opening negotiating tactic was an aggressive move to put Washington on the defensive and shift the emphasis away from the Americans' real target in China: the prisoners. Chou's strategy was calculated to put himself on an equal footing with Dulles.

At the second meeting in Geneva, Ambassador Johnson apparently refrained from stating American opposition on the question of verifying the attitudes of all Chinese nationals in the United States. Instead he emphasized that the conversations should be kept private, with no press admitted and no announcements made by either side concerning any meeting in any way except with joint concurrence or at least with prior notice from one side to the other. His purpose was to keep the Talks from being distorted into a propagandistic barrage, as had happened at Panmunjom. Significant in terms of the seriousness of Peking's early intentions concerning the Talks was Ambassador Wang's acceptance. To this day official transcripts of the records of all the Talks have been kept secret. As for substance at this second meeting, Ambassador Wang reiterated his initial proposals, while Ambassador Johnson asked that the names of Americans in China be confirmed.

Dulles' news conference on the day of the second meeting dramatized the Talks for the world press. He was hopeful that the Talks would be productive, had a good word for Premier Chou En-lai, visualized broad negotiations if Peking renounced the use of military force, and even left the door ajar for Chou's proposal on a collective peace treaty among Asian Pacific countries, including the United States. Dulles hinted at possible signs of a new phase of Chinese Communist relations with the rest of the world, and a possible course of action for Peking which could lead to a completely new status for the People's Republic of China. Some observers were optimistic. Mr. Menon of India even predicted that the Talks would be over in a week after they reached an agreement for a meeting of the two Foreign Ministers.[3] Some commentators even began looking for a new United States policy toward China and a reconciliation between Washington and Peking.

The third meeting on August 4 produced a deadlock.[4] Ambassador Johnson rejected the formula of a third party to verify the desires of Chinese aliens in the United States to return to mainland China. The Americans turned the formula down because it was tantamount to acknowledging Peking's jurisdiction over all Chinese nationals in the United States and the rejection of jurisdiction of the Republic of China on Taiwan over them. This, in turn, amounted to "backdoor" recognition of the sovereignty of the People's Republic of China. Ambassador Johnson expounded the legal position of the United States, based on its recognition of Chinese Nationalist sovereignty and its opposition to Peking's assumption of that sovereignty and jurisdiction.

Ambassador Johnson insisted that the Chinese Communists should immediately release the Americans held in China without attaching any conditions such as the Chinese negotiators were pressing. He emphasized that such release would demonstrate the readiness and willingness of the People's Republic of China to act in a more civilized manner than they had in the past. But Ambassador Johnson did not leave the matter there. He wanted the unconditional release of all Americans in the Chinese People's Republic. He saw no need for the Talks to get involved with Chinese nationals in the United States who were free to leave at any time. Nevertheless, as an apparently conciliatory gesture, he proposed to Ambassador Wang that the United States would agree to Peking's request for a third party to verify the wishes of those Chinese who said they desired to go to mainland China. If any Chinese wanted to go to Communist China and felt he was in any way prevented from doing so, he could report his situation and desires to a designated third party which, in turn, might interview and thus verify the Chinese desire. But Ambassador Johnson must have indicated at this meeting that the United States would not agree to subject any Chinese students to interrogation or investigation by a third party on Peking's direct request if they had not expressed any interest in going to mainland

China. The firm rejection by Ambassador Johnson apparently astonished the Chinese Communists. It produced the first of many deadlocks in the impasse between Washington and Peking.

But the public atmosphere remained optimistic and the talks meaningful. At his news conference on August 4, President Eisenhower made it clear that it was still premature to consider a Foreign Ministers' conference and sought to discourage speculation at that time of time of a subsequent "summit" meeting.[5] Much would depend on the Ambassadorial Talks to bring about first a release of all American citizens detained in China and, second, an agreement on renunciation of force.

By now the initial meetings had demonstrated that serious, businesslike exchanges on an agenda could actually take place directly between representatives of Washington and Peking. The Talks were not friendly, but they were more than mechanical. A certain amount of normal diplomatic courtesy and civility was introduced into the Talks at this early stage. The pejorative language and the combative atmosphere of Panmunjom gave way to the good manners and precise regularity of customary diplomacy, and "the atmosphere was relaxed and easy with urbanity and even the minimum social amenities." [6]

At the fourth meeting, the Americans again took the position that no discussion on Chinese nationals in the United States could take place until the forty American civilians in China were freed. Ambassador Wang repeated his position and insisted that the Americans agree to it. He also insisted that all Chinese prisoners in American jails be released before any interrogation and then be given the opportunity of returning immediately to the mainland. As in the case of all deadlocks between the two sides which have characterized the Talks, each side then began the process of reiterating its position word for word and requesting the other side to agree.

When the issue of the release of prisoners became stalled, the initial optimism and encouragement over the Talks nearly disappeared. It looked as though the whole process of Ambassadorial Talks would collapse. The fifth meeting was postponed for twenty-four hours. No progress was made on securing freedom for the Americans in China and the deadlock continued over Chinese in the United States, but the Chinese delegation attempted to create an optimistic impression. The American delegation made it clear that it was willing to rest its case and wait for the Chinese to make a move.

The sixth meeting lasted nearly two hours but amounted to a reiteration of the positions of both sides. The seventh meeting on August
16 was equally futile. Ambassador Johnson's deputy, Edwin Martin,
left Geneva. At his news conference the same day, Dulles admitted
that he was disappointed over the lack of progress inasmuch as he
had expected a prompt solution of the issue after Chou had said that
it could easily be settled with so few American nationals involved.
But he was determined to keep the Talks going, he said, as long as
there was any chance of getting the rest of "our people" out.[7] The
eighth meeting on the following day remained deadlocked for
nearly three hours. Ambassador Johnson continued to press for a list
of Americans in China; Ambassador Wang for custody and return
of the Chinese. Nine meetings were held up to August 20 without
approaching agreement on this issue.[8]

Three weeks after the optimistic beginnings, the State Department publicly expressed disillusionment in the Geneva Talks. Contrary to their extremely hopeful attitude in the first few days of
August, American officials now were discouraged, impatient, and even
infuriated by Chinese intransigence after eight or nine Talks. The
Americans considered it "blackmail" and "ransom" for the Chinese
to refuse to come to agreement on releasing Americans in China before discussing other subjects. At the end of August Washington
decided to slow down the pace of meetings from three to one a
week.

Then, suddenly, at the thirteenth meeting on September 6,
Ambassador Wang announced that 12 of the 40 American civilians
would be issued exit permits and released. The Talks began to move
toward some agreement on this first question on the agenda. The
discussions across the table then began to center on the substance
and form of a mutual announcement. The Americans had proposed
an English-language agreement in draft form, and the Chinese had a
different version in Chinese and English. The process of the negotiation then became a question of arriving at an agreed text and discussing the language of different drafts. For several meetings the
two sides worked on different drafts section by section, paragraph
by paragraph, sentence by sentence, clause by clause, and even word
by word. Nothing was left to chance by either side, for the difficulties of rendering Chinese and English into exact equivalents made
it necessary to insure an agreed understanding word for word in
both languages. The American side originally proposed a draft
agreement, but the negotiations went through many different ver-

sions. Finally Peking realized that the Americans would not be moved either on the issue of the immediate release of American civilians or on the question of jurisdiction over Chinese nationals in the United States. President Eisenhower and Secretary Dulles had followed these Talks closely and approved the instructions to Ambassador Johnson for each meeting. At last the Chinese agreed to a mutually acceptable formula. After both Governments had approved, the two Ambassadors issued a joint communiqué, following the fourteenth meeting on September 10, 1955.*

Analysis of the Negotiations

There are four aspects of this actual negotiation still well worth noting: the different ways in which both sides approached the principal issue, the negotiating of actual draft texts between the two sides, the difficulties and differences over terminology in English and Chinese, and the manipulation of the atmosphere, within the secret talks and in public for bargaining purposes. The issue would have seemed too simple to argue over: who were the civilians to be repatriated, where were they, and how would they be released and returned?

Negotiating tactics were in utter contrast. The Americans began with the one-track approach that only American civilians in China were involved and that no negotiation was needed about Chinese in the United States because those persons, as aliens, had been and were free to leave any time they wished to. For Ambassador Johnson the assignment was to obtain an agreement in writing on the terms and conditions for the immediate release of all Americans in China who wished to come home. However, the Chinese Communists complicated this issue as much as they could.

They rejected the one-way line and insisted on the "double or nothing" approach. Either the Americans would concede to negotiating similar terms and conditions for Chinese in the United States, or there would be no agreement at all despite the public assurances of Chou En-lai and Ambassador Wang before the Talks started. But then the Chinese further complicated the issue by changing it or adding subsidiary issues, one following another after each had been disposed of. They did this particularly concerning the Chinese in the United States. This delayed the negotiations until the Chinese had extracted all they could from the Americans. First Peking in-

* See Appendix B.

sisted that it should have political and judicial jurisdiction over all Chinese in the United States, which would have been tantamount to American recognition of the Chinese People's Republic. When Ambassador Johnson refused such jurisdiction, Ambassador Wang began insisting on an agreement guaranteeing the return of every single Chinese in the United States exclusively to the People's Republic of China and not to the Republic of China on Taiwan. When that tactic failed, he shifted to insisting that Ambassador Johnson produce a list of the names and addresses of all Chinese nationals in the United States. He demanded the release of all Chinese who were imprisoned in the United States regardless of their crimes and their sentences. Thus the seemingly simple matter of arranging for the return of American civilians became an arduous and exasperating matter of negotiating or disposing of a series of irrelevant or false subsidiary issues. They must have been designed to wear down the patience of the American negotiators.

As Colonel Ekvall had explained in his revealing study, the question of a third party was another one of those subsidiary issues which probably had not been anticipated in advance by the Americans and which rose to plague them. Again, the totally different outlook of Peking and Washington on international relations probably accounted for this particular problem. The difference was over relations with that third party. The United States proposed that the two respective governments conduct relations inside their own countries with the embassy of the third party, which would get in touch with the civilians. In one case the United States government would communicate with the Indian Embassy in Washington to ask it to help, or make representations on behalf of, specified Chinese civilians in the United States. By the same token, the government in Peking would give permission to the British Embassy there to do the same thing on behalf of American civilians in China. Peking, however, insisted that the government of the civilians in question should directly ask the third party to make the contact on behalf of its nationals, without referring to the host government.

As for the second aspect, the negotiations did come to grips with the real issue, which was to formulate the circumstances for such release and repatriation. This involved a standard procedure in bargaining and negotiating, of bringing the oral argument to the point where it became sufficiently precise to be drafted in writing. The Americans prepared the first draft. The Chinese insisted on making their own draft. Then there was a series of discussions and amendments of these drafts until hard bargaining over every word resulted in the final agreed version.

The hurdle of semantics in two very different languages is the third aspect to note in this or any other negotiation with the Chinese Communists. During this single negotiation of an agreement between Peking and Washington there was more at issue than the issue itself, and that was terminology. As Colonel Ekvall has shown at the negotiating table and in his book, negotiation in the two languages is complicated and often baffling because equivalents in each language frequently do not exist. Moreover, the nuances and multiple meanings in both Chinese and English can lead to confusion and ambiguity. They can also facilitate deliberate deception. Given the profound mistrust of the two sides, each had to be extremely careful before agreeing on terminology. Semantics were not merely part of argument—they became central issues.

The argument over the use of third parties increased in part because of difficulties over language. The Americans originally proposed that the English version for each government's action read "shall be authorized," and that the Chinese language version be virtually the same. By implication the government—Peking or Washington—would authorize itself to make this contact. The Chinese, on the other hand, proposed the English phrase of "shall be entrusted"; but in their Chinese text they used the Chinese characters which were translated back into the English as "mandated." This would imply that the third party would be empowered directly by the government whose nationals were involved—precisely what the Americans wished to avoid. The discussion of these subtle but important semantic nuances even came to the point of defining which phrase and verb was more courteous and polite, the Chinese, according to Colonel Ekvall, suggesting that "authorized" was harsh, overbearing, and lacking in courtesy. Eventually both sides came to agree on substituting "shall be invited" for "shall be authorized" inasmuch as the gesture of invitation has a traditional connotation in Chinese language and practice. However, the Chinese kept their "mandated" phrase in Chinese after accepting the much weaker terminology of "inviting." As the English version of the agreement was the only one intelligible to the world, it became the controlling one.

The fourth interesting aspect of this particular negotiation was the manipulation of the atmosphere, particularly by the Chinese Communist negotiators. While the Americans went about these Talks, correctly observing the agreement to keep them confidential, the Chinese Communists seemed to have indulged in a considerable amount of staging for effect and controlling of atmosphere for bargaining purposes. They created a synthetically favorable atmosphere, presumably to make the Americans well disposed to accept their terms. When the negotiations did not produce the results which Peking desired, its negotiators clouded the public atmosphere in an effort to put the Americans in a bad light and to embarrass them into making concessions.

Even the short first meeting immediately mirrored the contrast between the styles, motivations, and objectives of Peking and Washington in dealing with the issue and in establishing contact with each other, as Colonel Ekvall has reported in his version of the initial Talks. Peking hoped to acquire a new or better diplomatic status in the world of *de facto* and inferential *de jure* acceptance by arranging for a series of quasi-diplomatic exchanges and political agreements with Washington. Chou En-lai's "calculated piecemeal release" of Americans was designed to apply pressure on John Foster Dulles at crucial moments in order to attain Peking's objectives. Dulles, on the other hand, began these meetings with the single concrete objective of obtaining the speedy release of all the American prisoners in the Chinese People's Republic. He wished to avoid creating any atmosphere or giving any appearance which would in any way imply diplomatic acceptance or some political arrangement with Peking of a general unlimited nature. In contrast to Chou En-lai, Dulles intended to move slowly, cautiously, and reticently in any discussion and settlement at the Ambassadorial Talks. All these aspects appeared at the outset of the Talks at Geneva.

This one and only product of the longest diplomatic exchange on record had several interesting features. For the Chinese there had to be the image and appearance of equality in status and treatment with the United States. This first accord with the "enemy" was absolutely symmetrical in form for both the United States and the People's Republic of China. For the Americans, it was the substance that counted. In fact, only six key words were the heart of the matter: "expeditiously exercise their right to return." Washington and Ambassador Johnson interpreted them strictly and literally. This meant the unconditional and unqualified binding agreement to facilitate the return of all American nationals in mainland China who wished to return home. The State Department has since stated officially that the wording of the first numbered paragraphs in the joint agreement "was specifically designed to cover all categories of Americans known to be in Communist China, including those in prison." [9] The Americans had negotiated and concluded this agreement with the distinct impression and on the explicit assumption that it applied to all Americans in China who wished to return to the United States, regardless of whether they were in prison or not, irrespective of any charges or convictions by the Chinese Communist courts of violations of Chinese Communist laws, and notwithstanding whether they were civilian or military personnel. In other words, on the face of it, the agreement contained no hidden stipulations. It is interesting also to recall that this accord had all the features of a valid political contract, drawn up and signed in fullfledged diplomatic manner and language between two governments without diplomatic relations between themselves.

The Aftermath

Yet, however symmetrical and unconditional this one and only written agreement between Washington and Peking may have been, it did not lead to the quick settlement and removal of this item from the Talks, produce immediate and satisfactory implementation of the repatriation of civilians, or contribute to the easing of tensions and settlement of other issues between the two parties. In fact, the American assumption of its unqualified commitments led to continual argument and acrimonious exchange of charges and countercharges which have lasted to this day, with four Americans still unjustly and illegally held in Chinese jails even to the end of 1966. The agreement announced on September 10, 1955, turned out to be a meeting of men but not of minds on this first and seemingly easily settled item of the agenda.

At the time, it appeared that Chinese and American nationals would be returning to the country of their desire without any difficulty. In the People's Republic of China there was favorable reaction, stimulated, of course, by government leaders in Peking. The Communist press immediately put out the line that the People's Republic of China would make every effort to improve relations with the United States since a promising start had been made at

Geneva. The Communist press and radio welcomed the agreement because it encouraged conciliation and created confidence. Chinese officials, including Ambassador Wang, immediately began calling publicly for a Foreign Ministers' conference and trade relations with the United States as the next items for discussion and agreement. An editorial on September 12 in the authoritative *People's Daily* expressed pleasure at the "good beginning" which encouraged conciliation and created an atmosphere of mutual confidence between China and the United States "in the interests of improving relations between the two countries." The editorial expressed the hope that both sides would come to agreement in the second phase so that the Talks could pave the way to still further negotiations.[10] In the United States, however, the Deputy Under Secretary of State, Robert Murphy, one of the most experienced of American diplomats, used more circumspect language than Peking had when he stated in a speech that the Geneva Talks had "been attended by a certain success." [11] American officials were less vocal and positive about the implications of this first agreement than the Chinese Communists but not indeed about its execution. Washington's aim was the freedom and return of the remaining Americans. It immediately adopted a clear and simple position: the United States would not proceed to discuss any other matters until the remaining nineteen Americans were released. A few days after the announcement, Ambassador Johnson publicly rebuffed Ambassador Wang for his unilateral public disclosures and declared that it would be "premature to discuss other practical matters," referring to a Foreign Ministers' conference, "before carrying out the agreed announcement . . . regarding the return of civilians. . . ." [12] The United States would not consider moving to any other substantive question, particularly a Foreign Ministers' meeting, because the faithful carrying-out of the terms of the September 10th agreement "should be the continued task of the Geneva meetings and should provide a basis for proceeding to the discussion of other practical matters at issue." [13]

Again Ambassador Wang seized the initiative by resorting to publicity to force the hand of the United States. Prematurely and contrary to the joint understanding on announcements, he revealed on September 14 that the People's Republic of China intended to proceed immediately in the Ambassadorial Talks to discussion on establishing trade relations between the two countries and making arrangements for holding a meeting of the two Foreign Ministers forthwith.[14] Thus, the Chinese went over the heads of the American negotiators to the public, while the Americans were going into great detail and effort to implement the announced agreement on civilians. Ambassador Wang refused to discuss the implementation of that agreement while Ambassador Johnson refused to go on to the second item on the agenda.

Peking immediately began to exploit the issue of Chinese nationals in the United States, presumably for propaganda and bargaining purposes or at least to establish the kind of equal and reciprocal status with the United States that Peking seemed to insist on for psychological reasons. The issue of September 16 of *People's China*, Peking's English-language journal for presenting official views, carried an article on American obstruction of the return of Chinese students. It is interesting that Peking would have published such accusations immediately upon the signing of the accord on the return of civilians and at the very moment when a certain amount of optimism and conciliation was evident—at least on the surface. However, in this article Peking accused the United States government of intimidating, persecuting and obstructing Chinese students who wished to return to Communist China.[15] These untrue charges were vigorously rebutted by American authorities.

On September 19, Ambassador Wang issued another statement to the press denouncing the United States for refusing to talk about other matters until all Americans were out of China.[16] He said that he considered it regrettable that Ambassador Johnson had taken this position and warned that it would make it impossible to continue these talks. The Chinese were, in effect, negotiating an agreement which they had already reached. They were bargaining its implementation in return for beginning discussions and negotiations on the particular subjects which they wished to pursue.

Then, without public explanation, the Americans suddenly reversed their stand on the acceptable sequence of discussing Items 1 and 2 of the agenda. At the Ambassadorial meeting on September 20, they agreed to go on to the second item—"other practical matters"—provided the Chinese agreed to keep the implementation of the first item on repatriation of civilians open for discussion at each subsequent meeting in these Talks.[17] What this meant in practical terms was that Ambassador Johnson would continue to seek the release of the remaining 19 Americans while Ambassador Wang would press for discussions of topics under Item 2.

The tactics on the part of the Communists of first refusing to discuss an initial item on the agenda and insisting on moving to the next item exclusively, but then agreeing to simultaneous discussions has become standard procedure in Communist negotiations. The Talks after mid-September proceeded, therefore, to the second item on the agenda, on which the Americans at first remained silent; but in October they introduced the topic of renunciation of force,* whereas the Chinese immediately and at every session in September, October, and many thereafter in the first phase of the Ambassadorial Talks, sought a conference of the two Ministers and an ending of the trade embargo. Nevertheless, the return of the nineteen Americans and many Chinese students continued to hold the attention of both sides at Geneva.

Ambassador Johnson for several weeks refused to respond in any way to, or get involved in, Item 2 at all. He insisted on concrete evidence of immediate implementation of the September 10th Agreement. Ambassador Johnson kept pressing doggedly at each weekly meeting for information on the whereabouts of these remaining Americans and certification of their release and movement out of Communist China. However, Ambassador Wang refused to discuss the detained Americans but kept up the barrage of accusations against the United States of intimidating Chinese students in America. In his press conference of October 4, Mr. Dulles was asked whether the Geneva Talks were making any progress and whether there was any substance to the Chinese Communist charge of an American "slowdown." Mr. Dulles answered: "There is no slowdown that I am aware of. The whole operation is slow. It took us, as you know, six weeks to get agreement in relation to the first item on the agenda. . . . Progress in these matters is always slow and is seldom spectacular." [18] On October 3, Peking in the *People's Daily* accused the United States of obstructing the Talks and implied that there would be no further release of Americans if the United States continued to hold up the Talks.[19] The twentieth meeting took place on October 8 with continued pressure from Ambassador Johnson for the release of the remaining Americans but he received no satisfaction from the other side of the table on Item 1,[20] although there was an exchange of statements on the renunciation of force.

Meanwhile, Chou began to increase the public pressures on Dulles. The Peking press and radio began to show impatience and even anger over the Geneva Talks, directing thinly veiled personal

* See Chapter 4.

attacks against Ambassador Johnson and concentrating on Peking's single major objective at that time of proceeding quickly to a ministerial conference with Dulles.[21] On October 12 the *People's Daily* accused the United States of dragging out the Talks and insisted that the Chinese side had been faithfully carrying out the Agreement. The next day the *People's Daily* of October 13 and the Peking radio claimed that only 66 Americans remained in China.* Forty-seven were free to leave but so far had not applied for exit visas. The remaining 19 had violated Chinese law, Peking claimed. However, the Chinese authorities were examining each of these cases separately to decide the proper steps to be taken under the Agreement of September 10. In these comments, Peking charged that many Chinese nationals in the United States were unable to return home or were afraid to apply for exit permits. The government in Peking was not satisfied with the way in which the Agreement was being carried out by the American authorities. In these published statements, Peking also rejected the American effort requesting information at Geneva on "American servicemen missing in the Korean war." Peking considered this "completely groundless" and aimed at "creating tension." Instead, Peking pointed out that it had for some time proposed that the Talks proceed to discuss the embargo question and preparations for a ministerial conference, "in order to relieve Sino-American tension." The November 1 issue of *People's China* stated that the Talks had been hanging fire for over a month since September 10 and blamed the United States for this.[22]

Secretary Dulles was asked at a press conference on October 18 about the status of the Geneva Talks.[23] He noted that a certain number of American citizens had been allowed to return to the United States following the joint Agreement of September 10, while certain others had not been permitted to exercise that right "which they were supposed to have expeditiously." He noted that the United States had agreed to go on to Item 2 while reserving the right to reopen Item 1 at any time if it did not seem that the Agreement was being carried out in good faith. He informed the press conference that the issue of renunciation of force had been

* The Americans immediately pointed out that this total of 66 included two groups of Americans who had "defected" to Communist China; 17 Americans who were prisoners of war captured during the Korean War and who refused to return to the United States; and several other Americans who had decided to remain and live in Communist China.

discussed, that the matter of a trade embargo would be taken up, and that the question of a "further meeting" had also been raised by the Chinese at Geneva. The Secretary declined to go into the substance of these questions because of the mutual understanding not to release anything publicly except by mutual agreement.

During November and early December five more American prisoners were released from Communist China, but Washington, adamant on obtaining a total release, became discouraged over the prospects. On December 6, Mr. Dulles told a press conference that the Talks were not making as much progress as hoped for in view of the "lack of action" under the Agreement already reached, although he remained hopeful that it would be carried out.[24] Ambassador Johnson continued to press for the speedy implementation and expeditious return of all American citizens held in China. Again Peking suddenly resorted to the press to force his hand. Ambassador Wang issued a long denunciation of the Americans on December 15 for hindering the Talks and forcibly keeping Chinese nationals in the United States, despite Peking's "sincere efforts" and correct implementation of the September 10th Agreement.[25]

Washington reacted immediately and strongly. On December 16 the State Department formally charged the People's Republic of China with violation of the September 10th Agreement by refusing to free the 14 American citizens still in prison and protested their cruel and inhuman treatment. This American public statement denied Peking's charge that the United States was preventing Chinese nationals from returning to Communist China, pointing out that the Indian Embassy had so far failed to find or hear from a single Chinese in the United States who wished to leave. As for American nationals in China, the Department took this occasion to express its interpretation of the vital paragraph of the September 10th Agreement:

This declaration is simple, clear, and positive. It says that any United States citizen has the right to leave China, and that the Communists have taken or will take the necessary steps so that those who wish may leave "expeditiously." No distinction is made as between those in prison and those out of prison. All United States citizens who wish to leave should have been out of Communist China long before this. The continued holding of these United States citizens by the Communists is a violation of their agreed announcement, for which the United States must continue to protest.[26]

The Department ended this first of many public demands to Peking on this subject by hoping that the remaining American citizens would be "promptly" permitted to leave Communist prisons and to return home.

Beginning with the public volleys of December 15 and 16, the two sides launched a year-long battle of press releases. In early January a spokesman for the Foreign Ministry in Peking complained of the unsatisfactory state of affairs in the Ambassadorial Talks, accused Washington of "endlessly dragging them out," and set the record "straight" on both agenda items. Concerning Americans in China, the spokesman sharply disputed the State Department's statement of December 16 that there was no distinction made between those in prison and those out of prison. On the contrary, Peking claimed, this was a distortion of the September 10th Agreement because there was a distinction between "ordinary American residents" and "those who offended against the law." The spokesman went on to declare that the latter group must be dealt with in accordance with Chinese legal procedures, no time limit could be set on their release, and they had no right to request permission to return to the United States. "It is only when they have completed their sentences or when China has adopted measures to release them before the completion of their sentences that the question of their exercising the right to return can arise," the spokesman announced. He noted that his government had already "adopted measures" to release 27 out of 40 such "law breakers." And, of course, the spokesman added Peking's charge that Washington had failed to give Peking lists of Chinese in the United States and to "adopt measures" to enable any Chinese imprisoned there to exercise the right expeditiously to return to China.[27]

On January 11, 1956, Dulles was asked again at a press conference about the Talks, and he noted the "disappointing failure" to make the Talks useful, notably in giving the Americans in China "the right expeditiously to return."[28] Then Peking again resorted to the public attack on the Americans. Ambassador Wang issued a long statement on January 18 revealing much of the exchange regarding renunciation of force and the refusal of the Americans since September 10 to discuss the abolition of the embargo and preparations for a ministerial conference. He also accused the Americans of "haggling" over Item 1 of the Agenda, of violating the September 10th Agreement by "threats and obstructions," preventing "thousands" of Chinese from expeditiously exercising their right to return, and of refusing to furnish Peking with a "complete name list and information concerning the Chinese residents and students in the United States, thus making it difficult for India to carry out the tasks of a third country as specified in the Agreement." Regarding the Americans in China, Ambassador Wang remarked that "their number was not very large to begin with" and he added a new set of numbers and categories. Out of 59 law-abiding Americans, 16 who applied had departed. Among 40 who allegedly violated Chinese law, 27 had been released before completion of their sentences. Yet the American side kept raising "groundless charges" in the Talks to "shirk its responsibility" and to manufacture a pretext for "dragging out the Talks." [29]

The State Department replied on January 21 to Peking's statement with a long rebuttal on all these issues regarding both items on the agenda. Concerning repatriation, it again quoted the vital "expeditious" paragraph and noted that only six Americans had been released since September 10 and that thirteen Americans remained in prison, which agreed with Peking's count—the only feature about repatriation enjoying the concurrence of both sides. In this press release, the United States sought "the now overdue fulfillment by the Chinese Communists of their undertaking that the Americans now in China should be allowed expeditiously to return . . . not only for humanitarian reasons but because respect for international undertakings lies at the foundation of a stable international order." [30] As for Chinese nationals in America, the statement declared that any Chinese was free to leave for any destination, not a single one had been refused exit, and the Indian Embassy had not reported a single case of any Chinese being threatened or obstructed from leaving, nor any instance where the embassy had been impeded in executing its functions.

Peking immediately rebutted Washington with another long statement issued by the Foreign Ministry itself on January 24. It repeated accusations of American delays and Chinese views on Item 2, yet it did contain one interesting comment. The Foreign Ministry revealed:

The two items of the Agenda of the Sino-American Talks are interrelated. The American side has violated the Agreement on the first item and delayed progress on the second, and furthermore has issued a statement to distort once again the developments in the Talks and the substance of the discussion.[31]

On January 30, Chou En-lai included a long section on the Talks in his Political Report to the Second Session of the Second National

Committee of the Chinese People's Political Consultative Conference. He put the public "seal" or "chop" of the Peking leadership on the Chinese contention that it had been "faithfully complying" with the Agreement, while the United States government had not abandoned the use of all kinds of "threats and persecution" to prevent Chinese nationals from returning home. "If the United States Government continues to threaten and persecute them," Chou claimed, "it must bear full responsibility for wrecking the Agreement." [32] Testimonial stories by returning Chinese began appearing in Chinese periodicals purportedly to provide *prima facie* support for these charges.[33]

In early March Peking issued another repetitive press release attacking the United States for its dilatory, noncooperative role in the Talks. In rebuttal the State Department accused Peking of continuing to hold 13 American citizens as "political hostages"—the first time Washington had employed this sharp term—and for failing even to mention the issue of American repatriation in its statement.[34] In April Peking published another repetition of its version of the repatriation issue in an article entitled "The Truth About the Sino-American Talks." With persistence, Peking contended that it had carried out the Agreement, and given Washington full information on 59 "ordinary residents"; the 13 who had asked to be returned had left and the other 46 were free to leave at any time; and of the 40 imprisoned for crimes against Chinese law, 27 had been freed and sent home before serving their sentences. American civilians (but not prisoners) in China were free to contact the British Embassy. In contrast, the article claimed:

> The United States, on the other hand, has not only failed to carry out the terms of the agreement, but has even violated it. The United States government still refuses to give China proper information about Chinese residents in the United States. Chinese civilians in the States are still subject to all sorts of threats and hindrances, not the least of which is that they are compelled to apply for permanent residence in the United States as refugees and to secure entrance permits for Taiwan. The result is that thousands of Chinese who want to return to China still cannot do so. The United States government has also failed to take any steps in regard to Chinese imprisoned in the United States comparable to those China took with Americans who had committed offenses in China.[35]

In May United States officials publicly indicated that Peking had gone back on its word to the extent of refusing to release any more Americans until all Chinese in American jails were freed and that

Ambassador Johnson had sent in a "bitter" report about the Chinese Communists who were "deliberately holding thirteen Americans as hostages to get the United States to pay twice for the same pledge." [36] While making clear that release of Chinese criminals imprisoned in the United States could not be bartered for Americans, American officials announced on June 2 that any one of the 24 Chinese nationals still serving a sentence in a Federal prison would be free to go to Communist China if he wished to. Washington hoped that this concession, notwithstanding the strong protest of the Chinese government in Taipei,[37] would finally induce Peking to fulfill and honor its commitment to release the thirteen Americans in jail.

Earlier in May 1956, the Department of State had given the Indian Embassy a complete list of all Chinese convicts in Federal and State penitentiaries, a total of 34, and invited the embassy to interview them to ascertain whether they desired to be released for the purpose of going either to Communist China or Taiwan. The Chinese Communists refused to authorize the Indian Embassy to conduct these interviews, and they were carried out instead by the American National Red Cross. By the time the interviews took place, the normal parole process had reduced the number of prisoners from 34 to 24. The Red Cross found that out of the 24, one prisoner convicted of murder desired to go to Communist China, and two to Taiwan. All the others preferred to serve their sentences in the United States. The prisoner who expressed a desire to go to Communist China was deported toward that destination on October 29, 1956. He had then served two and a half years of a seven-to-twenty-year sentence for manslaughter.[38] Of the two prisoners desiring to go to Taiwan, one was deported on September 15, 1957; the other changed his mind and elected to serve out his sentence.

Although Ambassador Wang and the Chinese government accused the United States government of intimidating all Chinese nationals in the United States and preventing them from returning,* the United States government went to great lengths to facilitate such repatriation. It posted announcements in some 35,000 post offices regarding the terms of departure for any Chinese who so wished. Other means, such as radio and television, were used to bring this personally to the attention of Chinese in the United States. The Indian Embassy in Washington cooperated fully from

---

* Peking, of course, was embracing some 5,000 Chinese nationals in its campaign to get juridical custody over them all and influence them to come back to China.

the time of the September Agreement. The net result of this large-scale effort was so negligible as to be ridiculous. One Chinese criminal decided to return to China and then changed his mind in Hong Kong. No other Chinese national elected to go back under the terms of the September 10th Agreement, although many hundreds of Chinese on their own initiative and without reference to the Indian Embassy did leave the United States and returned to mainland China. Ambassador Johnson must have conveyed all these facts to Ambassador Wang across the table at several meetings.

From mid-1956 on, the Americans had to make several more statements in what had become a rather dreary, monotonous contrapuntal charge and countercharge in the battle of press releases. On June 12, 1956, the State Department had to issue another long rebuttal on the Geneva Talks and to repeat its earlier statements regarding repatriation of the thirteen Americans still in Communist prisons.[39] In mid-August, Peking put out another article in the *People's China* called "U.S. Stonewalling at Geneva." [40] This version of the issue of repatriation was more tendentious and exaggerated than ever. It now spoke of "tens of thousands" of Chinese detained and forcibly separated from their wives, children, and parents, and took an exactly opposite view from Washington on what had been agreed to eleven months before in September 1955 concerning the 40 Americans "guilty of offenses against Chinese law."

The return of such people to America was naturally a question which only China herself could decide on.

During the Geneva talks Ambassador Wang Ping-nan proposed that the U.S. Government should cancel all measures preventing Chinese residents and students in the U.S. from coming home. To facilitate matters he also suggested enlisting the help of third countries to speed up the procedure. These were reasonable proposals.

The U.S. on the other hand demanded the release of all American nationals, including spies and lawbreakers, within a specified time. China of course could not agree to this. A country has the inviolable sovereign right to deal with law-breaking aliens according to its own laws. American nationals violating Chinese law in China must be dealt with under Chinese law. The American representative, Ambassador Johnson, finally had to agree to this principle. Agreement on this item was therefore reached on September 10, 1955. Both sides declared that appropriate measures would be taken to enable each other's nationals to get home expeditiously if they wished. . . .

. . . The Chinese authorities also dealt leniently with the U.S. nationals who had violated Chinese law. Eleven of the forty American criminals were in fact released ahead of time when the Sino-American talks began.

Following the agreement China released another 19 before they had completed their sentences. China declared that, depending on their future conduct, appropriate measures would be taken regarding the remaining ten.

On September 24, the Department announced that it would not agree to shifting the discussions to, nor discuss, the question of relaxation of trade restrictions as long as the Chinese Communists continued to hold imprisoned American citizens as "political hostages." At the meeting in Geneva Ambassador Johnson had already informed the Chinese side of Washington's firm position.[41] In fact, he had never agreed to the "principle," as alleged by Peking, that Americans in China were divided into two categories.

Two months and several meetings later, Peking appeared to soften its intentions concerning Americans in China. In New Delhi for another visit with Nehru, Chou En-lai declared that American prisoners always had the chance of being released before their terms were completed. In Calcutta he said at a news conference that it was now up to the United States to make a move to obtain the release of the Americans, in view of the fact that there were Chinese nationals in the United States who wanted to return to the mainland but were still kept in United States jails. The next step for a Far Eastern settlement, he felt, should come from Washington inasmuch as it had rejected all his standing proposals: a ministerial conference, mutual contacts, cultural exchange, trade.[42] Sources in New Delhi then hinted, after Chou En-lai's visit with Nehru, that some ten Americans might soon be released from jail.[43] In early 1957, Chou En-lai himself intimated as much during a visit to Warsaw. Soon after in New Delhi he criticized President Eisenhower for mixing the question of United States prisoners in Communist China with the improvement of relations between the two countries.[44] Chou claimed that it was not correct to make relations conditional on the release of prisoners, although that was precisely what the United States was doing and intended to continue doing. Ambassador Johnson presumably made that perfectly clear in meeting after meeting in Geneva.

On January 29, in Katmandu, Nepal, Chou again hinted that Peking might consider exchanging American prisoners for Chinese convicts and that the Americans might be released before their sentences were up on evidence of good behavior. Meanwhile, Ambassador Johnson was reported to be disturbed over the complications which the issue of exchanging newsmen and the visit to Communist China of three American journalists would have on his efforts to insist on the full implementation of the September 10th Agreement.* In accordance with instructions, he insisted in the discussions regarding an exchange of newsmen that such visits could not be authorized or permitted by the State Department until all American prisoners were released. Otherwise his negotiating position would have been seriously undermined.[45]

By January 1957, the issue of repatriation had become befuddled and enmeshed in what, for the Americans, were the two extraneous issues of Peking's demand for repatriation of Chinese convicts in the United States and Peking's proposal for the exchange of newsmen. Both appeared to Washington to be Chou's means of bargaining human pawns in his larger objective of bringing the United States to the big table. Washington again felt compelled to join in the battle of press releases to set the record straight and correct the misleading distortions of Peking's "spokesmen"—meaning Chou—and its propaganda media.

In what was reported as a "harshly-worded statement," on January 29, 1957, the State Department added some basic clarifications and background about the initial Ambassadorial Talks which should have been disclosed much earlier.[46] This statement of January 29 described the September 10th Agreed Announcement as "an unqualified pledge and unequivocal promise" and the only "parallel commitment" made together by both governments. Washington again called for the expeditious release of the ten Americans now still in prison, and denied that the United States deliberately detained Chinese nationals in the United States inasmuch as the United States had done everything possible in the judgment of the State Department to expedite the return of any Chinese desiring to return home. But the statement went on to reveal something new to the public about the initial negotiations for that agreement on repatriations: First, no distinction between Americans in or out of prisons in Communist China was ever made or implied by either side in the first 14 Ambassadorial meetings. Second, Ambassador Wang had insisted on inserting an identical operative "expeditious" paragraph into the September Agreement to make the United States obligated in a parallel undertaking to permit Chinese nationals in the United States to return to China. Third, during the first 14 meetings

* See Chapter 5.

the Chinese Communists never mentioned Chinese convicts imprisoned in America. Fourth, the Chinese side accordingly never indicated that the Agreed Announcement was intended to cover them too. However, the statement went on to announce that the United States, seeking to dispel any question on these points had given the names of 34 such Chinese in American prisons to the Indian Embassy to check.* [47] Nevertheless, Peking had refused to authorize India to interview them, so Washington had asked the Red Cross to do so. When it did, normal parole had already reduced the number to 24, out of which one convicted murderer had opted to return to the mainland. By contrast, the People's Republic of China continued to violate the unconditional terms of the September 10th Agreement by detaining ten Americans and refusing even to let them communicate with the British Embassy in Peking as that Agreement specifically stipulated. The January 29th statement concluded that Peking's fulfillment of that one and only parallel commitment would determine the weight its future promises would be given.

Nevertheless, Chou En-lai was reported to have replied somewhat angrily a few days later when asked at a press conference, on a visit to Ceylon, whether his government would try to bring about better understanding with the United States by freeing the American prisoners, as President Eisenhower was suggesting. Chou said:

Let the United States continue not to recognize China. China will not topple. Why should we always listen to the words of the United States President? . . . The United States does not recognize China and has always obstructed China's being recognized by the United Nations. The United States is still hostile to China. . . .[48]

Although the number of Americans still detained in China dropped slowly from 10 to 6 in 1957, Americans became embittered and outraged by such repudiation of a pledge and such tactics of negotiation.

At the 65th meeting on February 14, 1957, the two Ambassadors met for some three hours to discuss the freedom of Americans imprisoned in China (from the American side of the table) and the freedom of American reporters to go to China (from the Chinese side of the table).[49] Again the press reports speculated that Peking's

* An Indian government spokesman in New Delhi confirmed official American statements, such as the one of January 29 and previous ones, that the Indian Embassy in Washington had not reported any cases of Chinese having been prevented from leaving the United States.

negotiators were trying to link the two issues for bargaining purposes. If Washington agreed to let American reporters go to China, Peking would release all the Americans. Secretary Dulles had let the implication arise at a press conference that such a bargain was taking place at Geneva, while President Eisenhower had indicated that a *"quid pro quo* arrangement" had entered the negotiations.[50] Ambassador Wang apparently continued to press for agreement on the entry of American reporters into China while Ambassador Johnson insisted at this 65th meeting on the release of all American prisoners before he would consider any other subject. The State Department, as he apparently continued to point out in the Ambassadorial Talks, refused to permit American correspondents to go into China on the ground that Peking illegally continued to hold ten Americans "as hostages" and that the United States government could not protect its citizens who took the risk of going to Communist China. This meeting reached no decision except that both sides would meet again in a month.

In June 1957, Dulles delivered a policy speech containing a stinging and comprehensive condemnation of the Peking regime in the harshest language probably ever used by that level of authority in Washington.[51] It was a pronouncement full of outrage, indignation, and hostility. American official anger over the issue of prisoners had finally erupted. Even so, he conceded that the United States could and would have dealings with such a regime where it served American interests, as in seeking to free the prisoners and to obtain a reciprocal renunciation of force. The State Department no longer restrained its vocabulary. The American Ambassador to Australia, William Sebald, told an audience there in July 1957 that Peking, "in defiance of commonly accepted standards of international behavior and decency and in utter disregard of the 1955 pledge at Geneva," was continuing to hold Americans on "specious charges and as political hostages in an endeavor to force political concessions" out of the United States.[52] In December 1957, twenty-seven months after the Agreement, and with 7 Americans released over the year but 6 Americans still detained, the Department issued another statement reporting that more than 80 meetings of the Ambassadorial Talks had sought and failed to secure the release of *all* Americans involuntarily detained in China. The statement declared: "The release of the Americans held in Communist China had been a major foreign policy objective of the United States Government." [53] The talks recessed for nine months in mid-December when Ambassador Johnson left Prague and the Geneva meetings to become Chief of Mission in Thailand. He had pressed with patient, dogged persistence at every meeting to have each one of these few Americans released.

During the long intermission of 1958, Peking continued to publicize its version of the issue of prisoners, which Washington considered completely false and distorted. Again the only point of agreement was on the number of six Americans remaining in Chinese prisons. Peking persisted in claiming that it had faithfully fulfilled its obligations, dealt leniently with "American convicts" and freed 34 out of 40 guilty of violating Chinese law, while the United States violated and undermined even the single Agreement between them, obstructed thousands of Chinese from returning home, confronted many with threats and persecutions and totally deprived them of their freedom to contact the Indian Embassy.[54]

Since the Ambassadorial Talks resumed in September 1958, the United States government has repeatedly raised the question at Warsaw of the few remaining Americans imprisoned in China. Time and again, apparently at nearly every meeting, the American Ambassador has called for their speedy repatriation. The United States government has not let the issue drop or ceased its efforts to dispose of it satisfactorily. In late 1958, President Eisenhower criticized Peking for continuing to do things which "we cannot possibly stomach," meaning Peking's refusal to honor its promise of 1955 to return all American prisoners.[55] In 1960 Prime Minister Chou En-lai appears to have brushed aside the whole issue of the American prisoners during his conversation with Edgar Snow.[56]

President Kennedy, at the beginning of his administration, expressed his concern about the American prisoners and instructed Ambassador Beam to raise this question, as well as other matters, at the first Ambassadorial meeting after his administration took office.[57] In January 1964, Secretary of State Rusk noted that Peking still refused to honor and fulfill its agreement, which had been made nine years before.[58] However, the government of the People's Republic of China has remained unyielding. The only consolation in the history of the single Agreement reached between Washington and Peking is that most of the American prisoners were eventually released and that no concessions were extracted from the United States in return.

CHAPTER FOUR

Impasse over the Renunciation of Force and over Taiwan

To return to the initial phase of the Ambassadorial Talks, the United States and the Chinese People's Republic took up the second item on the agenda, "other practical matters," a few weeks after agreeing, on September 10, 1955, to the return of civilians. However, Washington and Peking did not concur on how to proceed and which subjects to discuss.

Peking's Objectives

Peking did not publicly conceal its intention to move immediately in the Ambassadorial Talks to negotiate agreements for abolishing the American embargo on trade with Communist China and for arranging a Foreign Ministers' conference between Chou En-lai and John Foster Dulles. According to Peking's public explanations, the purpose of such a conference would have been to discuss the "relaxation and elimination" of tension in the Taiwan area. This was another way of saying, in the Aesopian semantics which Communists use to hide their real meaning, that what they actually wanted was Washington's total and immediate withdrawal from Taiwan. The conclusion of a ministerial agreement providing for American withdrawal from the Taiwan area apparently was Peking's price for a mutual renunciation of force in the area, which Washington sought. Peking made no secret of its determination to bargain with the United States for big stakes in terms of a non-negotiable *quid pro quo*. If the United States desired a relaxation of tensions in the Far East and some accommodation with China, Peking would only negotiate if Washington first agreed to deal with the People's Republic on the basis of virtual diplomatic recognition and to accept Peking's terms in advance. Peking thus sought several far-reaching concessions from Washington—removal of the Seventh Fleet from the Taiwan area, withdrawal of support for the Republic of China and President Chiang Kai-shek on Taiwan, and opening of trade between the People's Republic of China and the United States. In 1955–56 Peking attached considerable importance to the issue of the embargo and vigorously sought to get rid of it.

Rebuffing all these efforts, the Americans insisted on the immediate release of all American prisoners and on an agreement on the renunciation of force concerning Taiwan before Washington would consider discussing other matters. The Ambassadorial Talks actually harped for one year and some forty meetings on this one question of a so-called renunciation of force which, however, only the Americans wanted to discuss. While it is doubtful that Washington or Peking ever expected agreement on this deceptive and complex subject, they discussed it at length and exchanged seven different proposals.

Why Chou accepted Dulles' tactical maneuver and personal predilection for negotiating an abstract principle and juridical concept having universal application remains a mystery. Dulles related it specifically to the divided countries—Germany, Korea, China, and Vietnam. He had previously invited both the Soviet Union and the Chinese People's Republic on several occasions to accept this principle as the basis for negotiations with the United States.[1] Dulles often used the phrase "laying down the pistol," frequently remarking: "One cannot very well settle matters under the threat of a gun." The principle was particularly valid and necessary, in his view, in situations such as China or Vietnam where the outbreak of aggression and defense against it would automatically assume international proportions. He hoped to discover in the Ambassadorial Talks whether the Chinese Communists would accept this concept of a "cease-fire" in accordance with United Nations principles. Mr. Dulles was then seeking a simple unilateral statement from Peking, rather than any bilateral agreement or joint undertaking with the United States which would have compromised his policy of isolating the People's Republic of China.

By contrast, Chou En-lai, before the Ambassadorial Talks, had never shown interest in a renunciation of force. Communist victory had been achieved by force. Peking could seize Taiwan only by force. For Peking, then, its version of a principle of not using force was not an abstract concept but a self-serving necessity, implying the withdrawal of United States armed forces from the Taiwan area, "leaving Chinese territorial air free from further intrusions and China free from the threat of provocative war maneuvers." Chou emphasized that there could be no question of a cease-fire between the Chinese People's Republic and the United States because there was, in fact, no state of war between the two countries and because the peoples of both were "friendly toward each other, the Chinese people wanting no war with the United States." He preferred a "pact of collective peace" among the countries of Asia and the Pacific region, including the United States, in order to replace "antagonistic military blocs." Taking Chou's public statements at face value, it would seem that at the beginning of the Ambassadorial Talks Chou En-lai and Peking had an interpretation of the concept totally different from that of Washington. In other words, to Peking, any renunciation of force meant an unconditional but peaceful American withdrawal from Taiwan; whereas to Washington it meant an unconditional renunciation of efforts to take Taiwan by military means.

The Dialogue on the Renunciation of Force and over Taiwan

During 1955–56 Dulles and Chou, with their two Ambassadors at Geneva, proceeded, despite this foreseeable impasse, to seek an agreement. They exchanged seven proposals and counterproposals and issued public blasts and counterblasts at each other with no results. Washington submitted one oral and three written versions. Peking presented three written drafts.

It was not until several weeks after the joint announcement on the return of prisoners and the agreement to proceed to Item 2 of the agenda that the Americans introduced the subject of force into the Ambassadorial Talks. Until then, Ambassador Johnson had persistently argued at each meeting for the immediate and unconditional release of the Americans and had refused to discuss any other practical matter, such as ending an embargo or arranging a Foreign Ministers' Conference, pending settlement of that matter. Meanwhile, a certain amount of tension had built up over the offshore islands and Taiwan. At that point Ambassador Johnson introduced the subject of renunciation of force in the meeting of October 8, 1955.* He pointed out that progress in the Ambassadorial Talks could not be expected in the face of Communist threats to conquer Taiwan by force. Therefore, he suggested that both parties agree to announce that each would not use force in the pursuit of its objectives in g°neral, and in particular in the Taiwan area. He made clear that in the American view this should be a unilateral declaration, not a joint agreement, to be issued simultaneously but independently by both governments.

Ambassador Johnson did not present any written draft of such an announcement to Ambassador Wang. Instead he orally proposed the following points: (1) Policies between the United States and the People's Republic of China were incompatible in certain respects but should not lead to armed conflict. (2) The renunciation of the use of force was one of the practical matters for discussion between the two sides. (3) Only with such renunciation could other matters causing tension between the parties in the Taiwan area and the Far East be hopefully discussed. (4) Neither party needed to renounce legitimate policy objectives, but each should renounce the use of force to implement them. (5) It was "an essential foundation and preliminary to the success of discussions under Item 2 of the agenda that the parties renounce the use of force to make the policies of either prevail over those of the other," particularly in reference to the area of Taiwan. (6) The United States asked that the first matter for discussion under Item 2 be a declaration that "your side" would not resort to the use of force in the Taiwan area except defensively, while the United States would be prepared to make corresponding declarations, for such declarations would make it appropriate to proceed to the discussion of other matters "with a better hope of coming to constructive conclusions."

While the substance of this oral proposal was in line with the public indications of Dulles before the Talks began, the United States had now introduced the concept of two agreed-upon but separate declarations containing identical and parallel commitments and undertakings for both Peking and Washington. In format, this

* Appendix C contains the sequence of exchange and the full texts of statements and drafts which are now all on the public record regarding the issue of the renunciation of force. See Department of State Publication 6280 of February 1956 which reprinted its Press Release 37 of January 21, 1956, and Peking's English texts carried in *The New York Times* of January 19, 1956.

first proposal on a renunciation of force would have duplicated the separate but parallel Agreed Announcements on repatriation. It would have applied to all of East Asia, and particularly to Taiwan. As to procedure, the Americans agreed to discuss only this matter and refused to consider anything else under Item 2.

Peking's First Draft: After several ambassadorial meetings, Peking responded on October 27, flatly rejecting the American statement, and introducing the first written draft into the Talks.* This was a proposed joint agreement rather than a unilateral or parallel announcement on the renunciation of force. Ambassador Wang made four points in rebutting the American statement. First, the People's Republic of China had "consistently" advocated the peaceful settlement of disputes between the two countries without resort to force, in accordance with the Charter of the United Nations. Second, the People's Republic of China had previously proposed at Bandung that China and the United States enter into negotiations for the relaxation of tensions. Third, for the same purpose, the People's Republic of China was proposing in the Ambassadorial Talks that higher-level "Sino-American negotiations" be arranged and held to settle issues and reduce tensions. Fourth, the nonuse of force should not be confused with domestic tensions, for the status of Taiwan was a domestic matter which the Chinese People's Republic would settle by peaceful means if possible.

The preamble of Peking's draft bilateral agreement on the renunciation of force affirmed Article II of the United Nations Charter on peaceful settlement of international disputes and nonrecourse to force. The operative part of Peking's draft proposed that both governments settle disputes between them by peaceful means, "without resorting to the threat or use of force" and hold a conference of Foreign Ministers "to settle through negotiations the question of relaxing and eliminating the tension in the Taiwan area." In Peking's negotiating fashion, Ambassador Wang told Ambassador Johnson that the Americans, as members of the United Nations and subject to its Charter, should accept this draft without changes if they were sincere. But Peking's attachment of the principle of the nonuse of force to the Charter of the United Nations was conditioned upon a prior conference of the two foreign ministers which, in Peking's scheme, was the only way in which the Charter's principle could be applied to the nonuse of force. Chou En-lai was in

* Full text in Appendix C, No. 2.

effect telling Dulles that if he wanted renunciation of force and the restoration of peace in the Far East he should negotiate on China's terms. While pointedly omitting application of the principle to Taiwan, Chou had cleverly surrounded Dulles with a series of United Nations pledges, appealing to him as a "man of the United Nations" as much as a practitioner of international jurisprudence.

Washington might well have presumed that acceptance of Peking's adherence to the United Nations Charter would have conferred a respectable status on the People's Republic of China and possibly promoted its seating in the United Nations. President Eisenhower, Secretary Dulles, and the State Department were not inclined to deal with Peking in such a context or to meet with Chou on those terms, although they did not publicly or privately lock the door to a ministerial conference. Instead they directed the concept of the nonuse of force specifically to the Taiwan area and instructed Ambassador Johnson to reject Peking's general proposal.[2] The Americans found this initial draft unacceptable "because it would have made it possible for the Communists to claim that the proposal did not apply to the Taiwan area, which is the very place against which the Communist threats are directed, and to claim further that the United States had renounced the right to use force in self-defense." The Americans also rejected the Chinese draft because it called for an immediate meeting of the two foreign ministers. As Ambassador Johnson appears to have told Ambassador Wang, consideration of a higher-level meeting was neither appropriate nor acceptable "under existing circumstances," meaning the pressures of intimidation in the Taiwan area and the failure to implement the Agreement on repatriation fully and unconditionally. In fact, Washington opposed the draft announcement of a Foreign Ministers' meeting on the grounds that Peking's distinction between nonuse of force in international disputes other than in the case of Taiwan demanded three major and vital prior concessions from the United States: removal of the Seventh Fleet from the Taiwan Straits; withdrawal of support for Chiang Kai-shek; and ending of the embargo on United States trade with China.

The two Ambassadors continued to exchange many words on the renunciation of force for several meetings after October 27. Again to put pressure on Dulles, Chou apparently had a version of his draft leaked to the *Daily Worker* in London, contrary to the agreement on public announcements; but high sources in Washington discredited any idea that a conference between Dulles and Chou was imminent or even under way.[3] The Chinese were apparently annoyed that the American position continued to oppose specific references to provisions of the United Nations Charter in any agreed announcement or to a provision for a Foreign Ministers' conference. Peking publicly intimated that it would agree to an obligation of nonaggression and the nonuse of force under the United Nations Charter despite its lack of membership, provided that such a commitment did not apply to Taiwan.

Washington's First Draft: The Americans now had to counter Peking's draft renunciation and apparent leaks to the public. At the 25th meeting of the Ambassadors on November 10, 1955, Ambassador Johnson rejected the Chinese version, and submitted the first American draft of an agreed joint announcement.* Ambassador Johnson insisted that the seventeen Americans still imprisoned in China must be released, bluntly protested and denounced the leak of the Chinese Communist draft, and exploded Peking's "trial balloons" on a Dulles-Chou meeting.[4] Abandoning the idea of just a mere oral exchange on the nonuse of force, Washington now agreed to a parallel or joint written undertaking because Ambassador Wang had stated at a previous meeting that the People's Republic of China, though not a member of the United Nations, would agree to the obligation of its Charter not to resort to aggression.

The American draft of November 10 provided that both governments individually, but not mutually, would renounce the use of force in general and "with particular reference to the Taiwan area" except for individual and collective self-defense. Washington's proposal was for each Ambassador to inform the other that his respective government had renounced the use of force. In effect, this was a simultaneous, reciprocal exchange of identical pledges. It ingeniously, if somewhat ambiguously, combined a joint commitment with two single but simultaneous announcements. This first American draft made the renunciation of force apply specifically to Taiwan, yet did not prejudice or limit the peaceful pursuit of policies by either side and left both with the right of self-defense. Washington dealt only obliquely with the reference to the United Nations Charter. Washington's draft merely noted in a preambular, nonoperative way that the use of force "does not accord with the principles and purposes of the United Nations Charter."

* See Appendix C, No. 3.

Ambassador Wang rejected the United States redraft with the standard Peking argument that it confused international and domestic matters by demanding that the People's Republic of China accept the *status quo* of United States "occupation of China's territory" and renounce its sovereign right to liberate Taiwan. Ambassador Wang stated that such a position was

absolutely unacceptable to China. Taiwan is China's territory. There can be no question of defense so far as the United States is concerned. The United States has already used force and the threat of force against China in the Taiwan area. Therefore, should one speak of defense, it is precisely China which should exercise its right of defense to expel such force and threat. Yet the United States has demanded the right of defense in the Taiwan area. Is this not precisely a demand that China accept continued United States occupation of Taiwan and that the tension in the Taiwan area be maintained forever? [5]

Since the 25th meeting on November 10, 1955, Taiwan has remained the specific barrier to any agreement between Peking and Washington and the source of tension for more than 100 sessions of the Ambassadorial Talks. It would have seemed then that the two original drafts were so far apart, and the reiterated positions of the two ambassadors on behalf of Mr. Dulles and Mr. Chou so divergent, that this diplomatic duel over the renunciation of force could only be conducted in an abstract, unreal plane or suspended altogether. Yet it continued, and for six months the two sides engaged in an exchange that was devoid of substance.

Peking's Counter-Proposal: The Chinese made the next move. At the meeting on December 1, Ambassador Wang put forward a counterproposal considerably revised in appearance, if not in fact. Chou had a deceptively simple redraft submitted in order that the Talks "might progress," and the dialogue continue.

Peking now proposed a single agreed announcement by both governments that they settle disputes "through peaceful negotiations without resorting to the threat or use of force," and the two Ambassadors "should continue their talks to seek practical and feasible means for the realization of this common desire." * This new version omitted any reference to the principles and purposes of the United Nations Charter, and did not mention a conference of foreign ministers. It seemed as though some progress had been made, although Peking's second draft, of course, did not refer to Taiwan,

* Full text in Appendix C, No. 4.

the crucial issue. The counterproposal was significant for its brevity and the omission of a demand for a ministerial conference. However, it was not as simple as it seemed. Ambassador Wang explained that his government would agree to this new version of a renunciation of force only on the condition that the Ambassadors would immediately begin to discuss and decide upon the holding of a Sino-American conference of the two foreign ministers. It would not be possible, he made clear, to release any agreed bilateral announcement on the renunciation of force alone unless and until prior agreement was also reached at the Ambassadorial Talks for Chou and Dulles to hold a conference. Again in Peking fashion, the Americans were told to accept a Chinese proposal forthwith without change, for "if the United States Government sincerely wants to renounce force, it has no reason to drag out the talks instead of entering into agreement on our new draft." Chou's countermove meant the same thing in effect as his first draft. The redraft and Ambassador Wang's explanation in several meetings made clear that the renunciation of force would not necessarily apply to Taiwan.

The State Department considered the Chinese draft of December 1 somewhat of an improvement over the draft of October 27 because the latter omitted the paragraph on the Foreign Ministers' conference and favored the continuation of Ambassadorial Talks. This perhaps was a real concession because the thrust of Peking's position until December 1 was subordination of the Ambassadorial Talks to a Foreign Ministers' meeting. As we have seen, Peking considered negotiations at the ambassadorial level in Geneva merely an instrument for arranging substantive talks at the foreign ministers level. In effect, the Geneva Talks were merely "talks on talks" like those at Panmunjom in 1953 and 1954. The United States government, however, preferred to keep diplomatic discussions with Peking at the lower level. For this purpose, Washington was willing to discuss not only substantive matters but also vital concerns at Geneva.

Yet Washington found the Communist draft of December 1, if improved, still unacceptable, for it continued to avoid any mention of the Taiwan area and the right of self-defense. In several subsequent meetings in December, Ambassador Johnson did not immediately give any reactions to the Chinese counterproposal while Washington deliberated on its next move. He did not even refer to it neither rejecting, accepting, nor commenting on it in any way

Ambassador Wang continued at each meeting to urge its immediate acceptance, and demanded that the American side stop stalling. Dulles could not leave Chou with the last word in a disarmingly simple, if deceptive, proposition. Dulles had to continue the dialogue on the renunciation of force in the hope that he still might be able to extract a mutually acceptable and meaningful agreement from Peking, although that possibility was slight.

Meanwhile, Peking again publicly taunted Washington to force Dulles' hand and to embarrass Washington. In early January, a Foreign Ministry statement accused the United States of stalling on the agenda and declared that the state of affairs was unsatisfactory with the recesses between meetings becoming longer and longer. Peking declared that it would not consent to their endless "dragging out," for the embargo on trade with China and a ministerial conference demanded immediate action since they were of "concern to the whole world." In addition to a long defense of Peking's position on the repatriation of prisoners, the spokesmen called for agreement on the nonuse of force, again on Peking's terms:

If this means that China and the United States should, in accordance with the purposes and principles of the United Nations' charter, settle peacefully the disputes between their two countries without resorting to force, then there also is no reason why this question cannot be settled quickly.[6]

Washington's Revisions: Then in a three and one-half hour meeting on January 12, 1956, resumed after a New Year's intermission of several weeks, Ambassador Johnson finally commented on the Chinese draft of December 1, 1955, and countered with another American redraft.* It proposed a short joint undertaking of both governments to settle disputes between them "through peaceful means"—not "peaceful negotiations," an important distinction—and not to resort to the threat or use of force in the Taiwan area or elsewhere "without prejudice to the inherent right of individual and collective self-defense." This American counterproposal contained the identical final paragraph of Peking's draft to the effect that the two Ambassadors "should continue their talks to seek practical and feasible means for the realization of this common desire." This second American redraft apparently repeated an effort to narrow the difference and find some common ground with Peking's versions. Washington made these two short but significant amendments to Peking's proposal by inserting the idea of individual and collective self-defense and the words "in the Taiwan area or elsewhere,"

* Full text in Appendix C, No. 5.

and by using the phrase "peaceful means" rather than "peaceful negotiations." The exchange of drafts had now reached the point where Peking kept Taiwan out of all its versions and discussions, while the Americans kept putting it back in. The change from "negotiations" to "means" indicated Washington's sensitivity and aversion to any formal admission or contractual acceptance of continuous negotiations with the Chinese People's Republic, despite the reality of the continued contact in Geneva. The idea of "peaceful means" would imply a wide variety of channels or even vaguer contacts which would not include the commitment to formal arrangements for "negotiations."

Ambassador Wang immediately pointed out that the American redraft was just as unacceptable as the first one of November 10. In fact, he considered them substantially the same, because both American drafts "demanded" what his government had long since "firmly rejected": namely, any inherent right of the United States to individual or collective self-defense in the Taiwan area. In other words, the People's Republic of China was not going to restrict in the slightest way its intention to claim and to seize control of Taiwan by any means possible. This long, hard meeting took place amid increasing warnings from the Chinese against delays and stalling. There were even hints from the Chinese of breaking off the Talks.

Public Controversy: The Americans could not have guessed it at the time, but it is now apparent from a review of the record, that Chou had decided to make a dramatic move to put public pressure on Dulles. Instead of countering with another redraft or even making a strong oral rebuttal across the table, Peking, on January 18, 1956, without the required notification, suddenly revealed all the drafts and views on the renunciation of force that had been exchanged since October 8. For reasons of their own, the Chinese Communists decided at this stage to make a counterstroke in the form of a forceful denunciation of Dulles. Ambassador Wang was instructed to give a long summary of the Chinese viewpoint and the actual drafts on renunciation, as well as the Chinese position on repatriation. The statement rejected the American formula for a mutual renunciation of force as long as it was qualified by the right of individual or collective self-defense in the Taiwan area and repeated Peking's standard differentiation between "liberation of Taiwan" and tensions between China and the United States. Peking's main public thrust was the accusation that the Americans were deliberately dragging out the talks and refusing to agree "on the means for the relaxation and elimination of tension in the Taiwan area." The statement repeated the argument which Ambassador Wang had frequently used in the Ambassadorial Talks that the United States was demanding China's acceptance of the "status quo" of United States "armed occupation of Taiwan." Ambassador Johnson had often rejected this argument. Nevertheless, in its long statement of January 18, Peking went much further, and for the first time since the Talks began, attacked Dulles personally:

United States Secretary of State Dulles again openly cried out recently that in order to hold on to China's territory and infringe on China's sovereignty he would not scruple to start an atomic war. The United States aggressors imagined that this would frighten the Chinese people into giving up their own sovereign rights. But this attempt will never succeed.*

The long statement from Peking did not break off the Talks. Instead, with a certain imperiousness, the statement ended with the declaration that the Chinese side had already put forward "a reasonable proposal completely acceptable to both sides." The Talks should "speedily reach an agreement on the basis of this reasonable proposal and proceed to settle the question of abolishment of the embargo and the question of preparations for a Sino-American conference of the Foreign Ministers." "To drag out the Talks and carry out threats will settle no question," the statement concluded.[7]

The immediate American reaction was an angry denunciation and further explanation. Ambassador Johnson instantly issued a public protest deploring the Chinese release:

I am disappointed that the Chinese Communists have again chosen to resort to propaganda regarding the talks between Ambassador Wang and myself. At the beginning of our talks we agreed that progress could best be achieved by promptly announcing our agreements and refraining from public airing of our disagreements.

The statement to some extent reflects the progress that it has thus far been possible to make in seeking a commitment by the Chinese Communists to renounce force to achieve their objectives. However, the partial quotation and misinterpretation in the statement distorts and perverts the facts with regard to our discussions concerning the exact wording of such a commitment.

The statement also attempts to gloss over the stark failure of the Chi-

___

* The personal attack on Dulles may have been an allusion to the story in *Life* magazine of January 16, 1956. This was the famous article on how Dulles had brought the United States "back from the brink" in Korea, Indo-China, and Taiwan by applying a strong diplomacy backed with atomic weapons to avert a major war in the Far East.

nese Communists fully to carry out their commitments of September 10 expeditiously to release all Americans on Mainland China desiring to return.[8]

In this super-charged atmosphere, an ambassadorial meeting was nevertheless held on January 19, but no progress was made.

Then, on January 21, the State Department countered Peking's sudden public disclosure with a long release to "set" the record "straight," in view of the "misleading" statement issued by Peking on January 18. The Department published the full text of all the drafts, some of which Peking had edited, and briefly commented on each one up through January 18. The Washington release concluded that the Chinese statement apparently rejected the United States draft of January 12 because of the disagreement regarding Taiwan. The Department's statement of January 21 also explained the United States position on Taiwan, which it had reiterated many times in the Ambassadorial Talks, and which reflected Dulles' long-standing policy:

First, the United States is not occupying Taiwan and Taiwan has never been a part of Communist China. The claims of Communist China and the contentions of the United States with respect to this area are well known and constitute a major dispute between them. It is specifically with respect to this dispute that the United States has proposed the principle of renunciation of force and the settlement of differences by peaceful means. This is the principle which the Communists say they have accepted.

In this connection the United States has made completely clear that in renouncing the use of force neither side is relinquishing its objectives and policies but only the use of force to attain them.

Secondly, the United States has rights and responsibilities in the Taiwan area; also it has a mutual defense treaty. Accordingly it is present in the Taiwan area. The Communist refusal to state that the renunciation of force is without prejudice to the right of self-defense against armed attack can only be interpreted as an attempt to induce the United States to agree that if attacked it will forego the right to defend its lawful presence in this area.

The right of individual and collective self-defense against armed attack is inherent; it is recognized in international law; it is specifically affirmed in the Charter of the United Nations. No country can be expected to forego this right. Indeed, the Communists should be as anxious to preserve this right as is the United States.[9]

The Department's statement drew five conclusions at this stage in the Ambassadorial Talks: (1) thirteen Americans were still held in Communist prisons four months after the Chinese Communists had announced that they would take measures to expedite the return of

Americans in China; (2) the United States had proposed the renunciation of the use of force without prejudice to the right of individual and collective self-defense against armed attack in order that the discussions might take place free from the threat of war; (3) the United States had also made clear in the Ambassadorial Talks that this renunciation would not prevent Peking or Washington from continuing to seek their respective objectives and policies by peaceful means; (4) the Chinese Communists had nullified the renunciation of force by refusing to apply it to the Taiwan area and by refusing to include the right of individual and collective self-defense; and (5) the Communists seemed willing to renounce force "only if they are first conceded the goals for which they would use force."

At that juncture in the Ambassadorial Talks many wondered whether they would, should, or even could be continued. However, the State Department apparently did not wish to be responsible for breaking off the Talks or closing the door to further discussions. A continuation of the availability of the "little window of diplomacy" might still be useful. The Department's statement of January 21 used milder and more diplomatic language than Peking had for indicating essentially the same inclination toward prolonging the Talks. The Americans wanted to persevere to reach agreement on a "meaningful" renunciation of force, particularly in the Taiwan area, and at least to keep on probing Peking's intentions in this dangerous zone where miscalculations could have had critical consequences.

Three days later, on January 24, Dulles was asked at a press conference for his reaction to the Chinese charges of January 18.[10] After saying that the statement of the Department spoke for itself —he had probably drafted much of it—he declared that there was a "very sincere desire" on his part to achieve as rapidly as possible a "meaningful understanding" on a renunciation of force. Seeing some progress in that direction, he commented:

Negotiations with the Chinese Communists are usually slow and prolonged, as we know from past experience. But we are planning to go ahead; . . . and we continue to be patient and persistent in our effort to obtain a greater assurance of peace and renunciation of force in that area. . . . Obviously we would not be continuing the Talks unless we had some hopes and expectations of positive results coming out of them.

When he was asked why the Communists had broken the rule on secrecy, Mr. Dulles answered that it was rather traditional in these

matters for the Chinese Communists to break the general understanding about secrecy when they thought that they had a "good
propaganda position."

Also on January 24, Peking reissued a long repetition of its position, accusing Washington of "deliberate procrastination and obstruction." Peking reiterated its call for a Foreign Ministers' conference and for an end to the trade embargo. Peking's statement of
January 24, presumably reflecting what Ambassador Wang was saying in the Geneva Talks, bears lengthy quotation, to give the tone
and substance of Peking's position:

Nor have they been able to reach agreement on the question of renunciation of the use of force raised by the American side after having discussed the question for more than three months. It has been China's consistent stand that China and the United States should refrain from the use
of force and settle disputes between the two countries by negotiation,
particularly the question of the tension in the Taiwan area. . . . If the
principle of non-use of force between China and the United States is to
be realized, it is necessary to hold a Sino-American conference of the
Foreign Ministers to settle the question of relaxing and eliminating the
tension in the Taiwan area. . . .

The two items on the agenda of the Sino-American talks are interrelated. The American side has violated the agreement on the first item
and delayed progress on the second, and furthermore has issued a statement to distort once again the developments in the Talks and the substance of the discussions. This can only be interpreted as an attempt by
the American side to becloud the actual facts and hoodwink the people of
the world in order to continue to drag out the Sino-American Talks. The
American side expressed unwillingness in the talks to provide specifically
for the holding of a Sino-American conference of the foreign ministers;
on the contrary, it demanded that China accept that the United States
should have the right of self-defense in the Taiwan area. The United
States Department of State persisted in this unreasonable position in its
statement of January 21; and following the statement, an official of the
United States Department of State further declared that the United States
position on Taiwan was inflexible and "non-negotiable."

This only shows that the American side has no sincerity to settle
through negotiation the major dispute between China and the United
States, that the American avowal that each side should pursue its objectives and policies by peaceful means is nothing but a hoax, and that the
real intention of the American side is still to maintain and aggravate the
tension in the Taiwan area and pursue its so-called "brink of war" policy
of intimidation. . . .

The Sino-American Ambassadorial Talks have proved to be incapable
of settling such a major substantive question as the relaxation and elimination of tension in the Taiwan area. The Chinese side holds that a Sino-

American conference of the Foreign Ministers must be held, as this is the practical and feasible means for settling this question.

Since the United States has already used force and threat of force against China in the Taiwan area, a statement on the renunciation of the use of force by China and the United States must lead to the elimination of the force and threat of force employed by the United States in the Taiwan area, and cannot possibly be utilized to induce China to accept the status quo of United States occupation of Taiwan.[11]

Meetings at Geneva and public declarations then alternated for several months. The Ambassadors met again at Geneva for three hours on February 3 without any progress. They presumably reiterated in private their public positions. No more American prisoners were released. A general expectation grew that the Talks would be broken off. Peking, on March 4, released another statement unilaterally and without prior notification to accuse the United States of obstructing the Talks.[12] It again hinted that the Chinese might end them by indicating that Peking could not agree to the dragging out of these Talks. The March statement referred to Peking's original proposal of October 27 that the two sides agree to settle disputes peacefully under the United Nations Charter and proceed to hold a Foreign Ministers' conference to eliminate tension in the Taiwan area. Peking again offered the United States two choices: its formula of October 27 or its formula of December 1. As we have seen, each used a different set of words to say the same thing. Peking's viewpoint was that if the joint statement on mutual renunciation of the use of force was to mean anything, it should lead "to peaceful settlement of the dispute which the United States itself had provoked." For this, Peking proposed the holding of a Foreign Ministers' conference, while the United States demanded the right of individual and collective self-defense on Chinese territory, Taiwan, which was "tantamount to asking China to accept the present American occupation of Taiwan and interference with the liberation of the coastal islands."

The American reaction two days later to Peking's March statement was somewhat sharper in tone than Washington's statement of January 21 had been. The State Department said that the March 4th Chinese statement contained nothing new. Its failure to mention the Americans still in prison served to re-emphasize that these Americans were being held as "political hostages." The Department then went on to repeat its conclusions and the final paragraphs from its statement of January 21, quoted above.[13]

A week later Chou himself outlined Peking's stand on the impasse when he made a major report to the Chinese People's Political Consultative Conference. He declared that the government of the Chinese People's Republic had no objection to issuing a statement on the renunciation of the use of force by both sides which, he pointed out, the United States wanted. However, he claimed that since the United States had used force "to occupy China's Taiwan," an announcement on the renunciation of force by both sides must lead to removal of the force "already used by the United States and should not be allowed to bring about the legalization of United States occupation of Taiwan." Chou En-lai himself insisted that the principle of joint renunciation of force could be realized only by a conference of the two Foreign Ministers to solve the problem of "easing and eliminating the tension in the Taiwan area." He accused the United States of using the issue of renouncing force to maintain and heighten tension and not to eliminate it. He also charged the United States with introducing into its renunciation draft the idea of individual or collective right of self-defense for the purpose of maintaining the force, already used against China, "to legalize its occupation of Taiwan so that it can continue to make use of the Chiang Kai-shek clique to create a so-called 'two China' situation." China would not agree to any such objective, he declared. While willing to continue to seek an agreement at the Ambassadorial Talks, the Chinese People's Republic was opposed to this "prolonged dragging out of the Talks which prevents the solution to the tension in the Taiwan area." [14] As a special attraction, Chou repeated his proposal of July 30, 1955, for an Asian and Pacific collective peace pact that would include the United States. Two days later, on February 5, the influential newspaper, *Ta Kung Pao*, urged the parties to the Talks agree on a ministerial conference and warned that "prancing on the brink of war can lead to no good." [15] Chou's words now helped to identify explicitly what lay behind the vague phrase "eliminating tension in the Taiwan area." Peking meant the total elimination of the United States' power and armed forces from Taiwan. This position of Peking has never changed.

Final Drafts: One more round of drafts in the duel between Dulles and Chou over the renunciation of force was undertaken before the issue became a stereotyped repetition to be overtaken by other issues and situations. The next negotiating countermove at the Ambassadorial Talks came on April 19 when Ambassador Johnson tabled the following draft.*

* Full text in Appendix C, No. 6.

1. Ambassador U. Alexis Johnson, on behalf of the Government of the United States of America, and Ambassador Wang Ping-nan, on behalf of the Government of the People's Republic of China, agree, without prejudice to the pursuit by each side of its policies by peaceful means or its inherent right of individual or collective self-defense, to announce:

2. The United States of America and the People's Republic of China are determined that they should settle disputes between their two countries through peaceful negotiations without resorting to the threat or use of force in the Taiwan area or elsewhere.

3. The two ambassadors should continue their talks to seek practical and feasible means for the realization of this common desire.[16]

This draft significantly amended the Communist proposal of December 1, 1955, and the American counterproposal of January 12, 1956, by adding two important phrases. It added the necessary phrase "without prejudice to the pursuit by each side of its policies by peaceful means" to give effect to the Dulles policy of maintaining and seeking sovereign claims by peaceful means only. The new American draft made another significant change: it accepted Peking's phrase "peaceful negotiations" in place of Washington's preferred terminology of "peaceful means." As has already been noted, the reference to negotiations implied a commitment to use diplomatic channels or agreed-upon means of communications whereas "means" could imply a variety of indirect and vague possibilities. This redraft retained the two concepts of the inherent right of individual or collective self-defense and the renunciation of force or the threat of force in the Taiwan area, as well as elsewhere. Otherwise it was the same as Peking's draft of December 1. Secretary Dulles was in effect saying to Peking across the table in Geneva that it did not have to give up any of its political goals and that it could continue to pursue its political objective in Taiwan by political means. Thus, if the agreement on a meaningful renunciation of force, in the sense that Dulles understood it, could be reached, neither Peking nor Washington would agree on, or be obligated to abandon the pursuit of, any of its policies by peaceful means. Even if either side thought that it could achieve its objectives only by military or forceful means, it would have to give up such means and depend on peaceful ways. In the meantime, as the Americans went on to observe, each signatory would reserve the right of self-defense if the other broke its agreement and engaged in armed attack.

The Chinese reacted to this third American draft on May 11,

1956.[17] Ambassador Wang proposed that the two governments announce their determination to settle the Taiwan dispute by peaceful negotiations but added the definite stipulation that the two Ambassadors arrange for a Foreign Ministers' meeting to take place within two months.* This deadline was a peremptory variation on the old theme. The Americans, of course, did not accept this narrowing of the Chinese proposal and rejected the implied ultimatum of a meeting between Chou and Dulles in sixty days.[18] The next and last exchange on this subject was again a resort to public statements.

On June 1, Chou hinted that the Chinese might take another initiative with regard to the Talks. During a press interview in Peking, he charged that the United States was using the Geneva Talks "to try to legitimize her occupation of Taiwan by suggesting that both sides issue a joint statement guaranteeing the status quo of the island." [19] He again declared that the People's Republic of China could never agree to maintaining the present status of Taiwan but that it was ready to issue a joint statement to the effect that the two countries would be willing to use peaceful means to settle the dispute and "in accordance with this desire are ready to seek ways and means including talks at a Foreign Ministers' level to implement it." He again held out the prospect that the People's Republic of China would choose the peaceful rather than the military way to liberate Taiwan if conditions permitted, for he believed that the possibility of the "peaceful liberation" of Taiwan was becoming "brighter" every day, although the United States was "dragging out" the Geneva Talks. Washington, apparently discounting his interview as no more than a repetition of long-standing assertions and distortions, immediately pointed out that Ambassador Wang always insisted on a Foreign Ministers' meeting as a precondition to a renunciation of force, whereas Ambassador Johnson emphasized an unequivocal renunciation of force before discussions could be held on the question of an eventual ministerial meeting.[20]

Peking once more resorted to unilateral disclosure of the substance of the Talks to bring pressure on the Americans. On June 12, Ambassador Wang broke diplomatic silence and secrecy by releasing the text of the American proposal of April 19, the Chinese rejection of it, and their counterproposal of May 11.[21] The Americans immediately issued an explanation of their April 19th proposal. The Department of State took the position that the Chinese re-

* Full text in Appendix C, No. 7.

jection of the American proposal of April 19 amounted to a rejection of Peking's own proposal.[22] Of course, as we have seen, the American draft of April 19 was decidedly different from the previous Chinese Communist draft of December 1, 1955, because the Americans applied the renunciation of force to the Taiwan area, whereas the Chinese Communists excluded it. This was not an issue of semantics or an error in diplomatic drafting. It was a matter of real substance. The Department in turn rejected the "requirement" that the two Ambassadors be given only two months to reach an agreement "satisfactory to the Chinese Communists" or risk having the agreement on the renunciation of force lapse. Washington also indicated that there was not the remotest chance of a ministerial meeting as long as there was no release of American prisoners and no meaningful renunciation of force. In the State Department's view, the Chinese Communists could not object to American phrasing unless they had either determined not to join in a meaningful renunciation of force or intended to reserve for themselves the use of armed force if they were not assured in advance that they would gain their goals. According to the Department of State:

> The principle of the renunciation of the use of force is neither the abandonment of the right to pursue the attainment of objectives by peaceful means, or the right of self-defense. Nor does the principle of renunciation of force expire when one believes that he can better obtain his objectives by the use of force.[23]

The Department's statement ended with the intention to continue to seek "a meaningful renunciation of force." An official of the Department of State put the issue bluntly when he said that the long drafting on the agreement on renunciation of force had come down to a difference of only two significant words: "including Taiwan."[24]

Deadlock

Peking again publicly explained its version of the negotiations. In a report to the National People's Congress on June 28, Chou En-lai put the issue in the context of an American "plot to create two Chinas."[25] While rejecting a separate independent state of Taiwan, Chou reaffirmed that his government was willing to join the United States in a mutual agreement on the renunciation of force. But then he gave it the Chinese definition of eliminating "the United States occupation of Taiwan." He nevertheless believed that the Chinese drafts had taken the American views into consideration. But he insisted in his report that any joint announcement must provide for a Foreign Ministers' conference to put the principle of renunciation into effect by peacefully negotiating the dispute over Taiwan, implying a result favorable to Peking. However, he had been willing, he said, to compromise on the level of representation for this purpose by leaving it to the two Ambassadors to negotiate a peaceful resolution of the Taiwan dispute. He complained that the United States opposed a conference and even peaceful negotiations for this purpose. Instead the United States was attempting, he alleged, to drag out the Talks indefinitely in order to "freeze the *status quo* in the Taiwan area." He then put the Chinese case succinctly:

China cannot agree to issue an announcement of sole advantage to one side; nor can it tolerate the use of the Sino-American talks by one side as a tool to achieve its unilateral aims. China maintains that any joint announcement must be advantageous to both sides, and that continuance of the Sino-American talks is possible only on condition that it is advantageous to both sides.[26]

One of the highest officials in Peking, Liu Shao-chi, told the Eighth Congress of the Chinese Communist Party that his government had tried to settle disputes with the United States by peaceful negotiation and desired peaceful coexistence with United States.[27] However, the Chinese People's Republic would not acquiesce "in aggression," and wanted a Foreign Ministers' conference to "eliminate tension" in the Taiwan area.

The Peking press ridiculed and scorned Washington as the issues of renunciation of force, ending the embargo and arranging a conference deadlocked completely. One article chided Washington for inventing an entirely new tactic in negotiations which it called "delayed action diplomacy." These inspired commentaries, noting that Taiwan and the trade embargo prevented "rapprochement" between the two countries, confirmed Ambassador Wang's long efforts to arrange a discussion on an end to the embargo and to establish higher-level negotiations. These articles claimed that Peking had always stood for a joint declaration of a mutual renunciation of force and had tried hard at Geneva to find a mutually acceptable version. These articles also left the impression that the United States at Geneva had not closed the door to the possibility of a ministerial conference but was reluctant to do anything about it then. From the

Chinese Communist point of view, a ministerial conference was the only means possible for putting any mutual renunciation of force into effect, because only a high-level—not ambassadorial—conference could properly deal with the crucial issue of the "elimination" of the American presence in Taiwan. Otherwise, the reduction of tension would remain merely a "pious hope."

For Peking, Washington's position of "freezing the *status quo* in the Taiwan area" while refusing serious negotiations about such "elimination," and the status of Taiwan amounted to "a demand for the approval of aggression," [28] and represented the reverse of any renunciation of force. One newspaper bluntly criticized the Americans for not having any intention of negotiating an agreement or the "courage" to break off the negotiations. To the Chinese Communist government and its press, Washington, while trying "to kill time by keeping the pot boiling on the question of the renunciation of force," [29] was solely responsible for the deadlock in the Ambassadorial Talks.

If Washington had broken the deadlock by conceding a conference, can we speculate as to what Chou might have tried to negotiate or extract from Dulles? It is, of course, hard to say, since the Chinese Communists are disciplined negotiators who are skilled in concealing their purposes. However, it is possible to infer that Peking was seeking big-power status and had certain specific trade-offs in mind. For example, a Foreign Ministers' conference not only would have given Peking great international prestige, but it might have institutionalized a continuing conference at a higher political level as a trade-off by Peking for extending negotiations over Taiwan for a long time. And as to the advantages that Chou could have had in mind for Washington from a joint declaration of a mutual renunciation of force in this bargaining situation, there is just a small hint that Peking used the phrase "easing tensions" rather than "eliminating them" as a signal to indicate that any process of American withdrawal from Taiwan might be allowed to take place over a long period of time. In other words, the basic dispute between Washington and Peking would not have had to be solved all at once. The United States would not necessarily have had to "lay down the pistol," "eliminating" the American presence in the area through total and instant withdrawal.

For its part, Washington took the position at the time both in the Talks and in public that it would not explore these intimations even if they did exist until there was satisfactory evidence of compliance on two agreements: the return of all American civilians and the joint announcement of a mutual renunciation of force. In any event, the United States did not intend to make any concessions by trading away its relations with Taipei, particularly since the United States government did not want diplomatic relations or continuing negotiations with Peking. Washington wanted to isolate, not enhance, Peking.

Washington had to be particularly attentive to the reactions of Taipei, which was particularly disturbed by American efforts at Geneva to obtain a negotiated agreement with the Communists on the nonuse of force in the area of China and elsewhere. The former American Ambassador to Taipei, Karl Rankin, has written that Taipei was vehemently opposed to such negotiations and to the Ambassadorial Talks because it was felt that the very negotiations themselves as well as any agreements resulting from them could not help but lead to the establishment of diplomatic relations between Washington and Peking. In Taipei's view, any joint declaration or agreement between Peking and Washington would have promoted "Communist China's rehabilitation as a peace-loving nation." [30] But the discussion over force broke down in 1956, and never warranted the anxiety and hostility of the Chinese Nationalists.

Were the long hours of discussions on nonuse of force, an end to the embargo, and a ministerial conference just another Oriental shadow play or an American charade? Ambassador Rankin has written that he once reported that Washington did not expect Peking to agree to the American wording of a renunciation of force because Peking would insist on keeping Taiwan out of any such declaration on the ground that it was an internal Chinese problem and that in any case the United States would not trade "performance for a Chinese Communist promise." [31] Dulles no doubt would have liked to negotiate a successful agreement on his terms because it would have been a master stroke in his world diplomacy as well as a major political breakthrough in Asia. But it is doubtful that he ever had any expectations of arriving at a "meaningful agreement" with Chou on this particular issue. Instead, Dulles probably let it serve to foil and frustrate Chou's ploys for other agreements and rapprochement with the United States. The undeviating focus on the issue of force by Dulles and Ambassador Johnson served as a revealing gauge for probing and detecting Peking's intentions in 1956. It was

not only a good defensive maneuver; insistence on the issue of renunciation permitted the United States to manipulate it for other
purposes.

Chou also manipulated the issue to approach his real objective.
One American observer, analyzing these negotiations a year later,
concluded that Chou had let the Talks continue in 1956 not for the
purpose of coming to grips with any renunciation of force, the discussion of which was only a gesture to the Americans, but to
eliminate restrictions on trade with Communist China and to widen
the area of diplomatic relations with the United States.

In looking back at these issues, two comments which Dulles and
Chou later made reveal how far apart they really were and yet how
much each then realized the severity of the impasse. Dulles in 1957,
after recalling that Chou had made a dramatic proposal at Bandung
to sit down and negotiate with the United States, gave this version
of Chou's position regarding force:

> When the United States took him up and sought explicit reciprocal
> renunciations of force, his Ambassador, after presenting various evasive
> formulas, finally stated frankly that his regime did intend to use armed
> force to take Taiwan unless they could get it in some other way.[32]

Chou in 1960, after recalling that the Talks had been going on for
five years, gave his version of Dulles' stand.

> At the very outset, we proposed that disputes between China and the
> United States, including the dispute between the two countries in the
> Taiwan region, should be settled through peaceful negotiations, without
> resorting to the use or threat of force. The United States blocked all
> news of this proposal, but China later published it. Why did Dulles reject
> it? Because Dulles realized that reaching such an agreement implied that
> the next step would be discussions on how and when United States armed
> forces were to withdraw from Taiwan and the Taiwan Straits.[33]

With such divergence dividing the two principal negotiators, it is
understandable that in some forty meetings the Ambassadors could
find no common ground on that subject.

While their efforts now seem so futile, they at least have completed the preliminary negotiations for later use, should future circumstances ever require and permit a bilateral agreement for a
general cease-fire and nonrecourse to force. All that is needed are
the signatures—if the question of Taiwan is ever resolved. But for
most of the Ambassadorial Talks during the past ten years the issues
of nonrecourse to force, the trade embargo and a ministerial meet-

ing have been in limbo, although the Americans have continued to press, ritualistically, for the renunciation of force as a matter of form. Only during the acute crisis over the offshore islands and Taiwan in August–October 1958 did the issue of a cease-fire and the renunciation of force become a serious matter again. But in the summer of 1956, with the deadlock so obvious and the negotiations so fruitless on these subjects, Peking undertook a new initiative and turned to a proposal for the exchange of newsmen and other kinds of contacts with the United States.

CHAPTER FIVE

Peking's Proposals for Bilateral Contacts in 1956-57

The midsummer of 1956 was a more promising and less critical time in the Far East than elsewhere in the world, and Peking still followed the "Bandung Phase" of its foreign policy. Chou took advantage of a mellowing atmosphere to shift the terms of engagement and change the vocabulary of the dialogue, abruptly and publicly. It is ironic that the Communist regime in Peking, which controlled its press and its citizens, initiated this matter of travel and contacts, while the United States government, with its dedication to freedom, opposed it.

Peking's Opening for Exchange of Newsmen

Without warning, on August 6, 1956, the Peking government lifted its ban on American newsmen entering China.* In a surprise move, Peking cabled offers of visas to fifteen United States news-gathering outlets: newspapers, news agencies, magazines and radio-television reporters.[1] They were invited for a month's visit to the People's Republic of China as guests of the government, with no conditions imposed. This was probably designed to help improve Peking's chances of obtaining a ministerial conference with Dulles and bring about a relaxation of the economic restrictions imposed by the United States. Presumably Peking assumed that reporters filing favorable reports from China would help persuade the Ameri-

---

* As a result of the Korean War, Washington prohibited travel to and trade with Communist China. The State Department would not validate passports even with visas to go there. Newsmen as well as all other Americans were legally prevented from entering the People's Republic of China.

can public to loosen the cord which Dulles had tied around China. In any event, Chou's initiative had a dramatic effect.

The official American reaction was immediately negative. On August 7, in announcing its opposition, the State Department stated that, following a review of its passport policy, it had decided to continue the ban against issuing passports to anyone for travel to Communist China.[2] The Department turned down the invitation and prevented its implementation on the grounds that the Chinese Communist regime had created a "special impediment" by taking American citizens into captivity and holding them as hostages despite the Agreement of September 10, 1955. So long as these conditions existed, the Department's announcement went on, it would not be in the best interests of the United States for Americans to accept an invitation to travel to Communist China. Until the issues of principle on repatriation of civilians and renunciation of force were resolved, such "subsidiary matters" could not be broached.

Ambassador Johnson communicated this position to Ambassador Wang, at the next Ambassadorial Meeting.[3] In one sense the refusal of the United States to take up new issues until the two principal ones were resolved was consistent with its stand on other issues. But it also represented both an intense distaste for the Chinese Communist tactics of bargaining prisoners for newsmen, as well as a responsible concern for the welfare of American newsmen who might go to China under this invitation. The logic of the American position also provided an understandable pretext for Washington's disinclination to soften the general policy of isolating Communist China.

The reaction of the United States news agencies to the Department's prompt and firm response was equally immediate and negative toward Washington.[4] An editorial in *The New York Times* of August 8, 1956, stated its regret over the Department's ban. A day later *The New York Times* reported a general protest from the executives of leading American newspapers, press associations, and radio-television networks. Whether or not Chou En-lai had deliberately intended to turn the effective weapon of the Fourth Estate upon his adversary can only be guessed. In any event, the sudden invitation to newsmen had exactly that effect. The negotiations between Washington and Peking in the Ambassadorial Talks took on a new dimension. Although the American public had been generally sympathetic with Dulles' insistence on the release of Americans unjustifiably held in Communist prisons, and the diplomats and foreign offices of the world, particularly in Asia, were professionally interested in his negotiation over the renunciation of force, the issue of newsmen aroused public opinion leaders and diplomatic commentators. Dulles was faced with a particularly intense and difficult problem. Whatever the purpose may have been, had Chou intended merely to harass and embarrass his adversary without respect to the other issues at Geneva, he succeeded.

Chou En-lai, having introduced this issue in August 1956 and seen its impact on the American press and Dulles, pressed the initiative publicly and in the Ambassadorial Talks. At a banquet in Peking for a Nepalese cultural delegation Chou declared that the doors of the People's Republic of China were open for the world to enter, and that the purpose of the invitation to the Americans was "to enable them to see what we are actually doing." He indicated that the People's Republic of China was not concerned about the way American correspondents reported what they saw.[5] A number of American newsmen hurried to Hong Kong to await visas. However, Presidential endorsement of the ban came when on August 20 the State Department announced that the President had authorized Under-Secretary Herbert Hoover, Jr., to make clear the President's "full concurrence" with the policy statement of August 7.[6] State Department officials also let it be known that they hoped the President's endorsement would persuade American editors to countermand the reported plans of several correspondents to accept Peking's invitation and go into China without a visa. The home offices of the newsmen in Hong Kong then instructed them not to go into China without a visa and passport. On August 23 Peking advised these correspondents in Hong Kong that they would have to bring their passports if they intended to enter China.[7] This eliminated the possibility that newsmen granted a one-month visa from China would be able to accept without losing their passports on return to the United States where they would face legal prosecution and professional immobilization. Then, on August 23, Madame Sun Yat-sen—a vice-chairman of the government of the People's Republic of China—renewed Peking's bid for high-level talks with Washington.[8] At his news conference on August 31, President Eisenhower reaffirmed his support of the State Department's ban, stating that American reporters should not be permitted to enter Communist China while Peking detained Americans as "hostages." [9]

Meanwhile in the meeting of August 21, Ambassador Wang made a proposal to shift the discussions from the renunciation of force to the relaxation of trade restrictions and other kinds of contact. Ambassador Johnson turned this down on the same grounds that the proposal on newsmen had been rejected in Washington. The United States continued to insist on the release and repatriation of the few imprisoned Americans left in Communist China, and on a meaningful renunciation of force before there could be any consideration on the part of the United States of any other issue. It would hardly be reasonable to expect the United States to discuss a relaxation of trade restrictions, the State Department later announced, "when the trade that would result from such a relaxation would strengthen a regime which refuses to renounce the use of force against us." [10]

During the fall, Peking kept up its pressure for mutual contacts by trade, newsmen, and other exchanges. On September 21 Ambassador Wang released a unilateral statement in Geneva on his proposal of August 21 regarding trade, and continued at the Talks to seek agreement on a draft announcement to "improve Sino-American relations." [11] Ambassador Johnson reiterated Washington's opposition. On October 16 the Chinese Foreign Ministry released a statement in Geneva accusing the United States of having rejected the September 22 offer to eliminate existing barriers interfering with the freedom of contacts and cultural exchange between the two peoples. The Foreign Ministry made it clear that any leniency on releasing American prisoners depended on the improvement of "Sino-American" relations, adding that visits of American newsmen would help bring about the improvement. After referring to the invitation to American newsmen to visit the People's Republic of China, the statement continued:

It can be seen from the warm welcome expressed in American press circles that this step taken by China is in accord with the keen desire of the American people to know about China. So far as the Sino-American talks are concerned, agreement on certain questions which are easier to settle, such as this, not only would open the way for mutual contacts between peoples of the two countries but also would definitely improve the atmosphere prevailing in the Sino-American talks and help the settling of other issues between China and the United States.[12]

This clearly stated Peking's position in the first few years of the Talks that "subsidiary issues" could be settled before matters of principle.

A week later, on October 24, a high official in Washington, publicly commenting on the "conversations with the Chinese Communists," spoke of the "cultural bombardment" trained on the United States to allow scholars, musicians, artists, writers, and others to go to China. However, he indicated that Ambassador Johnson would continue his efforts until all American prisoners were released.[13]

In November, while on a visit to Cambodia, Chou En-lai went out of his way to talk to American reporters. At a press conference in Pnompenh he told them that they would be welcome to visit the People's Republic of China if they could get permission from their government. He remarked that antagonism had "dwindled some" between the two governments.[14] In Calcutta in early December Chou said that the initiative was now Dulles' regarding the release of the ten remaining Americans, for China desired peace and good relations with America and had made all the proposals for that purpose in the Ambassadorial Talks.[15]

Then, in December, William Worthy, correspondent for the weekly *Afro-American* of Baltimore, entered the People's Republic of China for a month's visit in defiance of the State Department's ban. He had assurances of support in any legal action against him by United States authorities and had waived all claims against the United States government in the event of personal injury, loss of property, or detention in Communist China. The State Department immediately deplored this visit as "against the expressed policy of the United States." [16] Two other American journalists, Edmund Stevens and Philip Hollington of *Look* magazine, also were reported to have entered Communist China.[17] The Department refused to validate the passports of all three correspondents. The American press and many of its executives protested publicly and privately to the United States government.

The State Department nevertheless announced that the three cases would be referred to the Treasury Department for suitable action in view of the relevant provisions of the Trading with the Enemy Act. In a press release of December 28, the Department announced that their passports would be valid only for return to the United States after they left China and again explained that the ban on travel to China was based on the consideration that Americans were still being held by the People's Republic of China as "hostages." [18] Thus, in six months Peking had thoroughly embroiled the Department of State, Secretary Dulles, and President Eisenhower in a contest of considerable intensity and even bitterness with much of the American working press and most of its leading executives. Moreover, the seemingly simple initiative of inviting fifteen American correspondents on a visit to China had opened a major moral, political, and constitutional issue among Americans over the right to travel abroad.

Chou En-lai tied the question of the entry of American newsmen to that of the exit of American prisoners. After noting in New Delhi in early December that the ten remaining Americans had a chance to be released "if their behavior were good," he hinted in January, during his third visit to Nepal in three months, that Peking would exchange Americans in the People's Republic of China for Chinese in the United States. He reaffirmed his "offer" to meet with Dulles and was reported as saying that "the People's Republic of China wants to be friends with the United States but even when we extend our hand they refuse to shake hands with us." [19] This may have been an allusion to the Geneva Conference of 1954 when Dulles had, in fact, refused to shake Chou's hand or exchange any civilities with him. But it also may have been a way of subtly expressing the negotiating position that Chou was trying to develop with Dulles.

Dulles remained firm and at his news conference on February 5, when queried about denying American reporters access to China, he replied:

. . . We don't like American citizens being used as a means of coercion against the United States Government. As you know, of course, the Chinese Communist Government has for some time been trying to get reporters—preferably those it picked—to come into Communist China, and it has repeatedly tried to use illegal detention of Americans in Communist China as a means to accomplish its ends in that respect. . . . I do not think under any circumstances that so long as the present state of at least semi-war prevails and we do not recognize that regime, that we would issue a passport valid for Communist China. Now, then, you get into all sorts of refinements, however, as to whether or not a correspondent wishes to go without claiming the protection from the United States Government. . . . But the issuance of passports to a regime which is not recognized is something which is never done.[20]

However, Dulles indicated that if the Americans in Chinese prisons were released, the administration would take a new look at the situation.

The American press was concerned and somewhat confused over this statement because the State Department had been criticized for using the issue of reporters going to China as an instrument of United States policy toward Communist China. Now Dulles had turned the tables in charging that it was Peking which was using newsmen as an "instrument of diplomacy." The policy of banning all travel by Americans to Communist China and all contacts between Americans and Communist Chinese—including but not limited to newsmen— was encountering steadily mounting public dissent and confusion, with very little manifest approval.

At this point, in February 1957, the State Department undertook a background briefing to justify and explain its policies.[21] These apparently were the principal points on the status of negotiations at Geneva: (1) Instead of fulfilling the commitment on American prisoners, the Communists at Geneva proposed cultural exchanges and invited various Americans, including newspaper representatives, to visit their country. Ambassador Johnson refused to consider this proposal while Americans remained imprisoned in violation of Peking's commitment. To compromise this American position would be a form of appeasement, and would bring no assurance of the desired result, since "there is no end to blackmail," once it is successful. (2) If the United States yielded under such pressure, the determination of friends and allies to resist "aggressive communism" would be weakened, the international leadership of the United States would be seriously undermined, and it would be difficult for Washington to urge others to stand unafraid and unflinching. (3) The policy on the ban had no special application to the press. Missionaries, scholars, relatives of imprisoned Americans, and others with cause to feel that their needs were compelling, had been similarly restrained on the same ground—that travel in Communist China was not in the public interest. This policy did not transgress the freedom of the press (guaranteed in the First Amendment) to collect and publish information. The State Department recognized the importance of the greatest possible flow of public information about conditions on the Chinese mainland, and had raised no issue of the skill or impartiality of American reporters to contribute to this flow of information. (4) However, the United States and the United Nations were in a state of unresolved conflict with Communist China. The President's Proclamation of National Emergency, still in effect, did not authorize trade with and travel in Communist China. (5) "Peiping" had specifically refused to renounce the use of force in the Taiwan area, which Congress had declared vital to American security and had authorized the President to protect by military means. (6) The United States had no diplomatic relations with "Peiping" and hence could not extend to United States citizens the normal diplomatic and consular protection proved needful by the fact that Communist China was still holding Americans as political hostages. (7) A regime, which had come to power by armed, Soviet-supported insurrection, was consolidated by a series of lawless acts, confiscated United States property without compensation, illegally imprisoned Americans without trial or due process, invaded South Korea, was constantly violating the Korean Armistice and the Geneva Accord by a military buildup in Vietnam, "now feels the need for respectability in the eyes of the world." As a first means it would "establish cultural exchange and trade relations with the United States" for which relaxation of our travel restrictions is a prerequisite. (8) If and when there are "constructive actions by 'Peiping,'" including the release of the American prisoners," that will mark a new situation "and the matter of the travel ban will, of course, be reviewed." This, in necessarily brief outline, was the State Department's case at that time.

The issue of newsmen and contacts came up for intensive exchange in the Ambassadorial Talks, which by late 1956 were reduced to only one a month. At the long 65th meeting on February 14, 1957, Ambassador Wang again pressed Ambassador Johnson for an agreement on an exchange of newsmen and others, reiterated a number of charges, and offered a number of enticements.[22] In reply, and again at the 66th meeting on March 14th, Ambassador Johnson pressed Ambassador Wang hard for the release of the ten Americans as a precondition to the consideration of any other subject except renunciation of force. However, after the 65th meeting, there was no public comment from either Ambassador on Secretary Dulles' implication at his press conference or on President Eisenhower's ambiguous remark at his news conference the following day that a *quid pro quo* had been received from the Chinese—newsmen for prisoners.

On April 2, 1957, the Deputy Under-Secretary of State, Robert Murphy, told the Senate Foreign Relations Committee that the State Department had no intention of permitting newsmen to visit Communist China as long as Americans were held there because to do so might well destroy their last chance for freedom; it would be giving in to "a form of blackmail." The anti-Communist leadership of the United States would be seriously undermined. "It would be most difficult for us to urge others, many of whom must depend in part on our strength, to stand unafraid and unflinching before the Communist threat," he claimed in familiar language. But Mr. Murphy went on to intimate that, if a formula could be found to permit coverage of conditions in mainland China "without affecting American lives and indulging in a form of appeasement by yielding to blackmail, we would all be greatly relieved." [23] At about the same time, Secretary Dulles told a news conference that the issue of exchange of correspondents was still under study, but he could not forecast any immediate change in policy at that time.[24]

Washington's Limited and Unilateral Shift

However, a change in policy was in fact under consideration and even underway. In a press conference on April 23 Secretary Dulles made the first of his several modifications, or "retreats" as others termed them, from the initial total ban on travel of newsmen and others to China. He invited the American news-gathering community to devise a way of sending a limited number of reporters to Communist China without breaking the general ban on American travel there. He suggested an experiment of a small group of newsmen selectively chosen as a pool on behalf of the entire American news-gathering community. In explaining this idea, Secretary Dulles revealed his attitude toward China:

It is a question of whether or not it is appropriate at this time to break down a barrier against Americans generally going into Communist China at a time when we are in a sense still in a state of war, at a time when Americans are subject to gross mistreatment already in Communist China, at a time when Communist China is seeking desperately to build up a pattern of so-called cultural exchanges with the Western countries, which it thinks will enable it to increase its hold over some of the countries in the Far East. . . . It is not a problem of our being worried in any respect about what the facts are. . . .[25]

Mr. Dulles was particularly loath to relax American barriers on "cultural relations," because to have done so might have weakened the resolve of some Asian countries to avoid contacts and relations with Peking. But a dribble of newsmen was perhaps controllable, and much less dangerous.

The implications of the modifications in United States policy proposed by Dulles for the news-gathering community were considerable. In effect, he turned the initiative back on them and took the pressure off himself to some extent, because they now had to decide among several options: (a) to acquiesce in the right of the total ban; (b) to defy it in theory or in fact; (c) to compromise with the State Department's modification on the ban without gaining the State Department's consent to the right of travel for reporters on bona fide news-gathering missions; (d) to negotiate among themselves on organizing a pool of reporters; and (e) to accept the practice that the dispatches and reports from this limited number of reporters would have to be used by the news-gathering community as a whole. These were hard decisions to make.

It was evident in this news conference as well as in later ones that Secretary Dulles had no intention of inviting Communist newspapermen to come on a reciprocal basis to the United States because he did not believe that it was practical and, in fact, he did not wish to grant visas to those whose credentials came from a regime unrecognized by the United States. In mid-May at a press conference, Dulles again had to respond to the heavy pressures over the constitutional questions of the right to travel and report raised by the American press, and particularly by a letter from Arthur Hays Sulzberger of *The New York Times*. Dulles stated that American rights were so "flaunted" by the Chinese Communists that it was "extremely disadvantageous from our standpoint to have Americans continue to go there," and that he had no intention of inviting Chinese Communist newsmen to come to the United States.[26] However, he repeated his idea of April that it might be possible for the American news-gathering community to devise a plan sufficiently limited that he would find it acceptable in terms of the objectives of American policy.

A few months went by while the State Department negotiated more with the American press on this issue than it did with Peking representatives at Geneva. Finally, in mid-July, a tentative arrangement with the American news-gathering community came close to agreement. At a meeting with a five-man group representing national news and radio-television organizations, Dulles consented to a limited number of newsmen going to the People's Republic of China for a trial period of six months. However, this meeting could not determine how many American organizations would wish to be represented in this arrangement or on what terms. The matter was temporarily left in abeyance while the news-gathering people went ahead to find out what the specifications of such an arrangement would be like.[27] In the meantime, the 69th Ambassadorial Talk on August 8, 1957, was as futile as its predecessors in resolving any of the issues, for each Ambassador repeated the well-known positions of his government.

But a new factor entered into the question of the right of travel when some fifty young Americans attending the Moscow Youth Festival in August indicated that they had accepted an invitation by Chinese delegates to take a three-week tour of Communist China. The State Department immediately announced that it opposed this trip but refrained from threatening disciplinary action. On August 13 the Department issued a press release to make clear and publicize the reasons for its ban on travel to China.[28] The State Department declared that "travel to Red China is not only contrary to passport regulations in force but would be subversive of the well-known foreign policy on which these passport regulations are based." [29] This was the strongest warning yet given to Americans who might consider traveling to Communist China. By these statements the forty-five or fifty young Americans in Moscow were warned that they might lose their passports and be liable to prosecution.

Then the Department subtly made another modification to facilitate the entry of newsmen into China. In a press release of August 22, it announced an "experiment" to allow 24 organizations to send correspondents, one for each organization, for a seven-month trial period to Communist China,* to permit "direct reporting by them to the American people about conditions in the area under Chinese Communist control." Passports would be issued "not restricted as regards travel to and on the mainland of China." But no photographers were included. Whether the period would be extended beyond seven months would depend on whether the newsmen were able to report freely on events in China and whether restrictions imposed by the

---

* The 24 organizations were: American Broadcasting Company, Associated Press, Baltimore *Sun*, Chicago *Daily News*, Chicago *Tribune*, *The Christian Science Monitor*, Columbia Broadcasting System, Copley News Service, Fairchild Publications, Inc., International News Service, McGraw-Hill World News, Minneapolis *Star & Tribune*, Mutual Broadcasting System, National Broadcasting Company, NEA Service, Inc., *Newsweek*, *New York Herald Tribune*, *The New York Times*, *Reader's Digest*, *Saturday Evening Post*, Scripps-Howard Newspapers, Time, Inc., United Press, *U.S. News and World Report*.

government in Peking would render their presence meaningless. The State Department did not indicate how this question would be decided. In any event, no reciprocal visas were to be granted Chinese newsmen.

In reversing its policy on American newsmen, and after noting that the Chinese Communist regime did not follow "the practices of civilized governments," which was an allusion to the forcibly-detained Americans, the Department did not explain its reasons for the modification. It merely declared that "new factors have come into the picture, making it desirable that additional information be made available to the American people respecting current conditions within China." The State Department hoped that the newsmen would be able to report on the Americans illegally held in Chinese prisons for whose fate there was deep concern on the part of the American people.[30] The Department refused to account for the "new factors" which had caused it to reverse and relax the total ban. That the American press was the principal reason, rather than the negotiations in Geneva, in causing this significant change was implied in the Department's conclusions that "this experiment" was founded upon "the desire to have the American people better informed through their own representatives about actual conditions in areas under Chinese Communist control." Who determined the desire on behalf of the American people was not indicated, although many correspondents and news executives believed as a matter of personal conscience and public duty that it was up to them and the American people and not some government official to decide when, where, and how the American people should be informed by a free press.

Two important points about the announcement of August 22 were its conditional and its nonreciprocal nature. The announcement specified not only a limited number of American news representatives, but stipulated that the relaxation of the ban was intended to make possible "direct reporting" to the American people about conditions in Communist China. The announcement also stipulated more as a matter of hope than of expectation that they should be able to report on the Americans in Chinese prisons. Apparently the State Department reasoned that the relaxation of this ban on total exclusion of American contact with China except at Geneva could be justified or rationalized on the grounds that the American reporters would file stories based on interviews or other valid information on the Americans still in Chinese jails. It is important to emphasize this matter of stipulations because the Chinese, during the first phase of negotiations on exchange of correspondents, made no conditions but then proceeded to reverse themselves when the Americans removed theirs.

The second important element in this announcement, for it affected the negotiations in Geneva, was the categorical opposition of Dulles and the State Department to consider any reciprocal arrangements for Chinese newsmen. The announcement of August 22 stated that "the United States will not accord reciprocal visas to Chinese bearing passports issued by the Chinese Communist regime." The announcement concluded with the statement that it did not change the basic policy of the United States opposition toward communism in China which Dulles had set forth in a major pronouncement of June 28, 1957, in San Francisco. In that famous speech, Dulles had predicted the "passing of communism," and expressed the conceptual foundation and basic outlook of the policy of isolating, weakening, and containing the People's Republic of China. He had declared that "we owe it to ourselves, our allies, and the Chinese people to do all that we can to contribute to that passing." [31] He had opposed cultural and commercial relations with Peking because they did not promote such "passing," any more than diplomatic relations or Peking's participation in the United Nations would. Despite the sternness and finality of his declaration, the issue of newsmen remained alive. In fact, Washington continued to explore possible ways of suitably sending American journalists into China while barring Chinese journalists from the United States. And Peking, despite Dulles' speech, even proposed a formal agreement on a mutual exchange of newsmen.

The question of nonreciprocity turned out to be the hurdle which either wittingly or unwittingly brought the Department's relaxation of the travel ban for newsmen, as well as the negotiations with Peking, temporarily to a standstill. In his press conference on August 27, when he was asked why the issue of reciprocity had been raised in the Department's announcement of August 22, Dulles explained:

We wanted to obviate any claim by the Chinese Communists that they would be entitled as a right to send a corresponding number of Chinese persons to this country. That we could not do under the law. As you know, the law hedges about very strictly the possibility of Communists coming to this country. There has to be a finding made by the Attorney General to permit any Communists to come. Whether or not he could make those findings in the light of the present relations that we have with Communist China and the lack of facilities that we have, I do not know. One thing I do know, which is that we cannot admit as a right a reciprocity claim on the part of the Chinese Communists, and we thought it best to make that clear in advance.[32]

When a correspondent asked him if the Department of State would admit some number of Chinese correspondents not as a right but as a matter of hard bargaining, Mr. Dulles left the door ajar to such a possibility by answering that such an application, if made, would be considered "under the law." Any such application, he went on to explain, would have to run the "gamut of the applicable law," which was "severe" and not an "improvised policy."[33] The reason was that the Chinese Communist regime had not been recognized by the United States. The Department might give "a separate piece of paper" to permit an individual to come into the United States. In this whole matter, Dulles was referring to the McCarran-Walter Immigration and Naturalization Act of 1952 under which the Secretary of State may recommend that the Attorney General waive the requirements and determine that a Communist individual, otherwise excludable by law, may enter the United States.

In the meantime, American officials tried in several ways to relax the virtual closure on Chinese newsmen. Senator Knowland followed up Secretary Dulles' press statements of August 27 by proposing "temporary news certificates" for Chinese newsmen.[34] As American newspapers noted, Dulles apparently accepted the Knowland plan in order to permit the entry of Chinese Communist journalists or athletes for the Olympic games.[35] Under the formula of visa certificates, each case would be decided on an individual basis under all applicable laws, and would avoid the issue of diplomatic recognition. To make some headway and show Washington's intentions, President Eisenhower approved permission for American newsmen to go to mainland China. Many speeded to Hong Kong expecting to get Peking visas under these new arrangements. Congressional authorities were prepared to waive the requirements for fingerprinting of Chinese Communist journalists. *The Christian Science Monitor* indicated that a *modus vivendi* on visits was approaching between Washington and Peking.[36] Others even reported at the time that Dulles would go so far as to allow Peking to set up a "permanent news bureau" in the United States under the conditions that (1) the United States could not grant reciprocity, (2) a certain number of Chinese Communist newsmen be admitted after each had qualified under United States laws, (3) they receive visa certificates but not regular visas on Peking passports, and (4) there be no time limit to this arrangement.[37] These conditions at least indicated the general manner which Washington was considering for handling this issue.

How wrongly had the Americans judged Peking! Despite the relaxation of the ban, and nothwithstanding the administrative openings for individual Chinese Communist newsmen to come to the United States, Peking turned down the arrangement. The *People's Daily* of Peking immediately rejected the State Department's "unilateral decision" of August 22 to permit 24 newsmen to go to China as "completely unacceptable" and charged that it had discourteously ignored the principle of reciprocity by ruling out the granting of visas to Chinese correspondents. According to this spokesman for Peking, the United States really wanted to collect intelligence through its newsmen, carry out subversive activities and "exacerbate feelings between the Chinese and American peoples." [38]

On September 8 *The New York Times* reported that Chou Enlai had told the group of young Americans touring China that American newsmen would not be permitted to enter China unless Chinese reporters received reciprocal rights to visit the United States. As he viewed it: "The State Department put an end to the matter by refusing reciprocal rights of coverage to Chinese reporters." [39] In a Geneva meeting, Ambassador Wang criticized the American offer because it said nothing about Chinese newsmen going to the United States and because it "absurdly" tried to specify the tasks of American newsmen in China. These were unacceptable conditions and stipulations to an exchange which Peking then wanted to be unconditional and reciprocal.

Then, at the Ambassadorial meeting on September 12, Ambassador Wang tabled the following draft agreement for a reciprocal exchange of news correspondents:

The Government of the People's Republic of China and the Government of the United States of America agree to give permission, on an equal and reciprocal basis, for correspondents of the other side to enter their respective countries for news coverage in order to promote the mutual understanding between the peoples of China and the United States.[40]

Ambassador Johnson immediately and categorically rejected this proposal. He carefully explained that he could not make such an agreement because reciprocity was impossible under United States law and because each visa must be considered on its merits. He also emphasized to Ambassador Wang that Peking had not demanded reciprocity in numbers or in any other respect when it made its original proposal in August 1956 for American correspondents to come to China. It was reported that Ambassador Johnson indicated at this session of September 12 that the United States government would consider and process the individual applications of Chinese Communist correspondents who wished to enter the United States. Of course, he gave no intimation of what their chances of receiving favorable action were. As a technicality this had to be left in doubt.

Again the Chinese did not leave their initiative on the table at Geneva. Bypassing the American government, they made their proposal public after the meeting of September 12 had adjourned. Ambassador Johnson had to make an immediate public rebuttal in Geneva. He stated that he had told Ambassador Wang he was astounded that the question of reciprocity had been raised, because when Peking had invited American correspondents to China, Ambassador Wang had specifically stated that it was not conditional on reciprocal United States action. Ambassador Johnson went on to state that the visa application of any Chinese Communist journalist would be accepted at any United States Foreign Service post and "considered on its merits under United States laws and regulations like any other visa application." He expected the Chinese authorities to consider American applications in the same manner.[41] The American position consistently predicated any discussion or agreement on the question of exchange of newsmen upon the implementation of the agreed-upon release and repatriation of all Americans in China.

Peking reacted promptly and strongly. The *People's Daily* accused the United States of "obstructing" the desire of the Chinese and American people to understand one another, and charged that the references to the Immigration Laws were a "pretext" to prevent normal undertakings and mutual understanding between the Chinese and American peoples. On September 16 Peking radio carried a statement of Ambassador Wang to the effect that Ambassador Johnson's public statement of September 12 was not only a subterfuge but an insult to the People's Republic of China, and denied that Peking had not honored the agreement of September 10, 1955, regarding the return of prisoners.[42] For the next three months at the Ambassadorial Talks both parties reiterated the same points. In public, the State Department challenged Peking to make visa applications for Chinese journalists, while Peking radio and the *People's*

Daily continued to attack the United States on the issue of non-reciprocity.[43]

One slight further American amendment on the ban on travel to China, which the issue of newsmen had raised so acutely, and which had been modified with such embarrassment for the United States government, was the corollary decision of the State Department at this time to issue passports to close relatives of the few Americans still imprisoned in Communist China. As in the case of the newsmen, the Department had for several years rejected the appeals of these relatives for travel to China. In December 1957 the Department decided that the renewal of requests from such relatives and the continued imprisonment of the six Americans for two years since the 1955 agreement made this specific relaxation necessary. The State Department declared that it was particularly conscious of the "prolonged and tragic" separation of these men from their families. Again, as in the case of the newsmen, the State Department's announcement of December 6 stated that it remained the general policy of the United States government not to issue or validate passports for travel to Communist China.[44]

Virtual Breakdown

Such was the situation at the 73rd meeting of the Ambassadors on December 12, 1957, Ambassador Johnson's last encounter before taking his new post in Bangkok. His finale was a characteristic meeting. He made his argument for the release of American prisoners, for an agreement on the renunciation of force, and for pooled arrangements for American newsmen, but against reciprocity for Chinese newsmen. He also had to reject a new and somewhat extraneous proposal from Ambassador Wang, who introduced a draft agreement between the two governments on "judicial assistance" for either government or nationals of either country desiring evidence or testimony in a court case involving either party. In this instance, an American judge had asked for evidence from Chinese Communist authorities regarding their charges of American germ warfare against China. The evidence was needed in the trial of an American who had continued to publish in China after the Chinese Communist take-over and who had later been repatriated to the United States where he faced certain accusations. Ambassador Wang made the gesture to the United States at this last meeting with Ambassador Johnson by officially stating that his government would be willing to provide such evidence through diplomatic channels if both governments entered into such an agreement.[45] Of course, American acceptance would have benefited Peking. Ambassador Johnson rejected this proposal because it would have been tantamount to establishing formal diplomatic relations with Peking. He had already rejected previous proposals for the same ostensible reason.

The shift to the subject of newsmen during 1956–57 produced one of the paradoxes of the decade of negotiations and discussions. Each side has completely reversed its position on nonofficial contacts. It is now all but forgotten that in 1956–57 the Chinese People's Republic pressed hard in the Talks at Geneva and in public appeals to have selected American newsmen freely come to China and to negotiate a simple agreement with Washington for the exchange of newsmen. Peking also proposed other kinds of contacts and travel between the two countries. Washington flatly rejected all these initiatives in meeting after meeting. Coming full circle by 1966, the United States has been vigorously proposing, and Peking has been adamantly turning down, the same unconditional exchanges which Peking had sought and Washington rejected in many ambassadorial meetings in 1956–57. However, during this decade, no mutually-authorized contact of a nonofficial character took place between any of the 700 million inhabitants of the Chinese People's Republic and 190 million Americans, except for a handful of Americans who travelled to China under special circumstances. The Talks on "contacts" produced no contact. Each remained a forbidden country with a closed door to the other.

During 1956–57 the Ambassadorial Talks could have produced an agreement on arrangements for exchanging newsmen and other categories of Americans and Chinese if there had been a desire to do so in Washington. Whether Washington handled this matter objectively, realistically, or wisely in terms of the best long-run interests of the United States remains open to serious question.

The principal issue for Washington regarding the Talks by the end of 1957 was whether or not to continue the Talks and contacts with Peking at all. Washington suspended its participation at the Ambassadorial level, and did not select a successor to Ambassador Johnson. It considered the options to lower their level, suspend them without terminating the original arrangements, or to terminate them completely. From Washington's viewpoint, Peking would not negotiate or honor meaningful agreements on major or minor issues, while frequently resorting to arbitrary and distorted disclosures of the Talks to apply pressure on Washington for negotiating and bargaining purposes. It seemed evident that Peking was exploiting the propaganda value of the Talks for its sole advantage. Washington apparently considered that the time had come for a pause in the Talks to take stock, warn Peking, and await results. The pressures from all the different events and personalities that had originally created the Talks had worn off. The United States considered that it had shown reasonableness in sitting down with Peking, but the Chinese People's Republic had proved to be a bad partner. Appearing futile and sterile for purposes of negotiation, the Talks in early 1958 seemed to have been ended, thus closing the little window of diplomacy.

The Chinese Communists expressed great concern, disappointment, and even anger over the breakdown when Ambassador Johnson left the Talks, when no replacement appeared, and when Washington did nothing to reinstate the Talks during the first half of 1958. Chou apparently wanted the Talks to continue. Peking evidently feared a short pause might lead to permanent paralysis. When Washington suggested Talks at the level of First Secretaries, Peking indignantly refused, insisting that Washington designate a new Ambassador for the Talks.

Peking, in a long statement on April 22, 1958, commented that the position of the United States on newsmen "flagrantly contravened the principle of reciprocity in international relations." The article stated that Peking hoped the "solution of certain questions in the interest of the people of the two countries would improve the atmosphere of the Talks and help resolve other issues."

The Ambassadorial Talks were finally resumed on September 15, 1958, in Warsaw with Ambassador Jacob Beam, and for much of the rest of that year concentrated on a new Taiwan crisis and the actual use of force. It was not until the spring of 1959 that the issue of newsmen was revived, after Dulles had left the State Department because of a tragic illness and Christian Herter, his successor, had reversed Washington's role and taken the political and psychological initiative on the issue of newsmen and mutual contacts. But Peking has never since shown any interest.*

* Chapters 9 and 11 continue with the handling of this issue by the Americans.

PART III

The Taiwan Crisis, 1958

CHAPTER SIX

The Ambassadorial Talks
in the Outbreak of the Crisis

The Taiwan crisis broke suddenly and explosively in the summer of 1958. The challenge it presented both to Washington and to Peking transcended in importance all the other issues they had faced. This was a critical question, or so it then seemed, of negotiating or fighting. Before long, Moscow was also involved. East Asia seemed on the verge of war.

Peking precipitated the Taiwan crisis probably for its own internal and external needs, but this cannot be documented. Perhaps the basic reason for the crisis was domestic: to create a "crisis atmosphere" to start an anti-rightist campaign, mobilize the masses, and launch the communes with a "great leap forward." Perhaps the need was external: to thwart any Moscow-Washington détente and to heighten tensions. Perhaps it was all these plus a real effort to get the offshore islands, without American counteraction if at all possible, but by force if necessary. A successful seizure of the islands might have been expected, perhaps in Peking's calculations, to produce enough pressures to compel Washington to concede to Peking's terms on Taiwan in resumed Ambassadorial Talks. What Peking had been unable to obtain for three years by diplomatic pressures in private talks and public ploys, it now seemed to seek by a two-stage play of force and diplomacy. Simultaneous with the bombardment and blockade of the islands, Peking's campaign implicated Moscow by extracting a limited commitment of nuclear support for the People's Republic of China and thereby warning the United States not to risk war on mainland China itself.

Washington reacted to Peking's violent venture and Moscow's diplomatic threats with an overwhelming show of nuclear and conventional power in the Taiwan area, greater than anything that had ever been assembled anywhere in the world. At the same time, Washington displayed resourceful diplomacy in the renewed Ambassadorial Talks to head off the seizure of the offshore islands and to seek to negotiate their status, as well as wider issues of consequence in Washington-Peking relations. The long battle of words at Geneva during 1955–57 over the renunciation of force turned into a critical test of nerves in 1958 on its use in the Taiwan Straits.

The determining factor in the outcome of the crisis was the collapse of Communist China's blockade of the islands and the nullification of Peking's use of violence by the Chinese Nationalist–American military defensive tactics. The American display of force and simultaneous use of diplomacy succeeded.

The role which the Ambassadorial Talks played in controlling the conflict should be carefully weighed and neither exaggerated nor underrated. The availability and utilization of this contact between Washington and Peking during the Taiwan crisis has been largely overlooked in current analysis of that period. Even President Eisenhower scarcely mentions the Talks in his memoirs regarding this Taiwan crisis. While the diplomatic record is long, intricate, and still secret so that we can only surmise what actually was said in Warsaw, it is clear that the Talks afforded a retreat from the brink for Peking, Washington, and even Moscow. This was no small achievement.

Throughout the crisis, from its outbreak on August 23 to its collapse on October 6, the two major themes of force and diplomacy alternated in world headlines, diplomatic messages, prestigious pronouncements, and secret deliberations in Washington, Peking, Moscow, Taipei, New York, London, New Delhi, Belgrade, and in many other chancelleries of state. In secret negotiations and public diplomacy Washington and Peking sparred, jabbed, and dodged over peace or war—not just over territory or politics.

Prelude to Crisis: June 30–August 23

Before the Taiwan crisis of 1958 broke out in late August, both Peking and Washington had publicly and privately demonstrated a willingness to continue the Ambassadorial Talks, at least in form if not in substance. When the crisis erupted, the avenue of diplomatic approach was again available, but the way had to be reopened. After six months of silence from Washington and declarations from Peking, the former took the initiative in mid-summer 1958 to arrange for the resumption of the Talks. However, Peking stayed silent until the crisis in the Taiwan Straits set the stage for the renewal of the Talks in September.

Peking issued a long attack on June 30 against the United States government and Secretary Dulles for "breaking" the agreement to hold Talks at the ambassadorial level. Peking castigated Washington for refusing to designate a representative of ambassadorial rank, for ignoring its March 26th letter and for "nonchalantly" offering a First Secretary to hold talks with a Chinese Ambassador. (Washington had apparently meant to have talks between First Secretaries of both parties.) It denounced the "imperialistic attitude" of the United States for using the Ambassadorial Talks to "deceive" the people of the world, to cover up its "sinister designs," to continue its "aggression" against China, to utilize Taiwan for "armed intervention" against Southeast Asia and to create "Two Chinas." Declaring that there was no reason whatever for the Chinese people to "pine for talks with the United States," Peking demanded that Washington designate a representative of ambassadorial rank and resume the Talks within fifteen days "counting from today." Otherwise, it said, the Chinese government would consider that the United States had decided to break off the Ambassadorial Talks.[1] Peking's statement was officially delivered to the United States Consul General in Geneva, as had been the previous practice in 1954 and 1955.

The United States government decided neither to accept the ultimatum nor suspend the Talks. Officials in Washington gave the impression that they were undecided on the resumption of Talks which had proved so futile and exasperating; nevertheless, they were aware of the need for maintaining a line of communication with Peking in order to seek the release of American prisoners, to reduce the danger of miscalculated hostilities, and to allay the perennial pressures on Washington to "talk" with Peking. All these considerations in 1958 echoed the origins of the Talks in 1955.* When Peking issued its ultimatum, Washington was in the process of formulating a proposal to resume the Talks at a new location, Warsaw. The State Department replied to Peking's ultimatum by stating that it had no intention of downgrading the Geneva Talks

* See Chapter 2.

or breaking them off and that it actually had been considering the selection of a new Ambassador and a new location. At his press conference on July 1, when asked if he intended to go on with the Talks to get the release of the four remaining American prisoners, Secretary Dulles replied that he certainly intended to continue them by every available means. He disclosed that a memorandum was being delivered to the Chinese Communists proposing a shift to Warsaw. Dulles indicated that, despite the "Chinese blast" of two days before, the United States would submit a proposal to Peking that the new United States Ambassador to Poland, Jacob Beam, be designated as the United States representative in the Ambassadorial Talks if Warsaw turned out to be an acceptable location. However, Washington decided to wait until after the two-week "ultimatum" had lapsed before delivering that proposal. The Chinese statement thus had just the opposite effect from the one Peking intended it to have. The Foreign Ministry in Peking immediately criticized the proposal to move the Talks to Warsaw and Dulles' refusal to accept the ultimatum. But on July 15 the ultimatum was extended for a few days in view of the fact that "the United States has declared its intention of resuming talks 'soon'" and that accordingly "a few days' delay is not objectionable." [2]

After the period of this ultimatum had expired, Washington instructed Edwin Martin at the Embassy in London to send a letter on July 28 to Ambassador Wang in Warsaw, officially informing him that Ambassador Beam had been appointed by the United States government to continue the Talks. Neither Ambassador Wang nor the Foreign Ministry immediately acknowledged this letter, however. On August 4, Ambassador Beam followed up by attempting to arrange with the Chinese Embassy in Warsaw for a meeting with Ambassador Wang on August 7. When the day came with no response from the Chinese Communists, the American Embassy in Warsaw sent an inquiry to the Chinese Communist Embassy, which merely answered that the matter had been referred to Peking.[3] Peking was silent for nearly a month with regard to the Talks, but not over Taiwan. Its failure to respond to Washington's overtures for more than a month was a significant and deliberate element in the Taiwan crisis.

At the very time that Ambassador Beam and Washington were trying to re-open the Talks, the crisis was approaching a climax. Nikita Khrushchev and Mao Tse-tung held a secret and significant four-day meeting in Peking from July 31 to August 3. They disclosed nothing in public then about Taiwan but subsequent revelations in Sino-Soviet polemics imply that they considered their responses in the Taiwan Straits crisis. At the time, however, the vague communiqué did not hint at any forthcoming crisis there and focused on the critical situation in the Near East.[4] But it did state that the two parties had had a full exchange of views on major questions in Asia and Europe and had reached "complete agreement on measures to be taken to oppose aggression and safeguard peace." The listing of the Defense Ministers near the top of the two delegations added to the belligerent tone of the communiqué, which declared that the aggressive bloc of Western powers was bringing mankind to the brink of war, that peace-loving peoples would "wipe out clean" the imperialist aggressors and establish eternal world peace, and that the "forces of peace and socialism" would overcome all obstacles and win a great victory. Peking's editorials interpreted the world situation to signify that the balance of power had changed and history would gradually unfold the full significance of the Mao-Khrushchev communiqué. And immediate history did— but in an unexpected way for Washington and a disappointing way for Peking. Nevertheless, President Eisenhower's memoirs reveal that he and Dulles were immediately aware that the Chinese had plans regarding the offshore islands and perhaps even Taiwan, and that American commanders were on the alert in early August.

Pressures and tensions built up in the Taiwan area immediately before and just after Khrushchev's visit to Peking, and the Chinese Communist press opened a radio and press campaign for "liberating Taiwan." Military movements and other preparations were evident along the Chinese coast which alarmed the Chinese Nationalists. On August 6, the Foreign Minister in Peking, Chen Yi, is alleged to have blurted out at a reception that something would be happening in the Taiwan Straits. That same day the Chinese Nationalists on Taiwan proclaimed a state of emergency in the offshore islands and the Taiwan Straits and began evacuating noncombat personnel from the offshore islands as precautions against the increasing Chinese Communist military activity on the mainland opposite the islands. The Soviet press began reporting "provocative actions and war preparations ordered from Washington on Taiwan" before the United States government had even begun mobilization. Moscow was denouncing publicly in advance what it anticipated Washington would have to contemplate.

Washington sharpened its tone and its attitude of hostility toward the Chinese People's Republic after trying to resume the Ambassadorial Talks and receiving no response whatsoever. On August 10, Dulles made an unusually strong public attack on the Chinese People's Republic, declaring that "we will do all that we can to contribute to the passing away of this regime." [5] In a lengthy memorandum of August 11, sent to all American missions abroad and also made public, the Department of State expounded its many reasons for the policy of nonrecognition of Communist China, viewed the passing away of communism in China as inevitable, rejected the "Two Chinas" solution, and warned of the consequences of the strong alliance between the Soviet Union and the Chinese People's Republic. [6]

The memorandum must have made an impact on Peking because it immediately denounced it as "shopworn," and the "occupation" of Taiwan as day-dreaming on the part of those who were unaware of their own "impotence," for China had the "determination and strength" to liberate Taiwan. In similar tones another article in the Peking press declared that the collapse of "imperialism" was inevitable, that the "imperialist camp" was a "paper tiger," "over-extended," "vulnerable" and "shaking in its shoes," and that the "forces of socialism" were overwhelmingly superior. [7] Peking must have assumed that the new rockets and sputniks had given its ally military ascendency and that therefore increased pressure on the "imperialists" was in order. At the same time a Soviet broadcast—significantly in the Chinese language only—assured the Chinese that they were not isolated in the world but had the support of the Soviet Union and all other socialist countries. [8]

During this prelude and build-up, President Eisenhower and the administration were studying what military action, if any, would be necessary if Chinese Communist forces actually launched a naval blockade, artillery bombardment, air attack, or amphibious assault on the offshore islands or on Taiwan. [9] After the President had received intelligence reports on such intentions as early as August 6, he immediately began to assess the developing circumstances and prepared to react against any or all of these contingencies. He concluded that Peking would launch an amphibious assault on Quemoy and possibly Matsu only if it were convinced that the United States would avoid intervention. The President and his advisers recognized, too, that they might "face the necessity" of using small-yield atomic weapons against Chinese Communist airfields, but the President specifically deferred having to make that decision until it became absolutely necessary. All these and other considerations were analyzed in the days before and after Peking triggered the crisis.

At the heart of the Eisenhower Administration's reaction was the conclusion that the future security of Japan, Okinawa, the Philippines, Vietnam, and Thailand would eventually be placed in jeopardy and the vital interests of the United States would eventually suffer severely if the capture of the offshore islands led to the loss of Taiwan. Consequently, the President decided, in advance, that the United States might be forced to intervene to save the offshore islands, that it would avoid expanding hostilities more than absolutely necessary, and that its initial reaction would be restricted to air strikes on Chinese Communist shipping or airfields near the offshore islands. These military and strategic considerations were precisely outlined in a revealing memorandum of understanding between the President and Secretary Dulles.[10]

The President and his advisers apparently discussed making a strong statement on United States intentions before any assault was made by Peking. Dulles favored it, but the Joint Chiefs of Staff did not. However, the government on Taiwan, and Chiang Kai-shek in particular, became increasingly uneasy. To reassure him, the President and Dulles agreed to use a letter of reply from Dulles to the Chairman of the House Foreign Affairs Committee, who had written Dulles on August 22, to issue a general warning and declaration of Washington's intentions. Dulles stated on August 23:

> It would be highly hazardous for anyone to assume that if the Chinese Communists were to attempt to change this situation [Taiwan's control of the islands] by attacking and seeking to conquer these islands that this act could be considered or held to a "limited operation." It would I fear, constitute a threat to the peace of the area. Therefore, I hope and believe that it will not happen.[11]

However, the implied warning came too late.

Outbreak of Crisis: August 23–September 15

On August 23, Peking suddenly and massively began a well-prepared campaign of interdiction by artillery and air bombardment to blockade and capture Quemoy and Matsu. Chinese Communist batteries on the mainland launched intensive bombardment of the offshore islands, while Chinese Communist coastal radios beamed broadcasts directly to the uneasy people on the islands warning them of imminent landings of the Chinese Red Army, demanding surrender of the islands, and appealing for defectors. Yet, the Peking radio and press did not at first inform the Chinese public about these military and political developments, nor link the attack with Peking's theme of the 'liberation of Taiwan," which had been so prominent in early August. Peking now avoided this theme and continued to withhold a response to the American moves to reopen the Ambassadorial Talks. Peking's internal propaganda began to bombard the Chinese people with Mao's new campaign for establishing people's communes, the establishment of which was decided by a resolution of the Central Committee of the Chinese Communist Party soon after the military attack on the islands was launched. Moscow ignored the Taiwan situation for several days after August 23. Indeed, on August 24 *Pravda* finally published remarks which Khrushchev had made on August 13—ten days after the Peking communiqué of August 3 and ten days before the outbreak of the bombardment—that "at the present time, it seems to me, there is no cloud from which thunder could roll." [12]

The Americans had anticipated a cloud—perhaps of a very different kind—and reacted instantly to Peking's bombardment of the islands. The President ordered some limited supporting measures. Two more carriers were added to the Seventh Fleet, making a strength of four. All United States forces in the area were placed on a "readiness alert," prepared for immediate war operations. Naval forces were to be prepared to escort Chinese Nationalist supply ships to the three-mile limit off the offshore islands. Naval and air power, with nuclear armaments, rapidly augmented the strength of the Seventh Fleet in the Taiwan area. These movements were not secret; some were even deliberately publicized to signal Peking and Moscow. On August 27 President Eisenhower declared that the offshore islands were more important to the defense of Taiwan than they had been in the Taiwan crisis of 1955, because there was now a "closer interlocking" between the defense system of the islands and Taiwan. [13]

On the same day, the Chinese Communist army commander opposite the islands broadcast to the garrison on the islands that China was determined to liberate Taiwan as well as the offshore islands and warned that the landing on Quemoy was imminent. The

State Department seized on this local broadcast to reissue Dulles' warning that a resort to force by the Chinese Communists would not lead to a limited operation.[14] On August 31 *Pravda*—which does not speak with the same authority in diplomacy as the Soviet government—warned that any power threatening the Chinese People's Republic was also threatening the Soviet Union, which would provide China with "the necessary moral and material help in its just struggle."[15] Yet, there was still no official public reaction from Peking's Soviet ally. On September 4 Peking declared a twelve-mile coastal zone to be Chinese national waters which would have had the effect of closing off the offshore islands. However, the United States rejected this claim and continued to escort Chinese Nationalist supply ships to within three miles of the offshore islands.[16] Nevertheless, the artillery bombardment was efficiently and thoroughly sealing them off. On September 5 *Pravda* stated: "The instigators and organizers of this latest military venture in the Far East should not calculate that a retaliatory blow will be confined to the region of the Taiwan Straits and offshore islands. They will receive a crushing rebuff which will put an end to United States military aggression in the Far East." According to *Pravda*, the Chinese People's Republic had sufficient strength to counter "the aggressors fully." *Pravda* also indicated that the Soviet Union would not "remain inactive" or "quietly watch" United States military preparations in the Pacific, and "the Soviet people" would extend to "the Chinese people" every form of assistance.[17] While these and earlier statements in *Pravda* were directed by the Soviet government, they did not yet represent any responsible undertaking or official commitment of Moscow in the crisis. They were effective generators of atmosphere on the psychological plane rather than significant indicators of action at the military or diplomatic levels. And *Pravda* carefully limited itself to Peking's capabilities, not Moscow's, at this stage in the outbreak of crisis. The Chinese press and radio were also limiting the range of the crisis by avoiding any reference to the possibility of nuclear war or to the use of nuclear weapons by Washington or Moscow in the Taiwan Straits. But Chinese internal broadcasts indicated that Peking was focusing on the islands and possibly Taiwan, which strengthened the hand of the President and Dulles.

At the outbreak of the crisis Peking had undertaken a determined and successful siege of the offshore islands.* Peking must have calculated that the blockade by bombardment would force the garrisons of some 90,000 troops on the offshore islands either to surrender and lay down their arms when denied any supplies or reinforcement from Taiwan, or to face defeat in the battle with Chinese Communist forces following their assault on the island across the four-mile water divide. Peking must also have calculated at first that the United States would not intervene militarily and that the limited venture of seizing the offshore islands would succeed quickly before the Americans could take steps to prevent it.

With its supposition of Soviet superiority over the United States and its calculation of Soviet support with matériel and, hopefully, nuclear aid, Peking could have estimated that seizure of the offshore islands was possible without American interference. If Washington could do nothing, Peking would advance its objectives of regaining Taiwan, obtaining international recognition, and ending its isolation. In the event that the United States resorted to aerial bombing of the mainland—its only obvious method of breaking the blockade—Peking might rely upon a number of pressures to cause the Americans to withdraw. Such attacks would threaten an escalation of war in the Far East with the U.S.S.R. American as well as world opinion might create such opposition that Washington would have no option but to withdraw.

This may have been the reason behind Peking's month-long silence following Washington's initiative in August for resumption of the Ambassadorial Talks. Peking avoided any contact with Washington and sought to discourage any American intervention in the limited objective of taking the offshore islands by quick effective actions. From August 23 to September 4, Peking carefully avoided mentioning "liberation of Taiwan" in its foreign propaganda and stalled the reopening of the Talks in order to strengthen their position.

In early September Peking could have assumed that if the blockade continued successfully, the United States would be forced to enter into negotiations, would have to accept Peking's occupation of the offshore islands, disengage the Nationalist forces there, perhaps compromise on Taiwan and even allow the Chinese People's Repub-

---

* I am much indebted to Tang Tsou's study, *Embroilment Over Quemoy: Mao, Chiang, and Dulles* (Salt Lake City: University of Utah Press, 1959) for the analysis and description of the blockade and counterblockade during the whole Taiwan crisis of 1958.

lic to replace the Republic of China in the United Nations at the forthcoming session of the General Assembly. These were great objectives, although perhaps not easily attained. In the event of the failure of the negotiations or Washington's rejection of them, Peking could at least count on pressures from neutrals as well as allies of the United States to mediate the dispute or bring it to the United Nations—again on terms favorable to Communist China when the General Assembly opened on September 18. Whatever Peking's strategy was, the successful outcome depended on a subtle and sophisticated blend of force and diplomacy that could bring about a victorious Chinese Communist blockade, a defeated Chinese Nationalist garrison, a demoralized Chinese Nationalist regime on Taiwan, a public display of all-out Soviet support, an unyielding position in diplomatic maneuvers, avoidance of direct provocation of the United States or the Chinese Nationalists over Taiwan, and pressure of world and domestic public opinion against an American attack on mainland China.

However, this well-orchestrated combination of force and diplomacy led to a different kind of confrontation and result than Peking apparently foresaw. The United States did intervene militarily and diplomatically, beginning on September 4. That was the turning point. As already noted, the President and Secretary Dulles had been assessing the situation and planning their strategy for a month. By early September the alarm of Chiang, the pressure of allies, and Peking's campaign persuaded President Eisenhower and Secretary Dulles to make their position clear before the world. The United States would do two things: prevent the seizure of the offshore islands by force, and keep the door open for negotiations. Peking had been at least partially correct in its assessment of Washington's difficulties: Washington was under heavy pressure from many governments and American public opinion to be conciliatory and to relieve the crisis. As the effective blockade and military crisis seemed to near a critical point, Secretary Dulles took the initiative in the public diplomacy which led to the Ambassadorial Talks and which provided an alternative to the military collision course.

On September 4, after approval by President Eisenhower, Secretary Dulles issued two dramatic statements which offered the alternatives of peace or war. He left no doubt that the United States would defend Quemoy. The first statement stressed the olive branch of peace. It was read officially to newsmen by Secretary

Dulles in Newport, Rhode Island, where the President was staying. After reviewing the situation in the Taiwan Straits in detail, the statement expressed the hope that the Chinese Communist regime would not use armed force to achieve territorial ambitions and warned that any such naked use of force "would pose an issue far transcending the offshore islands and even the security of Taiwan. . . . [and] would forecast a widespread use of force in the Far East which would endanger vital free world positions and the security of the United States." The United States, Dulles noted, had not abandoned hope that the Chinese Communists would stop short of defying the will of mankind for peace. He then recalled that the United States had made a sustained effort in the extended negotiations during 1955–58 between the representatives of the United States and the Chinese Communist regime to get "a declaration of mutual and reciprocal renunciation of force except in self-defense." He concluded his statement with the pointed admonition that such a course of conduct constituted the "only civilized and acceptable procedure" and that the United States intended to follow that course so far as it was concerned "unless and until the Chinese Communists, by their acts, leave us no choice but to react in defense of the principles to which all peace-loving governments are dedicated." [18] As to diplomacy and negotiations for peace, both the President and Secretary Dulles implied that they wished to move the crisis to the conference table through the Ambassadorial Talks despite the month of silence which followed Washington's proposal to shift the Talks from Geneva to Warsaw. The official statement also implied that the United States government would not avoid resort to force in the Taiwan Straits if compelled to do so. It noted that the President had not yet felt called upon to make the decision on the employment of United States armed forces but that he would not hesitate to do so if the circumstances required it.

The second statement stressed the arrows of war. In an unofficial comment for background, answering reporters' questions on Dulles' prepared statement on the same day, a "high administration official," not named, asserted unequivocally that the United States would take strong action to defend the offshore islands if the Chinese Nationalists were unable to cope with the attack by themselves. He implied that United States bombing of the Chinese mainland might become part of the defense of Taiwan itself. He did not mince his words in this "unattributed" but obvious signal to Peking.[19] On

September 5, Senator H. Alexander Smith, the senior Republican on the Far East Subcommittee of the Senate Foreign Relations Committee and a close confidant of Dulles, authoritatively stated that the Administration was preparing to fight in the Taiwan crisis if forced to.[20]

Since early August Dulles had been aware of Chou's stratagem of using military force on the offshore islands and simultaneously fending off the Americans through diplomatic means before reaching for Taiwan. Dulles did not let Chou carry out this daring plan. Perhaps somewhat sooner than he might have wished, due to intense allied and other public pressures, Dulles got President Eisenhower's approval of the solemn but discreetly-worded intimation toward negotiations. It stressed diplomacy and hinted at force only as a last resort. The unattributed statement was Dulles' "tour de force" in the crisis. Dulles was convinced and resolute that he had to present a prompt, precise, and unqualified limit to Chou beyond which he could not go without definitely provoking hostilities with the United States even over the offshore islands. Many persons objected to drawing the line there, but Dulles defined his brink without any bluff. Dulles and his advisers hoped that the message would induce Chinese leaders to accept the bid for negotiations and to respond with a specific proposal. Dulles apparently assumed that, in any case, Peking would continue pressures of a limited interdictional nature on the offshore islands. By September 4-6 Washington was still deeply concerned that Chinese Communist artillery interdiction might succeed in defeating or demoralizing the garrison on Quemoy.

But by September 5, Dulles' tactics of the preceding two weeks had apparently left no doubt in Peking or Moscow that the United States was ready for either alternative of force or diplomacy, and that it was indeed prepared for hostilities against the People's Republic of China, if compelled to respond. Moscow must have immediately understood and responded to the American declaration of intentions, for *Pravda* issued a warning on September 5 that a United States resort to force could not be confined to Taiwan and the offshore islands, but would involve the mainland and the Soviet Union by implication. Peking quickly responded to the call for a resumption of the Talks and thus Dulles' immediate purpose was achieved; Peking had acted on the message of September 4, and Washington was relieved that the crisis was under control. Washington apparently assumed that if Quemoy could be successfully resupplied in the next two weeks and the blockade broken, Peking would end the crisis.

What actually took place in Peking and what developed in the exchange of messages with Moscow regarding Dulles' initiative remains a fascinating but unknown diplomatic secret. In any event, after less than two days in actual time, on September 6, a Radio Peking broadcast specifically proposed the resumption of the Ambassadorial Talks at Warsaw. This important decision came rapidly, by the usual standards of "reaction time" for most governments. Chou En-lai made the statement to the Supreme State Council, then meeting in Peking. It was broadcast over Radio Peking and published in the Peking press. While it was not actually transmitted officially and directly to the United States government by any diplomatic channel, the statement was specifically authorized by the Government of the People's Republic of China and was interpreted as an official reply to Dulles' statement on September 4.[21]

Most of Peking's significant response—four long paragraphs out of six—was devoted to the standard, familiar claims of the Chinese People's Republic regarding its sovereign rights to Taiwan and the offshore islands and the Chinese government's "unshakable" determination to liberate its sovereign territories "by all suitable means at a suitable time" without any foreign interference. And the statement repetitively charged the United States with unlawful interference in China's internal affairs, infringement on China's territorial integrity and sovereignty, and open threats of aggression in the Taiwan Straits area. Chou claimed that the government in Peking had proposed "time and again" since August 1955 that the two parties should issue a statement declaring their intention to settle the dispute between China and the United States in the Taiwan area through peaceful negotiation and without resorting to the threat or use of force against each other, but the United States had refused, he said, to issue such a statement and had suspended the Talks unilaterally, contrary to Dulles' assertions on September 4. Chou En-lai went on to make the crucial proposal for resuming the Ambassadorial Talks, and to accept the American proposal in effect, in the following terms:

After the Chinese Government demanded in July this year that the talks be resumed within a set time-limit, the U.S. Government did not make a timely reply, but it has ultimately designated a representative of ambassadorial rank. Now, the U.S. Government again indicates its desire to settle the Sino-American dispute in the Taiwan area through peaceful negotiation. To make a further effort to safeguard peace, the Chinese Government is prepared to resume the ambassadorial talks between the two countries. But the danger of war created by the United States in China's Taiwan area has not been reduced thereby. In view of the fact that the U.S. Government often acts differently from what it says and often uses peaceful negotiation as a smokescreen to cover up its actual deed of continuously expanding aggression, the entire Chinese people and the peace-loving people all over the world must not relax in the least their struggle against U.S. interference in China's internal affairs and against U.S. threat to the peace of the Far East and the world.[22]

Peking's official statement ended with a warning that the United States would have to bear the responsibility for all the "serious consequences" if it persisted in "aggression and intervention against China" and imposed war on the Chinese people, who had every right to liberate their own territory "by all suitable means at a suitable time."

Peking's response together with Dulles' initiative set in motion the resumption of the Talks, but Peking's statement seemed more belligerent and threatening than conciliatory and constructive, even though it used the same expression, "to safeguard peace," as Mao and Khrushchev had in their communiqué. Chou sounded defensive, not responsive, but this may have been used to cover up the resort to diplomacy. He also distorted the situation by refusing to acknowledge that the Americans had gone to much effort in August to contact Peking's representatives in order to resume the Talks which Peking had chosen to ignore.

Dulles' unofficial warning on September 4 with its heavier emphasis on Washington's readiness to use force to defend Quemoy, rather than on its initiative toward the alternative of diplomacy, probably determined Chou's response of September 6. It must have been the threat of military intervention by the United States, coupled with the military deployments underway, which convinced Mao and his colleagues that the Talks had suddenly become necessary. There was perhaps little to be gained but much to be lost by ignoring several American overtures for renewal of the Ambassadorial Talks at Warsaw. Had it not been for the growing threat of American military intervention, Peking probably would have continued to try to settle its claim over the offshore islands in its own way, by force if necessary, within the confines of Peking-Taipei relations and without involving the United States. However, the

American strategy of diplomacy with force and the influence of Soviet diplomacy apparently persuaded Peking to accept the Talks as one means of circumventing American intervention.

It is still impossible to determine whether or not Peking would have taken the initiative to propose resumption of the Ambassadorial Talks if Dulles had made no such gesture either on September 4 or at any time before the military situation turned into a stalemate and then a defeat for Peking, as will be outlined below. All that can be said is that Ambassador Wang apparently had already left Warsaw for Peking at the time of Chou's proposal to resume the Talks. Peking may have expected resumption at a later time. The circumstantial evidence that he had left suddenly for consultations indicates that Peking may not have been considering such an initiative. Eventually, perhaps within thirty to sixty days after August 23, Peking might have sought some kind of negotiation with the United States to confirm its expected victory over the offshore islands and to settle on its terms, possibly in the General Assembly of the United Nations in session in New York City. Whether Peking would have timed its diplomatic initiative only two weeks after its military campaign had begun seems doubtful.

Dulles' sudden offer to resume negotiations or face the consequences of fighting the United States confronted Peking with different options. It was now clear that the offshore islands could not be taken, nor Taiwan demoralized, without provoking American military intervention. Peking could not keep the United States uninvolved and therefore a diplomatic response was unavoidable. The new situation, however, allowed Chou to exploit his bid for resumption of the Talks to gain some advantages for Peking. It demonstrated Peking's moderate and conciliatory attitude, which lessened neutralist and other anxieties over the possibility of a major war. It cultivated a favorable image for Peking in the world. It did not force the issue of whether Soviet military and nuclear support was available in the face of the American military build-up and the official Soviet reserve and reticence—which lasted until September 7 when the resort to diplomacy appeared confirmed in Washington as well as in Peking. It might indeed have been Moscow's counsel, or even diplomatic pressure from other friendly governments, that induced Peking to respond so quickly to Dulles' gambit. In any case Peking may have assumed that talking while fighting—one of Mao's classic tactics—would serve to minimize the risk of an American attack on Chinese positions, on the assumption that Washington would not be likely to resort to force if it had initiated and undertaken diplomatic negotiations. Peking, moreover, could also procrastinate by delaying any immediate date set for an ambassadorial meeting, to gain time for military pressures to strangle the Nationalist garrisons and to face Washington at Warsaw with a military *fait accompli* on the islands. Chou's diplomatic gambit also took into account some important American individuals and close allies who strongly opposed Dulles' policy on the offshore islands. Peking apparently estimated that Washington urgently and seriously desired to negotiate the crisis rather than prolong military or diplomatic maneuvers while losing support elsewhere.

Peking was right. Washington's allies and friends were indeed putting tremendous pressure on Dulles to go to the negotiating table. The President of the United States himself accepted Chou En-lai's proposal with greater alacrity than Chou had shown in his response to Dulles' gesture. Even before receiving any official version of Chou's statement over Radio Peking, the White House issued a statement taking "particular note" of the reported radio statement indicating the Chinese Communists were prepared to resume the Ambassadorial Talks "which they had recently interrupted." The White House hoped Chou was responding to Dulles' policy statement of September 4, which urged that "armed force should not be used to achieve territorial ambitions although such renunciation of force need not involve renouncing claims or the pursuit of policies by peaceful means." That was the course, the statement declared, which the United States would "resolutely" pursue. As for the Talks, the White House stated:

The United States has sought to implement that policy in its past talks at the ambassadorial level with the Chinese Communists. On July 28, 1958, and subsequently, we have sought a resumption of these Talks. If the Chinese Communists are now prepared to respond, the United States welcomes that decision. The United States Ambassador at Warsaw stands ready promptly to meet with the Chinese Communist Ambassador there, who has previously acted in this matter.[23]

Eisenhower gave no details for resuming the Talks, but added a repetition of the original American qualification issued in 1955 that the United States would not be a party to any arrangement prejudicing the rights of the Republic of China.

The immediate Soviet press reaction was endorsement of and

even acclaim for Peking's offer to negotiate—a reaction which betrayed Moscow's reluctance either to escalate Peking's military venture or to underwrite Peking's political claims. Then Moscow made its first public official move in the two weeks' crisis of force and diplomacy. It was after the public exchanges between Washington and Peking at the highest level had set the stage for the renewed negotiations that Chairman Khrushchev sent a very long discursive letter dated September 7 to President Eisenhower.[24]

The letter blamed Washington for the "dangerous situation" and direct threat of "military conflagration," but appealed for sense and moderation. It warned against taking the military alternative under any circumstances and announced in general, indefinite, and unconditional terms that the Soviet Union would support the People's Republic of China. Khrushchev plainly emphasized that China was not alone and had "true friends" ready to go to its aid at any moment in case of aggression. China's security interests were "inseparable" from those of the Soviet Union. He stated that "an attack on the Chinese People's Republic, which is a great friend, ally and neighbor of our country, is an attack on the Soviet Union." This implied "any" attack from either the United States or Nationalist China, and by any means, including nuclear attack. The Soviet Union would do everything possible, Khrushchev declared, to defend the security of both states, and the interests of peace in the Far East and the whole world. In ascribing to the political and military actions of the United States the blame for the "abnormal and dangerous situation" in the Far East, he stated that it required the withdrawal of American forces from Taiwan—an endorsement and support of Peking's political claims and position at the Ambassadorial Talks. He put the responsibility for peace or "a dangerous hotbed of war" fully on the future actions of the United States government. However, the letter made no mention of Soviet support for an attack by Peking on the islands or on Taiwan, and refrained from threats or provocations as such against the United States.

But Khrushchev, like Eisenhower, played on two themes: diplomacy as well as force. The letter seemed to intimate an anxious preference for moderation and limitation of the crisis. Khrushchev said he was anxious to find a "common language" with President Eisenhower to halt "the present movement downward on the inclined slope"; to remove tensions in the Far East by the common efforts of the Soviet Union, the United States, the Chinese People's

Republic, and other countries; and to turn toward united efforts for a useful contribution in the interest of world peace. Khrushchev also emphasized the Soviet Union's firm position on peaceful coexistence and "not allowing the beginning of military conflicts." Yet, significantly and curiously, the letter did not mention or even hint at the Ambassadorial Talks. Perhaps this silence indicated that Moscow had urged Peking to respond immediately to Dulles' initiative and had not wanted to irritate Peking's sensitivities by making it appear as though Peking had made a diplomatic retreat at the hands of Soviet and American diplomacy. *The People's Daily* in Peking had already declared that Chou's gesture should not be viewed as "empty noise."

Khrushchev's letter was presumably timed and phrased to discourage the United States from taking effective military measures to break the blockade: conventional aerial bombing of the Communist artillery positions or denial of the mainland opposite the islands through use of low-yield nuclear weapons. Such a threat of Soviet retaliation might have partly served to channel the crisis into the resort to diplomacy. There is no doubt that this letter alarmed the world as well as Washington. Moscow took substantial risk in supporting Peking, but it was an effective use of public diplomacy. While the letter stopped short of stating unequivocally that Soviet foreign forces and nuclear weapons would be employed on behalf of China, the letter contained no hint that such would not be the case. On September 8, no one could take it for granted that the Soviet Union's military power could be ignored. While the letter was somewhat ambiguous, it did betray considerable concern, even alarm, over the crisis and the need to control it.

The substance and phraseology of Khrushchev's letter were evidently intended to appeal to President Eisenhower to negotiate genuinely with Peking and to settle the dispute peacefully. The order and emphasis of subjects within the letter seem to indicate that negotiations at Warsaw just for the sake of negotiations and for reducing the danger of war and violent conflict were more important in Moscow's view than Washington's consideration of Peking's terms of unilateral withdrawal and concessions. Obviously, Moscow did not expect Washington to capitulate. It is a significant confirmation of this interpretation that the Soviet government broadcast a press report on September 9 by an Associated Press correspondent that Moscow's strong and threatening letter was sent "after Chou

En-lai agreed to the resumption of talks on the ambassadorial level," that the letter was aimed at "reducing the immediate threat of war for the sake of Taiwan," and that Khrushchev's message contained a frank appeal of the Soviet government for "talk instead of war." [25] The Khrushchev letter, this broadcast, and Soviet press endorsement indicated that Moscow of course would retaliate with force if necessary to defend China *proper*, would not get involved in limited hostilities over Taiwan or the offshore islands, and would encourage diplomacy, subtly and indirectly, for negotiations between Peking and Washington.

Moscow could have assumed on September 6 and 7 when the Khrushchev letter was already dispatched that President Eisenhower's administration would probably proceed to negotiate in Warsaw rather than react militarily in the Taiwan Straits to his implied threats and warnings. Also Moscow must have known that Peking's probe was limited to the Nationalists and avoided the Americans. In other words, Khrushchev could use strong and even unacceptable language with impunity on the diplomatic front because he was confident the military bluff would not be called. Of course, as already noted, there is always the element of chance as well as choice in diplomacy, for Khrushchev's letter could have been drafted before Dulles' statements of September 4 or dispatched coincidentally on September 6 separately from Peking's reaction. However, it is more likely that the letter, which does seem hastily composed, was drafted after the diplomatic option appeared and in coordination with Peking's reaction.

Washington understood the implications of the letter's dual theme. On September 8, the day after President Eisenhower received Khrushchev's lengthy warning, the President relieved pressures and tensions further by emphasizing the diplomatic route with a conciliatory gesture. In a public statement he assured the Soviet government that he would study Khrushchev's note fully, but added that he would welcome Soviet concern more over the threat to the peace posed by Communist China's use of armed force to achieve territorial ambitions than over the alleged actions of the United States.[26] Thus Washington publicly called for Moscow to do what it apparently was doing secretly with Peking but could not openly admit.

Official Chinese confirmation of Washington's acknowledgement of Chou's proposal for resuming the Talks came from Mao himself.

Apparently, this was the first and only time thus far on public record that Mao Tse-tung had ever concerned himself publicly with the Talks. On September 8, Mao announced to the Supreme State Council that he was "hopeful about the Ambassadorial Talks between China and the United States that are expected to be held in Warsaw soon." [27] He personally attached considerable importance to them and emphasized their timeliness. Underscoring the fact that the whole world would be focusing on them, Mao said that they might "lead to some results provided both sides had the sincere desire to settle the questions at issue." "Some results" presumably meant for him the return of Taiwan and the assumption of a proper status in the world for his People's Republic. In other words, negotiations would be successful if Washington conceded to Peking's terms. Inasmuch as Mao did not have to mention the Talks to the Supreme State Council, nor have his statements publicized, since diplomatic tasks were usually left to Chou, the fact that Mao did single out the Talks and lent his august position in 1958 to endorse their significance and assure their outcome probably indicated that he and his colleagues assumed at that stage that the chances looked favorable for those "results." Or perhaps Mao had to put his unassailable stamp on the Talks to contain his "hawks," dampen the crisis, avoid American military action and take whatever he could out of the venture. It is also possible that Mao and Chou now were unsure of the outcome and had to go to Warsaw, for they disclosed nothing in advance about precisely what they desired or expected to result from the resumption of the Talks, using even vaguer and more ambiguous phrasing than they had in 1955 when they proposed negotiations with the United States.

The Americans were more forthright on details than they had been in 1955, before the Talks began. Dulles—negotiator and trader, tactician and policy-maker—now called the moves. At a press conference on September 9, he disclosed that the United States might make another attempt to get a renunciation of force in the Taiwan Straits, which was not a new or surprising position for him to take. But he now went further. He suggested abandoning the "ritual" of past negotiations with Peking in order to deal with specific matters. He believed that there was "quite a lot" to negotiate, in fact. He even intimated that if the Talks were successful, then a "very constructive new element" might develop with "further consequences," which he of course did not disclose. Dulles hoped that the Talks would at least reach specific agreement on a *modus vivendi* or a cease-fire agreement which would assure that issues would not be resolved by violent aggressive action that would risk war. This could include a renunciation of force, he said, or be couched in more detailed or specific terms rather than in generalities. Asked whether he had a "number of papers" of substance in his "bag" which he did not want to disclose in advance, Dulles answered:

The things I am talking about are matters which relate to the use of force or the disuse of force in the Taiwan Strait area. But I think the matter can perhaps be dealt with in a more specific way rather than in abstract generalities and that it might not be useful to repeat the ritual of the last three years. . . . If there were a meaningful renunciation of force in the Taiwan Straits area, that would alter the situation in a great many respects and probably have consequences.

As before, Dulles was clearing the way for Peking to widen the range of matters at issue for a possible trade-off of mutual advantage. To make his public words credible and real, he had already instructed Ambassador Beam to inform the Chinese Communist Embassy in Warsaw on the same morning of September 9 that he was ready to carry forward the Talks in Warsaw.[28]

As he spoke, however, the fighting between the Chinese Nationalists and Communists was growing in intensity, and American naval ships were escorting Nationalist supply convoys to the three-mile limit. The Nationalists and Americans were working out several techniques to break the blockade, but it remained tight. The situation on the islands would soon become desperate. Force on the Communist side could win victory before diplomacy could bring about the disuse of force. The matter had reached such a critical crossroad that President Eisenhower on September 11 addressed the nation by television to inform the American people of the grave danger of war and to explain the alternative.

As far as he was concerned, he said, there could be negotiations but no appeasement. Asserting that there would be no retreat in the face of armed aggression and that the United States was prepared to fight if necessary over the offshore islands, the Pesident recalled the statements of Dulles, Chou, Mao, and himself on the resumption of negotiations. He believed that the "way of negotiation" was far better than a resort to force and that there was some hope that such a better way might be followed. As he put it:

That way is open and prepared because in 1955 arrangements were made between the United States and the Chinese Communists that an Ambassador on each side would be authorized to discuss at Geneva certain problems of common concern. . . .

The Secretary of State, in his September 4th statement, referred to these Geneva negotiations. Two days later, Mr. Chou En-lai, the Premier of the People's Republic of China, proposed that these Talks should be resumed "in the interests of peace." This was followed up on September 8th by Mr. Mao Tse-tung, the Chairman of the People's Republic of China. We promptly welcomed this prospect and instructed our Ambassador at Warsaw to be ready immediately to resume these talks. We expect that the talks will begin upon the return to Warsaw of the Chinese Communist Ambassador who has been in Peiping.

Perhaps our suggestion may be bearing fruit. We devoutly hope so.

If the bilateral talks between Ambassadors do not fully succeed, there is still the hope that the United Nations could exert a peaceful influence on the situation.[29]

The President did not go so far in his television address as Dulles had done in his earlier press conference to suggest the general nature of the position which the United States would take at the resumed meetings of the Ambassadorial Talks.

However, in his reply of September 12 to Khrushchev's letter of September 7, President Eisenhower sought to use the influence of diplomacy not only on Khrushchev but through Khrushchev on Peking. The President, of course, disagreed with Khrushchev on the origin of the Taiwan crisis and rejected the accusation contained in Khrushchev's letter. The President went on to welcome the willingness of Peking to resume the Ambassadorial Talks. He pointed out, however, that the United States representative at these Talks had tried for three years by every reasonable means to persuade the Chinese Communist representative to reach agreement on mutual renunciation of force in the Taiwan area, but the latter insistently had refused to reach such an agreement. The United States hoped, he said, that "an understanding can be achieved through the renewed Talks which will assure that there will be no resort to the use of force in the endeavor to bring about a solution of the issues there." Then the President turned to Moscow to use the influence of its diplomacy on Peking.

I regret to say I do not see in your letter any effort to find that common language which could indeed facilitate the removal of the danger existing in the current situation in the Taiwan area. On the contrary, the description of this situation contained in your letter seems designed to serve the ambitions of international Communism rather than to present the facts. I also note that you have addressed no letter to the Chinese Communist leaders urging moderation upon them. If your letter to me is not merely a vehicle for one-sided denunciation of United States actions but is indeed intended to reflect a desire to find a common language for peace, I suggest you urge these leaders to discontinue their military operations and to turn to policy of peaceful settlement of the Taiwan dispute.[30]

The President assured the Soviet government, and indirectly the government of the Chinese People's Republic, that the United States would earnestly respond on its part if the Chinese Communist leaders could be persuaded "to place their trust in negotiation and a readiness to practice conciliation."

The stage had finally been set for the Talks. It is remarkable that all these exchanges between the highest levels of authority in Washington and Peking at a time of extreme crisis were conducted indirectly and publicly without much direct or formal communications via diplomatic channels either in Geneva, where the precedent already existed for both Washington and Peking, or in Warsaw where a telephone call, a letter, or a meeting of staffs could have exchanged acknowledgements and confirmations of these important declarations. Even Moscow's letter to President Eisenhower had to be classified as public diplomacy. In this crucial period, vital communications between Washington and Peking were transmitted by statement to the press and by radio broadcasts. Only this arms-length exchange confirmed that a message of proposal or acceptance had been actually sent and in fact received.

The actual preparations for resumption of the Talks were undertaken by official contacts between the two embassies, with the Polish government serving as go-between. On September 12, Ambassador Wang returned to Warsaw from Peking following consultations with his superiors. In a statement to reporters on his return to Warsaw, he indicated that his government was "most anxious" to negotiate a settlement with the United States, although he held the United States responsible for the Taiwan crisis.[31] And, more to the point, Ambassador Wang immediately informed the American Embassy in Warsaw that he was prepared to resume the Talks and to make arrangements for a meeting within the next few days. This was the first time, apparently, since the Taiwan crisis had broken out that the two governments or their respective embassies were directly in touch with each other about re-establishing contact. On

September 13, the State Department announced that the two Ambassadors had communicated with each other to make arrangements for facilities and personnel, including interpreters.[32] The officials of the embassies of the United States and the Chinese People's Republic used the telephone, letters and mutual visits to arrange an ambassadorial meeting on September 15.

After the offer of the Swiss government to use its embassy was declined, the Polish government made the old, aristocratic Myslewicki Palace available for the Talks. This was a small eighteenth-century building constructed by the last King of Poland in the first year of the American Revolution, called the "hunting lodge." The Polish government selected a traditional drawing room on the second floor, removed the old and faded damask-covered chairs which had been placed around in this elegant setting for genteel conversation and installed two long shiny mahogany tables facing each other, Panmunjom-style. Each side again had its separate waiting room and entrance into the meeting room.

And divided they were, as in Panmunjom, when the Ambassadorial Talks were resumed on September 15, 1958, after a lapse of nine months. Unlike the talks in August 1955, no genial mood and favorable atmosphere surrounded the Talks this time. The military situation was tense and unfavorable for Washington. All the public diplomacy of the past two weeks could have left no doubt that Washington and Peking stood at opposite ends of the spectrum.

Ambassador Wang was reported to have told diplomats in Warsaw, before he returned to Peking for consultations, that his government would not agree with Washington to anything which cast any doubt on Peking's determination to get control of Taiwan and the offshore islands. For its part, Peking radio on September 15 launched the Talks with the uncompromising declaration that the Chinese People's Republic would be ready to wait "five to ten years" to settle the problem in order to get Taiwan. Peking commented also on President Eisenhower's reply to Khrushchev and on the Ambassadorial Talks themselves to the effect that the letter was not "a bad thing if it is not aimed at deceiving world opinion" since the Chinese People's Republic would never tolerate "the expansion of United States aggression in China's inland waters or Chiang Kai-shek's continued occupation of these islands." The Soviet press took up the refrain, denounced President Eisenhower, expressed doubts on the sincerity of the United States in resuming the Talks and supported Peking's claims to the offshore islands and Taiwan.

For its part, Washington indicated it was seeking a renunciation of force so that the Republic of China would in effect continue to maintain sovereignty and control over Taiwan and the offshore islands. Washington wanted such a renunciation preceded by a cessation of hostilities in a *de facto* or agreed-upon cease-fire to stop Peking's blockade by bombardment, naval action, and air attacks. The significant diplomatic difference between Washington and Peking on the eve of the Talks was Dulles' intimation of constructive, new consequences and policy changes if hostilities were stopped in the Taiwan Straits and force foresworn at Warsaw. Peking showed no public mood for negotiation and conciliation as the President and Dulles understood them. Again, as in 1955, there was no meeting of minds even before the meeting of men. It was no wonder then that officials in Washington were pessimistic about the resumption of the Ambassadorial Talks at Warsaw.

Military developments on the eve of the Talks in 1958 extended the diplomatic breach between Peking and Washington. The crisis for the islands was nearing its peak. The combined reaction of Chinese Nationalist and American resources had not yet affected, let alone broken, the blockade. On September 15 the Chinese Communist blockade seemed impervious to the efforts of the Chinese Nationalists to run either its ships through for landing supplies or its planes for air drops. Nor did the United States appear ready to bomb the mainland and perhaps start a war of serious consequences. No one then could foresee that the first successful Nationalist naval run to Quemoy, which landed supplies on September 14, would begin the shift of the military advantage and diplomatic initiative away from Peking.

CHAPTER SEVEN

Ten Talks at Warsaw

After a lapse of nine months, the Ambassadorial Talks resumed on September 15, 1958, with world-wide, front-page attention. On a sunny afternoon, in the quaint setting of the eighteenth-century "hunting lodge," the American and Chinese Communist Ambassadors opened their first session in Warsaw in an exceedingly strained atmosphere. Their ten sessions wrote a remarkable chapter in the diplomatic history of Washington, Peking, and Moscow. Even if the other 120 meetings had produced nothing else, those ten meetings in 1958 would have justified the twelve years of Talks.

In the park outside, carefree strollers, women with baby carriages, and a few flute players went about, apparently unaware of the drama about to unfold. The two delegations arrived separately at the front door and were escorted, without meeting each other, to separate rooms. Then a Polish protocol officer brought each delegation in by different doors to place them on opposite sides of the mahogany tables in the drawing room. Each side nodded stiffly to the other and solemnly sat down, while a large contingent of journalists waited impatiently downstairs to give the expectant world some word of hope.

If the status and caliber of the participants alone determined success in diplomatic negotiation, the encounter at Warsaw would have been well qualified to succeed. Ambassador Wang had the credentials of a long-time party stalwart, a revolutionary enjoying the confidence of Mao and Chou, and a high official having access to the top leadership in Peking. Furthermore, Ambassador Wang had dealt with Americans during World War II, attended the Geneva Conference and conducted 73 Ambassadorial Talks at Geneva with the subtle skill and sheer imperturbability of Chinese diplomatic tradition. Ambassador Beam, although not yet a "veteran" in the sense of having long experience in negotiating with the Chinese Communists, had the impressive credentials of a capable professional in diplomacy. He was well known for the qualities required in just such negotiations: ingenuity and incisiveness, stamina, persistence, as well as perspective. Moreover, he had the confidence of Dulles and, through the Secretary, direct and quick access to the President. He was well assisted by Ralph Clough, an extremely able Foreign Service Officer.

What actually transpired in the ten successive Talks, from the 74th on September 15 to the 83rd on November 8, is still a diplomatic secret. Neither Washington nor Peking has revealed the actual record of each meeting. Yet the probable sequence and general substance of this negotiation can be partially detected and surmised from various public sources. Rather than guess at the actual exchange across the tables meeting by meeting, this reconstructed narrative groups the sessions at Warsaw to sketch in the probable presentation and evolution of the proposals and counterproposals of both sides. In addition to the news on the Warsaw meetings themselves, a continuous interplay of declarations and commentary from Peking, Washington and Moscow during these eight critical weeks helped to illuminate publicly what was occurring secretly.

The Opening Exchanges

The first two sessions of the resumed secret Talks, on September 15 and 17, certainly must have spelled out the initial positions, proposals, and reactions of each side.[1] Peking seems to have taken the initiative, apparently fearing that its readiness to resume negotiations at Warsaw might be misinterpreted as weakness. The Chinese Communist government, and presumably Ambassador Wang, accused the United States of undertaking military provocations, war threats, and aggression against China in the area of the Taiwan Straits. The Chinese statements demanded that the United States promptly end all such "aggressive acts." Peking reiterated its longstanding exposition that Taiwan and the offshore islands were China's territory and that the Chinese People's Republic had assumed sovereignty over all of China. The government, therefore, had "inalienable rights" to this sovereignty and to the territory of China. However, the United States was challenging China's sovereign rights, just like "a robber" questioning the claims of a rightful owner to his property before taking it away. The United States government, according to Peking, expressed the desire for peaceful talks, but insisted on continuing its "occupation" of China's territory. Rather than continue "aggressive acts" against China, the United States should halt its war provocations which had become the "most dangerous" United States military venture since World War II.

Therefore, Peking demanded that, if the Talks were to succeed and tension be eliminated, the United States must remove its military forces and its "occupation" from Taiwan and the Taiwan Straits. This could be done, it was apparently suggested, by agreeing to a particular kind of renunciation of force in the entire area. Peking's proposal for such a declaration presumably would have meant the immediate removal of Chinese Nationalist garrisons from the offshore islands and the simultaneous withdrawal of American military forces from the Taiwan Straits and off the island of Taiwan itself. Accordingly, the only subject acceptable to Peking for negotiation with Washington was the timing and procedure—not the principle—of such withdrawal. At the same time, Peking distinguished between the treatment it proposed for the offshore islands and that for Taiwan. There were nuances in sequence and method.

The initial position of the United States at Warsaw appears to have been equally clear and equally general. Washington proposed a joint agreement declaring an immediate cessation of hostilities or cease-fire, to include the Chinese Nationalist forces. If such an agreement were reached and put into effect, then the Ambassadorial Talks could proceed to negotiate a lasting and specific application of a renunciation of the use of force in the area. Washington apparently wished to emphasize that it strongly desired a peaceful settlement and a prompt, effective cease-fire. As publicly explained, the Americans proposed negotiating and establishing "equitable conditions" which would have eliminated provocations from both sides but which would have left the claims and counterclaims of each side open to subsequent negotiation and resolution by peaceful means without the threat of war and military pressure. The Americans apparently wanted an immediate order for all firing to cease, but the guns left in place, so that the diplomats could propose, discuss, and negotiate agreement on specific measures of a military and nonmilitary character to establish "an atmosphere of security." The American proposal apparently was general, deliberately designed to leave the exact geographical area and specific method of application somewhat ambiguous, to be settled in subsequent negotiations. Dulles in his public remarks emphasized, however, that it would be constructive for the Ambassadorial Talks to move away from argument over issues of abstract principle, such as a general renunciation of force, and to get down to the urgent if difficult practical problems involved in the mechanics of a cessation of hostilities. Unlike the 1955–56 exchanges on the renunciation of force, Washington now wanted to emphasize the specific rather than the general and to avoid issues of principle. The intent was to circumvent any bid by Peking for recognition as the price for a cease-fire or a negotiated settlement, as some Communist press sources were intimating.

It is thus apparent that from the outset the two sides stood at opposite poles. Both wanted to eliminate a key feature in the situation but, in fact, their proposals meant eliminating the substance of the other's position. Peking demanded that the Americans withdraw from Taiwan, and Washington proposed the conclusion of an agreement on cease-fire. Dulles and Chou, and their two Ambassadors, again had met in a head-on collision where the resumed battle of words paralleled that of guns several thousand miles away.

The government of the Chinese People's Republic adamantly rebutted Washington's proposal for an immediate cessation of hostilities. For many reasons Peking denounced the proposal as the same old "trick," just an "old plot in a new disguise." There could be no question of a cease-fire because the two powers were not at war. Going over old ground, the Chinese position emphasized that tension in the Far East was caused solely by the United States in its "seizure and occupation of Chinese territory," in its increasing military provocations and war threats, and in its obstruction of China's "rightful liberation" of its territory. These actions by the United States were causing a serious international dispute between the two countries, which should not be confused with China's domestic problem of the unfinished civil war. Liberation of all of China's territory, according to the Chinese Communist position, could take either the form of force or the form of peace, but the decision was the prerogative of the People's Republic of China. The United States should cease interfering in China's internal matters and instead eliminate its armed intervention in the Taiwan area, to make the "peaceful liberation" of Taiwan possible. It was utterly illogical to Peking, therefore, for the United States to ask China to renounce force and to cease hostilities in its own territories while the United States continued to build up its military strength and its "illegal occupation." Peking apparently rejected Washington's proposal for an immediate cease-fire as a primary condition for further negotiations because it avoided what appeared to Peking to be the really crucial question. And Peking indicated that it was "absolutely impermissible" for the demand of a "cease-fire to be made on it, and equally inconceivable that the Chinese People's Republic or any sovereign state could even consider it." A cease-fire would have "legalized" United States occupation of Chinese territory, covered up "war provocations" along China's sea coast, and placed the whole Far East in a "state of permanent tension" which could explode at any time into global war. Peking therefore rejected a preliminary cease-fire on principle. It objected to the cease-fire in general and to Washington's specific proposals for reduction in forces because both would have left the Republic of China in possession of the offshore islands and would have maintained Nationalist garrisons on the offshore islands, contrary to Peking's primary objective of destroying or removing those garrisons and taking control of the offshore islands preliminary to obtaining control over Taiwan itself.

Nevertheless, the Americans apparently continued to suggest at Warsaw that, subject to a general and effective cease-fire, there were several ways to lessen or remove the "provocative features" on and around the offshore islands and to bring about a stabilization of the area. For one thing, the military forces on the islands could be reduced by stages until they were substantially diminished or entirely removed. The offshore islands could then remain "non-militarized" or "neutralized" without garrisons or military personnel from either side. For another thing, the guns and air forces on the mainland and the air forces from Taiwan could have been drawn back. Washington seems to have intimated in these initial Talks at Warsaw that the offshore islands, if so neutralized, could be placed under some form of trusteeship by the United Nations so that sovereignty or political control could be deferred for future negotiations. Thus, Washington, despite the immediate deadlock over cease-fire versus withdrawal, appears to have probed for different variations of a cessation of hostilities and changes in the military and administrative control of the offshore islands to see whether Peking would be interested and willing to negotiate an agreement. Under severe political and military pressures, Washington was ready and even anxious to negotiate an alteration in the status of the offshore islands so that they would no longer contribute to the fundamental dispute over Taiwan.

But Peking would hear none of this. Its strong opposition to any agreement on a cease-fire or to any "thinning out" meant that it would turn down the proposal for eventual neutralization of the offshore islands following the reduction or removal of "provocative features" if such an agreement required retention of sovereignty and administration by the Republic of China and not its total abandonment of control. Peking probably kept reiterating that the United States should stop its military deployments and its war threats. If it did, tension in the Far East would be naturally eased for Peking because almost by definition, whenever the United States abandoned the use of force and "armed intimidation," tension would end. For that reason, according to Peking, the question for negotiation and settlement at Warsaw did not lie in any proposal for a cease-fire, reduction of forces, or any "neutralizaton." The key to eliminating tension, in Peking's view, lay in an agreement on the part of the United States to withdraw its forces from the Taiwan area. Otherwise, tension would remain indefinitely. Therefore, their removal was the "urgent and specific" question to be settled in the Ambassadorial Talks. If the United States government was really sincere, it would immediately enter into negotiation for such withdrawal. Then, the Talks would have a successful outcome. Moreover, adding to some opening insinuation of Washington's insincerity, Peking immediately began to accuse the United States of stalling and sabotaging the Ambassadorial Talks, although they had hardly gotten underway, by refusing to address itself to the real issue—American withdrawal in principle.

After rejecting the American proposals regarding a general cease-fire, Peking seems to have made significant counterproposals of its own which would have established its version of a specific cease-fire in fact. Peking apparently indicated that it would permit Chinese Nationalist forces on the offshore islands to withdraw safely and peacefully to Taiwan over a specified period of time without any military hindrance from Chinese Communist forces if the United States ceased its "war provocations." By differentiating the offshore islands from Taiwan, and Chinese Nationalist withdrawal from the American presence in the Straits, Peking apparently wished to discuss and transact detailed terms and conditions between the two Chinese parties for an effective cease-fire and evacuation. But Peking seems to have withheld discussion—let alone negotiation—of the timing, scope, and procedure of American withdrawal until the United States government had committed itself to a prior agreement on the principle of such withdrawal. Peking did indicate that it would agree to a truce or cease-fire if it were guaranteed that Chinese Nationalist forces would be totally removed from the offshore islands—not just thinned down.

The exchange of lengthy presentations and rebuttals, abetted by considerable public commentary after the first two meetings, amounted to an immediate impasse in the negotiating positions of Peking and Washington. Peking sought the negotiation of detailed arrangements for Chinese Nationalist withdrawal at once from the offshore islands but only American agreement in principle on its withdrawal from the whole Taiwan area. In contrast, Washington insisted first upon the actual establishment of a cessation of hostilities as the preliminary and absolute condition to any discussion or negotiation of other matters. The United States emphasized that it would not negotiate or make other agreements "at gunpoint." For Washington a cease-fire was essentially a technical state of no shooting and a return to the military *status quo* with no political implications or consequences. Those were to be transacted by negotiation without military pressures. For Peking, a cease-fire seems to have been essentially an institutional process for gaining a change in the political *status quo* with major military and political consequences for the offshore islands, Taiwan, and the People's Republic of China.

During the two initial meetings of the Ambassadors at Warsaw, the military and diplomatic situation intensified noticeably and favorably from Peking's viewpoint. Chinese Communist batteries began using their heaviest artillery pieces and deep penetration shells to smash the Nationalist counterbattery fire from Quemoy. The Chinese Communist air force began strafing Nationalist ships in the Taiwan Straits. Holding the military advantage, Peking apparently assumed it could dictate the terms of negotiation. Peking expressed the hope that the Ambassadorial Talks would find a "real way to remove the danger of war which has arisen in the Taiwan Straits area," and anticipated "some results." Accordingly, Peking tried to fan fears of escalation by warning that "there is no time to lose," for "the situation in the Taiwan Straits may explode at any moment into war between the United States and China." [2]

The issues at Warsaw immediately emerged at the United Nations. Soviet Foreign Minister Gromyko spoke up for Peking in his formal address of September 18 before the United Nations General Assembly when he reminded the world that the Chinese People's Republic was not alone and had faithful allies "to beat off the aggressor." [3] Attacking Dulles for his "open and crude threat of force," Gromyko's formal address significantly ignored the resort to diplomacy in the Ambassadorial Talks at Warsaw just as Khrushchev's letter of September 7 had. Soviet public silence on the Warsaw negotiations seemed to underwrite Peking's resort to force and its military odds. By contrast, Dulles on the same day told the General Assembly that the United States preferred negotiations at Warsaw and a political solution.

We hope that a peaceful settlement can be found. Talks are going on between the United States and Chinese Communist Ambassadors at Warsaw. We seek a prompt cease fire and equitable conditions which will eliminate provocations and leave for peaceful resolution the different claims and counter claims that are involved. The United States reserves the right to bring this matter to the United Nations, if it should seem that the bilateral talks between Ambassadors are not going to succeed.[4]

He also told a luncheon group in New York that the Ambassadorial Talks might start constructively if the two sides could move away from talking about issues of principle and get down to practical matters. A spokesman for the United States later explained that the practical matter which Dulles had in mind was a specific cease-fire in the area of the offshore islands. The issue of principle which he wished to avoid was the broad question of United States recognition of the People's Republic of China. His representative at Warsaw apparently had been instructed not to accept Peking's initial proposal for Chinese Nationalist withdrawal from the offshore islands, but to suggest a concrete variation. If the Chinese Communists agreed to a cease-fire, then the United States in a year or two, when the situation was calmer, would have tried to persuade Chiang Kai-shek to return his offshore island garrison to Taiwan so that the islands could then be neutralized. However, Peking rejected this counterproposal, insisting on the immediate removal of the Nationalist forces from the offshore islands and spurning the proposal for neutralization on the grounds that the islands belonged to the Chinese People's Republic. Dulles was also reportedly working toward an arrangement to evacuate Chiang's forces and to put the islands under the Trusteeship of the United Nations, although Washington understood from the initial discussion at Warsaw that Peking would reject this idea too.

While both sides were far apart after two meetings, they had modified their opening moves. But the military advantage seemed to remain with Peking, and was perhaps even improving. The actual military situation surrounding the offshore islands seemed dim indeed to the military analyst of *The New York Times,* Hanson Baldwin, and the alternatives appeared to be a resort to war or to the United Nations if neither side conceded anything at Warsaw.

At this key stage in the tense diplomatic and military situation, just *after* two ambassadorial sessions in Warsaw, the Soviet government made a major move to support its ally and to encourage the resort to diplomacy. On September 19, Khrushchev sent Eisenhower a long, abusive letter. This letter is an interesting item in the history of contemporary "crisis control," and an especially significant feature in the triangular relations among Moscow, Peking, and Washington at this time. First, the letter was an exercise in nuclear deterrence of a sort. Moscow warned the United States that it faced atomic retaliation by the Soviet Union and expulsion by Communist China from the Taiwan area. He declared:

. . . if the People's Republic of China falls victim to such an attack, the aggressor will at once get a rebuff by the same means. . . . An attack on the People's Republic of China is an attack on the Soviet Union. We have a treaty of friendship, alliance and mutual assistance with the great friend, ally and neighbor of our country . . . and may no one doubt that we shall completely honor our commitments. Therefore, I would like to appeal to you once more not to bring the atmosphere to red heat. . . .[5]

Repeating Peking's thesis, Khrushchev said neither the Soviet Union nor Communist China was frightened by "atomic blackmail." He asked President Eisenhower to remember that the Communist side could use atomic and hydrogen weapons too. He had gone to Peking in August, he recalled, to make it clear that the Soviet Union would never be a party to "intervention" in Chinese internal affairs. Khrushchev told the President that he and Mao had reached "full unanimity of views. . . . on the main thing, that is on the necessity of continued determined fight against all forces of aggression and support for forces working for peace." Moreover, the Soviet government "resolutely rejected" the idea of "Two Chinas." Thus, the Soviet letter of September 19 seemed stronger than the Soviet letter of September 7, not only in raising the threat of atomic retaliation but in mentioning the Sino-Soviet Treaty of 1950.* Nevertheless, Khrushchev's letter did soften its threat of nuclear retaliation by carefully refraining from implying that the territory of the United States would be attacked. The letter avoided specifying the "aggressor" or the target area for such retaliation. It also did not indicate that Soviet-controlled atomic weapons and Soviet-manned means of delivery would be used, and permitted the logical inference that a nuclear exchange, if undertaken by Chinese forces, could only occur in the local theater of operations around Taiwan. Moscow retained the nuclear initiative vis-à-vis Peking.

In retrospect, the interesting feature of Khrushchev's letter concerning the Warsaw Talks was not Moscow's threat of nuclear retaliation but its endorsement of diplomacy. This was the Soviet government's way of applying force and diplomacy. It used the Warsaw Talks as part of its strategy of "crisis control." The Soviet letter of September 19, despite its belligerent and insulting tone, put great emphasis on the use of diplomacy. This time, after the Talks had begun, Moscow seemed to attach a good deal of importance to them. Khrushchev lauded what he called the many initiatives of the Chinese People's Republic to relax tension in the Far East. Among other things, he said the Chinese People's Republic had repeatedly urged both parties to declare their readiness to solve disputes in the Taiwan area by peaceful negotiations, not by relying on force or the threat of force. The Ambassadorial Talks had failed, the letter claimed, only because the United States had refused to adopt this attitude and had broken off the negotiations unilaterally. Therefore, the Soviet government had welcomed the "initiative" of the Chinese People's Republic and was glad that its efforts in resuming the Talks had met with a favorable response from Washington. The Soviet government hoped that the United States would at last take a "reasonable, realistic attitude" at the Ambassadorial Talks. By Moscow's explicit definition, such an attitude would have meant American acceptance of the "historic changes" in China, cessation of American support for Chiang Kai-shek and the Chinese Nationalists,

---

* That pact obligates each party to respond automatically with all the military means at its command if the other party is subjected to attack—and is therefore in a state of war.

American recognition of the Chinese People's Republic, withdrawal from the Taiwan area, and respect for the sovereign rights of the Chinese People's Republic in the spirit of coexistence. Khrushchev's letter agreed with Peking that it had no recourse "but to expel the hostile armed forces from its own territory which is being converted into a bridgehead for attacking the People's Republic of China."

Taken together, Moscow's belligerent threat and diplomatic emphasis seemed to be signalling Washington in three directions: not to attack the Chinese mainland, not to involve the Soviet Union involuntarily in hostilities with the United States, and not to frustrate negotiations in Warsaw. If the tone and language of the letter seemed extreme and bombastic compared to the earlier one, it may have been due to some over-reaction in Moscow to Washington's threatening build-up of force in the Taiwan Straits. Moscow may have jumped to the conclusion that the Americans were about to use their massive power to intimidate and even forcefully punish Moscow's ally—as the Americans were now in a powerful position to do. Moscow's over-reaction probably was designed to counteract its version of Washington's over-reaction, in a process of psychological escalation, so to speak, which only a precise and credible diplomacy using reliable communications can minimize.

From this standpoint, then, the important feature to note about the letter of September 19 in the context of the Ambassadorial Talks is not its contents but its timing. It was delivered *after* Washington and Peking had resumed the Ambassadorial Talks, held two meetings, and exchanged their respective opening positions at Warsaw. The abusive tirade from Moscow was delivered at a time when serious exchange was taking place in Warsaw. Moscow's warning came after Washington had emphatically registered its wish for a cease-fire and a peaceful settlement of the crisis. Tensions were declining when Khrushchev's temper appeared to be rising. Yugoslav official sources, even before seeing Khrushchev's letter of September 19, were already saying that the Taiwan crisis was ebbing and would soon die down without provoking a war.* [6] Peking had in-

---

* The Yugoslavs, first to sense the trend, claimed that it was Peking's purpose to manufacture a crisis without causing major hostilities because Peking needed an atmosphere of war hysteria at home in order to generate support and overcome resistance to the communes and the Great Leap Forward; and because Peking wanted to block Moscow's initial attempts in 1958 to ease international tensions and improve relations with the United States to facilitate Soviet economic expansion and Soviet aid to developing countries, particularly in Asia. Peking feared and opposed all this.

volved Moscow in the Taiwan crisis, but Moscow had proclaimed all-out support for Peking only when assured that its Chinese ally would use diplomacy and not push the crisis over the brink and involve it in major hostilities. Moscow could then diplomatically use the Talks to talk forcefully with little risk. The real crisis was over.

In fact, while the Ambassadors met tensely and the world waited anxiously, Mao Tse-tung and Liu Shao-chi, then Peking's two top leaders, spent the last ten days of September in the countryside, casually visiting various construction and social projects. These were activities seemingly unconnected with the zone of crisis. Mao's itinerary centered on iron and steel production, a university, several communes and meetings with workers, farmers, students, teachers and the people's militia. Liu went out among the people, as the Peking press put it, and traveled far and wide in many towns inspecting education and land projects. Apparently they both returned to Peking at the end of September. Whatever the purpose of these tours, the account of their visits in the Peking press was benign and normal, and as far removed from the atmosphere of crisis as possible.[7] It was after their return to Peking at the end of the month that they extracted themselves from their venture in the offshore islands and their defeat in the Taiwan crisis.

Washington, however, took an alarmed view of Khrushchev's intentions, perhaps not having at that time the same perceptions as Belgrade had into the relations between Peking and Moscow, and not aware that the two top men of China were wandering around the spacious and rolling Yangtze valley. Accordingly, the White House instantly refused to accept Khrushchev's letter and instructed the embassy in Moscow to return the signed copy to the Soviet Foreign Ministry because its "abusive and intemperate" language and "inadmissible threats" rendered it unacceptable under established international usage.[8] Such finality in handling high-level correspondence seldom occurs in diplomatic practice. But the administration could not leave Moscow's move there. The White House—not the President—issued a second impersonal public statement to refute and counteract Khrushchev's spurned letter. The White House, noting Soviet support for the policy of the Chinese People's Republic to expel United States forces from Taiwan, stated that it was tragic for "Soviet military despotism"—a Dullesian phrase—to encourage the use of force to achieve "expansionist ends." In contrast, the statement emphasized that the United States was seeking a peaceful solution through the Ambassadorial Talks in Warsaw and that it "was not easy to negotiate under such threats as the Soviet Union now makes." The statement deeply deplored such threats and termed the Soviet viewpoint "grotesque and dangerous."

In point of fact, the Americans had reacted strongly to the Soviet letter precisely in the way Moscow apparently did *not* want them to react: Washington officially treated the letter as a threat, far more serious and consequential in diplomatic usage and international practice than a warning. During the next few days, Administration officials declared that the United States would indeed use nuclear weapons in the defense of Quemoy if it had to, notwithstanding Khrushchev's threat.[9] Concentrating more forces in the Far East, Washington warned Peking and Moscow of its willingness and ability to carry nuclear attacks to the mainland, if forced to, despite Khrushchev's letter.

Peking then added its verbal barrage of diplomatic denunciation. Foreign Minister Chen Yi declared on September 20 that "no force on earth" could stop the Chinese People's Republic from recovering Quemoy and Matsu,[10] and objected to the United States concentrating such a large amount of naval and air power in the Taiwan Straits area to engage in "armed provocations against our country." Peking obviously did not find Washington's simultaneous use of diplomacy and force to its liking. Chen Yi asserted that the Chinese government was "profoundly enraged" by Dulles' statement at the United Nations General Assembly, making the "extremely preposterous" proposal of a "so-called 'cease-fire.'" Particularly nettling to Peking was Dulles' suggestion that the dispute might be taken away from the Warsaw Talks to the United Nations where, Chen Yi pointed out, "the People's Republic of China has been unjustifiably deprived of its rightful place." He repeated Peking's long-standing willingness "to settle" Sino-American disputes "through peaceful negotiations without resorting to the threat or use of force." According to the Foreign Minister the withdrawal of United States' armed forces from Taiwan and Taiwan Straits was the urgent question to be "settled" in the Ambassadorial Talks.

Meanwhile, the Taiwan crisis seemed more serious than ever to Washington, still confronted by many political and military pressures. While Dulles and his advisers apparently had hoped that the

Ambassadorial Talks at Warsaw might immediately break the deadlock in the crisis and bring about a real cease-fire, the wide divergence and instant impasse made Washington fear that Peking's intention was to force a military showdown with the United States. Officials in Washington now seem to have concluded that Peking was increasing pressure to test Washington's nerves and see how far it could be pressed to give in. The administration apparently decided to hold to its firm initial position of cease-fire first and negotiations second, for it was still assumed in Washington that some kind of peaceful compromise over the offshore islands could be reached even if it had to be arranged through the United Nations.[11]

There, as well as in other capitals, the allies of the United States and other governments were intensely and constantly urging Washington to keep the Talks going and even to open communications with Peking in several other ways: by raising the Talks to a Foreign Ministerial level or even to Heads of Government; bringing "Southeast Asia powers" such as Great Britain, France or India into the Talks; arranging direct conversations between the Chinese Nationalists and the Chinese Communists; taking the issue to the United Nations with Peking's participation; and inviting Peking to the disarmament discussions at Geneva. As if all these pressures on Washington were not considerable, the Chinese Nationalists added a further twist of the screw on Dulles by announcing that they would not accept "thinning out" of Nationalist forces on the offshore islands or any notion of their "neutralization." In fact, the Chinese Nationalist Ambassador in Washington warned that his government might even launch air attacks against Chinese Communist gun emplacements on the mainland.[12] The government of the Republic of China or Taiwan stiffened its attitude toward the Warsaw negotiations, which it had never trusted.

The military situation, however, had changed dramatically by the fourth week in September, altering the course of the Talks and the Taiwan crisis. By September 22 the previously impervious blockade of the islands had been successfully and continuously breached. For eight days the Chinese Nationalist navy, under the protection of United States convoy ships, had run the artillery blockade and reached the islands with enough supplies for Quemoy to feed both the garrison and the people and to build back reserves. Of tactical and even strategic significance in running the blockade was the landing and emplacement of 8-inch guns which could fire nuclear warheads as well as extend the range of the Nationalist counterbatteries so as to cover most of the Chinese Communist artillery positions opposite Quemoy. The artillery balance could be shifted in favor of the Nationalists without direct American combat intervention. Moreover, the Chinese Communists were losing fighter aircraft to the Chinese Nationalist air force and were even avoiding ir combat. The Chinese Communists began to ease up on their artillery bombardment. The military confrontation was coming to a turning point, but it was too early for Washington to be certain that the blockade by bombardment had, in fact, been definitively turned.

As for the effect of the military shift on the Warsaw Talks, United States officials wanted to allow more time to see whether some arrangements for a cease-fire and elimination of provocative measures could actually be negotiated. Even with only two Talks on the record on the Taiwan crisis, the State Department was still impatient to get a cease-fire while the military situation remained critical and the military measures taken by the Nationalists and the Americans were having some effect. Peking also seemed willing to "spin out the Talks" and let its military pressure do the work of extracting the price it wanted. But the impact of the military shift on diplomacy was not felt for several more days.

At the next two meetings in Warsaw, on September 22 and September 25, Washington and Peking continued to develop their respective arguments in their deadlocked dialogue on variations of cease-fire and withdrawal.[13] Washington must have kept probing for discussion of its various formulas. Peking responded that the United States proposals or suggestions were all "absolutely unacceptable." Peking reiterated its denunciations and emphasized the need for a cease-fire to cover Chinese Nationalist departure from the offshore islands. Hinting that the Talks would get nowhere, Peking presumably objected to the "unreasonable" public statements of Dulles in Washington and at the United Nations which in Peking's view prevented progress at the Ambassadorial Talks and evidently created suspicion in Peking as to Washington's intentions. Peking declared that the expansion of United States "aggression" from Taiwan to China's own coast would not be permitted and that the United States could not deprive China of its right to recover all these islands by whatever means it chose, including military force.

Peking's rejection of the United States proposals for cease-fire and negotiations was based on a series of considerations previously announced. First, the United States wished to impose its various proposals on China by increasing military and political pressure on the Chinese People's Republic in spite of the obvious fact that China had strongly refuted these proposals publicly and in the Ambassadorial Talks. Whatever the various forms of Washington's proposals, they were only meant to disguise Washington's primary objective of holding Taiwan. The United States was deliberately creating a deadlock by insisting in these meetings on negotiation of these "preposterous proposals." This was delaying settlement of the real issue of American withdrawal, while the prolonged deadlock served as Washington's pretext to prevent China from defending itself against "aggression" and recovering its own territory. Second, the United States was increasing pressure at the United Nations and on its allies to endorse the United States position in the Talks and thus to bring even more pressure to bear on China, under the United Nations flag. And, third, the United States was intensifying its "warlike activities" in the Taiwan Straits to threaten the negotiations at Warsaw, and, failing to impose its will at the conference table, to prepare "to plunge itself and its allies into a major war with China." Peking declared that the American tactics of either pressurized negotiations or preparatory war were doomed to failure. Yet Peking kept urging Washington "to sit down and conduct the Talks in sincerity."

Peking also criticized Washington for avoiding principles and concentrating on the mechanics or details of a cease-fire. This in turn was "totally impermissible." It was just another way for the United States to insist on its right of resort to force for the sake of "individual or collective self-defense" in the Taiwan area, while depriving China of the right to resort to force to liberate Taiwan. Peking denounced these various American proposals for a cessation of hostilities far more aggressively than it had attacked the proposed agreements for renunciation of force during the negotiations in 1955–56. Peking claimed that the cease-fire meant war, not peace. This was the crux of Peking's rationale used for "resolutely" rejecting the American proposal. If China accepted, according to this rationale, the United States would occupy the offshore islands and start war on China. Or if China tried to rebuff the "provocations" of the Chinese Nationalists, the United States would do the same thing. The only way to advance the Talks, Peking repeated, was to get rid of this "absurd proposal" and negotiate United States withdrawal from the area.

Washington apparently kept trying to focus on just those provocations and various ways for reducing them. The United States would have found any of various arrangements for the cessation of hostilities and provocative actions acceptable and feasible, provided such arrangements would not involve either side in a surrender to force, or the threat of force, or in the abandonment of any claims or counterclaims. During four meetings in Warsaw the United States had by now evidently elaborated a two-stage proposal in considerable detail. First, the United States had proposed and argued for a formal agreement to establish a simultaneous, general cease-fire in the area so that negotiations not "at gunpoint" could take place. The Americans kept insisting on a cease-fire before agreeing to proceed to any other business. And the cease-fire would involve all sides to be fair and effective. Then, at that second stage, the United States was proposing that, after a cease-fire was in effect, negotiations be immediately undertaken and agreements reached over the disposition of the offshore islands. The Americans outlined a succession of possible formulas to reduce tension. A reduction or scaling-down of the respective armed forces had been offered. In turn, this could have been followed by some form of demilitarization, neutralization, or even trusteeship of the offshore islands. Finally, Washington apparently hinted that it might agree to refer the status of the offshore islands to the World Court for a judicial settlement of their future.* Seemingly, the American proposals were offered either as separate options or in a packaged transaction or were spelled out in detail for the purpose of taking the "thorn out of the side of peace." However, Peking never responded to any of them, rejecting them outright while denouncing the American version of a cease-fire and insisting on separate withdrawal of Chinese Nationalist and American forces.

After the third meeting in Warsaw on September 22, 1958, Peking resorted to a well-known negotiating tactic of creating outside pressures on an opponent to strengthen one's position inside the conference room. Peking used its diplomatic channels with certain other countries, and briefings for the Communist news media, to

---

* Dulles implied in his news conference of October 14, 1958, that Ambassador Beam had even suggested judicial settlement. *Department of State Bulletin*, Vol. XXXIX, No. 1010, November 3, 1958, p. 682.

circulate an aide-mémoire couched in threatening terms against the United States.[14] Accusing the United States of a campaign of "deliberate aggression" against the Chinese People's Republic, the memorandum focused on getting the Chinese Nationalist forces out of the offshore islands and the United States out of the Taiwan area. This aide-mémoire warned that, if the United States refused, Communist China would throw United States forces out of the Taiwan area. If the United States retaliated, the Soviet Union would aid Peking. Diplomatic sources in Warsaw, following up on the aide-mémoire, reported that the Chinese Communists considered the Talks a failure and that Peking had been "enraged" by the American proposals for a cease-fire which would have permitted retention of the offshore islands by the Chinese Nationalists. To promote these side pressures, Peking had an article published by a Polish newspaper, accusing the United States of using the Ambassadorial Talks to "mask war preparations," to impose a cease-fire to tie Peking's hands, and to "plot taking the matter to the United Nations even just as the Ambassadorial talks had begun." Chinese Communist representatives in Warsaw and Peking let it be known that they would not give up their demand for Nationalist withdrawal from the islands and their insistence on some tangible measure of political recognition from the United States. Unless the United States made concessions at Warsaw on the situation in the Far East, Peking warned that the crisis would soon become worse elsewhere. The *Peking Review* of September 30 then remarked that the Chinese Communist newspapers were keeping a "weather eye" on the Talks.

After four Talks at Warsaw had made the deadlock evident, the Soviet press launched one of the bitterest campaigns which had appeared for a long time against the United States, and began alerting people to the threat of war over Taiwan. The Soviet press campaign showed no intention of compromise in Moscow or Peking and denounced the suggestions advanced by the British Foreign Minister and President Eisenhower that the Soviet government use its good offices in Peking to effect a compromise. The Soviet press reflected great sensitivity to the notion that it take action to try to persuade Peking to move away from its military course and toward a compromise. Perhaps that was what Moscow was actually doing. The Soviet press kept referring obliquely to the Ambassadorial Talks, without reporting much on their status or progress, charging the

United States with a lack of sincerity in its attitude toward the Talks and assailing the American proposal for a cease-fire.

After four meetings, Dulles restated the American position in an important speech in New York on September 25. While welcoming the willingness of Peking to resume the Talks and to settle issues by peaceful means, he deplored Peking's and Moscow's rejection of the American proposals. "So far, however, both the Chinese and Soviet Communists publicly reject in advance any settlement involving a cease fire or which deals only with the offshore islands. They demand Formosa itself and the withdrawal of United States' defensive forces from the Western Pacific area." [15] Dulles thought that a readjustment of military deployment which would strengthen the United States position, meaning the regroupment of Nationalist forces out of the islands and onto Taiwan, would be desirable. However, he felt that such a redeployment would be reckless in the face of Chinese Communist threats, backed by the Soviet Union, to expel United States forces from the area. Nevertheless, the United States, he said, was prepared to negotiate the dispute over the offshore islands, and would find acceptable any arrangement which did not surrender to force while eliminating those features which could "reasonably" be regarded as "provocative." The diplomatic impasse was now well summed up by Joseph Alsop, who wrote that Peking's rejection of a cease-fire had called Dulles' hand in what James Reston of *The New York Times* had described as a game with two of the sharpest players in the profession, Mao Tse-tung and Chou En-lai.[16]

On September 26, Peking radio confirmed that the negotiations at Warsaw were stymied. It again repeated the rejection of the United States proposals at Warsaw for a cease-fire, portrayed the Ambassadorial Talks as deadlocked, and described the crisis as "explosive." [17] Peking instantly attacked Dulles' speech of September 25 and his idea of "eliminating those features which could be reasonably recognized as being provocative." This was "bandit logic" to Peking. Confidently it predicted that the People's Republic of China would deal the United States a "fatal blow," and demanded that Washington take the "only way out" by withdrawing from Taiwan.

Meanwhile, the Chinese Nationalists were reinforcing their control of the offshore islands by continuing to run the blockade and to build up the stockpile of food and ammunition. The biggest convoy yet to reach Quemoy unloaded approximately 200 tons of supplies on September 27. The American Secretary of the Air Force declared that the United States was ready to use nuclear weapons if necessary and that Matador missiles were now located on Taiwan. The Chinese Communist air force received its heaviest defeat in the air battles over the Straits on September 28 when skillful Nationalist pilots shot down 24 of 26 MIGs and Sidewinder missiles accounted for the other two. American and Chinese Nationalist observers felt that the military situation was definitely improving. Chiang Kai-shek declared at the end of the month that the Chinese Communists had been checkmated militarily and their blockade had been nullified; his forces would hold the offshore islands, and would take unilateral action in retaliation, for, he stated, "the time is now." Negotiations with the Chinese Communists, including the Warsaw Talks, Chiang stated, were futile.[18]

Dulles Probes

On the eve of the fifth meeting at Warsaw on September 30, a United States official disclosed the current negotiating situation in a confidential letter to several Congressmen summarizing a background briefing in Washington.[19] According to press accounts of this communication, Peking had taken an "all or nothing position," concentrating not on the offshore islands, but on getting Taiwan by diplomatic or military means. Peking's representatives had demanded that the United States withdraw entirely. Only then would Peking be willing to talk about the length of time such a withdrawal would take. If the United States would agree to proceed with such a withdrawal, then the problems between the Chinese Communists and the Chinese Nationalists would solve themselves. At four meetings in Warsaw, the United States representative had countered with the two-stage proposal previously outlined, first on a cease-fire and then on the offshore islands. The letter stated that Ambassador Beam had made this proposal several times at the meetings in different ways in order to find a mutually satisfactory formula—reduction in forces, demilitarization, neutralization, trusteeships, and even referral of the status of the offshore islands to the World Court. The Chinese Communists not only were entirely unwilling to discuss a *bona fide* cease-fire, but they did not even want to hear the United States' proposals spelled out to make Quemoy less of a "thorn." The Chinese side continuously rejected a general cease-fire as a frame of reference for any negotiations and refused to conduct any exchange of discussion on negotiations about that kind of unconditional cease-fire. As a result, Ambassador Beam had never been able to develop any exchange on the second stage of the American position. Apparently, the only point that Washington found encouraging about Peking's attitude after these two weeks was Peking's willingness to continue the Talks and at least go through the motions of negotiations. Only if its blockade failed might Peking give up its "all or nothing" attitude, the Congressmen were informed.

At the long 78th session on September 30th—the fifth to be held at Warsaw—the United States presumably continued to press for a general cease-fire and for the second stage of various negotiated arrangements regarding the withdrawal or thinning out of Nationalist forces from the offshore islands.[20] By now it had made as many concessions or proposals on the application of a cease-fire and on readjustments regarding provocative features in the situation as were practical and prudent. Peking, rejecting Dulles' proposals as a "cover up" for his "war intrigues," apparently continued to demand a total withdrawal of United States forces from the area as the only solution. At this meeting, Peking protested the use of Sidewinder missiles, accusing the United States of "extended aggression" against China. After the meeting Chinese Communist representatives publicly charged that the United States was endangering the negotiations by letting the Chinese Nationalist air force use American Sidewinders, some of which had landed on the Chinese mainland. This created a new military situation from Peking's standpoint and endangered the Talks. However, despite the lack of progress, neither side appeared interested in breaking them off or hurrying them up.

Five sessions had still failed to obtain any agreement on a cease-fire or reach concrete results. While both parties at first had dealt with the offshore islands and Taiwan as a whole, each used an opposite emphasis. The American proposals were specific about the offshore islands and vague about Taiwan; the Chinese Communists were specific about Taiwan but vague about the islands. The two sides may even have moved farther apart. Peking kept separating Taiwan from the offshore islands issue and differentiating between specific arrangements with the Chinese Nationalists and a general proposition for the United States. The United States must agree in principle to withdraw entirely from the Taiwan area, but Peking would be willing to discuss a suitable timetable for such withdrawal whenever agreement was reached for it to begin. Once the United States agreed to withdraw, the Chinese Communists and the Chinese Nationalists would settle their outstanding problems themselves. In other words, the United States was to give up Taiwan and abandon the Chinese Nationalists altogether. Peking obviously did not want to have the United States proposals on the offshore islands detailed in any way.

Washington, however, went on to develop its two-stage proposal: first, a formal cease-fire so that real negotiations not at gunpoint could be made possible; and second, agreements on specific measures to relieve tensions in the Taiwan Straits, including thinning out of forces, demilitarization, neutralization, trusteeships, or a judicial settlement. It even hinted that a cease-fire and other arrangements could lead to a Foreign Ministers' meeting, as Dulles later intimated publicly. American officials were at least encouraged that Peking was willing to hold the Talks at all and to continue with them. Robert Murphy, the Deputy Under Secretary of State, explained that the five Warsaw Talks represented a practical attempt, using customary diplomatic means, to arrive at a peaceful settlement, the American objective being first to obtain a cease-fire. While there had been no progress, he did not despair of the possibility that "there may be developed a situation of *de facto* tranquility." [21]

In the meantime, a curiously tantalizing and still mysterious sidelight to the negotiations had occurred. At some point after the Talks began, Peking probably used diplomatic channels outside the Warsaw machinery reportedly to try to convey a vague signal to Washington that an interim basis might be found first to deal with the offshore islands and then later, at some indefinite time, to take up the question of United States withdrawal from Taiwan itself. This report was never confirmed, however. The State Department denied the story at the time, and American diplomatic officers involved in the matter asserted that there was no truth whatsoever to the story. It apparently played no part in the Talks as such. On the other hand, American correspondents and knowledgeable diplomatic sources insisted then and still maintain that some kind of "signal" was sent from Peking and was received in Washington. While this could have amounted to no more than a planted hoax, mistaken reporting, or sincere misunderstanding, it should be mentioned as an incident in the difficult dealings between Washington and Peking.

According to press reports,[22] this signal apparently was transmitted orally and informally from the Peking Foreign Ministry to its embassy in Oslo, then to the Norwegian government which in turn transmitted it to the United States delegation at the United Nations General Assembly and, finally, to the State Department when the Norwegian Foreign Minister visited Washington in late September. This new position seemed to some diplomats and the press at the time to differ from the stand Ambassador Wang had taken in the first two meetings, in that immediate and total withdrawal of United States forces was not demanded. There was speculation at the United Nations that by implying a willingness to discuss the offshore islands first and separately from the Taiwan issue, Peking was coming nearer to the American proposal. Inaccurate and full of wishful thinking as this interpretation might have been, Peking, however, seemed to be shifting its position, possibly in part because Moscow had begun urging moderation. Public opinion was building up against Peking, and pressure was being brought to bear to prevent Peking from undertaking any extension of military action, particularly an assault on the islands. There was also pressure on Peking to agree to make separate arrangements for the offshore islands and for Taiwan. The counterblockade was proving effective, while the success of military operations against the offshore islands seemed increasingly dubious in the light of the massive power which the United States had already moved into the area. It was claimed that Peking had chosen to signal Washington through a third party because the positions at Warsaw had become so rigid and because hostility between the two governments had intensified. In any event, whether there was any intent at all in Peking to send a signal to Washington or whether an actual signal, however vague, reached Washington, it would not have contradicted other available indications that Peking had its own two-stage strategy for getting the offshore islands first and then moving on to Taiwan later. Perhaps the "signal" reflected Peking's initial confidence that it could get them by a combination of military and diplomatic means in a double sequence. In that context, the "signal" was only meant to confirm what was obvious to Peking and to convey its intention or readiness to divorce the two subjects and settle them on its own terms.

Either this alleged signal from Peking or some other diplomatic indication may have stimulated Dulles at his news conference on September 30 to make some remarkable statements and intimations.[23] As it turned out, this was his last detailed public comment on China before his death. His remarks appeared, particularly to the Chinese Nationalists, to suggest a dramatic shift in his attitude toward the Taiwan issue and the Chinese People's Republic. He indeed implied that basic and substantial changes in United States policy could take place under certain conditions, although he purposely left those conditions undefined. He focused his attention and emphasis on the desirability of a *de facto* cease-fire and a reduction of Nationalist forces on the offshore islands, and he expressed hope that the military confrontation in the area as well as the diplomatic encounter at the Ambassadorial Talks would move toward increasing stabilization and decreasing danger. He believed that the Talks had kept the situation from deteriorating into major hostilities for three years. In addition, he felt that a Nationalist withdrawal from the offshore islands could take place only after a "reasonably dependable" cease-fire, even on a *de facto* basis without any signed document at Warsaw.

Dulles also significantly suggested that any renunciation of force by Peking in the area would have to apply equally to the Chinese Nationalists, because it would be "quite impractical and quite wrong" to ask Peking alone to abandon the use of force. He even endorsed the heretical and controversial notion that the offshore islands could be "abandoned" without an adverse impact on the defense of Taiwan if there were a dependable cease-fire. In any event, the Nationalists could not return to China, for he did not believe that "just by their own steam they are going to get there." The Ambassadorial Talks could go on indefinitely to discuss the political issues, he said. He made clear to Peking, as Ambassador Beam must have, too, at the negotiating table, that a reciprocal renunciation of force did not involve a renunciation of claims by either side. In other words, the Taiwan problem would be comparable to claims such as in the cases of Korea, Vietnam, India, Pakistan and Indonesia, as he had often explained. But he ruled out any consideration of the Taiwan crisis as a civil war or a purely internal affair, because, in Dulles' view, it involved outside powers. The Soviet Union had a Treaty and commitment to support the Chinese People's Republic and was prepared to back it "to the hilt," while the United

States would certainly live up to its Treaty of Collective Self-Defense with the Republic of China. As a very practical situation, then, it would be quite unrealistic to consider a clash between these two sets of forces as a purely civil war without any effect on international peace.

But the most important, if elusive, comment Dulles made in this news conference was his indication that there was a possibility "of some important changes" in United States policy, provided there was some "response" from Peking. As he put it, "Our policy in these respects is flexible and adapted to the situation that we have to meet. If the situation we have to meet changes, our policies change with it." [23] This intimation echoed his public hints of September 9 when he implied that new, constructive, and significant consequences—including a Foreign Ministers' conference—could result from any first-stage agreement at Warsaw on a dependable cease-fire. Now, President Eisenhower immediately supported the position of his Secretary of State to the effect that a cease-fire, as understood by the West, would create "an opportunity to negotiate in good faith." Both the President and the Secretary apparently still assumed, at least in public, that mutual sincerity and common interest on both sides were present at Warsaw.

However, these conciliatory statements of the President and Secretary of State—and presumably the flexible efforts of Ambassador Beam in Warsaw—did not move Peking any nearer to a resolution of the conflict. In fact, they may have helped to shut off the possibility of negotiations on the offshore islands just as they might have gotten underway. In fact Peking now recoiled from further negotiations, except to seek Washington's capitulation although that had now become even more unlikely.

Chou Recoils

On September 30, Chou En-lai made a curious speech at the National Day Reception in Peking on the important occasion of the Ninth Anniversary of the founding of the Chinese People's Republic.[24] Devoting nearly half of his statement to the Taiwan crisis, he repeated all the familiar accusations against the United States: committing aggression against China, concentrating huge naval and air forces in the Taiwan Straits area, "playing with fire on the brink of war," interfering in an internal Chinese affair, and "preposterously" demanding a cease-fire that was only a plot. Chou En-lai added a new and even more unconciliatory note, which seemed to diverge widely from the purported signal transmitted through the Norwegian government calling for a negotiated settlement. He said: "Demonstrations of several hundred millions of our people . . . against U.S. aggression and the movement to arm the whole people . . . are a forceful answer of the Chinese people to the U. S. aggressor."

Why the sudden hardening after September 30 on Peking's part in Warsaw and elsewhere? Was it due to the coincidental interaction of Dulles' flexible position, United Nations action, and a possible shift in Moscow's position? During the last few days of September the Soviet press muted Khrushchev's nuclear threat, played down the issue of the Sidewinders and the United States military build-up, and ignored Washington's challenge that nuclear weapons might be used if necessary for the defense of the offshore islands. On September 30, the occasion for the same anniversary at which Chou En-lai had delivered his uncompromising statement in Peking, Khrushchev in Moscow totally ignored the Taiwan crisis and Soviet support for the Chinese People's Republic. With the United States military position now virtually unassailable and the offshore islands secure, Peking really needed a Soviet nuclear shield and even Soviet nuclear weapons, in addition to other moral and material support. However, at this point, after five meetings at Warsaw and clear indications from Eisenhower and Dulles that Washington wished to negotiate the question of the offshore islands and even other issues, Moscow apparently denied such support to its ally and sought a compromise on both fronts, diplomacy and force. Moscow apparently did not cooperate with Peking in "rebuffing" the United States to assist Peking in the attainment of its national objectives, or at least to prevent the defeat and humiliation which were becoming imminent. In fact, Moscow may have feared that Peking was too eager to fight the United States with Soviet help.*

Moreover, on October 5, Khrushchev made a public clarification of Moscow's attitude quite as significant in its way as Dulles' remarks had been. And assuredly this statement must have been privately delivered to Peking in advance, that is before the sixth

* These inferences are taken from a study of the documents in the Sino-Soviet conflict, published in 1960–1964 by both Moscow and Peking.

Warsaw ambassadorial meeting on October 4. Khrushchev now declared:

> . . . we have not interfered and do not intend to interfere in the civil war which the Chinese people are waging against the Chiang Kai-shekite clique.
>
> It is the inalienable right of every nation to settle its internal affairs as it sees fit. Their intention to regain Chinmen [Quemoy] and Matsu and to liberate Taiwan and the Penghu Islands is the Chinese people's internal affair.[25]

Khrushchev indicated that only an American attack on the Chinese People's Republic—meaning only the mainland—could result in Soviet military involvement. The Soviet Union would stay out of any Chinese Nationalist-Chinese Communist conflict, since that would be only a continuation of the Chinese civil war. Moscow seemed to be qualifying its support for "China's lawful actions" and "sovereign rights." Notwithstanding the bombastic utterances of a few weeks before—made safely *after* the negotiations were started —the Soviet government now appeared to be disengaging from the Taiwan matter. Soviet weapons apparently would not be committed to Peking in its campaign to regain its sovereign territory despite the fact that that has always been Peking's prime objective in foreign policy. The Soviet Union was putting a limit on its role as a backer of Communist China in its dispute with the Chinese Nationalists and the United States. From any objective view this would also have had the effect of easing the Taiwan crisis into a "Two Chinas" solution, Peking's anathema.

Many factors were accordingly moving the Taiwan crisis toward a significant change by the time of the 79th Ambassadorial Talk on October 4. The political and military situations were shifting rapidly. Dulles was intimating important new changes. Moscow was disentangling itself from the conflict, leaving Peking to work it out with Washington or to handle the situation in its own way. The possibility of a political separation of the offshore islands from Taiwan seemed to be emerging. By early October, the practical effect of Washington's and Moscow's positions was to infer a "zone of limit" and a "way of exit" for the conflicting interests and sets of forces. An unspecified zone was emerging in the Straits between the offshore islands and Taiwan to separate military sorties or provocative activities from mainland China or from Taiwan. This tacit line could have differentiated the offshore islands, juridically, as well as militarily and politically, from Taiwan; and this exit, in turn, would have extricated everyone from an undesirable and disastrous collision. In another unpredictable and coincidental overlap of different national interests, Washington and Moscow both judged that the conflict over the offshore islands did not warrant a nuclear war, that the settlement of the issue could be separately negotiated at Warsaw, and that Taiwan's future status should be resolved politically, not militarily.

We can only surmise from the veiled revelations in the subsequent polemics that, at this crucial point in the Taiwan crisis, some voices in Peking were heard in favor of war with the United States with Soviet nuclear support. However, Moscow apparently rejected hostilities and opted for negotiation, and withheld nuclear support.

One would have assumed that under these fluid and unfavorable circumstances Peking would have changed Ambassador Wang's instructions. Here was a chance to negotiate the Nationalist garrisons off the islands, stop Nationalist hostilities against the mainland, and set in process a way to return the offshore islands eventually to Peking's control and jurisdiction. And Peking could perhaps have negotiated such agreements without having to get involved in a side negotiation of a renunciation of force specifically regarding Taiwan. Peking might at least have had the islands, kept its claim to Taiwan intact, and continued its "unshakable determination" to liberate that "sovereign territory" at a suitable time. But Peking did not seize the opportunity at Warsaw. The Chinese leaders in Peking discarded diplomacy and negotiations, ignoring the wisdom of Demosthenes, who warned that, unlike generals, diplomats have only words and opportunities in their arsenal, and opportunities once lost cannot be restored with any amount of words.

To judge from Peking's public declarations and commentary, the 79th meeting of the Ambassadorial Talks in Warsaw on October 4, 1958, appears to have been the historic and significant dividing-line in the ten Talks and perhaps even in the decade of negotiations and contacts between the United States and the Chinese People's Republic.[26] That encounter of the Ambassadors might have provided the opportunity to discuss Dulles' intimations of significant consequences in a joint effort to stabilize the situation in the Taiwan Straits. Instead, it can safely be presumed from Peking's public attitude at the time that the Chinese side denounced Dulles' statements of September 25 and September 30, and rejected all his proposals. Moreover, Ambassador Wang probably added a particularly violent denunciation of the idea of "Two Chinas." For a week before the 79th meeting Peking had already attacked the American position day after day with what Peking called the "bandit logic" of John Foster Dulles. The more Dulles seemed to be suggesting compromises or variations on a settlement, the more Peking excoriated him. The American proposals made at the Ambassadorial Talks were described as "a despicable hoax" and a "trick." Peking viewed Dulles' proposed changes in policy as completely "deceitful and insincere." According to Chou En-lai and his colleagues in Peking, Dulles wanted China to submit to American military provocations and to cease taking punitive measures against the "bandit Chiang army." Another deception of Dulles, according to the Peking radio and press, was his "scheme" of abandoning the use of force and establishing a cease-fire in order to "bind the hands and feet" of the Chinese people. Peking kept declaring that the United States government was not acting "sincerely" at the Ambassadorial Talks, was trying to drag them out, and was using them to cover up its "aggressive schemes." Indeed, a long Peking commentary of October 4, referring to the 79th Ambassadorial meeting, noted that Dulles and other leaders of the United States government were trying to create the impression that some kind of change was taking place in United States policy in the Far East. But Peking proceeded nevertheless to give short shrift to the idea that any such change was actually under way. Washington's statements were dismissed as no more than a continuation of Washington's "lunatic policy."

Arguing strenuously against the cease-fire and the "Two Chinas," Peking linked these two "plots" or "schemes" of Washington together for the first time. Peking's sudden denunciations of the "Two Chinas" idea in connection with a cease-fire on the offshore islands —presumably repeated in its secret statement in the Ambassadorial Talks of October 4—were particularly interesting and significant at this particular juncture. The "Two China plot" seems to have been a new theme in the Warsaw Talks on the Taiwan crisis, although not in Washington-Peking dealings. Chou now accused Dulles, in effect, of trying to establish Taiwan as another independent country and government beside the People's Republic of China, for this "scheme" to create "Two Chinas" was allegedly intended to carry out the aim of invasion and conquest of the Chinese mainland. According to Peking, "the Kuomintang clique" was just a tiny "remnant" of the Chinese civil war, propped up by its Treaty with the United States and American military forces. Peking now declared that it would have no part of the "Two Chinas," denounced any step in that direction, and protested against what it apparently alleged was Washington's "plot" to manipulate the Taiwan issue into an agreement at Warsaw for "Two Chinas." Peking "resolutely" would not stand for this because it was "absolutely impermissible." The whole idea was anathema to Peking. Yet what remains surprising and obscure about the timing and motivation of Peking's sudden introduction of the "Two Chinas" theme was Washington's evident disclaimer of the idea at the very same time. Washington was clearly not trying to promote any such idea at Warsaw or elsewhere. Yet Peking announced that the two Ambassadors now had the task, among others, of negotiating Washington's abandonment of its "scheme" for "Two Chinas."

The almost frenetic rejection of the "Two China plot" at this particular time may have betrayed a fear on Peking's part that the diplomatic and military tactics of Dulles, Khrushchev, and the United Nations were coincidentally combining—or deliberately conspiring —to maneuver Peking into an embarrassing and untenable position of separately treating the offshore islands and Taiwan, which Peking had earlier implied itself. Now Chou suddenly was linking the two inseparably into one Taiwan issue perhaps to thwart Dulles, Khrushchev, and others in their "plans" to create "Two Chinas." Yet the reason for this sudden denunciation of the United States for its so-called Two Chinas plot was not at all clear at the time—nor is it now. Perhaps Peking reacted so strongly actually because acquiescence in the two-stage American negotiating position could have led to the possibility of Peking's takeover of the offshore islands following their evacuation by Chinese Nationalist forces if Chiang could have been persuaded to acquiesce—a doubtful prospect at best at that time.

But such takeover or mere demilitarization would have set the stage for a subsequent separation under any of Washington's proposals—reduction of forces, demilitarization, neutralization, trusteeship, judicial settlement—and the Chinese mainland, Quemoy and Matsu might have become divided physically, politically, and juridically from Taiwan. Many governments, India in particular, were seeking some such settlement by separation to dampen the crisis atmosphere in the Taiwan Straits and to reduce the risk of a nuclear exchange. By indicating to Peking just at this time that it favored a cooling-off of the crisis, Moscow may also have had the effect of influencing Peking away from any settlement by separation. For its part, Washington continued to argue strenuously for agreement on a cease-fire, various measures for preventing hostilities in the area, several possible arrangements for dealing with the islands, and a definitive agreement on a reciprocal renunciation of force. The notion of an arrangement for "Two Chinas"—a highly complicated and controversial concept—was apparently not in the Dulles "bag of tricks" at all. Yet, Washington's position at Warsaw may have seemed to advocate the concept of "Two Chinas" to Peking leaders, and thus may have contributed to Peking's abrupt shying away from the course of the discussion at Warsaw.

Peking, nonetheless, gave no sign of wanting to break off the Talks entirely despite the hardening deadlock. However, at the 79th meeting on October 4, Peking's chief delegate to the political talks at Panmunjom in 1953–54, Huang Hua, appeared in the Polish hunting lodge as a member of the Chinese Communist delegation. For those who had sat across the table from him in Korea, his presence could not have been considered either auspicious or helpful in view of the violence and intensity of his attacks at Panmunjom. Further negotiations did not take place as the military situation turned against Peking. The Ambassadors could only agree at the 79th meeting to a six-day recess and a return to longer intervals between meetings. Peking then took unilateral action in snubbing the Warsaw Talks to call off the Taiwan crisis.

In the early morning of October 6 the Chinese Minister of National Defense, Peng Teh-huai, suddenly issued a dramatic and curiously composed broadcast to his "compatriots" in Taiwan, Penghu, Quemoy and Matsu.[27] "Of all choices," he began, "peace is the best." There is only one China, not two, in the world, he asserted. The Americans would leave the garrisons on the islands in the "lurch," he warned, asserting that Dulles' statement of September 30 was the clue. Then he announced that, out of "humanitarian considerations," the bombardment of the islands would stop for seven days, beginning immediately. The Chinese Nationalists would be free and unhindered in bringing in supplies to the islands, provided there were no American escort. The issue between China and the United States, he said, was "United States invasion and occupa-

tion of Taiwan and the Taiwan Straits." That issue should be settled, he said, through negotiations between the two countries at
Warsaw. The issue of China's internal problems should be negotiated between "you and us." The wording and structure of the
message appear to have been hastily and even clumsily drafted indicating that it may have been decided precipitately.

In any event, this broadcast began a unilateral *de facto* cease-fire
and truce which Washington had been seeking in some form for
three weeks at Warsaw. Washington was at first dubious of the
effectiveness or sincerity of this unilateral and temporary cessation
but hoped that Peking would make a formal proposal at the next
Ambassadorial Talk which would confirm the *de facto* cease-fire and
lead to a regular and even permanent solution to the problem of
offshore islands. Dulles wanted the *de facto* cease-fire extended indefinitely in time and negotiated at Warsaw into formal, dependable
arrangements.

However, Chou En-lai and Foreign Minister Chen Yi immediately
dashed any such possibility. On October 7 Chou En-lai was reported to have told several Japanese visitors in Peking that he rejected the Dulles version of a cease-fire and demanded that the
United States pull its troops out of Taiwan "lock, stock, and
barrel." He apparently went on to allege that "some people in the
world are trying to split Taiwan from China and put it under international control." [28] This could have been an allusion to Khrushchev, or at least an inclusion of him, in view of the fact that
Peking's polemics against Moscow during 1960–63 used the semantic signal of "some people" to mean Khrushchev and his colleagues
in Moscow. Chen Yi specifically accused the United States of trying, under cover of the cease-fire, "to poke its nose into Quemoy
and Matsu and to make permanent the splitting of China in order to
facilitate the realization of its plot to create 'two Chinas.'" The
Chinese government, he said, was willing "to settle Sino-American
disputes through the Warsaw negotiations, but they will never
allow the United States to misrepresent one China as 'two Chinas'
and to distort China's internal affair into an international dispute."
Chen Yi warned the United States not to misinterpret the temporary cease-fire as weakness or as an equivalent to the United States
proposal for a cease-fire. He declared again that the Chinese People's
Republic would liberate Taiwan and stand for no foreign interference. The announcement of October 6 and Peking's other state-

ments had already made it clear that the *de facto* suspension of hostilities was not a general cessation in terms of a mutual cease-fire. It
was unilateral. Moreover, it was conditional upon the United States
ending its escort to Nationalist ships.

After all the interplay of complicated diplomatic and military
moves, Peking ended up in a stark position. On October 9 the Foreign Ministry publicly rejected a permanent cease-fire, denounced
United States escort operations as "open and flagrant intervention"
in China's internal affairs, and protested the "aggression" by un-
precedentedly huge armed forces in the Taiwan area and the intrusion
into China's territorial sea and air space. Insisting that the United
States should stop all this, the Foreign Ministry demanded that, "instead of haggling about a so-called cease-fire, their ambassador
should sit down to negotiate seriously in Warsaw, consulting with
our representative on concrete ways and steps to withdraw all
United States armed forces from Taiwan and the Taiwan Straits." [29]
Peking had decided on a unilateral, non-negotiated cease-fire.
Now there was only one kind of negotiation and agreement which
Peking would continue to seek at Warsaw: American *capitulation*
in a unilateral and irrevocable withdrawal and American *consulta-
tion* with Peking only over methods and details. And that was an
invitation to deadlock and stalemate, not maneuver and transaction
in Washington-Peking negotiations.

On October 10, the two Ambassadors met for the seventh time at
the 80th meeting for two and one-half hours. [30] As the State Department had already publicly indicated, Ambassador Beam pressed for
the establishment and an extension of the *de facto* cease-fire on a
mutual and regular basis which Washington stated was its "whole
purpose" at Warsaw. Ambassador Wang presumably read the statement of October 9 into the record in addition to repeating many
other demands. Officials in Washington indicated that Ambassador
Wang, again refusing to discuss a cease-fire with Ambassador Beam,
had reiterated the demand that the United States leave the Taiwan
area and the Western Pacific. No negotiations in any real sense were
now being conducted in Warsaw regarding the Taiwan area. Instead, the Chinese Communists unilaterally issued a report on the
Talks which the State Department considered distorted because the
Chinese Communists, ignoring all the proposals on a cessation of
hostilities and provocative actions in the Talks, harped on their
original demands for a complete withdrawal of United States forces

from the Taiwan area, and attempted "to assume a posture of being champions of peace and sweet reasonableness whereas all the world knows that the attacks on these offshore islands were . . . started by the Chinese Communists."

According to Washington, Peking had adopted this rigid position and implemented a unilateral *de facto* cease-fire for three reasons.[31] First, the blockade by artillery bombardment had clearly failed and obviously could not work. Peking had to retreat and not lose face. In that context it could not negotiate in the Ambassadorial Talks. Second, the combination of military and diplomatic tactics had stirred up the neutrals and other governments to put pressure on Peking to work for the unpalatable proposal of accepting Taiwan's status in return for a permanent settlement of the offshore islands possibly but not necessarily under Peking's control. Apparently, Peking had first tried to deflect this pressure of the neutrals and others for such a double solution by agreeing only to a settlement on the islands, as Peking may have hinted in September, without renouncing its claim to Taiwan or its insistence on freedom of action to seize it. However, the rapid and brilliant success of the Chinese Nationalists in breaching the blockade probably influenced Peking to reject even the idea of negotiating on the offshore islands for fear of a settlement on Taiwan by separation. Third, the *de facto* cease-fire with its blatant appeals to the Nationalists was an obvious attempt to undermine and embarrass relations between the Chinese Nationalists and the Americans by casting doubt on American intentions and even exploiting Washington's willingness to negotiate the offshore islands as a "sell out" of Free China.

On October 14, the day after Peking ordered a two-week extension of the *de facto* cease-fire, Dulles in a news conference gave his version of what he termed had been the "bargaining position of a tough negotiation." He had tried unsuccessfully to introduce the question of the islands for negotiation in the Ambassadorial Talks. He had not gotten from any source, he revealed, anything to indicate that a "deal" could be made with the Communists which was confined to the Quemoy and Matsu situation. Nothing said at Warsaw or elsewhere in any statement of Peking had suggested to him that it was possible to "strike a bargain" with the Communists in terms of the offshore islands. They were after something bigger, in Dulles' view. They sought to drive the United States out of Taiwan and the Western Pacific. Under these circumstances, he was no longer planning to urge a reduction of Nationalist garrisons on the offshore islands as he had intimated on September 30. He now closed that opening for Chou in their final round together. Yet, for the third time in this crisis, Dulles intimated that significant results could come out of the Ambassadorial Talks and United States negotiations with Peking if it negotiated a dependable cease-fire. As he put it for the last time:

If there were anything like a dependable cease-fire in the area, there would automatically, almost as a matter of cold logic, come about quite considerable changes in this situation. . . .
   If the total of it all added up to something that we felt that we could rely upon and that efforts would not be used by the Communist side to take these islands by force, then I think one can see that logically certain consequences would flow from that.[32]

Dulles had repeated this theme of "consequences and changes" in his news conferences of September 9 and 30 and now on October 14. Ambassador Beam had apparently probed the possibilities and outlined variations on this theme, including even a ministerial meeting, at half a dozen sessions. The message was surely communicated to Peking in full. Peking seemed not to want to hear it, or believe it if it were listening. These were consequences alien to Peking's interests and foreign to Peking's perspectives.

Four more Ambassadorial Talks were held, more or less *pro forma*, on the issues of cease-fire, withdrawal, and the Taiwan situation, until the effort stopped in early November. There was now nothing new to add or say in the deadlock. Both sides put forward their respective and familiar arguments and listened to the anticipated rebuttals.[33] Peking and Washington reverted to the *status quo* insofar as the offshore islands and Taiwan were concerned.

But when Dulles went to Taiwan in mid-October he negotiated an understanding with Chiang Kai-shek to reject the use of force, if at all possible, in seeking a return to the mainland. The Dulles-Chiang communiqué stated that "the mission of the Republic of China resided in the minds and hearts of the Chinese people" and "the principal means of achieving that mission would be the implementation of the three principles of Dr. Sun Yat-sen—nationalism, democracy and social well-being—and not necessarily the use of force." In the meantime, while Dulles was on Taiwan, the Communists broke the cease-fire for a few days by shelling the offshore islands intermittently. Defense Minister Peng put out another Order of the Day, directed at the Chinese Nationalists and aimed at separating them from the Americans.

After Dulles left Taiwan, Peking ordered a unilateral *de facto* cease-fire or truce to be effective every other day on even dates; that is to say, Chinese Communist batteries would fire at the off-shore islands only on the odd dates of the months, although they would not necessarily do so. However, the order suggested that the Chinese Nationalists should not try to bring in supplies on these odd dates to avoid possible losses. This was another way of probably saving face over the political and military defeat which Peking had just undergone and another effort to drive a wedge between Washington and Taipei.

On November 1, Foreign Minister Chen Yi, before the tenth meeting of the Ambassadors on November 7, closed the door on any meaningful Talks in Warsaw regarding Taiwan for the indefinite future. He stated to Gordon Clark of the *Montreal Star* that Peking would give no guarantee to anyone on the renunciation of force, that the Americans must withdraw from the area, and that Taiwan together with the offshore islands had to be liberated by one means or another. Chen Yi insisted that the Taiwan area be treated as a whole without splitting it up in any trusteeship, neutralization, or some other United Nations formula. Reflecting the outlook of Mao and his colleagues, Chen Yi declared that time was in their favor, not in favor of the United States. He held out hopes for the Ambassadorial Talks but stipulated that their results depended on whether the United States would withdraw from the Taiwan area. He was confident, he added, in a peculiarly Chinese fashion, that he would see such a withdrawal before "my hairs turn completely white," some ten to twenty years from then.[34]

Nine years have elapsed and he is still waiting. After the tenth encounter at Warsaw in the 83rd session of November 7, Ambassador Beam went to Washington for consultations to report on the Talks. The Taiwan crisis was over. As it soon turned out, the duel between Dulles and Chou had closed forever. Never again did the Yenan revolutionary and the Wall Street lawyer confront each other.

CHAPTER EIGHT

The Aftermath of the Crisis

The Taiwan crisis produced an aftermath of immediate silence, and enduring discord. Chinese Communist and American leaders went through a profound, long-lasting experience in those ten Talks in Warsaw, the effects of which we are still feeling in many respects. To understand subsequent years of American dealings with Peking we need to examine the conduct and impact of those Talks as a whole. What results, positive and negative, did they have for Washington, Peking, and Moscow? Why did they produce no agreement and explore no new approaches? Did they have a negative effect on the Ambassadorial Talks and American dealings with Peking by institutionalizing misunderstanding on both sides, widening the gap between them, and reinforcing the illusions and suspicions of each? And what effect did the experience in Warsaw and the crisis in the Taiwan Straits have on Sino-Soviet relations?

Washington's Outcome

The Americans had pressed for and initiated the resumption of the Talks. The ten meetings of the Ambassadors in September–November, as well as the general statements of President Eisenhower and the specific remarks of Secretary Dulles, indicate conclusively that the United States government was willing and ready to enter into negotiations not only in good faith but with a view to reaching agreement and undertaking mutually satisfactory arrangements. Perhaps that was the American illusion. Dulles looked upon the initial meetings in Warsaw as genuine attempts to settle differences over the offshore islands and on other issues. He preferred the Ambassadorial Talks to any Foreign Ministers' meeting for initial negotiations and preparation of draft agreements. Had the Ambassadorial Talks achieved those aims, he would have agreed to a conference with Chou, who preferred the ministerial level and resented Dulles' refusal to come to a meeting.

The Americans apparently believed that they had achieved something useful in the ten Talks at Warsaw. Robert Murphy, Deputy Under-Secretary of State, remarked on November 11 that the United States government had approached the Taiwan crisis with "imagination" and a willingness to seek an improvement of the situation. He believed that Washington's policy had gained initial success by bringing about a *de facto*, if fragile, cease-fire. But he indicated that Washington was continuing to hope for more than that. The United States government still had in mind an agreement with Peking for establishing a cessation of hostilities, similar to the one in Korea and Indochina, which could "last indefinitely." [1] On November 18, Dulles remarked that the United States would continue its unsuccessful efforts to obtain an agreement regarding the Taiwan area, but he was not hopeful. "We are now negotiating to end the hostilities in the Formosa area," he said, and "we seek reciprocal renunciations of dependence upon force to achieve political objectives." He noted, however, that the Chinese People's Republic had consistently rejected these proposals.[2] On December 4, in his last formal statement regarding Peking before his death in the spring of 1959, Dulles returned at length to his familiar arguments for nonrecognition, but did not even refer to the Warsaw negotiations on the offshore islands and the situation in the Taiwan Straits, although he reaffirmed the expediency of the "almost constant negotiations" which the United States had pursued with Communist China at Panmunjom, the Geneva Conference of 1954, and in the Ambassadorial Talks in general.[3] In January, Robert Murphy noted that the United States was hopefully continuing to maintain "an informal contact" with Communist China through the Ambassadorial Talks in Warsaw. He also pointed out the frustration which Peking had encountered after its unsuccessful attempt to capture the offshore islands.[4] Also in January, Dulles said that he was still seeking, in the Warsaw Talks, to assure the Chinese that "force should not be relied upon by either side to bring about the reunification of China." [5] But in February 1959 Assistant Secretary of State Robertson told a Senate Committee that Communist China would accept "no compromise on Taiwan." As he put it:

The only settlement they are prepared to negotiate is the withdrawal of the United States from the entire Taiwan area, the capitulation of the free Chinese government on Taiwan, and the seizure of that big island along with its 650,000 well-trained military forces. They refuse to renounce the use of force in the Taiwan Straits.[6]

And in mid-March Robertson reported that Peking had stubbornly refused during all 87 meetings at Geneva and Warsaw to renounce war "as an instrument of national policy." [7]

The aftermath for Dulles in the last few months of his life was thus increasing disappointment and firmness regarding Peking, the offshore islands, and Taiwan. On the eve of his death, he expressed the belief that cession of the offshore islands to Communist China would have led to disaster. Communist China would have begun its objective "of driving us out of the Western Pacific, right back to Hawaii and even to the United States." Just what power Peking possessed to accomplish this feat, Dulles did not explain. But he was sure that to give the islands over to Peking would promote war and not prevent it and, as he put it, would just whet their appetite. It would crack the morale of Chiang Kai-shek and the people of Taiwan. To the end of his life he felt certain that his use of diplomacy and force in the Taiwan crisis had convinced Peking of American firmness in the event of an assault on Quemoy. In the aftermath of the crisis, as well as at is height, he would have recommended the President's use of nuclear and other power if necessary. He came out of the crisis apparently persuaded that Peking had rejected real negotiations and was no longer interested in any reciprocal transactions.[8] Yet Dulles had achieved a qualified success through the Ambassadorial Talks and deployment of power.

On balance, it was Washington's diplomacy at Warsaw and its display of power in the Western Pacific which produced the truly significant results of the ten talks. Dulles won in his last encounter with Peking. He established a *de facto* stabilization of power along a tacitly delimited line. To produce this significant stabilization in such a complex triangular relationship requiring the sensitive reactions and restraints of all three parties, Dulles' negotiating techniques included not only leaving an escape hatch for his adversaries, but also a well-marked limit or parameter on each side of the way out. In an effort to show both firmness and flexibility, he had to give Peking "the maximum possible reason for acting in a calm manner and helping to restore peace in the Straits without weakening the morale of the whole Pacific area." His press conference of September 30, as his sister later wrote, was designed to convey this attitude of firmness and also to acknowledge Peking's diplomatic soundings

outside the Warsaw Talks for an "accommodating attitude." *
Dulles implied that the United States would withdraw its forces
from the area around the islands if Peking ended their bombardment, and also that Washington would perhaps proceed to discuss
other arrangements and show flexibility in its policies if Peking
showed some willingness to cooperate. Peking, however, refused to
negotiate a new political *status quo*, whereupon American power
produced a new military *status quo*.

American officials believed that their conduct of the negotiations,
especially their emphasis on a cessation of hostilities, had brought
about at least a *de facto* cease-fire. Diplomatic and military factors
in the crisis then combined to produce a *de facto* stabilization. That
set the stage for an indefinite tacit but recognizable longitudinal line
or zone of limits in the Taiwan area, similar to the horizontal lati-
tudinal zones in Korea and Vietnam. The United States government
even fortuitously gained the tacit acknowledgement of the Soviet
government for this restraining line in East Asia during the negotiations at Warsaw. Moreover, Moscow's endorsement of the Ambassadorial Talks and unwillingness to support the use of force over the
question of Taiwan facilitated Washington's quest for stabilization
in Asia through peaceful means even if it infuriated Peking. Dulles'
strategy of force and diplomacy served to remove Taiwan from the
threshold of global war for some time; but it remained the core issue
in Peking's relations with Washington.

Peking's Balance Sheet

For several months after November 7, Peking was unusually
reticent and silent about the Ambassadorial Talks and the Taiwan
crisis, particularly where Moscow was concerned. On the anniversary of the Sino-Soviet Treaty in February, for example, Peking restricted itself to praising the "Chinese people" for foiling the "aggressive plans of United States imperialism" in 1958, noting, however, that the Chinese people were "solidly backed by the Soviet
Union and other fraternal countries." It was not until April 18,
1959, at a National People's Congress and after six more meetings of

* See especially Miss Eleanor Dulles' account of her brother's diplomacy
during this crisis for these quotations and other points, *John Foster Dulles:
The Last Year* (New York: Harcourt, Brace and World, 1963), pp. 178, 180–
181.

the two Ambassadors at Warsaw, that Chou En-lai finally alluded publicly to the Taiwan crisis. Yet he apparently said nothing about the past negotiations. He remarked briefly that United States "imperialism" occupied "our Taiwan, and threatened China, constantly requiring the strengthening of defenses." Although he made no report of the crisis and negotiations of 1958 on Taiwan, he spoke with the same vehemence against the "Two Chinas plot" as Ambassador Wang apparently had in Warsaw seven months before and as Peking leaders and publications had continued to do. Blaming the United States for the lack of diplomatic relations between the United States and China and for their current bad relations, Chou declared:

We have not gone swashbuckling to the United States, we are not blockading the United States, occupying its territory or creating two United States of America. There is only one United States of America in the world. Likewise, there is only one China in the world. Taiwan is an inalienable part of Chinese territory. We are determined to liberate Taiwan, Penghu, Quemoy and Matsu. All U.S. armed forces in the Taiwan area must be withdrawn. The Chinese people absolutely will not tolerate any plot to carve up Chinese territory and create "two Chinas." [9]

Although they had frequently had experience with the power of the Seventh Fleet and the vigor of the diplomacy of Dulles, Mao and Chou began talking pungently and bitterly about the "impotence" and "demise" of the United States. Mao refurbished his own thesis about the United States being a "paper tiger," and hanging itself in its own "noose." He laid down the dictum that "the enemy rots with each passing day while for us things are getting better daily." "The deathbed struggles of the imperialists and all other reactionaries will never save them from final extinction," he asserted. All these reactions of silence or anger in the aftermath of the Taiwan crisis intimated that Peking was sorely frustrated and disappointed. What had they wanted and expected out of the resumption of the Talks?

The Chinese response in 1958 to negotiate with Washington was much vaguer in purpose than Chou's original initiative in April 1955, when he proposed "to enter into negotiations . . . to discuss the question of relaxing tension in the Far East and especially the question of relaxing tension in the Taiwan area." In contrast, the offer in 1958 merely proposed the resumption of the Talks "to safeguard the peace." Chou did not specify where it was to be safeguarded, made no mention of "negotiations," and kept his aims hidden. Chou's statement of September 6 gave the impression that he wished "to settle" the issues, rather than "to negotiate" them. Perhaps Peking's vagueness betrayed its doubts and uncertainty. It is also possible that in early September the Peking leadership wished to settle the issue by imposing the result; their failure to achieve this aim caused them bitter frustration.

Peking evidently went to Warsaw with the idea that the Ambassadorial Talks would not be a little window for an exchange of views, but a back door for the United States and the Republic of China to exit in a retreat by surrender and capitulation; while there, they intended to bring about a stalemate after probing Dulles' intentions. Very few commentators or analysts of the period have given sufficient weight to this diplomatic version of the Taiwan crisis in Peking's strategy and tactics. V. P. Dutt of India may have come close to the actualities when he concluded that Peking had adopted the two-pronged policy of diplomacy and force with the notion that it would compel the United States to retreat. He suggests that Mao may have believed that this "rather unsophisticated formula" would make it possible to "sit down with them around the negotiating table and extort concessions from them." And even if this strategy failed, Peking's creation of a crisis would have helped in any event to whip up emotions inside China where acute domestic problems remained, and to sabotage any attempt on the part of Moscow toward an accommodation with the United States and a settlement of tensions.[10]

But what precisely did Mao and Chou seek through their combination of force and diplomacy? At first, from September 6 to about September 25, at least through the fourth meeting of Ambassadors, Peking perhaps expected to get a forced or negotiated change in the offshore islands. As indicated in the preceding chapter, Peking appears for a certain time to have separated the islands and Taiwan in a two-stage military and diplomatic strategy: first, control of the islands would be obtained and then a deteriorating situation created which would facilitate the ouster of the Americans from Taiwan and demoralize the Chinese Nationalists and bring about their collapse.

According to collateral interpretations from Communist sources, Peking was developing a political and military distinction between the offshore islands and Taiwan until around September 25 when

Washington's proposals for a cease-fire, the exchanges in Warsaw, and the trend in the United Nations raised the possibility of the actual segregation of the two areas by international sanction and military realities. Until that time Peking apparently believed it could obtain the little islands either by military means or by bargaining.* Its single purpose in this first stage could have been to demand concessions from Washington by exploiting the superior military position of the Chinese Communists vis-à-vis the Chinese Nationalists. Thus, Peking may have calculated that, by September 15 when the Talks were resumed or sometime during the last two weeks of September, its blockade would have so strangled the Nationalists on the islands that Washington would have had to comply with unilateral terms for Nationalist evacuation. Evacuation of Taiwan would then have followed logically, hastened by the force of public opinion in the United States and the protests of foreign ministries around the world.

When the blockade failed and negotiation of the islands, not necessarily on Peking's terms, became the sole diplomatic alternative, Peking dropped its idea of a two-stage strategy. Pressures also mounted on Peking from all sides to treat the matter diplomatically and settle the issues in two separate categories. Peking must have feared that it would not only be defeated in its basic purposes of removing the Chinese Nationalists from the islands, but that it might also lose its claims on Taiwan through international as well as American maneuvers. In these circumstances, Peking decided to close that door at Warsaw, keep open the possibility of an eventual "settlement" on American withdrawal from Taiwan, say nothing new in the meetings, and proceed with a unilateral cease-fire for the indefinite future. This would render the Ambassadorial Talks inactive but would leave the possibility open for negotiating an American withdrawal from Taiwan. It is significant to note Peking's constancy and singleness of purpose in the negotiations over the years.

Consequently, it can be agreed that Peking did derive some gains

---

* I am indebted to Mrs. Alice Langley Hsieh for discovering the subtle distinction between the offshore islands and Taiwan drawn by Peking during the first three weeks of September. She also refers to the same indication in an article by Anna Louise Strong, a sympathizer of Peking, who wrote in November 1958 on Peking's double strategy in the Taiwan crisis. See Mrs. Hsieh's *Communist China's Strategy in the Nuclear Era* (Englewood Cliffs, N.J., Prentice-Hall, Inc., 1962), pp. 124, 127–128.

out of the Ambassadorial Talks and its strategy of a combination of force and diplomacy during the Taiwan crisis.* Moscow made a more explicit and public commitment of support, including nuclear support, for the security of the Chinese mainland than the Soviet government had ever publicly made before in connection with the Taiwan issue and the threat of American attack. While Moscow had not gone as far in backing Peking's venture to reclaim its Taiwan "province" as Peking would have liked, nevertheless Peking had received a nuclear shield and checkmated an American nuclear threat. Peking's resort to the Ambassadorial Talks and its show of force probably served to produce the Soviet commitment and warning. Moreover, the position taken by Washington in and out of the Talks had the effect of restraining Chinese Nationalist use of the offshore islands for "aggressive" or "provocative" actions against the mainland. This was a net gain for Peking. Such a windfall could not have developed for Peking without the intercession of the Talks at Warsaw. And finally, Peking kept the islands linked to Taiwan and retained a line of direct approach to the Chinese Nationalists in one, not two, Chinas. Of course, Peking could have negotiated new arrangements for the offshore islands, but apparently it did not judge that course to be in its long-range interests.

However, the venture did result in a major setback for Peking: far from obtaining American withdrawal from Taiwan, it generated a greatly increased long-term American deployment of all-inclusive forces into the Taiwan area. Just as Peking's strategy in Korea in 1950–53 had ended by insuring American presence on the Korean Peninsula on a long-term basis, so also in 1958, its action resulted in more American military might on its doorstep rather than less, whereas negotiation could have prevented it altogether. This is all the more significant in that Peking's major objective over the past fifteen years has been to remove American power from Asia and the Western Pacific. From this standpoint the Warsaw Talks produced a strategic miscalculation and diplomatic blunder of major proportions for Peking.

The aftermath left Peking more restricted and less able than before to "liberate" Taiwan by any combination of means. Peking had totally misjudged the new balance of forces. Chou had misread

* "Sino-American Relations and the Future of Formosa" by O. Edmund Clubb, *Political Science Quarterly*, Vol. LXXX, No. 1, March 1965, pp. 1–21, contains a good analysis of the balance sheet.

Dulles. Perhaps that explains why Peking's reaction, after the failure in the ten Talks at Warsaw, was henceforth to focus solely on Taiwan and American withdrawal and to result in complete stalemate.

The Elusive Negotiation That Never Was

What might have happened had Mao and Chou seriously considered Dulles' proposals for genuine negotiations and his intimations of a potential change in United States policy? This tantalizing question will remain one of modern Asia's unanswered questions and lost opportunities. Their failure to do so represents a major setback for the Ambassadorial Talks. The Eisenhower administration in 1958 hoped for a real negotiating process leading to a series of far-reaching agreements on the offshore islands, the renunciation of force, the status of Taiwan, and eventual relaxation in Sino-American relations. However, Mao's government would not even discuss or probe American intentions.

The public record verifies that, in those ten meetings at least, American officials tried to probe for a common negotiating basis with Peking. Variations of American proposals were presented in detail at Warsaw and a genuine effort made to settle differences. Dulles was prepared to move toward reciprocal compromises which would have adjusted some of the tensions in order to create a *de facto* and even a *de jure* stabilization of the area, particularly in the immediate vicinity of the offshore islands. Those ten meetings in Warsaw gave Washington an opportunity to seek to loosen its position somewhat in its relationship with Peking and Taipei, begin a diplomatic movement toward changing the manner of disposition of the offshore islands, establish a reciprocal agreement on the renunciation of force on the part of the Nationalists as well as the United States vis-à-vis the Chinese Communist mainland, and set up ground rules to prevent invasion of the mainland and ensure cessation of provocations in the Taiwan area. Moreover, if these significant modifications had occurred, even more far-reaching changes in United States policies toward the Chinese People's Republic might have ensued. In the resumed Talks at Warsaw, the United States position not only was much more flexible and suggestive, but it was also far more concrete and practical than it had been during 1955–56 regarding the exchanges and counterproposals on the abstract principles of a renunciation of force. In 1958, Washington wanted agreements with Peking and was negotiating earnestly and resourcefully. Washington's signals in private Talks and public hints must have demonstrated to Peking that it was seriously interested in negotiating at least on the offshore islands and perhaps on much more basic issues. Why was the effort so elusive and the opportunity lost?

Even if any such real negotiations had occurred in Warsaw, they might still have failed. The psychological barrier, the ideological divergence and the stilted diplomacy, all intensified by limited hostilities and threats of war, probably would have frustrated any such negotiation. But it probably was Peking's singleness of purpose in seeking Taiwan that explains its refusal to respond to Dulles' hints that "interesting consequences and changes" were both logical and possible results of a real cease-fire. Peking did understand the implications of Dulles' proposals but refused to take heed. Dulles held out a *quid pro quo* for negotiation in the Western sense of negotiation, hoping to encourage Chou into a real bargaining position. However, it may have seemed to Chou that Dulles hung a little carrot at the end of a big stick. Although Dulles kept hinting throughout the Talks that the relative size of the carrot and stick might well change if results were certain, Chou would not play this game. He was not interested in conducting any such bargaining with Dulles. Taiwan, in principle, was the single target.

It can also be conjectured that Dulles' willingness to negotiate with Peking at that particular time may have been less than welcome to the Chinese Communist leaders. With a massive campaign of domestic economic mobilization and political rectification under way, they probably did not want a lessening of tensions with the United States or an improvement in relations with the "arch enemy." In fact, a worsening of the relationship provided a new sense of danger and a sharper image of a "devil" for stimulating the Chinese masses and the Chinese intelligentsia to accept Peking's new communes and "great leap forward." Moreover, accommodating Washington would have made it difficult for Peking to hold its hard Marxist-Maoist line for dealing with the world and opposing any Soviet détente or relaxation with the West.

Washington's clear intentions and diverse tactics may also have made Peking shy away from the "carrot." Did the Americans say too much publicly? Did they and others at the United Nations indulge in too extensive a public discussion of dividing the islands and

Taiwan and "internationalizing" the Taiwan problem? It is a reasonable conclusion that the ten Talks at Warsaw were handicapped by these excessive side-effects and the public diplomacy on both sides. Perhaps Dulles overreached himself in his public statements in September, putting Chou openly on the defensive. No doubt Washington's public statements were carefully coordinated with its secret statements in Warsaw, but were the former not excessive? Moreover, unofficial statements or unattributed "leaks" out of Washington during the course of the first five Talks, together with considerable and often inaccurate press speculation, may have hampered the delicate negotiations and insinuations about "changes and consequences." Perhaps the very vagueness of the hints was harmful. We cannot say with certainty, but it is a fair presumption that the general inclination in Washington, New York, and many world capitals toward some new internationally-sanctioned division of the Taiwan area was premature and overpublicized. Although more discretion and less publicity would not necessarily have facilitated a secret agreement privately arrived at by diplomacy, the inference is inescapable that public diplomacy did not help the Talks deal with the crucial substance of the negotiations or provide the elusive opportunities to proceed to far-reaching matters beyond a cease-fire agreement. Moreover, Washington did not, and perhaps could not, realize the repercussions on Moscow and on Sino-Soviet relations of its diplomacy and use of force in the Taiwan crisis.

Moscow's Escape Hatch

In the aftermath of the Taiwan crisis, Moscow's similar silence and reticence with regard to the Warsaw Talks concealed its reactions to its role in the crisis, the triangular interplay among the three governments, and the resultant discord in Sino-Soviet relations. Moscow hardly mentioned the Taiwan crisis or the Ambassadorial Talks for months. The 21st Congress of the Soviet Communist Party in January ignored the subject. The anniversary of the Sino-Soviet Treaty in February 1959 skirted the matter, although the Treaty must have certainly been brought up during the Taiwan crisis. The Soviet press ignored Moscow's role in that crisis and merely remarked that the efforts of the Chinese People's Republic, with the support of peace-loving forces," halted United States "aggression" a few months before.

Nevertheless, the conclusion seems to be valid that the Ambassadorial Talks provided a timely and useful opportunity for Moscow in its public diplomacy and secret maneuvers. Whether or not Moscow exploited the Talks during the Taiwan crisis is not clear, but the Talks seem to have made it possible for Moscow to make a commitment to Peking without an unconditional guarantee and a warning to Washington without an unlimited risk. Having a diplomatic alternative between Peking and Washington, Moscow could pledge its general support to the defense of mainland China with the calculation that the Soviet Union's armed forces and nuclear weapons would not be called into play. Moscow could also threaten the United States, using unusually abusive language, in the expectation that the United States would probably not overreact and bring about all-out war over China.

As already noted, the Soviet commitment appears to have been limited to the eventuality of an American attack by conventional and nuclear arms on the mainland of China, as distinct from military engagements with Peking's forces at sea or in the air in the Taiwan Straits or in Taiwan itself. According to Edgar Snow's version following his visit to Peking in 1960, Khrushchev's two letters implied that "The Soviet guarantee was limited to a defensive war by China against any attack backed by the United States; apparently it did not extend to an offensive by China against American armed forces in the Taiwan Straits." The establishment of this "equilibrium of power," in Snow's analysis, allowed the tension to begin to relax.[11]

The safety valve or escape hatch for Moscow in a safe commitment and redeemable risk has been noted by many students and commentators on Sino-Soviet relations.[12] They have pointed out with emphasis that Khrushchev's strong and unqualified support for Peking on September 7 came *after* Chou En-lai's acceptance of Dulles' proposal to resort to diplomacy and forego force. Until Peking had offered to resume the Talks and set their arrangements in motion on September 6, the Soviet government and press had withheld all-out military commitment to get involved with the United States for the protection of the People's Republic of China. At the time, Moscow indirectly encouraged the Americans to note that Khrushchev's letter was sent after the diplomatic engagement was confirmed.

The Chinese Communists themselves have also confirmed this conditional before-and-after character of the Russian commitment. Five years later when the polemics between Moscow and Peking reached high intensity Peking verified the timing and sequence of Soviet support in the letters of September 7 and 19:

Although at that time the situation in the Taiwan Straits was tense, there was no possibility that a nuclear war would break out and no need for the Soviet Union to support China with its nuclear weapons. It was only when they were clear that this was the situation that the Soviet leaders expressed their support for China.[13]

This version of the crisis would appear to apply more to the second than to the first letter, which was sent while American power was still building and before the Talks began and the blockade was breached. In general, it may be said that, taking Peking's interpretation either literally, or with the necessary allowance for exaggeration in such polemics, the conclusion is valid that the return to the Ambassadorial Talks was significant—and perhaps even crucial—in permitting Moscow to make a genuine and effective guarantee of support for China's defense and a timely and unequivocal warning to Washington. Those two letters did follow, first, the agreement between Washington and Peking to reopen the Talks and, second, the holding of the first two meetings on the 15th and the 17th of September, which began in a negotiating and even bargaining framework. And of course the Soviet government must have known exactly what was occurring in the Polish hunting lodge. However, the risks were much greater for Moscow on September 7 than on September 19.

The facts support Peking's interpretation that the Soviet government declared its support only when it appeared that real risks of actual hostilities were less than perhaps had been assumed on all sides before September 4, and that some sort of peaceful settlement was possible. Of course, it can be argued that the Chinese interpretation was based on their implicit assumption that they never had any intention of maintaining the blockade and forcing a limited or nuclear confrontation between the Soviet Union and the United States. Peking felt it had made its position clear to Moscow in early August when Mao Tse-tung and Khrushchev had met in conference.

Yet, the later Chinese versions leave the agreements reached between Moscow and Peking on the use of diplomacy and force unclear and uncertain on several points. Edgar Snow has implied that Peking's action with regard to the offshore islands was intended to obtain the islands by negotiation alone. Anna Louise Strong also has written that Peking believed it could get them "by warfare or bargaining" but without major hostilities. Dutt has concluded that the leaders in Peking at first estimated that they would win in Warsaw. The subsequent polemics exchanged between Moscow and Peking imply that there may not have been a clear and complete understanding between them on how far they could safely proceed in August and September 1958. Peking claims that Moscow declared its support only when it felt it was safe to do so, and that it was Peking which prevented the outbreak of war. Moscow, for its part, claims that it deterred war in 1958, facilitated negotiations, and saved China from aggression and nuclear attack from the United States.* These spirited exchanges between Moscow and Peking on the Taiwan crisis were undertaken first in private and later divulged in public largely in the subsequent and different context of China's desire to create a rationale for proceeding to develop its nuclear capability. To uphold that position, Peking had to claim that it did not need Soviet nuclear support in 1958 and that the Soviet guarantee was conditional and unreliable in that critical instance. In Peking's eyes, Moscow was more interested in negotiating the matter at Warsaw than in pressing the issue to a showdown in the Far East in 1958. Later Moscow wanted to discourage and prevent China's nuclear development by discrediting any such rationale. Moscow has claimed that its nuclear protection had safeguarded China in 1958 against the United States and that this protection would be perfectly adequate for all future contingencies. According to the Soviet view, Mao apparently had agreed in September 1958 that during the Taiwan crisis Soviet, rather than Chinese, production and possession of nuclear weapons was acceptable and indeed preferable. The Soviet government statement of September 21, 1963, quotes Mao as saying in September 1958 that the Chinese People's Republic "need not organize the production of such weapons, especially considering the fact that they are very costly," [14] which implies that Peking had agreed to leave the weapons in Soviet hands. Peking's attitude on nuclear power and many other matters changed after its diplomacy failed in the Taiwan crisis. Each time that Moscow has since made its claim for "staying the aggressor's hand" in the Taiwan crisis, Peking has sharply and categorically denied Moscow's assertion.

* A very useful and more detailed discussion of the nuclear aspects of the Taiwan crisis is developed in Morton Halperin's *China and the Bomb*, cited, pp. 55–62.

Whatever the Sino-Soviet arguments over the nuclear role in 1958 may have been, it seems evident that Moscow's position was considerably eased by the resumption of the Ambassadorial Talks. If the assumption is made that Peking had persuaded Moscow that the Taiwan crisis would pressure Washington into making concessions during these negotiations, then Khrushchev's letter of threats as well as Moscow's support for the Warsaw Talks had the effect of underwriting Peking's demands for virtual capitulation by Washington, provided, of course, that the blockade was successful.

The opening of the Talks and embroilment of Washington and Peking in extended negotiations saved Moscow from becoming drawn into a conflict, the terms, timing, and results of which it could not control. The Talks, bolstered by the two letters, were the safety valve and escape hatch to avoid forfeit of decision. If the military situation turned against Peking and risked all-out commitment of Soviet armed forces and nuclear weapons, the Ambassadorial Talks were available as a safety valve to reduce increasing pressures leading toward an uncontrollable crisis. When Washington had established overwhelming force vis-à-vis China in East Asia, and the choice became available in late September to escalate the hostilities by turning over nuclear weapons for Chinese Communist use, or to provide Soviet nuclearized units to break the Nationalist-American counterblockade, Moscow did not change the equilibrium of Soviet-American power or the rules of engagement, but rather reinforced the decision to resort to diplomacy by stepping out of the dispute over the offshore islands and Taiwan.

The conclusion must remain, until other evidence is available, that the Ambassadorial Talks had a useful and perhaps even vital effect on the control of this crisis insofar as Moscow and Washington were concerned. Each viewed the Talks in a different way but both were anxious to resolve the crisis by diplomacy and without recourse to war, even though both used the threat of force to assure a diplomatic and limited objective.

It is hard to establish the effect of Moscow's threat to use force on the final outcome. Some have suggested that it had a major influence in abating the crisis, while others have maintained that the danger had receded by the time Moscow served notice on Washington. Certainly it is true that Khrushchev's letter of September 7 came after Dulles and Chou En-lai had found a political way out of the crisis through diplomacy. However, Moscow's risk in its warning to Washington and commitment to Peking was more substantial on September 7 than on September 19. At the time of the first letter there was no certainty of retreat, avoidance of hostilities, and relief from crisis. In fact, the military confrontation around Quemoy remained critically in Peking's favor. The blockade was well on its way to success. Washington had massed impressive military might in the area and showed unmistakable willingness to use nuclear weapons if necessary. The first Soviet letter preceded these military developments. It should not, therefore, be suggested that Moscow's diplomatic actions came "after the peak of the danger had already been passed" in early September, or that Moscow's initiatives came when there was comparatively little danger of attack on the Chinese People's Republic, or that Khrushchev's statements, firmer and tougher than earlier Soviet broadcasts, played little part in the solution of the crisis.

It would be more correct to recognize that the first Soviet letter had a dual purpose. It strongly warned Washington not to attack mainland China by airborne bombardment or with nuclear weapons to neutralize Peking's artillery positions. It also may have had the effect of persuading Peking to conduct negotiations with Washington in such a way that the crisis would be resolved without limited or general war. In other words, the Soviet Union had an escape route at Warsaw, but its threat to use force and the influence of its diplomacy were designed to persuade Peking and Washington not to use force and instead to exhaust the possibilities of diplomacy. Moscow took the chance that Washington would hold back its forces and that Peking would unleash its diplomacy. But the danger was a very real one.

As John R. Thomas has so rightly noted in his excellent study of Soviet reaction in this crisis,[15] and as others have pointed out, Moscow spoke softly, carefully, infrequently, and unofficially before September 6—at the time of greatest danger from military miscalculations by Peking or Washington and when there existed no diplomatic alternative. As it became clear that the Chinese People's Republic would not be able to seize the islands by interdiction, and that the United States would not have to introduce armed forces other than convoys outside the three-mile limit, the prospects decreased that the Soviet Union would have to implement its threat. If Moscow did indeed urge moderation on Peking during the crucial period of September 4 to September 6 when Chou En-lai agreed to the resumption of the Talks, the increasingly menacing stance of Moscow thereafter must have been designed to assure the renewal of the Talks. This cautious behavior for controlling and even resolving a dangerous conflict presumably reflected Moscow's desire not to challenge the United States in a head-on military collision over the issue of the offshore islands and Taiwan. The leadership in Moscow wished to set limits to the use of force by the Soviet Union, the Chinese People's Republic, and the United States. With the decision to reopen the Talks confirmed by September 7, Moscow extended a pledge of all-out support against the United States and the Chinese Nationalists. After the first two Talks and the American build-up, Moscow limited its guarantee of September 19 to conditional nuclear retaliation against United States forces. When Khrushchev sent his uncommonly intemperate letter to Eisenhower, the Nationalist convoys had already begun a successful pattern of breaching the blockade. The violence of Khrushchev's tirade increased as the risks decreased. Moreover, as a bargaining position was being developed by both parties in and out of Warsaw in late September, Moscow muted its apparent nuclear support for defending the mainland, subdued its attention to the crisis, and sought to disengage itself from the situation.

The critical point of decision for Moscow and Peking arose when it became clear that the massing of American military force and the combined American-Chinese Nationalist techniques for breaking the blockade were succeeding. Toward the end of September or the first two or three days of October the issue for Peking and Moscow probably was whether or not to escalate the military confrontation in order to save the blockade. That would have meant using greater elements of Chinese Communist forces and probably nuclear weapons against American forces and the heavy guns on Quemoy, as well as the Nationalist supply ships and the American convoys. The Soviet Union evidently rejected this option, insisted on resort to diplomacy and then tried to extricate itself from embroilment over the islands and Taiwan. Mao was willing to challenge Dulles; Khrushchev apparently was not.

These limitations on the use of force, the question of nuclear weapons for China, and the capitalization on the Ambassadorial Talks to avoid a war even at the cost of defeat for Peking appear to have intensified the growing embitterment between Peking and Moscow. There are still important gaps in our knowledge and understanding of the exact role of the Talks in the triangular relationship at the time. If the Talks were a safety valve for Moscow, they also put pressure on Peking, and certainly reinforced Peking's bargaining position. For the first part of the crisis Peking and Moscow were probably working in harmony, but only for a short time.

It was after the first five Talks, the American build-up, and American readiness to use nuclear force, if necessary, that Moscow and Peking seem to have diverged. The Taiwan crisis in both its military and diplomatic aspects left "much ill feeling on both sides," as Professor Zagoria has stated, and "looms as a major factor in the current Sino-Soviet dispute," as Mr. Thomas put it in 1962.[16] And the existence of the Ambassadorial Talks played a part, even if a small one, in this crucial development of our time. In view of President Eisenhower's reference to United States negotiations over the islands for "removing the thorn in the side of peace," it is ironic, if coincidental, that Khrushchev later told the Chinese Communists that "one sometimes has to live not among fragrant roses but admidst thorns," meaning Taiwan among other places. He told Peking in October 1959, in effect, to live with the situation for a long time. Peking felt differently. It can be conjectured, as Edgar Snow does, that Moscow's refusal to stand resolutely by Peking with regard to the Taiwan Straits and to commit nuclear weapons, and its preference for diplomatic solutions to differences between Peking and Washington led Mao and his colleagues to conclude that the Soviet leadership was unreliable as well as corrupt in Marxist-Leninist terms. If Peking could not count on Moscow to go the whole length in helping it regain part of its national "territory," then the relationship was scarred if not doomed from that time on.[17] Had there been no diplomatic option available for Moscow, it might have been easier for Peking to have extracted more unequivocal Soviet support on the grounds that military acton was the only option and therefore the single correct course. The Talks, however, provided an opportunity for Moscow in 1958, 1959, and ever since, to urge a political solution to the Taiwan question which in turn has become anathema to Peking.

Diplomats Without Diplomacy

If diplomacy is defined as the management of relations between states, it can fairly be said that, since the deadlock following the

Taiwan crisis, the two diplomats meeting occasionally in Warsaw have not engaged in diplomacy.

By late spring of 1959, Washington—as well as Moscow—had apparently concluded that Peking had assumed an uncompromising posture regarding major issues of principle. Just as Moscow apparently had decided to change its relations with Peking, the United States had also come to the conclusion that there was little to be gained or expected from the Ambassadorial Talks with regard to any diplomatic agreement on Taiwan and the nonuse of force in that area. After 89 Ambassadorial Talks, including the 89th, at which the United States took a new initiative, Assistant Secretary Walter Robertson described the status of these Talks as they had continued in the aftermath of the Taiwan crisis:

In the 89 Ambassadorial Talks which are still continuing, we have attempted to negotiate with the Chinese Communists on various issues envenoming our relations. They have shown no disposition whatever to settle these issues. Instead they have consistently taken an intransigent all or nothing stand. They have rejected every formula we have proposed to reduce tension in the Taiwan Strait. It is their position that the issue is non-negotiable except on their terms: that the United States get out of Taiwan. They have made it clear that they will accept no solution for Taiwan other than Communist possession of it. . . . What the Peking regime is interested in is capitulation to its demands, not negotiations.[18]

While this statement reflects the strong reaction of a high official very much involved at the time in such negotiations, it does convey the fact that during the previous sixteen meetings, i.e., since the Taiwan crisis erupted and the Ambassadorial Talks were resumed on September 15, there had been no real negotiation between the two parties.

Complete acceptance of its position was all Peking would settle for; it has continued to hold that position ever since. Washington's efforts to find ways of reducing the tensions in the Taiwan Straits have met with intransigence. There has been no real negotiation since the ten Talks on the Taiwan crisis. Nevertheless, during 1959–61 a new Secretary of State and then a new President tried to relax positions and loosen communications between Washington and Peking, but without any success.

PART IV

Washington's Initiatives Rejected

CHAPTER NINE

Washington Initiatives in 1959-61

During these two years the Ambassadorial Talks changed tone and shifted terms. Reversing themselves, the Americans now took the initiative to try to negotiate new contacts and improve relations, while the Chinese rebuffed these approaches. The frustrations of the previous years of Talks contributed to a deadlock and perpetuation of a total impasse. Dealings between Washington and Peking also became entangled in the evolving Sino-Soviet rift. The impasse at Warsaw inclined the Americans to break the deadlock and the Chinese Communists to keep it.

The First American Initiative

In May 1959, the United States decided to seek agreements with Peking, particularly on an exchange of newsmen, despite the sharpening antagonisms and divergence between Peking and Moscow, the singular obsession of Peking to retrieve Taiwan, and the hardening hostility of the Chinese Communists at Warsaw. In the spring of 1959, after Mr. Dulles had left the State Department because of his fatal illness and Christian Herter had become Secretary of State, Washington began its attempt to revive negotiations in the Ambassadorial Talks. It was felt that the previous American position had been too rigid, and that given the evolving political situation in the world, the United States should take the political and psychological initiative at Warsaw on the issue of newsmen. Consequently, one of Herter's first acts as Secretary of State was to challenge Peking publicly to let American newsmen go to China and Chinese Communist newsmen come to the United States, thus reversing the previous positions of Washington and Peking on this issue.

On April 23, 1959, the State Department announced in a press release that it would extend for another year the validation of the passports of some thirty-three American newsmen to go to Communist China. The announcement also stated that if any *bona fide* Chinese Communist newspaperman should apply for a visa, the Secretary of State would consider recommending to the Attorney-General a waiver under the law so that a visa could be granted. The statement went on to reiterate that United States law did not permit the Department to do what Communist China had demanded; namely, to agree in advance to an equal number of Chinese Communist newsmen even before their identity was known.[1]

Nevertheless, at the 89th meeting on May 19, 1959, Ambassador Beam apparently was not able to make any headway on the exchange of correspondents or on a renunciation of force.[2] The Chinese reiterated their demand for United States withdrawal from Taiwan. A *London Times* editorial commented that the "delegates who had marched in by different entrances to the hut at Panmunjom in Korea had set a pattern in the stiff relations between the United States and China."[3] At the very same time, the Department issued passports to former Governor W. Averell Harriman, as a correspondent, and to Vincent Sheean, the writer, valid for travel to mainland China, but Peking refused them visas.[4]

During four more meetings in 1959, the issue of newsmen came up and Ambassador Beam pressed Ambassador Wang for his government's agreement. Toward the end of 1959, on November 12, when Secretary Herter was asked at a press conference if he favored an exchange of journalists between the two countries, he answered: "We have been trying to advance that very objective for some two years now without any success whatsoever."[5] The United States informed Peking in general terms at the Ambassadorial Talks from the 89th to the 98th sessions that it would make explicit its willingness to admit Chinese Communist correspondents.

The terms of the April announcement presumably were amplified for Ambassador Wang in detail. If a Chinese Communist correspondent applied for a visa, the Department of State was prepared to consider making a recommendation of waiver to the Department of Justice so that the visa would, in fact, be granted. The Americans were virtually saying that the visa would be granted and that the matter of waiver was procedural and not substantive. Nevertheless,

Ambassador Wang, on behalf of his government, appears to have continued in these meetings to demand an unconditional reciprocity in the numbers and handling of newsmen and to reject Washington's stipulations even when they were explained. Peking did not like treatment by waiver. Ambassador Wang objected to the American position on the constitutional qualifications and legal requirements regarding visas. Thus, he parried Ambassador Beam by insisting on the removal of conditions, stipulations, and qualifications of any kind. And, of course, Ambassador Wang never weakened in his insistence on United States withdrawal from Taiwan.

The Sino-Soviet Rift

Meanwhile, Peking and Moscow proceeded from their initial difference on tactical emphasis over Taiwan in 1958 to a critical rift on strategy in October 1959 when Khrushchev visited Peking. The Americans, unsuspecting of the extent or even the existence of the split, were trying to develop negotiations, contacts and agreements with Peking. Khrushchev's significant visit followed several historic events. In 1959 Peking attacked Tibet and hardened its attitude toward India and Laos. Then Moscow dealt a severe blow to Peking by renouncing its secret agreement to help China develop a nuclear military capability. Moscow publicly declared its neutrality in the Sino-Indian dispute without consulting Peking in advance and subsequently gave military aid to India. Peking kept the Taiwan situation near a boiling point throughout 1959. Khrushchev's visit to the United States and the understanding he reached with President Eisenhower in the "Camp David spirit," that international questions should be settled by peaceful means through negotiation and not by force, was a major landmark in Soviet-American relations.

Following his talks with President Eisenhower, Khruschev immediately flew to Peking for the Tenth Anniversary of the founding of the Chinese People's Republic where he repeatedly counseled his Chinese comrades in public and in private against the use of force—and privately applied his admonitions specifically to Taiwan. We now know that he urged Mao, Chou, and other leaders in Peking to do the very things which the Americans were urging at the Ambassadorial Talks: that is, not to resort to force over Taiwan, to renounce force by agreement in that context, and to settle that outstanding international question by negotiation. In a public speech at a banquet in his honor on September 30, 1959, Khrushchev disclosed to the Chinese Communists his impression that President Eisenhower and his supporters recognized the need to relax international tensions. Consequently, Krushchev declared that "we must . . . do everything on our part to exclude war as a means of deciding controversial questions; these questions must be resolved through negotiations." Claiming that "we have no need of war at all," he admonished his highly-placed, powerful listeners not to "test the stability of a capitalist system by force," and reminded them that Marxists "condemn wars that are predatory and imperialistic," recognizing only "wars of liberation, wars that are just." [6]

The leaders in Peking expressed shock at Khrushchev's "absurd view," and their subsequent hardened position at Warsaw with regard to Taiwan may well have been caused by Khrushchev's position. According to the Chinese version, he privately told them that the question of Taiwan was an "incendiary factor" in the international situation, creating an atmosphere of an "imminent great war." The Soviet government sought those conditions which would ease international tensions and eliminate war, recognizing that there was always more than one way to solve every complicated question. Chinese sources state that Khrushchev cited Lenin's "temporary concession and sacrifice" in recognizing the anti-Soviet Far East Republic in Siberia during the Russian Revolution.[7] In his public speech upon his departure, Khrushchev did remark that "we Communists of the Soviet Union [thus excluding the Chinese Communists] consider it our sacred duty, our primary task . . . to utilize all possibilities in order to liquidate the cold war." [8]

Peking leaders and the Peking press gave the Soviet Chairman the silent, cool treatment when he arrived, while he spoke, and as he departed. Mao did not meet him at the airport or see him off. No joint communiqué appeared on the visit—unusual in modern diplomacy and curious for the customarily verbose Communists. The Chinese deleted his admonitions for negotiation and against war in the Chinese language texts of his speeches. In stark contrast, Chinese pronouncements were militaristic and belligerent, proclaiming that no foreign country would be allowed to interfere with Peking's "liberation of Taiwan." Nothing was then said publicly about the Soviet "revision" of Peking's policies toward force and its renunciation, or Taiwan. But the "revision" must have echoed the soundings which

Peking had apparently heard a year before when the Soviet Union declared its intention not to interfere in China's civil war or internal affairs just as Ambassador Wang was denouncing the "Two Chinas" plot at Warsaw. Later, in revealing Khrushchev's statements on Taiwan, Peking declared that it had believed he was asking China to agree to the United States "scheme" of creating "Two Chinas." In rebutting Khrushchev and rejecting his "absurd view," the Chinese leaders also claimed that Khrushchev had made a "series of speeches" accusing China of "craving war like a cock for a fight." Soviet leaders have explained this significant episode by denying the Chinese charges and saying that they had sought only a peaceful resolution to, not a forcible seizure of, Taiwan.

This historical indication of Sino-Soviet divergence is mentioned here in connection with the Ambassadorial Talks and Washington–Peking negotiations because it apparently affected them somewhat. Peking obviously began to resist what it considered to be a *de facto* understanding between Moscow and Washington on any joint or parallel moves toward "Two Chinas" or toward indefinite acceptance of the *status quo* of Taiwan and the offshore islands.[9] It is easier now than it was then to understand Peking's ever greater intransigence and obsession over Taiwan after 1958.

Aware of some of this growing *contretemps* in Peking, the Under Secretary of State, Douglas Dillon, used a major speech in early October to probe the Sino-Soviet position with regard to Taiwan and the Warsaw Talks. In commenting on Peking's rejection of Khrushchev's position on the renunciation of force, he recalled that the United States in 1958 had welcomed Chou En-lai's efforts to resume bilateral Ambassadorial Talks and had hoped that an acceptable cease-fire would be arranged. Mr. Dillon went on to describe the status of the Talks in 1959 at the time of Khrushchev's visit to Peking and after nearly twenty meetings of the two Ambassadors since September 15, 1958:

The Peiping regime has demonstrated absolutely no disposition to make the slightest move toward an agreement on a cease-fire or a renunciation of force. Its recalcitrance at the negotiating table has been maintained since the talks were resumed at Warsaw more than a full year ago.[10]

He expressed the hope that the Chinese Communist authorities would heed the advice of the Soviet Union and adhere to Chairman Khrushchev's proposition that differences must be settled by negotiation, not by force. He also repeated the American warning that an attempt to seize Taiwan and the offshore islands was just as likely to embroil the world community in total war as the launching of any other type of war. "There can be no exceptions in the matter of peaceful settlements of disputes," he warned. He attached at least partial responsibility to Moscow for guaranteeing the peaceful conduct of Peking, a role which Moscow evidently did not relish for reasons which are now known but of which the State Department was probably then unaware.* In any event, Washington's efforts in Warsaw were futile. Two months later, the two-hour meeting of the Ambassadors on December 8, 1959, brought the two sides no nearer to any agreement.

In view of all these related developments it is logical to assume that sometime in late 1959 or early 1960 Peking reassessed its position vis-à-vis Moscow and Washington and decided as a matter of strategy to put *struggle* for the "international proletarian movement" first and *negotiation* with "imperialism" second on the Communist agenda. The issue of negotiations *per se* with Washington, which included the Warsaw Talks, became embroiled in bitter, violent, and secret controversy in the Communist world. While the Americans were pressing even harder in 1960 for agreements with Peking, the Chinese Communists were rebuffing the Russians on their version of peaceful coexistence and negotiations related to war, peace and nuclear arms. This study is not the place to repeat or analyze this development, which has been described so ably elsewhere. But we should note that the issue of negotiations with "U.S. imperialism" and the related contentions with Moscow came to affect the Chinese attitude toward the Ambassadorial Talks in 1960–61.

In January 1960, Peking publicly, and for the first time, rejected Moscow's position on disarmament as a basis for negotiations. The 95th meeting in Warsaw on January 19 made no headway on the issues of prisoners, renunciation of force, newsmen, or Taiwan. In February, at the end of the Warsaw Pact meeting in Moscow, the Chinese Communists declared that President Eisenhower's State of the Union Message proved that the United States was preparing "new tricks" to gain what it had failed to get by "old tricks," that

---

* In fact, Khrushchev sent President Eisenhower a letter on October 21 which denied any such responsibility and declared that the Taiwan issue was an internal one for the Chinese to settle. This may have meant just what he told Mao—the U.S.S.R. did not favor force or war concerning Taiwan.

its "imperialist nature" would not change, and that American imperialism remained the "arch enemy of world peace." [11] The 96th meeting in Warsaw in February seemed to confirm Peking's lack of interest in any relaxation of tensions and its increasingly hardening line.

The Hardening Line

In March 1960, Peking suddenly threw a new and serious obstacle into the conduct of the Ambassadorial Talks when it indicted and imprisoned Catholic Bishop James Edward Walsh for "espionage." He had lived in China for years. Earlier, he had been invited to leave but had refused, had been held incommunicado for seventeen months and then imprisoned. At the meeting of March 22, Ambassador Beam strongly protested this "inexcusable act," charging the Chinese People's Republic with "complete indifference to humanitarian principles," with "callous disregard" for the universally accepted standards of international law and behavior among civilized nations in refusing to give any details about the Bishop's health or the charges against him despite repeated requests in Warsaw for a year and a half.[12] Ambassador Wang apparently tried to defend his government's sudden move, but the attempt seemed lame. Washington was profoundly provoked and the Ambassadorial Talks were severely jolted.

The incident raised the question for Washington whether there was really any usefulness in continuing the Talks. It was noted that 96 meetings had produced no meaningful agreements other than the initial one on repatriation. American officials pointed out that Washington had failed in its efforts at Warsaw to persuade Peking to give up the use of force, to release all Americans as provided in the 1955 Agreement, and to accept the admission of American newsmen into China. Washington did concede that the channel at Warsaw had produced arrangements for mail and packages to be delivered to the prisoners. And ultimately, American officials hoped, some kind of link with Peking might be useful. Nevertheless, Peking ignored the protest and let the arrest stand, presumably to discourage the Americans from pressing for the entry of newsmen.

Then, in April, Peking published a lengthy, defiant polemic against the Soviet Union and the United States in "Long Live Leninism," which has become the first major declaration of ideological opposition to Moscow's theses of coexistence, relaxation of tensions, negotiations, and avoidance of war. Peking declared that "wars of one kind or another always occur" until the imperialist system and the exploiting classes come to an end, and denounced the Russian leaders for "doing their utmost to camouflage U.S. imperialist policies of aggression and war, and to present imperialism and Eisenhower, the chieftain of U.S. imperialism, in favorable light." None of the new techniques of atomic energy or "rocketry" had changed Lenin's analysis of imperialism and the proletarian revolution in the least, according to Peking. "On the debris of a dead imperialism, the victorious people would create very swiftly a civilization thousands of times higher than the capitalist system and a truly beautiful future for themselves." [13]

In May 1960, Chou En-lai virtually killed any chance still remaining to negotiate an exchange of newsmen when he publicly announced in a visit to Nepal that both sides must first sign an unconditional and reciprocal agreement, something the Americans at Warsaw had been saying was literally impossible on constitutional grounds and over which they had been attempting to arrive at a compromise in a mutually satisfactory way.[14] But at least Peking was talking in terms of negotiation. Then the 97th meeting scheduled for May 16, the day the Summit Talks in Paris collapsed so dramatically over the U-2 incident in the Soviet Union, was postponed at Ambassador Wang's request until June 7. On June 5 Chou En-lai denounced "United States aggression" in strong language.[15]

Nevertheless, Ambassador Beam tried a new approach to the issue of newsmen. At the 98th meeting of the Ambassadorial Talks on June 7, the two Ambassadors held a two-hour discussion devoting much of it to the issue of newsmen, which Ambassador Beam had intended to take up in May and had had to defer because of the postponed meeting.[16] Ambassador Beam strongly urged that an exchange of newsmen would help each country learn about the other and relax tensions. He proposed that he and Ambassador Wang issue parallel individual and simultaneous agreed announcements, coordinated by both governments, on the admission of newsmen into the two respective countries. Similar in form to the one of September 10, 1955, on repatriation and the unagreed proposals on renunciation of force, the announcements would have been a simple understanding by which the two governments would agree to accept each other's newsmen on a basis of equality and reciprocity. Ambassador Beam also proposed that the United States version of this announcement would contain the following explicit statement of the position which the United States had held since August 1957:

The government of the United States of America, subject to the Constitution and applicable laws and regulations in force in the United States and in accordance with the principles of equality and reciprocity, will admit to the United States newsmen of the People's Republic of China in order to permit direct reporting about conditions in the United States. Newsmen of the People's Republic of China who are admitted to the United States will be accorded the same facilities for news reporting as are generally accorded newsmen from foreign countries in the United States.

Peking neither responded immediately at Warsaw to this proposal nor referred to it at the 99th meeting over a month later.

During June, Peking's representatives took an uncompromising stand at several secret Communist meetings. In Peking, at the annual session of the World Federation of Trade Unions, the Chinese representative repeated Peking's thesis that interest in serious and business-like negotiations with the West was naive, war was inevitable under imperialism, "war maniacs" remained, and opposing local wars should not be dismissed indiscriminately. In secret sessions he ridiculed "summit meetings" and demanded that priority be given to the struggles of the peoples, stating: "To win world peace, the struggle of the world's peoples and diplomatic negotiations carried out by the Socialist countries should go hand in hand." At the Rumanian Party Congress in Bucharest two weeks later, the Chinese delegate charged that "U.S. imperialism is the arch enemy of world peace," whose "aggressive and predatory" nature will never change, while Khrushchev violently attacked the Chinese leadership. The Soviets and most Communist participants apparently rejected the Chinese "aversion to negotiations." [17]

During the ensuing summer months events moved in diverging directions. Moscow abruptly terminated its aid to China but continued to seek a détente with Washington despite the collapse of the Summit Meeting. Senator John F. Kennedy urged a flexible readiness for revision of China policy, called for improved communication with Peking, and suggested that Communist China be included in a Test-Ban Treaty. American opinion, particularly among the Democrats, seemed to be moving slightly toward moderating hostility to China. Nevertheless, Peking increasingly stressed its "Hate the United States" theme and took a very hard public line against Washington. For the most part, Peking ignored the thaw in the United States. In preparing for the all-important conference of Communist parties to be held in Moscow in November 1960, the Chinese Communists secretly pushed their position for struggle and against negotiations, apparently objecting to the idea of Moscow and the majority of Communist parties that it was possible and desirable to prevent a third World War and to negotiate with the "imperialists." But, perhaps in an effort to counter the growing opposition on all sides to Peking's intransigence, Chou, at a Swiss reception in Peking on August 1, suggested a "peace pact" in the Pacific that would include the United States. However, it was a conditional gesture, not a proposal.

Peking's Formal Stalemate and Reversal of Position

In the late summer of 1960 the government of the Chinese People's Republic formalized its new position on opposing negotiations with the Americans and determined that no "minor or subsidiary issues" could hence forth be discussed or settled at Warsaw until the primary issue of Taiwan was disposed of. This was, of course, a complete reversal of its original position held during the first two years of the Ambassadorial Talks that negotiation and agreement on subsidiary issues would make it easier to come to an understanding on matters of principle. Peking apparently indicated its opposition to any negotiation except over the Taiwan issue for the first time on August 30, 1960, in a private interview with Edgar Snow, the contents of which were not immediately conveyed to the State Department. Presumably Washington had no way of knowing that a major shift in Peking's position was under way.

Chou En-lai then told Mr. Snow that a pact of mutual nonaggression among the countries of Asia and those bordering on the Pacific could not be concluded without diplomatic relations between China and the United States, and that such relations were inconceivable "without a settlement of the dispute between the two countries in the Taiwan region." [18] He noted that the Ambassadorial Talks had been going on for five years and that the Chinese government had first proposed that the Taiwan dispute and all disputes should be settled through peaceful negotiations, not by a resort to the use or threat of force.* After reiterating the standard Peking position that, concerning Taiwan, the dispute between China and the United States was an international question whereas military action between the Chinese People's Republic and the Republic of China was an internal question (meaning that the use of force to conquer Taiwan was a sovereign and autonomous Chinese Communist right), Chou En-lai went on to suggest that parallel talks and solutions could be reached separately between Peking and Washington on the one hand and Peking and Taipei on the other.

Then he explicitly laid down the fundamental and continuing stipulation in Peking-Washington relations before it was officially put to the Americans at Warsaw:

In the talks between China and the United States agreement on principle must after all be reached first before concrete issues can be settled. The two points of principle on which agreement should be reached are:

(1) All disputes between China and the United States, including the dispute between the two countries in the Taiwan region, should be settled through peaceful negotiations, without resorting to the use or threat of force; and

(2) The United States must agree to withdraw its armed forces from Taiwan and the Taiwan Straits. As to the specific steps on when and how to withdraw, they are matters for subsequent discussion. If the United States Government ceases to pursue the policy of aggression against China and of resorting to threats of force, this is the only logical conclusion which can be drawn.[19]

When Mr. Snow asked Chou whether these two principles had been discussed at any length in the Ambassadorial Talks, the Prime Minister replied that the first principle was put forward by Peking at the end of 1955 and the second principle in the autumn of 1958. When asked whether the second principle included the questions of the timing and manner of American withdrawal from Taiwan, Chou would only answer that the United States government must agree on the principle of withdrawal first before such concrete matters could be taken up. When Mr. Snow later tried to draw from Chou a formula for the neutralizaton of Taiwan, a Pacific nonaggression pact, disengagement in Korea and Vietnam, China's admission to the United Nations, and Sino-American diplomatic relations, Chou answered that "such questions would belong in the realm of diplomacy, once principles were agreed upon." Chou also told the British journalist, Felix Greene, at this same time, that no improve-

---

* Already referred to in Chapter 4.

ment in relations between China and the United States could come about unless there was a settlement of the Taiwan issue.[20]

Peking then shifted its stance at Warsaw. The 100th meeting on September 6, 1960, was an historic occasion in the twelve-year history of the Talks, for it marked their transition from the diplomacy of negotiation to that of stalemate. That day was the dividing point. Three months after the American initiative in presenting a draft agreement on newsmen and after substantial solidification of Peking's position in the Sino-Soviet cleavage, Ambassador Wang at this 100th meeting locked the window on further negotiations at Warsaw except on capitulatory terms for Washington. He specifically rejected the American draft of June 7 on an exchange of newsmen, refused to agree to issue a simple parallel statement, and substituted a Chinese counterproposal. He first objected to the phrase in the American proposal that the United States admit Chinese Communist journalists "subject to the Constitution and applicable laws and regulations in force," even though it was clear that the Chinese Communists were expected to make a parallel qualification which would have rendered both releases identical and reciprocal in form and substance. He then proposed the following joint announcement on the exchange of newsmen, which in effect foreclosed any further transaction at Warsaw until Washington accepted this draft in its totality:

In order to seek to eliminate estrangement between the Chinese and American peoples, to make a preliminary improvement in the present relations between the two countries, and furthermore to impel the two countries to settle peacefully in accordance with the five principles of mutual respect for sovereignty and territorial integrity, mutual non-aggression, non-interference in each other's internal affairs, equality and mutual benefit and peaceful coexistence, the question of withdrawal of all U.S. armed forces from China's territory of Taiwan and the Taiwan Strait area, the governments of the two countries have agreed on the following provisons to enable correspondents of each country to enter the other for news coverage on an equal and reciprocal basis.

1. The two governments agree that correspondents of their own countries who desire to enter the other country for press coverage must apply to the government of the other country for approval, and that the number of correspondents of the other side whose entry is approved by the two governments must be equal each time.

2. The two governments agree that neither of them will obstruct the entry of approved correspondents of the other side by any laws and regulations now in force or promulgated in the future.

3. The two governments agree that correspondents of the other side whose entry has been approved will enjoy the same facilities for news

coverage as enjoyed by correspondents of their own countries in the other country.

4. The two governments guarantee that correspondents of their own countries entering the other country for news coverage will not engage in activities contrary to the aims mentioned in the preamble of the present agreement.[21]

Ambassador Wang presumably explained the "reasonableness" of his government's new proposal and called on Ambassador Beam to accept it.

However, Ambassador Beam immediately rejected it, apparently on the grounds that it deliberately entangled the exchange of newsmen in so many unacceptable conditions and stipulations. Acceptance of the Chinese draft would have automatically meant United States acceptance in principle of Peking's claim to Taiwan. The United States would have had to set aside its laws and regulations if any of those would have barred a newsman selected by the Peking government. The proposal would have required the United States to guarantee the professional conduct of American correspondents. Contrary to constitutional prohibitions and requirements placed on the government with respect to freedom of the press, it would have linked the admission of American correspondents to political conditions and concessions unilaterally imposed upon and undertaken by the United States. Paragraph 4 of the Chinese counterproposal would have seriously limited the normal and legitimate freedom of the press to report. In addition, the counterproposal would have required the executive branch to ignore the Constitution and the Congress and act contrary to the laws of the land by agreeing in advance to accept any Chinese newsman selected by Peking to come to the United States for purposes of reporting. While instantly rebuffing Ambassador Wang, Ambassador Beam apparently urged that the other side reconsider his reasonable proposal of the previous June.

Following this historic dividing point five years after the first and only agreement, the State Department took the public initiative to issue extensive comment on the impasse. A long press release of September 8, containing the text of Peking's and Washington's proposals and the reasons for Ambassador Beam's instant rejection of the Chinese counterproposal on September 6, concluded reluctantly: "The rejection of Ambassador Beam's proposal follows the similar rejection by the Chinese Communists of every other initiative of the United States Government designed to make possible an exchange of newsmen." In the State Department's view, Peking had no "serious interest" either in reporting by its own newsmen from the United States or reporting by American newsmen from the Chinese mainland, and Peking opposed a reciprocal exchange of newsmen in view of the fact that it had rejected Washington's proposal and put forward "a totally unacceptable counterproposal." Nevertheless, the Department stated that it would continue to press for a satisfactory solution. Likewise, on September 8, Secretary of State Herter, in commenting on this impasse in an important policy speech on world developments, noted that Peking was "seeking to use the admission of American correspondents to extract political concessions," and conjectured that the Chinese Communists were afraid of objective reporting, "which we believe would be helpful," and probably wished to hide unfavorable internal developments in the Chinese economy and its system of communes. He nevertheless hoped that in due course a reciprocal and equal admission of newsmen into both countries could be arranged.[23]

Peking's preamble in its counterproposal was manifestly objectionable and unacceptable to Washington. It must have been inserted to frustrate any further negotiations in view of the obvious intention of the Americans in the Ambassadorial Talks, certainly made evident at the 98th meeting, to seek a narrowing of the differences and a formulation of some feasible understanding and agreement on the exchange of newsmen. Until September 1960, Peking had not yet indicated that it was totally impossible. But the Chinese counterproposal on the newsmen and their rejection of the simple American draft were totally inconsistent with the public and negotiating position which Peking had taken previously before reversing its position.

On September 13 the Foreign Ministry in Peking followed up the 100th meeting with a public statement on the issue of an exchange of newsmen and the fundamental bar to subsidiary negotiations with Washington. It claimed that although the Chinese had put forward many "reasonable proposals" during the past 100 meetings of the Ambassadors, the Americans had rejected all of them. Accordingly, the Foreign Ministry declared that there was no need in the future to "waste time" again on "minor questions" inasmuch as fundamental issues should first be settled. In Peking's words:

The facts prove that so long as the United States Government still persists in its policy of hostility and aggression against China, still persists in occupying China's territory of Taiwan by armed force, and continues to scheme to create "two Chinas" all efforts made by the Chinese side for first settling the individual questions are of no avail.[24]

The Foreign Ministry's statement, however, did have to acknowledge that the American proposal had the "aim of promoting understanding between the Chinese and American peoples and improving relations between the two countries." Still, the statement ambiguously rejected the American arrangement on newsmen because of its "other motives which cannot stand the light." While the tone was more civil than polemic, Peking's declaration seemed much more final than that issued by the State Department on September 8, although both accused the other of rejecting all proposals.

At the 101st meeting, on October 18, 1960, Ambassador Wang apparently used Peking's public words to the effect that "so long as the United States Government . . . persists in occupying Chinese territory by force . . . all efforts for the settlement of other questions are of no avail and there is no need in future talks to waste time on minor questions." All the many subsequent attempts and considerable efforts by the United States to resolve the issue over newsmen have since encountered the same argument that progress on any issue will be possible only when "the principal question between the Chinese People's Republic and the United States" has been resolved through United States withdrawal of support from the Republic of China, or, more generally, when the United States has ended its "policy of hostility" toward the Chinese Communists. During this period Ambassador Wang began serving official protests at Warsaw on the Americans for alleged violations of Chinese sea and air space, which ever since have appeared regularly in the Communist press and which have been duly registered in Warsaw every time.*

A few weeks later the historic Moscow Conference of eighty-one Communist parties took place to cover the entire range of the issues which had evolved in the dispute between Moscow and Peking during the past two years. With the Warsaw Talks in a state of stalemate, the Chinese Communists were well prepared for the Moscow conclave, for they were unencumbered by any compromising negotiations with "U.S. imperialists." At the conference they argued

---

* Most of these alleged violations seem to involve American planes flying over Coral Reefs which China claims in the South China Sea between Vietnam and the Philippines.

for the position that peaceful coexistence was only a tactical move, not a general objective. The West could only be forced into making concessions and could not be cajoled, maneuvered, or negotiated into useful agreements. While the Chinese did not exclude occasional negotiations with the United States and the West for immediate tactical gains, or for the contributions to the long-range Communist strategy of liquidating imperialism, Peking evidently did not believe that even such narrow negotiations would have much value.[25] The Russians and many others disagreed. They also rejected the Chinese thesis that local wars, namely Chinese seizure of Taiwan, are probable and desirable and that even a third world conflict might benefit the "socialist camp." In these critical Communist negotiations over strategy and tactics for dealing with the United States, Peking had to compromise in the final declaration, which represented a collation of theses and postponement of divergencies. Peking could not persuade those present that the "forces of socialism" had surpassed the "forces of imperialism" during the past three years and that first priority should be given to forming a broad united front against "imperialism to oppose U.S. policies of aggression and war." [26] Reflecting this split, the 102nd Ambassadorial Meeting on December 1 resulted in a deadlock once again.

Peking's Rejection of President Kennedy

Just a few days before President Kennedy's inauguration in 1961, the Central Committee of the Communist Party of China, in a resolution on the Moscow Conference, reconfirmed the Chinese theses on the need for vigilance against both "U.S. Imperialism" and peaceful coexistence by negotiation. Peking declared itself in sharper terms than ever as the Kennedy Administration was about to take over: "The United States, the chief imperialist country of our time, being the biggest international exploiter, the world gendarme, the chief bulwark of world reaction and modern colonialism and the main force of aggression and war of our time, is the main enemy of the peoples of the whole world." [27] Peking appeared to ignore some shifts in American opinion toward China during the election. Or perhaps it would be more correct to infer that Peking was so aware of the evident movement in American attitudes and actual shift in Washington's position at Warsaw during 1959–60 that it fiercely rebuffed the new administration before the "New Frontier" even had a chance to try to pry open that "little window of diplomacy" again.

The Chinese Communist press had castigated Senator Kennedy during his election campaign and as President-elect. During the initial months of his administration when most governments followed a wait-and-see policy, the Chinese Communists defiantly slammed the door shut on the new President in a barrage of unusually personal vituperation. The Peking press and official statements constantly portrayed President Kennedy and his administration as a more dangerous form of "imperialism" than the previous Republican administration under President Eisenhower and the "arch-enemy," John Foster Dulles. Peking was bent on denying the new administration any opportunity to probe for diplomatic openings or any points of contact with the People's Republic of China. Perhaps also the reason lay in the indications during the election campaign and in the testimony of Secretary of State Rusk before the Senate Foreign Relations Committee in January that the new administration might try to liberalize relations with China, and Peking sought at the outset to nullify any such efforts before they could even get started. Available evidence indicates that Peking was constantly alert to the intentions and activities of the Kennedy administration; it is paradoxical that the controlled Peking press contained relatively unslanted news accounts of American affairs, despite its abusive treatment of President Kennedy. Likewise, Peking apparently was interested not only in maintaining the Warsaw Talks but in converting them to an effective means of sounding out Washington's intentions and communicating Peking's intentions.

Peking's suspicious and hostile attitude toward the Kennedy administration during its first months in office is confirmed in Peking's secret periodical called "Bulletin Of Activities," published by the General Political Department of the Chinese People's Liberation Army and meant "for Chinese eyes only" and not for public disclosure under any circumstances.* The Bulletin of April 25, 1961, minced no words about the Kennedy administration: it was "more reactionary, treacherous, elusive and deceitful" than Eisenhower's. Despite appearances that Kennedy was "comparatively realistic, loving peace, and desirous of relaxing the world situation," the "facts"

---

* Twenty-nine issues of this secret publication have fallen into American hands and have been issued in translation by the Hoover Institution on War, Revolution and Peace in Palo Alto.

proved to Peking that "the cards he played in Laos, Cuba, and the Congo did not show any indication of relaxation." According to this Bulletin, "Kennedy wants to walk on two legs: on the one hand to raise American technology to the highest degree of perfection in order to reduce the missile gap and on the other hand to enlarge the standing army, develop conventional weapons, and prepare actively for a limited and sublimited war." Referring to his press conference of March 8, 1961, quoted below, Peking secretly instructed its military cadres to be "very watchful of this smiling tiger which looks relaxed externally but tense internally" and called his words concerning Sino-American relations "pompous and somewhat bewildering." Consequently, Peking had concluded in the April 1961 Bulletin that "it is better to maintain a frozen relationship between China and the United States, with a continued impasse for many years." Putting the statement of policy in another way, the secret Bulletin declared that "the present situation is to stand firm against the United States and maintain a peaceful coexistence with many other countries." Professors Tang Tsou and Halperin have interpreted these internal statements of Peking's policy to mean that negotiation with the United States is transitional and a secondary question in a world-wide struggle which will bring about the end of imperialism and the prevalence of socialism. Moreover, according to their interpretation of the Bulletins, Peking regarded Taiwan as part of this world-wide struggle and could not yield to the United States in allowing it to hold Taiwan by force. In short, to take these Bulletins at face value as purely internal communications, the Chinese Communists in 1961 were in no mood to negotiate with the new administration.[28]

President Kennedy's Policy on Communist China

Any policy toward relaxation of tensions between Peking and Washington or any American effort at Warsaw toward reaching substantive agreements would thus have seemed well beyond realization when the New Frontier moved into Washington, with the zest of youthful energy, a drive for pragmatic innovation, and an air of hopeful expectation. It was thought that the new generation moving in with a strong mood for change would certainly take up the issue of relations with China. Indeed, the installation of the New Frontier in Washington led many to expect a new initiative toward Peking, particularly on an exchange of newsmen. Although immediately preoccupied with the critical issues of Cuba and Laos, it did concern itself with the Ambassadorial Talks.

John F. Kenndy began and remained throughout his presidency disturbed and baffled by Peking's instant and constant antagonism toward him and his administration.* Although willing to try, President Kennedy had little expectation of reaching an understanding with China or developing a new relationship between Washington and Peking. With that manner of calculated practicality which characterized his administration, his handling of the China Problem was both expedient and perceptive. He took up those matters which he could deal with and deferred the others. He decided to postpone any major effort to change relations with Communist China and to let that be a principal, and perhaps the principal, foreign policy issue during his second term. As he viewed the prospect of tackling the China problem in terms of presidential powers and options, he realized that any substantial redirection of American policy on China would require a more receptive Congress and a more understanding public. He was reluctant to divert presidential resources to bring about a change in policy on China during 1961–63 when domestic and other foreign policy issues had higher priority.

But President Kennedy took the long view in dealing with Communist China, knowing that he would, sometime during an eight-year period in the White House, have to take the leadership in an American rethinking and reorienting of attitudes toward the most populous country in the world. He did not regard the long-standing American policy of rigidity as "magical and permanent," according to his biographer, Theodore Sorensen. The President hoped for lessening of tensions and normalization of relations between the Chinese People's Republic and the West, preferred "good will" toward and from Peking and hoped that its "extremely belligerent attitude" would change. He believed that eventually the Chinese could be persuaded that peaceful coexistence with their neighbors would represent "the best hope for us all." Looking ahead, President

* The summary of President Kennedy's attitude and strategy regarding the China question is based primarily on *Public Papers of the Presidents of the United States: John F. Kennedy*, Vols. 1961, 1962, and 1963 (Washington: United States Government Printing Office, 1962–1964); Theodore C. Sorensen, *Kennedy* (New York: Harper & Row, 1965), pp. 665-666 and 755; and Arthur Schlesinger, Jr., *A Thousand Days* (Boston: Houghton, Mifflin, 1965), pp. 479–483 and 514. See also Roger Hilsman, *To Move a Nation* (Garden City: Doubleday and Co., 1967), chapters 22–24.

Kennedy felt that the passage of time, the change of leadership, isolation from world contacts, internal requirements, and failure of aggression would all persuade the Chinese on the mainland to amend their attitudes. For some time at least, during 1961, he did privately consider the case for seeking a major change in China policy, including United States support for a "Two China" formula in the United Nations. While he discussed this with his advisers, he did not proceed with the idea in view of the evident attitude of the government in Peking and the probable resistance he would encounter in the United States, to say nothing of other difficulties.

He focused, therefore, on the immediate specific issues in *ad hoc* dealings with Peking on the basis of expediency. Since a *modus vivendi* and a wider approach with China did not look promising during 1961–63, his China policy concentrated on the narrower and more practical problem of keeping the door ajar to the future possibility of expanded relations. His main concerns centered on Peking's belligerent attitude and nuclear potential. These, to him, were clear and immediate dangers. Accordingly, he hinted early in his administration that he would sympathetically consider an approach from Peking for American shipments of food. He was willing to undertake some degree of suitable trade with the People's Republic of China, and he decided to try to expand official and unofficial contacts. As he put it once to Sorensen: "If we could lessen their malevolence, I'd be for it."

He was deeply troubled about Chinese Communist hostile intentions in Asia and toward America. He intended to see if something could be done to allay them. On January 25, 1961, only five days after his inauguration, he noted: "There has been a rather belligerent attitude expressed toward us in recent days by the Chinese Communists, and there is no indication, direct or indirect, private or public, that they would respond favorably to any acts by the United States." [29] His first annual message to the Congress of January 30 introduced his theme of the Chinese Communist menace to Asia, which often appeared in his private remarks, public comments, and presidential actions during his three years in office. In a press conference on February 8, he predicted that the United States would be severely tested in the next four years by the belligerence which marked the Communist bloc, "particularly the Chinese Communists." His concern centered on China's use of force, view of war, and development of atomic capabilities. Therefore, he wanted to probe for any flexibility on the Communist side that might lead to a relaxation of Peking's belligerent posture and to some restraints in its nuclear developments. Without harboring any illusions, President Kennedy decided to continue the effort, at least for a while, to sound out Peking on the possibility of reaching a *modus vivendi*.

In view of all these considerations, the new President and the New Frontier decided to start with the Ambassadorial Talks in Warsaw and to take a new initiative, however depressing the prospects. Soon after his inauguration, President Kennedy was asked in a news conference what he intended to do about the five Americans still imprisoned in Communist China. He replied:

There were many conversations in Geneva as well as in Warsaw on the problem of the Americans who have been detained, some of them way back since 1951. This is a matter of continuing concern. And as long as those men are held, it will be extremely difficult to have any kind of normal relations with the Chinese Communists. There are other matters which affect those relations too. But this is certainly a point of the greatest possible concern. Now, we have asked for a delay in the meetings which take place in Warsaw, between the United States representative and that of the Chinese Communists, from February to March, because they have become merely a matter of form and nothing of substance happened. But I'm going to make it very clear that we are concerned about those men in China.[30]

During this postponement, the new administration appraised the situation and elected to resume the effort to negotiate an exchange of newsmen. The State Department sent Ralph Clough, a veteran of these Talks, to Warsaw with special instructions for Ambassador Beam to make a new start at the 103rd meeting of the Ambassadors in March in order to try "bridging the political gulf" between Washington and Peking.[31] The State Department indicated publicly that Ambassador Beam on behalf of the new administration would continue "quiet diplomacy at Warsaw," where he would raise the issues of the five remaining American prisoners and the renunciation of force, in addition to the question of newsmen.

This first encounter of the new administration in the Ambassadorial Talks drew considerable diplomatic and journalistic interest. There apparently was general hope in Washington that Peking would either respond favorably to the new initiative of President Kennedy or at least withhold its public reactions and engage in genuine negotiations in Warsaw. At the 103rd meeting on March 7, 1961, Ambassador Beam tried a new approach on the question of newsmen to circumvent the Chinese Communist refusal to discuss "minor questions." In brief, he stated that if each side selected an equal number of the other's correspondents from a list of names submitted by the other, the Chinese Communists' demands for reciprocity would be met. However, despite their strong initiative in favor of exchanges between the two countries, the Americans were as mistaken in these premature hopes as they were astounded by the sharp abruptness of the Chinese rejection of the American proposals on the release of American prisoners, exchange of newsmen, and renunciation of force. Ambassador Wang apparently read from long-familiar instructions to the effect that none of these matters could be arranged as long as the United States "occupied" China's territory of Taiwan. He left the distinct impression that Communist China was not interested in improving relations with the United States.[32] Peking thus immediately rebuffed the Kennedy initiative toward conciliation and proclaimed a policy of contention in taking a fiercely uncompromising view of the Kennedy administration in particular and the United States government in general, for reasons going far beyond the specific issues at Warsaw.

At his news conference of March 8, the day after the Warsaw meeting, President Kennedy was asked if he would comment on the latest word from Warsaw that the Chinese would not consider the admission of 32 American correspondents nor the release of American prisoners in view of the fact that there had been some hope "that if we could exchange correspondents with the Chinese that it might be a step toward more harmonious relations." President Kennedy replied:

Well, that was our hope and if they are unwilling to do that, of course that hope has been dimmed. They have been, as we know, extremely belligerent toward us, and they have been unfailing in their attacks on the United States . . . I think part of that has been because they recognize that the United States is committed . . . to maintaining its connections with other countries, committed to its own defense and the defense of freedom. But they have been extremely harsh in their attacks upon us, and I would like to see a lessening of that tension. That is our hope from the beginning. But we are not prepared to surrender in order to get a relaxation of tension.[33]

He made clear then, as he did later,* that his administration had no

* On the occasions of Vice President Johnson's visit to Taipei in May 1961, in which the author participated, and the visit to Washington in June 1961 of the Chinese Nationalist Vice President.

intention whatever of changing United States policy toward the Republic of China. On March 9 Secretary Rusk told a press conference that he was disappointed with the results of this meeting of the two Ambassadors although the general tenor of the Talks was civil.[34]

A week later Peking publicly rejected President Kennedy's initiative, demanded that the United States withdraw from Taiwan, and accused it of preventing an accord in Warsaw, while Peking's leadership intensified its personal attack on President Kennedy, Mao Tse-tung calling him even more dangerous than President Eisenhower. A Peking newspaper on April 20 labeled President Kennedy a "100 per cent imperialist gangster."[35] In this embattled atmosphere the Talks relapsed into stalemate. No real exchange in a negotiating sense was yet possible at Warsaw.

Nevertheless, the Kennedy administration continued to hope for some break in this impasse. The prospects were as disappointing as the results during the first six months of his efforts, as the President noted at a news conference on June 2, 1961.

But I will say that since long before I assumed office and in the first days of our new administration, before really any actions were taken, the attacks upon our Government and the United States were constant, immediate, and in many cases malevolent. The debate which took place last fall between the Communist parties indicated that the Chinese planned to take an extremely belligerent attitude and role towards us and those with whom we are associated. We hope that policy changes. We want good will. But it takes two to make peace, and I am hopeful that the Chinese will be persuaded that a peaceful existence with its neighbors represents the best hope for us all. We would welcome it. But I do not see evidence of it today.[36]

However, in the summer of 1961 the President became interested in the possibility of sending food and other materials such as CARE packages to China for humanitarian purposes, if Peking showed any interest. He also was tentatively prepared to develop any feasible possibility of trade in nonstrategic goods.[37]

But Peking rather defiantly kept its doors shut tight and never gave the Kennedy administration a chance to relax tensions with the Chinese people or with the Chinese People's Republic. In fact, Peking took an increasingly hostile view of President Kennedy's strategy of peace, flexible response, and military preparedness. The rejection indicates the underlying factors in Peking's long-range view: the inevitability of doom for the United States and the priority of struggle in accordance with the "national liberation" idea. These and other factors probably accounted for Peking's reversal in 1959–61 to rebuff all American initiatives to open contacts and improve relations.

*   *   *

After reviewing this record of American initiatives during 1958–61 and noting the complete reversal of Peking from following a versatile diplomacy of negotiation during 1955–57 to a rigid diplomacy of stalemate in 1960–61, the question arises as to why Peking and Washington changed sides in their diplomatic encounter. Why did the government of the Chinese People's Republic so persistently reject the new overtures and proposals of the Americans, which were similar to what Peking itself had sought so strenuously in the first period of the Ambassadorial Talks? Several hypotheses can be advanced.

Perhaps the first reason for relegating diplomatic negotiations and the Ambassadorial Talks to "second place" lay in the logic and theory of Chinese Communist ideology, which is always so important to analyze in determining their motivation and action whatever the objective situation may be. As the Sino-Soviet clash originated and spread throughout the Communist movement as a whole in 1959–61, an extensive exchange of arguments developed over the benefit, danger, and nature of negotiations *per se* with the non-Communist world, and particularly with the United States. The Chinese Communists took the position that negotiations were dangerous, of limited value, and to be subordinated to the superior interests of the "struggle of the masses" and the advance of the "international proletarian movement." It would appear inconsistent, to say the least, for the Chinese leadership to carry on serious negotiations and to exchange real concessions with the Americans at Warsaw on the one hand, while denouncing or deprecating negotiations with the "imperialists" on the other, either at Communist meetings or in their exchanges with the Communist party of the Soviet Union during the crucial period of 1950–60. As long as this major schism in the so-called Communist camp over peaceful coexistence and negotiations continued, it was probably difficult for Peking to undertake negotiations with the Americans on any subject of mutual interest unless there was a decisive and virtually unilateral benefit for the Chinese People's Republic. Obviously, Washington's concession of Taiwan would qualify for "negotiation" under these terms. And Peking carefully kept open, and publicly pointed to, the Ambassadorial Talks for that single purpose.

In the second place, conditions inside China changed substantially for the worse from 1955-57 to 1959-61, as even Peking's documentation has acknowledged. In the early period China had wanted to demonstrate its progress. But the collapse of the Great Leap Forward, with its agricultural and industrial breakdowns, widespread popular dissatisfactions resulting in thousands of refugees and many more thousands of would-be refugees, caused the Peking leadership to seal the country to almost all foreigners. At this juncture, American pressure at Warsaw for an exchange of newsmen presumably had to be blocked "resolutely," as the Chinese Communists are fond of saying. Furthermore, the American "foreign devil" in Peking's tireless tirades was essential for whipping up emotions to mobilize Communist China's huge population into the communes and to spur any "leap" at all. This convenient and indispensable symbolic stimulus would not have seemed very credible or persuasive to the Chinese populace if American newsmen were traveling about the countryside making friends with Chinese people. In this instance, the issue over the Taiwan Straits was simply an effective barrier to American visitors. The impact and personal appeal of President Kennedy for some intellectuals and young people on the mainland may have frightened the old leaders in Peking and may have made it necessary for them to blacken Kennedy's image with their scorching invective. In 1961, there was more reason than ever to shut out the Americans and the Kennedy image, while keeping the Chinese people in a new isolation, a modern "Great Within" to surpass the old imperial closure of China to foreigners.

Yet a third reason for the reversal of the Talks probably lies in the very real impasse over Taiwan. Gaining undisputed sovereignty over the offshore islands and Taiwan and preventing any sort of "Two Chinas" have become the vital, primary and all-important objectives of Peking's foreign policy in its relations with the United States and even the Soviet Union. Peking entered and conducted the Talks primarily—even exclusively—to gain that objective. All else was either incidental or instrumental to the regaining of Taiwan. Mao and Chou have used different tactics to negotiate Taiwan. In the era of the Bandung spirit and Communist China's internal progress, Chou experimented, to no avail, with some concessions and favorable conditioning in an effort to persuade President Eisenhower and Secretary Dulles to talk about Taiwan. Then Peking tried a frontal attack and belligerent diplomacy to seize the offshore islands for paving the way toward Taiwan. This tactic not only failed to get Taiwan but also substantially lessened Peking's prospects to do so. Washington tightened its hold on the area, while Moscow washed its hands of the matter. Thereafter, Peking had no alternative in the Talks but to stop the diplomatic exchange, stand its ground, and wait, however long, to change the balance of forces or the evolution of history. Warsaw had become the waiting place for cues and notices of the day when the Americans would be escorted away from Taiwan. In the meantime, and for the indefinite future, Peking, as well as Washington, could tediously maintain the small link at Warsaw and perhaps use it discreetly and advantageously only for specific notifications.

CHAPTER TEN

1961-66: Asian Crises and Nuclear Deadlock

During 1961–66, the Ambassadorial Talks changed considerably in scope and were held much less frequently. In fact, there were only twenty-seven meetings in five years. Paradoxically, however, their significance had been increased. Dispensing with any formal agenda, the two governments have talked about many matters covering a wider range than had been originally intended. Although Washington and Peking have not reached any agreements, they have conveyed a broadening range of attitudes and intentions. In an interview with *U.S. News and World Report*, published on July 4, 1966, Ambassador Gronouski summed up this important expansion on the basis of his own experience in Warsaw:

. . . over the years there have been any number of situations which have come up where it has been very useful for both the United States and Communist China to be able to get their points of view and positions across very clearly and distinctly. . . .

Just the fact that the talks are going on and that both sides obviously want them to go on—just this communication that is happening between the United States and Communist China—I think is important in itself.

They provide a forum for discussing a whole series of issues that confront both nations, in Southeast Asia particularly, but also throughout the world. The very seriousness of the situation in Southeast Asia makes these meetings even more important. We are in a position to express our point of view very clearly, so that neither side makes any mistake with respect to what attitudes and positions are on the other side.

. . . One reason why I think these talks are important is that they provide the opportunity for us to put forth, from time to time, suggestions aimed at reducing the tensions between us. And while I can't suggest that we've made great progress in this area, I'm always hopeful that having this vehicle to make these kinds of proposals and to raise these kinds of questions will one day prove fruitful.

Washington has used this two-way channel—and perhaps Peking has, too—to lessen the chances of policy miscalculation and increase the precision of policy presentation. Consequently, the Ambassadorial Talks now provide one of the prime functions of effective diplomacy: identifying and establishing the outer limits as well as the central thrust of both governments in a variety of disputed areas.

For purposes of reliable and sensitive communication, both sides must have attended conscientiously and efficiently to the mechanics and procedures of these altered Talks. The two delegations are composed of highly competent diplomats and linguists. The staffs on both sides have taken meticulous care to make exact and reliable translations and interpretations. The principals have undoubtedly dissected the phraseology, emphasis, and composition of each statement of the other side during and after every meeting to detect and catch any nuance which might indicate any shift in position, however tentative. Evidently, both sides have carefully considered and prepared their positions with high-level approval. During twenty-seven meetings there were few major official revelations of the exchange such as plagued the early phase of the Talks. Yet, enough fragments have been pieced together to suggest that during 1961–66 the issues discussed covered Laos, Taiwan, the Test-Ban Treaty, nuclear disarmament, and Vietnam.

Laos

The first subject for communication of position and intention was the crisis over Laos in 1961. The international implications were ambiguous, for the United States might have had to intervene militarily during the difficult initial stages of arranging the Geneva Conference, while Peking's position appeared uncertain and equally unpredictable. A miscalculation could have occurred. Apparently at the Ambassadorial meeting in March 1961, President Kennedy warned Peking that the United States would be compelled to intervene militarily, however unwillingly, if a cease-fire did not precede the opening of negotiations in Geneva. This message was also conveyed to Soviet officials in Moscow and Geneva.[1] Then, a few months later, according to unofficial press sources, Ambassador Wang, on Peking's instructions, informed Ambassador Beam that the government of the Chinese People's Republic was serious about wishing to negotiate an acceptable settlement for the neutralization of Laos and hoped that the United States government would cooperate in reaching a final agreement at the Geneva Conference. Peking apparently used the Ambassadorial Talks to convey directly to Washington that it did not wish to press the issue to a test of force in Laos, and to confirm its policy of supporting an international guarantee for Laotian neutrality. Since uncertainty over Peking's sincerity and intentions was a critical factor for Washington in determining its strategy regarding the Laotian question in 1961, Peking's notification at the Ambassadorial Talks in Warsaw helped to permit Washington to participate, on its part, in the difficult negotiations at Geneva. There, until the Agreement on Laos was concluded a year later, the American representatives sat at the multilateral conference table with Peking's representatives, who repeatedly denounced the United States in rather extreme language.

No bilateral discussion took place in Geneva between the Americans and the Chinese Communists, although President Kennedy urged Ambassador W. Averell Harriman, the American delegate, to develop any social or other contact with Chou En-lai and the other members of the Chinese delegation that might seem helpful. The American delegation did not directly take part in the secret negotiations involving the Chinese delegation and others outside the plenary sessions. Instead, the British and Russian delegates, as third parties, met with Chou En-lai or his deputy separately or jointly to work out difficult compromises. In fact, the men from Washington and Peking made little direct contact with each other at Geneva during 1961–62. On one occasion, when a few members of the American delegation went to a Chinese Communist reception by invitation in 1962, the hosts from Peking seemed as surprised as they were embarrassed. The Chinese Communists again avoided direct and visible contact with the Americans at Geneva just as they had in 1954 and at Panmunjom in 1953. However, they maintained a controlled and inconspicuous relation with the Americans at Warsaw.

With regard to Laos, which was the principal issue to be negotiated in 1961 and 1962, both sides seemed to prefer the formality of the relationship in Geneva and Warsaw. When President Kennedy was asked at his news conference of October 11, 1961, about his reaction to an informal suggestion made by the Chinese Communist Foreign Minister for ministerial-level talks with the United States if the latter took the initiative, the President avoided the issue by noting that the United States was already conducting conversations with the Chinese Communists over Laos at the Geneva Conference, and that there were many channels through which "any exchange of views" could take place, including the Ambassadorial Talks in Warsaw. He saw no evidence that the Chinese Communists wished to live "in comity" with the United States in the same way that the United States desired to live in friendship with all people.[2]

Taiwan

As the crisis over Laos was moving toward resolution in Geneva in 1962, the Taiwan problem again took on crisis proportions. The issue of the resort to force with regard to Taiwan confronted President Kennedy, as it had President Eisenhower, with the necessity of notifying Peking authoritatively and persuasively of the precise limits of United States policy in that area. In June of 1962 the Chinese Communists began making military preparations and deployments near the offshore islands in reaction to the Chinese Nationalist government's statement of its intention to harass or even invade the mainland to take advantage of the deteriorating conditions there. In this worsening situation, and in light of the fact that the negotiations in Geneva over Laos had reached a critical point of decision, Ambassador John Moors Cabot was instructed at Warsaw to raise the issue of Taiwan and make a statement of American intentions.

On June 23, 1962, at a special meeting, he reportedly informed Ambassador Wang that the United States would not support any attempt of the Chinese Nationalists to assault the mainland and that the United States did not associate itself with the declarations of the Chinese Nationalists to that effect.[3] The purpose of this unilateral and confidential notification in Warsaw was to prevent a Taiwan confrontation and to relieve what might have been a really exaggerated fear in Peking of imminent attack. Such a fear could have led to a serious miscalculation in Peking, resulting in an unwarranted decision to resort to force in the Taiwan Straits. The United States no doubt also carefully indicated that it was just as opposed to the use of force by the Chinese Communists as by the Chinese Nationalists, except in self-defense.

The general tenor of the American declaration on this particular crisis in Taiwan was then confirmed in public by President Kennedy at his news conference of June 27, which he opened with a prepared statement. After noting that the situation in the area of the Taiwan Straits was a "matter of serious concern" to the United States government, he stated that it was important for the American position to be clearly understood:

Our basic position has always been that we are opposed to the use of force in this area. In the earlier years President Eisenhower made repeated efforts to secure the agreement of Communist China to the mutual renunciation of the use of force in the Taiwan area, and our support for this policy continues.[4]

However, President Kennedy strongly reaffirmed his predecessor's statements that the United States would defend Taiwan and the offshore islands if necessary. He went on to reiterate the 1955 statement of Secretary Dulles that the treaty arrangements with the Republic of China "make it quite clear that it is in our mutual contemplation that force shall not be used." "The whole character of the Treaty is defensive," he emphasized.

After these public and private reaffirmations of the Kennedy administration's position on the Taiwan Straits, the crisis abated, the Chinese Communist military movements shifted, the *status quo ante* prevailed. Peking presumably did not relish another military confrontation with the United States. During the next four weeks the Geneva Conference was concluded with conciliatory statements, even from the Chinese Communist representatives. However, in regard to intrusions from Taiwan, Peking used the Ambassadorial Talks at the 114th meeting to protest the alleged violation of Chinese mainland airspace by a U-2 airplane.[5]

It is important to note that this significant discussion of the renunciation of force and the Taiwan issue in mid-1962 facilitated the even more significant exchange in 1963–64 on the nuclear problem. In 1962 at Warsaw, the Chinese representatives appear to have accused the United States of "sabotaging" general disarmament.* As a rebuttal, the Americans apparently handed over to the Chinese a United States government booklet setting forth the detailed position and proposals of Washington on disarmament.† Ambassador Cabot apparently asked for the reaction of the Chinese side after it had studied the document. This was the cue for the subsequent unique

---

* This interpretation is made retroactively from the later public comments as described in the next section of this chapter.

† *Blueprint for the Peace Race: Outline of Basic Provisions of a Treaty on General and Complete Disarmament and a Peaceful World* (Washington: United States Arms Control and Disarmament Agency, 1962).

exchange on nuclear disarmament summarized below in this chapter.

Disarmament in the Ambassadorial Talks

President Kennedy's disturbing assessment of Communist China and his profound concern over the potential proliferation of nuclear weapons brought the nuclear issue to Warsaw in 1963 and 1964 for an extensive exchange of views.* These discussions constituted the single, and perhaps the only possible, diplomatic attempt by a non-Communist government to bring the Chinese People's Republic into the test-ban association, develop disarmament discussions, and come to grips with Peking over the issue of nuclear proliferation. While the United States efforts at Warsaw failed in that regard, its initiative at least served to produce a simultaneous exchange of communications and notifications on general disarmament and nuclear diffusion in a new kind of "diplomacy by elusion" in which each party deftly tried to avoid the other's presentation. The subject of disarmament and nuclear weapons was, of course, a new topic for discussion at Warsaw, not strictly speaking on the agenda, although it fell into the open-ended category of "other practical matters of interest to the two sides" agreed on in 1955. It was taken up in Warsaw apparently for three reasons: President Kennedy's long-standing concern, the conclusion of the Test-Ban Treaty on August 5, 1963, in Moscow, and Peking's own utilization of the Warsaw channel to communicate with the United States in connection with the banning of nuclear tests and Peking's own nuclear policy.

Throughout his administration President Kennedy felt troubled more by the foreboding menace of China's potential nuclear capability than he was by the unilateral character of its leaders' hostile attacks on him personally and on the United States generally, or even by the danger of Peking's miscalculations in critical confrontations. He never had illusions about the likelihood of reaching agreements with Peking or changing its attitudes on the issues and subjects long undertaken in the Ambassadorial Talks. Nor did he anticipate any general *modus vivendi* with China. But from the outset of his administration, and particularly during his last year, he was con-

* This section, like Chapter 7 on the Ten Talks at Warsaw on the Taiwan crisis, is an interpretive, impressionistic narrative of what is likely to have occurred across the tables. It is based largely on public comments from Washington and Peking, as well as on some secondary sources.

cerned—and deeply so—about the implications of China's acquisition of a nuclear capacity.*

In late 1962, the tone of sharp antagonism toward the United States increased in Peking, particularly after the Cuban missile crisis and the Chinese Communist military involvement with India in October. Against this background, President Kennedy made some of his most comprehensive comments on the Chinese People's Republic to express his growing concern with regard to imminent developments which would make China a dangerous nuclear power. The problem, he felt, assumed greater proportions because of China's policy of struggle first and negotiations second. On December 3, 1962, he remarked to a Japanese trade delegation that, while the alliance between Western Europe and the United States barred an advance by the Soviet Union into Western Europe, there was no such assurance in the East where the "major problem" was emerging:

Our problem now, of course, is that with the rise of the Communist power in China combined with an expansionist, Stalinist philosophy, our major problem, in a sense a major problem, is how we can contain the expansion of Communism in Asia so that we do not find the Chinese moving out into a dominant position in all of Asia with its hundreds and hundreds of millions of people in Asia, while Western Europe is building a more prosperous life for themselves. . . . There are a billion people in the Communist empire operating from central lines and in a belligerent phase of their national development. So that I think this is a period of great danger for Asia. . . .[6]

A few days later he predicted to the Economic Club of New York that his successor in office would have to deal with "the problem of a China which is carrying out an expansionary policy with nuclear weapons and missiles." [7] In his famous radio and television interview of December 17, 1962, he pointed to the "constant determination" which the Chinese Communists showed in the "most militant form" to settle for nothing short of a totally Communist world, in contrast to Soviet policy, and he commented:

The combination of these two systems in conflict around the world in a nuclear age is what makes the sixties so dangerous. . . . We would be far worse off—the world would be—if the Chinese dominated the Communist movement, because they believe in war as a means of bringing about

---

* Stuart Alsop has reported that this subject troubled President Kennedy "more deeply" than any other (*Saturday Evening Post*, January 1, 1966), a fact often observed by the President's advisers and appointees, including the author.

the Communist world. . . . The Chinese Communists believe that by constantly hitting, and if war comes, a nuclear third world war, they can survive it anyway with seven hundred and fifty million people.[8]

The nuclear issue so haunted President Kennedy in 1963 that he involved the Ambassadorial Talks in it, though with little success. That was also the year of the Nuclear Test-Ban Treaty, and its negotiation was one of President Kennedy's principal objectives. One of his primary concerns in the last few months of his life was Communist China's refusal to adhere to the ban and its determination to develop nuclear capability. It was his hope to see China join in nuclear disarmament rather than engage in nuclear diffusion. However, the evidence was clear that China would explode its first nuclear device in about two years.

At a news conference on January 24, 1963, he indirectly included the People's Republic of China when he expressed the hope that many other countries would sign the Test-Ban Treaty once it was negotiated.[9] Six months later, after making a strong plea in his famous speech at the American University on June 10 for peace, the test ban, and general disarmament, he said in a news conference that failure to negotiate a treaty in 1963 would "greatly" increase the prospect that there would be additional nuclear powers in " '64, '65, or '66" and that he would regard that as a "disaster . . . [and] a highly explosive and highly dangerous situation." He noted that "it is proposed in the treaty that those who sign the treaty would use all the influence . . . in their possession to persuade others not to grasp the nuclear nettle." [10] When he addressed the nation on July 26 after Great Britain, the Soviet Union, and the United States had negotiated and initialled the Test-Ban Treaty, President Kennedy declared that "we have a great obligation . . . to use whatever time remains to prevent the spread of nuclear weapons, to persuade other countries not to test, transfer, acquire, possess, or produce such weapons." [11] In a press conference on August 1, he emphasized the importance of widespread adherence to the agreement. He specifically hoped for Peking's willingness to sign, too, though he was skeptical that it would.* "We have received no encouragement," he noted, "but we would like the Red Chinese to come into the agreement. It looks like they will not, but it would obviously be in the

---

* Chairman Khrushchev indicated to Ambassador Harriman in Moscow that the Soviet government did not expect Peking's adherence, would not undertake to seek it, and was not dissatisfied with or concerned about ignoring and excluding Peking. (See Sorensen and Schlesinger, cited.)

interests of world peace." [12] When a correspondent asked him at this same news conference to assess the power and threat of Communist China, he reiterated his deep concern, in a relatively long and candid answer, that a nuclearized, militant China would confront the world with the most difficult and menacing situation since the Second World War. He again pointed to a "great powerful force" in China, surrounded by weaker countries, and organized by the government along "Stalinist lines," not only internally but externally, and calling for international war to advance the final success of the Communist cause.

We regard that as a menacing factor. And then you introduce into that mix, nuclear weapons. As you say, it may take some years, maybe a decade, before they become a full-fledged nuclear power, but we are going to be around in the 1970's, and we would like to take some steps now which would lessen that prospect that a future President might have to deal with.[13]

As a result of his assessment, the United States strove to obtain Peking's association even with a limited test ban so as not to "find the world in as great a danger as it could be in the 1970's" from Communist China.

It was highly unlikely that Peking would have responded favorably to any "steps" to limit its nuclear development in the summer of 1963 when President Kennedy and the State Department began the task of probing and persuading at Warsaw. The intimations were that Peking had already protested officially in 1962 and 1963 to the Soviet government that it "not infringe on China's sovereign rights and act for China in assuming an obligation to refrain from manufacturing nuclear weapons," and that China "would not tolerate the conclusion, in disregard of China's opposition, of any sort of treaty between the Soviet government and the United States which aimed at depriving the Chinese people of their right to take steps to resist the nuclear threats of U.S. imperialism, and that we would issue statements to make our position known." [14] Peking did indeed declare its defiant and independent course in refusing to adhere to the treaty. During and after the negotiations in Moscow on the Test-Ban Treaty, the Chinese Communists called for total prohibition and complete destruction of all nuclear weapons and castigated the Test-Ban Treaty in violent terms, describing it as a "betrayal and capitulation," a "big fraud," a "joke peace" giving a "false sense of security."

One of the major themes running through Peking's many public diatribes against the Treaty was rejection of what Peking called "the nuclear monopoly of the nuclear powers." Peking opposed the negotiations and denounced the Treaty mainly because they were aimed at restricting non-nuclear countries, "especially the non-nuclear socialist countries from ever gaining nuclear self-defense capability." It was a "tripartite treaty . . . aimed at tying China's hands." [15] An article in the *Peking Review* of August 9 dissected President Kennedy's televised statement of July 26 and his news conference of August 1, quoting some of his remarks, and concluding that he intended by these very words to have the Treaty prevent non-nuclear "socialist countries from possessing nuclear defense capabilities" and to use "opposition to China as a bait to explore the possibility of reaching a comprehensive détente with the Soviet Union." [16] In an official statement on August 15, Peking declared that the "object of U.S. imperialism in advocating the prevention of nuclear proliferation is not all to manacle itself but to manacle socialist countries other than the Soviet Union." The statement went on to argue for nuclear proliferation in the "socialist countries," [17] allegedly because nuclear weapons in their hands would help peace. Subsequent official Chinese statements of September 1 and September 6 in the Sino-Soviet polemics hammered more on Peking's opposition to the Treaty, to "nuclear monopoly," to prevention of China's nuclear development, and to the Soviet "betrayal." [18] In fact the thrust of Peking's verbal onslaught in mid-1963 was more heavily directed against Moscow than Washington.

If the Soviet government did not try or was unable to persuade Peking to desist from testing and producing nuclear weapons, it is all the more commendable that Washington, Peking's ideological "archenemy," would even try to use its one channel of communication with Peking to attempt to reverse the direction of Peking's nuclear policy. Under President Kennedy's direction, Washington took advantage of the opportunity offered by the Talks in Warsaw to involve China in the Treaty and engage Chinese leadership in the whole question of arms control and nuclear diffusion. Once again, however, the result was stalemate.

After the Treaty was initialled on July 25, the issue evidently arose immediately in Warsaw. In an energetic campaign to sidetrack the Treaty, the Chinese Communists issued an official public statement on July 31 denouncing the Treaty and calling for "complete, total, thorough, resolute" prohibition and destruction of nuclear weapons. Copies were sent with accompanying letters to many governments making an official counterproposal. Peking took the unprecedented step of using the Ambassadorial machinery at Warsaw to communicate directly with the President of the United States on this matter. In a letter of August 2 to Ambassador Cabot, Ambassador Wang enclosed a letter from his government to President Kennedy calling for complete disarmament in substantially the same terms as its public statement of July 31.* In brief, that public statement and the private letter to President Kennedy urged all nations to agree on: (1) the destruction and prohibition of all nuclear weapons and their means of delivery or testing; (2) measures to carry that out, including the dismantling of all foreign bases and withdrawing all nuclear weapons with their means of delivery from abroad; the establishment of nuclear-weapons-free zones in Asia and the Pacific region, including the United States, the Soviet Union, China and Japan, as well as zones in Central Europe, Africa and Latin America; the refraining from exportation and importation of nuclear weapons in any form and the technical data for their manufacture; and the cessation of all nuclear tests including underground ones; and (3) the convening of a conference of all heads of government to discuss the destruction and prohibition of nuclear weapons and the implementation of the above steps. While the public statement had contained a violently polemical and propagandistic attack on the Soviet Union for joining in the Test-Ban Treaty, as well as an attack on United States "imperialism" and President Kennedy, the letter to him omitted these gratuitous remarks and mainly stressed Peking's proposals for a conference to take the above steps to bring about complete disarmament. Having received this letter to President Kennedy via the Ambassadorial channel at Warsaw, the Americans were then able to pursue the issues of Chinese Communist adherence to the Test-Ban Treaty and nuclear diffusion at the very next meeting on August 7, 1963.

The 118th meeting in Warsaw on August 7, lasting three and one-half hours, was a significant one in the history of the Talks.[19] *The New York Times* report from Warsaw noted that this particular meeting had special interest because it was the first held since the breakdown in the Moscow-Peking talks in July 1963 and the signing of the Test-Ban Treaty in Moscow on August 5. The report specu-

* Appendix D.

lated that the Chinese would outline their views on the Treaty at this meeting and that the Americans would explain their position, in addition to raising other problems. Apparently, Ambassador Wang first brought the subject up when, in presenting the full substance of the public statement and private letter, he argued for a world conference and total elimination of nuclear weapons. Ambassador Cabot had the occasion to ask Ambassador Wang to clarify what his government had meant by a complete ban on nuclear weapons. The Americans could have noted that it was inconsistent for Peking to advocate complete disarmament while calling for the mobilization of forces against "imperialism." Nevertheless, the Americans probably spelled out the general position of the United States on the stages of disarmament and the methods of control and inspection as contained in the American booklet transmitted to the Chinese side in mid-1962, as already noted. The Chinese Communist delegation apparently ignored the American presentation and probably repeated once again the contents of the letter to the United States government.

A month later, at the 119th Ambassadorial meeting on September 11, which lasted some two and one-half hours,[20] Washington again responded partially to Peking, whose total uncompromising opposition was evident by then to all. Vehement attacks on the Treaty had continually appeared in the Chinese Communist press, radio and official public statements. Instead of directly answering the Chinese draft proposal for a world-wide conference, Ambassador Cabot evidently tried to develop several approaches to have an exchange on the issues. He could have asked Peking to follow up its counter-proposal by answering specific questions on the general issue of disarmament. The Chinese Communist representatives had already received the various criteria advanced by the United States government for developing a detailed program of disarmament and arms control with verification and inspection. Ambassador Cabot now gave them more documentary material on disarmament. Ambassador Cabot must have also noted that President Kennedy's speech of June 10 apparently had been misinterpreted by Peking,* for his government hoped that all nations, including the Chinese People's

* A *Renminh Rih-Pao* statement on June 21, 1963, called it a "most cunning and vicious move" in President Kennedy's strategy for peace that required the "people of the whole world [to] maintain greater vigilance than ever before." This statement was quoted in *Peking Review,* Vol. VI, No. 26, June 28, 1963, p. 14.

Republic, would adhere to the Test-Ban Treaty, and that the Chinese People's Republic would reconsider its rejection. He asked the Chinese delegation to clarify Peking's contradictory position according to which universal and complete disarmament could be realized, but only after "imperialism, capitalism, and all systems of exploitation" had been eliminated, which evidently would require the use of force including use of nuclear force. During the exchange on the subject of arms control and the Treaty, the Americans, judging by their later public intimations, concentrated on such questions as what steps should be envisaged to achieve disarmament, what should be the balance of forces, what machinery was essential for adequate inspection and verification, and what safeguards would be necessary to monitor atomic testing.

In expounding the American views, the American representative at Warsaw apparently reiterated the request for Peking's comments on the United States government booklet regarding disarmament, already handed over to the Chinese in Warsaw in 1962. It seems probable that Peking never acknowledged the booklet and ignored the comprehensive oral presentation of the Americans. Nevertheless, the Americans apparently reasoned that this booklet, other material, and the detailed exposition of the basic questions on disarmament and the role of nuclear power would bring the essentials as well as the complexities of this crucial issue to the attention of the leaders in Peking, perhaps for the first time, or at least with a different emphasis and in another context. If these meetings were typical, it can fairly be said that the Chinese representatives responded only by referring repeatedly to their letter of August 2 to President Kennedy and other Chiefs of State which contained their public proposal of July 31. Perhaps they did not then consider the Ambassadorial Talks the proper place for an exchange on disarmament. They apparently evaded the American questions on disarmament or inspection, while the Americans did not respond directly to Peking's proposal for a world conference.

The 120th meeting on November 14 apparently did not advance the mutual presentation of views very much. Neither side gave any indication of an intention to consider or accept any part of the other's proposals; they merely exchanged their public "credentials" on disarmament. But the tone was civilized. Perhaps this disappointing exchange at Warsaw was on President Kennedy's mind that same day when he held his last press conference. It is significant that he made his final assessment of Communist China in much the same vein and tone that he used just after he was inaugurated, nearly three years before:

When the Red Chinese indicate a desire to live at peace with the United States, with other countries surrounding it, then quite obviously the United States would reappraise its policies. We are not wedded to a policy of hostility to Red China. It seems to me Red China's policies are what created the tension between not only the United States and Red China but between Red China and India, between Red China and her immediate neighbors to the south, and even between Red China and other Communist countries.[21]

American attempts in 1963 to deal with the tension were rebuffed and frustrated. Neither side met the other. For another eleven months this diplomacy of circumvention on the "nuclear nettle" lay static until the Chinese People's Republic, as expected, exploded its first atomic device on October 16, 1964.

Peking then appears to have duplicated its procedure of August 1963 by making a long public statement on October 16 and inserting much of it in a letter of October 17 to President Johnson and all other heads of state. Ambassador Wang again sent a covering note to Ambassador Cabot in Warsaw requesting him "kindly" to transmit Peking's letter to President Johnson.[22] In it, Peking seemed to rationalize China's nuclear development in the face of world concern by deriding the Test-Ban Treaty as a "big fraud" and blaming the United States for holding on to a "nuclear monopoly" and causing nuclear proliferation around the world. Both the public statement and the official letter again proposed that a "summit conference of all the countries of the world be convened to discuss the question of the complete prohibition and thorough destruction of nuclear weapons." Having forced its way into the nuclear orbit, Peking now made a new proposal for a world-wide pledge not to use nuclear weapons. As a first step, the letter urged that a summit conference should reach an agreement to the effect "that the nuclear powers and those countries which will soon become nuclear powers undertake not to use nuclear weapons, neither to use them against non-nuclear countries and nuclear-free zones, nor against each other." The statement and the letter also made the unilateral declaration that "China will never at any time and under any circumstances be the first to use nuclear weapons." In response, President Johnson, in a statement on October 18, denounced the Chinese detonation, deplored the "nuclear spread," called on Peking to join the Test-Ban Treaty, and assured non-nuclear nations of "strong support" from the United States in the event that they were faced with "some threat of nuclear blackmail." [23] On October 23, the State Department called Peking's proposal for a world conference "neither serious nor constructive." According to *The New York Times* dispatch from Washington, State Department officials considered it a "sucker proposal," pointed to the Warsaw channel for a dialogue if Peking had anything to say and disclosed that "we haven't heard anything constructive from them yet." [24]

The three-hour 125th Ambassadorial meeting on November 25, according to immediate and later press reports, spent much time on Peking's "emergence as an atomic power," on the test ban, the Chinese atomic detonation, Peking's proposals, and general disarmament.[25] Peking apparently introduced a new proposal for a bilateral U.S.–China renunciation of first use of atomic weapons. Ambassador Wang apparently first presented Peking's broad case for arms control and accused the United States of "obstructing and sabotaging world disarmament which all the peoples of the world want"—just what Washington accused Peking of doing. Including Peking's earlier proposals for a nuclear-weapon-free zone in the Pacific and total destruction of atomic weapons, Ambassador Wang then probably stressed the need for agreements not to be the first to use nuclear weapons. Peking considered this concrete proposal against "first use" as "practical, fair and reasonable, easily feasible," and involving "no question of control," [26] thus deflecting or eluding the American emphasis on verification and inspection. If all countries agreed in principle, the danger of nuclear war would be reduced, according to Peking, and an important initial step would be taken toward complete prohibition and thorough destruction of nuclear weapons. There could then be discussion on the specific questions of halting all tests, prohibiting the export, import, proliferation, manufacture and stockpiling of nuclear weapons, and finally of the destruction of existing weapons.

But Peking tried to commit Washington—with its vast atomic arsenal—to an agreement with China on "no first use" of nuclear weapons (China had none to pledge at that time, of course) pending the convening of a world summit conference. Ambassador Wang reportedly submitted a specific draft proposal to Ambassador Cabot for a formal joint agreement—as distinct from a world-wide multilateral agreement—not to be the first to use nuclear weapons against each other. This was a variation on the idea, which the Chinese had expressed publicly at the time of their nuclear explosion in October, that a summit conference of nuclear and potential nuclear powers should agree that no one be the first to use nuclear weapons. The United States government would have no reason at all to reject this proposal, Peking's representatives probably declared, in echo of many past statements in the Ambassadorial Talks.

Ambassador Cabot, however, apparently responding in much the same way as in 1963, avoided or circumvented the Chinese proposals by stressing the essential factors regarding disarmament, which had already been expounded from the American side and which, in effect, served to disparage the validity and feasibility of the Chinese proposals for general or bilateral agreements. The Chinese Communists were again pressed to discuss the stages, inspection systems, and safeguards which should be obligatory for disarmament agreements but which need not upset security arrangements for any country. Ambassador Cabot presumably inquired why the Chinese government had not yet signed the Test-Ban Treaty and again requested Peking to adhere to it. He also presumably repeated Washington's urgings that Peking participate in international conferences on disarmament. Ambassador Wang likewise continued to elude and circumvent repeated American attempts at dialogue on the nuclear issue in American terms.

Significantly, Peking's proposal for a bilateral agreement with the United States on a joint "no-first-use" pledge was the first and only initiative for a negotiated transaction advanced by Peking since it stopped negotiations with Washington in 1960, subjecting any further discussion or agreement to American willingness in principle to withdraw from Taiwan. In making this exception to its rigid principle on Taiwan, Peking was demonstrating some willingness to conduct diplomatic talks on the nuclear issue. The fact that Peking did not immediately disclose its proposal publicly, referring to it only obliquely in late December 1964, may have indicated Peking's seriousness. On the other hand, Peking's reticence may only have betrayed its sensitivity to public disclosure of any readiness to enter into negotiations with Washington. Perhaps Peking did not want Washington's rejection publicly known. Moreover, Peking's proposal may have amounted to no more than a clever means to throw the "nuclear nettle" back at Washington. In any event, because of Washington's rejection, we shall never know whether this one gesture on the part of Peking away from stalemate would have engaged both parties in a meaningful dialogue for the first time since the Taiwan crisis of 1958.

The United States immediately took the position that Peking's proposal for a joint pledge on "no first-use" of nuclear weapons was a device to cover up Peking's unwillingness to participate with most of the governments of the world in efforts to cease nuclear testing. Ambassador Cabot apparently indicated that the United States government could not consider or accept a simple declaration in words that could not be verified or enforced in view of the fact that no provision was made for inspection and verification. The only relevant aspect of an exchange to seek agreement on disarmament, according to Washington, was a comprehensive system of arms control such as the United States was advocating at the Disarmament Conference in Geneva. Washington used the Ambassadorial Talks not only to deflect Peking's proposal but again to communicate its over-all position of disarmament. But a dialogue evidently never materialized, and another opportunity was thus lost in the Ambassadorial Talks. A month later when the presence of American atomic submarines stirred up attention in Japan and East Asia, Peking publicly disclosed that it had proposed a formal bilateral agreement with the United States not to be the first to use nuclear weapons against each other. What Peking may have calculated from Washington's rejection of this proposal, in the light of stepped-up developments soon thereafter in Vietnam, was not made apparent until mid-1966.

The Talks may have avoided further detailed discussion on disarmament in 1965, as Vietnam became the critical issue between Peking and Washington. After several heated exchanges in 1963 and 1964, both sides had by 1965 notified each other of their respective views on the nuclear issue, presented a considerable amount of unilateral commentary, and offered divergent proposals. However, there was no response across the table from either side to questions, requests for details, or any effort to reach some understanding. The Chinese avoided direct response to the broad area of inspection and control, although they reacted indirectly by claiming that pledges against first use made "control" measures unnecessary. The Americans, for their part, tried to draw out the Chinese but sidestepped the issues of "atom-free zones" and "no first use." Typical of the diplomacy of stalemate and elusion in the Ambassadorial Talks, the dichotomy on disarmament was complete. In February 1965, the

Deputy Assistant Secretary of State for Far Eastern Affairs, Marshall Green, summed up the impasse:

> They have set their terms for disarmament talks. In 1962 and again in 1963 we asked the Chinese Communists for their views on specific disarmament problems and received no answer other than the demand that we forthwith agree to a destruction of all nuclear stocks—unverified—and to send our President to participate in a gigantic conference of Heads of State (this latter a device to divert the world's attention from their refusal to sign the partial nuclear test ban agreement).[27]

A year later, on February 12, 1966, Assistant Secretary of State for Far Eastern Affairs, William Bundy, disclosed that Washington envisaged Peking's participation in international conferences on disarmament under workable arrangements but that Peking's attitude, particularly since its nuclear tests, had "given no ground for supposing that she is prepared to enter disarmament discussions with any constructive position." [28] Until the spring of 1966, apparently nothing significant occurred on the nuclear issue at Warsaw while Washington and Peking sparred over Vietnam and other matters.

Then, Peking's third nuclear test of May 9, 1966, once again stirred up the nuclear debate at Warsaw, this time publicly. Another "detonation statement" defended the development of tests and weapons as a means of opposing "the nuclear blackmail and threats of U.S. imperialism" and "United States–Soviet collusion for maintaining a nuclear monopoly and sabotaging the revolutionary struggles of all oppressed peoples and nations." [29] However, the statement made no new overtures. It merely referred to Peking's proposals of 1963 and 1964 for a world summit conference for prohibition and destruction of nuclear weapons, alluded to the American disregard of its proposals at Warsaw, and reiterated its unilateral renunciation of any first use of nuclear weapons. But significantly, in addition to this announcement, Peking for the first time publicly called attention to its "no first use principle."

At a banquet on May 10, 1966, for visiting Albanian comrades, Chou En-lai officially revealed that China had suggested a formal reciprocal commitment and that the United States had turned down the proposal.[30] The position of Peking appeared to be that Washington's rejection of the joint pledge was another justification for Peking's development of nuclear weapons. According to a report in *The New York Times*, Peking had earlier made the proposal at Warsaw, while Washington had rejected it in order not to deny itself the deterrent power to counter aggression by the Chinese Communists, who did not then have nuclear capability. The next day a State Department spokesman confirmed that Washington had indeed rejected Peking's joint pledge, in addition to a general renunciation by nuclear powers, because Peking's proposal did not represent "a constructive step toward the paramount problem of controlled disarmament." [31]

The Chinese Communists were reportedly informed at Warsaw that a pledge without enforceable controls would be useless and would not constitute a sufficient guarantee, nor would it contribute to disarmament. Instead of merely outlawing the use of nuclear weapons, the United States had proposed banning aggression in any form to "get on with verified disarmament on a balanced basis and in a manner consistent with the security interests of all countries." In its talks with Peking on disarmament, the United States, the spokesman indicated, had advanced many of the same proposals as it had laid before the Geneva Conference on arms control, such as the two key proposals of a cut-off in the production of fissionable materials for nuclear weapons and a freeze in the number of strategic delivery weapons. Apparently Peking had not responded at Warsaw to these proposals either, the State Department spokesman indicated.

A week later, when asked to comment in a news conference on Prime Minister Chou En-lai's statement, Secretary Rusk for the first time publicly revealed Washington's position on the Chinese Communist proposal and Washington's bilateral discussions on nuclear disarmament:

Well, we are aware of their proposal on that. But we did not—and that proposal has been made by others and it has been made publicly from time to time. But we did not accept the Chinese Communist proposal because we believe that these disarmament measures should be carried out under strict and effective international control so that all parties can be assured of honoring their obligations. Mere declarations on such matters would not be adequate.

And so we are very much concerned about that, that any measures that involve the prohibition or the control of nuclear weapons should deal with the question of verification and inspection. We have ourselves put forward some very far-reaching proposals about limiting nuclear weapons and freezing and possibly reducing nuclear weapons delivery vehicles. You recall that the first Chinese proposal was made in connection with their own nuclear tests. They had refused to sign the Nuclear Test Ban Treaty and they have made certain suggestions which seem to be an attempt to soften the impact upon world opinion of their gross failure to cooperate in a world-wide effort to limit the further spread of these weapons.

Now, we have suggested that they ought to be associated with a preparatory committee, the so-called exploratory group, which might try to work out arrangements for a world disarmament conference. But we have had no indication from the Chinese that they are willing to do that. They have not responded constructively on those occasions when we ourselves have raised the disarmament question in our bilateral talks. We are prepared to sit down with them, as we have said many times, to talk about disarmament, such problems as the proliferation of nuclear weapons, but we can't take up these great issues of war and peace solely on the basis of unverified declarations which may or may not mean anything.

We have had a fairly recent agreement with Peiping, the Agreement of 1962 on Laos, and we can't find that Peiping has lifted a finger to assure that that agreement is complied with. Indeed, we have every reason to believe that they have encouraged its violation, both in terms of keeping North Vietnamese troops in Laos, contrary to the agreement, and using Laos as an infiltration route into South Vietnam, contrary to the agreements. So we would like to see an organized peace, arrangements which can be reliable, in order to get on with these great tasks of disarmament and assuring the safety and the independence of countries large and small.[32]

But Washington could not leave Chou En-lai's public initiative unchallenged.

If press sources are accurate regarding a private statement made by Senator Gore, Chairman of the Disarmament Subcommittee of the Senate Foreign Relations Committee, Washington apparently responded at a specially called Ambassadorial meeting of May 25, 1966, with a significant addition to the Chinese Communist proposal. Ambassador Gronouski reportedly inquired officially, but in a tentative and exploratory fashion, whether China would consider agreeing to a two-part joint pledge providing for Peking's adherence to the Test-Ban Treaty and Washington's agreement to Peking's proposal for "a no-first-use" pledge on nuclear weapons.[33] A State Department spokesman apparently refused to comment on reporters' questions regarding this press story, emphasizing that the Warsaw Talks were confidential. He very cautiously noted Peking's purported interest in agreements on the use of nuclear weapons and Washington's interest in getting from Peking some clarification of its statements and some indication of whether it was serious at all about workable arrangements for disarmament.[34]

These public comments on the American side evidently upset and angered Peking, for it soon reacted publicly, although it had been the first to divulge the subject of the joint pledge on the occasion of its third nuclear test. Contrary to its customary reticence, and without waiting to convey its response privately at the next meeting in Warsaw or calling a special meeting of the Ambassadors, Peking issued a violent public denunciation of Washington's "blare of publicity" and its suggestion for a two-part mutual pledge.[35] The statement specifically attacked the State Department for its spokesman's comment and the press story based on Senator Gore's purported revelations. In Peking's version, Chou En-lai's statement of May 10 had caused "turmoil" in the United States, throwing the United States government into a very awkward position. Two paragraphs in the statement made the same points twice:

In these circumstances at the Sino-American ambassadorial talks on May 25 the U.S. Government proposed that the Chinese Government consider linking its non-first use of nuclear weapons draft agreement to the U.S.-British-Soviet treaty on partial cessation of nuclear testing. Then on June 3, the U.S. Government disclosed the content of this proposal through the *New York Times* to the effect that "neither would be the first to use nuclear weapons, providing the Chinese would agree to stop their atomic testing. . . ."

At the Sino-American ambassadorial talks, the U.S. Government proposed to consider the Chinese proposal not to use nuclear weapons first in conjunction with the tripartite partial nuclear test ban treaty. Then it deliberately disclosed the contents of this in a blare of propaganda. The purpose behind all this is also to induce China to join in the so-called disarmament talks. In 1965, when the 20th Session of the United Nations General Assembly passed a resolution for a world disarmament conference, the U.S. and Soviet representatives in the assembly sang a duet, one saying that there was the "possibility" of admitting China to the conference and the other declaring that China's participation in the conference was "essential." Recently, on the same day that the *New York Times* disclosed what went on at the last Sino-American ambassadorial talks, the U.S. State Department spokesman, Robert McCloskey, said: "'We are, of course, always interested in whether there is any indication that the Chinese Communists might be seriously interested in workable disarmament agreements. . . .'"

Peking's statement bluntly told Washington that its efforts "to sound out our reaction" would be in vain. The double pledge was a "fraud," "swindle," and "preposterous proposal." The Test-Ban Treaty was a "criminal concoction by the two nuclear overlords . . . to consolidate their nuclear monopoly, to bind all peace-loving countries hand and foot, and to hoodwink the people of the world."

The government in Peking declared again that "at no time and in no circumstances" would it subscribe to that Treaty nor attend any disarmament conference at the United Nations or outside it.

Such things as the tripartite treaty, the world disarmament conference, the prevention of nuclear proliferation, and the linking of China's non-first use proposal to the tripartite treaty on partial cessation of nuclear testing are all aimed at restricting and depriving China and all other peace-loving countries of their legitimate right to develop their own armed forces for self-defense and their right to possess and develop nuclear weapons. In a word, they only permit the United States to carry out all-round arms expansion while forbidding the peace-loving countries of the world and particularly the Asian and African countries to possess armed forces for self-defense.

According to Peking, the most acute international question was Vietnam, not disarmament.

The deadlock on disarmament continued at Warsaw in the summer of 1966 although Peking and Washington had been exchanging views on Vietnam for over a year in the Ambassadorial Talks. The diplomacy of elusion on nuclear disarmament became the diplomacy of collision on Vietnam. The talks on the nuclear issue were derailed after a small and tardy start.

Vietnam

During 1965–67, the principal issue argued between Washington and Peking at Warsaw was indeed Vietnam. Both sides have used the Ambassadorial Talks to convey their respective public and official positions. Insofar as each has expressed its attitude, the danger of careless or ignorant miscalculation originating from lack of communications has probably been somewhat reduced, although willful or unwitting distortion or misreading of respective intentions cannot be wholly discounted or prevented. At least both Peking and Washington appear to have carefully prepared their respective presentations on Vietnam and to have meticulously recorded, translated, and studied what each side said. In several meetings at Warsaw—to judge by various partial press accounts—the United States apparently has conveyed to Peking a comprehensive statement of its general policy on Vietnam, which, briefly paraphrased from its public statements, covered the following familiar points:

Readiness to live at peace, leaving neighbors alone and complying with agreements, is the key to peace in Southeast Asia. The United States is looking for a peaceful settlement through many contacts. The missing element is Hanoi's failure to cease aggression. The United States remains determined to help stop aggression in South Vietnam and will take all necessary steps to do so. However, the United States has no designs on the territory of Vietnam, North or South, nor any intention of seeking to overthrow the Democratic Republic of North Vietnam. Moreover, the United States does not wish to pose any threats to the security of the Chinese People's Republic.

In addition to these public and private assurances, Washington presumably also called for the cessation of all Communist aggression and infiltration against South Vietnam and suggested a political settlement using the 1954 Agreement at Geneva as a basis of departure for discussion.

Peking's Ambassador seems to have given no indication that either Hanoi or Peking was prepared even to acknowledge these assurances or to stop supporting military activities in South Vietnam. Instead, Peking repeated its public and well-known position that the United States should cease its "criminal" and "imperialistic" attacks on the Vietnamese people and withdraw completely, immediately, and unconditionally.[36]

At the 126th meeting on February 25, 1965, just after American bombing of North Vietnam began, the United States government apparently communicated a fairly long statement to Peking to make clear its position with regard to South Vietnam, North Vietnam, and Communist China, as the Secretary of State indicated in his press conference immediately afterwards. Secretary Rusk disclosed that there had been such a discussion at Warsaw but that it had revealed "nothing new in the known positions of the two sides"; nor was it evident to him that the North Vietnamese Communists were prepared to stop doing what they were doing.[37]

The 127th meeting on April 22, 1965, lasted three hours and again involved an important exchange on Vietnam, according to a report in *The New York Times*.[38] This meeting apparently amounted to an official conveyance of what had been publicly stated by both Washington and Peking. Ambassador Cabot presumably presented the substance of President Johnson's comprehensive speech of April 7, 1965, calling for unconditional discussions, an independent neutral South Vietnam, and a comprehensive development of Southeast Asia including North Vietnam. Ambassador Wang presumably rejected these overtures, put forward Hanoi's four points for "settlement," and again demanded United States withdrawal from Vietnam. The June 30th meeting undertook another "switchboard" operation to communicate the views of each side.[39] We can be sure that each delegation has scanned every word and dissected each syllable to detect any nuance of change in tone or emphasis on the critical issue of Vietnam.

Ambassador Cabot was transferred from Warsaw to a new assignment in September. After his last Ambassadorial Talk on September 15, the 21st in his tour of duty in Warsaw, he told the press that the Talks had served a "useful purpose" as a channel of communications but had made little or no progress toward reducing tensions in the Far East. He also did not reject a reporter's question that he had conveyed a warning from Washington to Peking not to intervene militarily in the serious Pakistani-Indian dispute. However, the report from Warsaw to *The New York Times* indicated that American diplomats really believed that the Ambassadorial Talks were "not so much negotiations as listening to Radio Peking" and had not really served as a channel of communications on the Vietnamese crisis.[40] In any event, the Americans, according to another press report of late November 1965, made it "crystal clear" in the Warsaw Talks that Washington had no intention of invading China or crushing North Vietnam, and was seeking a peaceful settlement on acceptable terms.[41] On December 15, Ambassador Gronouski had his first encounter with the Chinese in Warsaw. Press reports indicate he stated that the serious issues of Southeast Asia and Vietnam took up much time, although both sides kept the exact exchange secret, as usual. Peking's statements on Vietnam at that meeting presumably contained the same points as those contained in a Foreign Ministry declaration, issued on January 11, 1966, which condemned "U.S. imperialism for its atrocious acts of aggression" and sought to "expose the U.S. plot of peace talks." [42]

In 1966, Washington and Peking continued their private exchange of notifications on Vietnam during the Ambassadorial Talks. Reportedly the Ambassadors discussed the war in Vietnam at their long meeting on March 16. Ambassador Gronouski told newsmen that "Ambassador Wang and I have had a serious talk about the current situation in the Far East." Ambassador Wang remarked that no progress had been made.[43] However, at the meeting of May 25, Ambassador Gronouski reportedly proposed to Peking and Hanoi a reciprocal lessening of hostilities as a basis for peace negotiations. The United States would stop bombing North Vietnam if Hanoi, in turn, would completely stop sending its troops to South Vietnam and accept international verification by some acceptable system of inspection and control. This offer on Vietnam accompanied the American proposal, made at the same meeting in Warsaw, for a mutual pledge with the People's Republic of China on "no-first-use" of atomic weapons. According to press accounts, Hanoi spurned Washington's peace offer as another "peace offensive fraud." Peking rejected Washington's position on Vietnam at the next Ambassadorial meeting in September. The newspaper accounts of the offer conveyed at Warsaw on May 25 for a reciprocal undertaking with Hanoi were also based on Senator Gore's private revelations.[44]

The Soviet government then became involved in the Washington–Peking exchange regarding Vietnam. But this resumption of the triangular interaction was far different from the experiences of 1958 concerning the Taiwan crisis or of 1954–55 when Moscow tried to bring Peking into a "Big Five" Summit Conference. In 1966–67, Moscow seemed to be accusing Peking of secret collaboration with Washington over Vietnam in the Ambassadorial Talks. Peking, in sharply denying these alleged Soviet insinuations, did reveal that Vietnam was an issue discussed in Warsaw. In early August, in the course of meetings of the Chinese Communist party, Peking took the unusual step of publicly describing the Ambassadorial Talks to rebut what Peking commentators called Soviet vilification. On July 28, the Soviet newspaper *Pravda* had printed an article on the "Sino-American Dialogue" with excerpts from the interview in *U.S. News and World Report* [45] with Ambassador Gronouski, who had said, among other things, that the Warsaw Talks were "useful" regarding Vietnam. Apparently sensitive to Soviet insinuations regarding their talks with Washington in Warsaw, the Chinese Communists reacted sharply against both Moscow and Washington. Since *Pravda* reported that its readers had asked for additional information about the Warsaw Talks, Peking obliged Moscow bluntly:

The Sino-American ambassadorial talks have been dragging on for more than 10 years and have long ceased to be news. Because China takes a firm Marxist-Leninist stand and absolutely refused to haggle about principles, the United States has failed to gain anything from the Sino-American talks. At these meetings, as on other occasions, China has severely condemned the bloody U.S. crimes of aggression in Vietnam and the U.S. "peace talks" swindles on the Vietnam question. It has firmly supported the Vietnamese people's sacred struggle to resist U.S. aggression and save their country. For *Pravda* to insinuate that China is making some political deal with the United States on the Vietnam question is the height of absurdity! [46]

It is interesting that Peking would go to such lengths to declare that the United States had gained nothing from the Ambassadorial Talks—which paralleled the American appraisal.

At the next Ambassadorial meeting on September 7, 1966, the Chinese Communist representatives strongly condemned the United States again on Vietnam, and rejected Washington's offers of reciprocal lessening of hostilities and a peace conference. After the three-hour meeting adjourned, Ambassador Wang took the unusual step of releasing the entire contents of his secret text to the press.* Violently attacking the "U.S. government's expansion of its war of aggression against Vietnam," predicting its "disgraceful failure," and denouncing its "smokescreen of peace talks," Peking's statement for the Ambassadorial Talks declared that the crux of the Vietnamese question was not gradual de-escalation of the war but immediate and complete withdrawal of "the U.S. aggressors from Southern Vietnam." Peking went on to inform Washington that "U.S. imperialist aggression against Vietnam is aggression against China," and that "the Chinese people are ready to undertake maximum national sacrifices." This statement ended with the warning that Washington would be committing a "grave historical blunder" if it underestimated the determination and actions of the Chinese people to support the Vietnamese people to fight through to the end to "thorough victory."

Why did Peking take this unusual step for the first time in many years? Apparently there was a dual reason: the evident publicity, and the possible correspondence of views between Moscow and Washington regarding diplomacy on Vietnam and the Ambassadorial Talks. Ambassador Wang declared that the United States government had "time and again" violated the mutual agreement on the confidential nature of the Talks by unilaterally revealing their contents, while "the Soviet revisionist leading clique" had followed up by conducting a great deal of propaganda about a "Sino-U.S. dialogue." Apparently Peking believed that it was entitled to make a

---

* Appendix E contains the full text with explanation as carried in *Peking Review*, Vol. IX, No. 38, September 16, 1966; only a partial text was published in *The New York Times*, September 8, 1966.

unilateral release of its statement to enable "all the just-minded people of the world" to see the stand taken by the Chinese Communist government in the Ambassadorial Talks on Vietnam and thus to expose the "deceptive propaganda" of the United States government and the "profuse nonsense" of the "Soviet revisionist leading clique." This sharp and rigid language suggests that the conjunction of Washington's conciliatory diplomacy with Moscow's inclination for a political rather than military solution accorded with Peking's policy of reducing the negotiations to a stalemate. However, due to internal and external reasons, Peking felt constrained to repudiate both Moscow and Washington and bar the way to any overtures toward a cease-fire and peaceful settlement. For his part, Ambassador Gronouski adhered to the confidential rule regarding the secret exchanges across the tables and made no public rejoinder. In the meeting he presumably rejected Peking's charges of "aggression," while restating Washington's assurances and desire for peace.

However, Moscow did not leave the last word on "collusion" to Peking. In late November 1966, *Pravda* published a long and significant editorial concerning "events in China" apparently designed to set forth the Soviet position on the "cultural revolution" and the "Red Guards." The Soviet editorial, to counter Peking's charges that all contacts of the Soviet Union with the United States were collusion with "imperialism," remarked that "the Chinese leaders at the same time do not miss a chance to develop relations with capitalist countries, including the United States." *Pravda* referred to Chen Yi's remarks on the Warsaw Talks in his conversation of September 1966 with Japanese political representatives and quoted them to the effect that "Peking does not necessarily exclude the idea of talks with the United States." After noting that the "Western press" had been stressing the "purely verbal escalation" conducted by Peking against the United States, *Pravda* found it "not surprising" that the "bourgeois press" was circulating reports about "China's tacit agreement with the U.S. and other capitalist countries, which are suited by China's present policy." [47]

Three weeks later, the Soviet *Literary Gazette* on December 20, 1966, ridiculed Chinese charges of Soviet-American collaboration by countercharging that it was China which was, in fact, "colluding" with Washington, and that American military escalation in Vietnam had been taken only after Washington had made "careful soundings of Peking's reaction." Chinese charges appeared to Moscow, according to the *Literary Gazette,* to be no more than a "smokescreen designed to camouflage the readiness of the Chinese leaders for rapprochement with the United States and other imperialist countries, and are quite satisfied by the present position of Mao Tse-tung and his group." [48] Curiously, this article in the *Literary Gazette* used a few correctly translated but misleadingly incomplete excerpts from the author's article in the October 1966 issue of *Foreign Affairs* on "American Dealings with Peking" to substantiate these charges of Peking's "collusion" with Washington, although the author would insist that no such interpretation of his article or this book could be made except by distortion.

In any event, the Chinese Communist leadership reacted quickly. According to the *Peking Review* of February 10, 1967, American imperialists, Soviet revisionists and their "pawns" had "spouted out rumors to the effect that China has privately 'assured' U.S. imperialists that so long as they observed certain principles China would prescribe certain limits of its aid to Vietnam." Peking also referred to a Soviet publication which carried "a lie fabricated by the *Paris-Jour* and the *Washington Post* alleging that China has a 'secret agreement' and 'tacit understanding' with the United States on the Vietnam question." As the *Peking Review* defined this foreign allegation, China would not take any direct military action in Vietnam and would not allow any military action to occur on its own territory which might pave the way for the United States to attack China, while for its part, the United States had agreed not to launch a military attack on China. Moreover, Peking noted that "Indian reactionaries were spinning the same fairy tale concerning the Sino-American Ambassadorial Talks in Warsaw," for the *Times* in India had carried a story on January 24 from Washington that the United States had "implicitly obtained this assurance" from Peking through the Warsaw Talks to the effect that China would abstain from direct intervention in Vietnam if the United States did not attack China or invade North Vietnam. According to the *Peking Review,* the Soviet, American, and Indian versions of any such tacit understanding amounted to "a new criminal design of imperialism, revisionism and the reactionaries in their unholy alliance against China" and "a lie which could not stand the light of day." The article ended with a vehement statement of China's determination to remain firm through all circumstances in aiding Vietnam to resist "U.S. aggression." [49] Subsequent Peking commentaries have made the same objections more vehemently.

Meanwhile, the Ambassadors had met again at Warsaw on January 25 apparently to exchange views on the situation in Southeast Asia and other matters. According to the *The New York Times,* the Warsaw Talks had enabled the United States and Communist China to have a "guarded exchange" in order to avoid "a direct encounter over Vietnam." [50]

In these several meetings during 1965–67, Peking and Washington have talked directly about each other's policies and actions in Vietnam and Asia. Hardly speaking the same diplomatic language, and locked in a bitter struggle, the two adversaries have maintained the exchange and have continued to listen, perhaps in bitter frustration, to each other's claims and countercharges. From the American viewpoint, the Chinese representatives have apparently confirmed in these secret Talks what Peking has been declaring and warning in public. Perhaps the same in reverse is true for Peking. In the delicate process of accurately detecting intentions, it has probably been of considerable value for Washington at least to know that Peking said the same thing officially in private as in public. Without the Talks, Washington and Peking would have had to depend on public statements alone and on second-hand reports about each other's attitudes and policies regarding Vietnam. At least the Warsaw Talks provided an opportunity for efficient communication. Thus far the Talks have not changed the situation in Vietnam or opened the way to negotiations on this critical area; but perhaps they have at least implicitly set forth the extent of the interests and delimited the boundaries of the conflict, which is an accomplishment in itself.

CHAPTER ELEVEN

Unsuccessful American Efforts for Bilateral Contacts

During the four years 1963–67 of Ambassadorial Talks, the United States government vigorously but unsuccessfully tried to persuade the Chinese People's Republic to agree to an exchange of newsmen and other nonofficial contacts between the two countries. The United States government repeatedly emphasized that contacts would be useful, pressed Peking to work out detailed arrangements in the Ambassadorial Talks, and liberalized its conditions for such exchanges. Nevertheless, Peking adamantly rejected every suggestion and overture, steadfastly adhering to its basic position that no individual issue can be negotiated until the United States agreed to vacate Taiwan.

In fact, by 1967, a dramatic and significant contrast had emerged. Washington was upgrading the Talks, campaigning for contacts and conciliation with the Chinese People's Republic, cautioning against an unending or inevitable state of hostility, and suggesting the desirability of "an era of good relations." Peking, on the other hand, said less than Washington about the Talks, though continuing them, spurned Washington's liberal approach, and girded itself for an inevitable struggle "throughout this historical era."

Washington's Initiatives

To recapitulate, Washington's new interest in contacts began to take shape in June 1960 with an initial draft on an exchange of newsmen. Peking circumvented that initiative in September 1960 with a counterproposal so full of political conditions that Washington would not discuss it. In 1961, the Kennedy administration pushed at Warsaw for an exchange of newsmen and made a comprehensive proposal for nonofficial, private exchanges of newsmen, scientists, scholars, doctors, and others. This American initiative reflected President Kennedy's interest in exploring every avenue to bring about a change in relations with Communist China during his administration. Peking vociferously rejected all these initiatives and feelers, with no acknowledgement whatsoever of the exploratory, even conciliatory, new attitude in Washington in 1961. From Peking's viewpoint, this was all a "trick" to disguise the "cunning plots" of the "imperialists" who should cease their "aggression" and "provocations" against the Chinese People's Republic, get out of Taiwan, and stop blocking the "legitimate rights" of the Chinese people. We may suppose that this uncompromising repudiation of the Kennedy administration's initial gesture to create a better basis for a rational, sensible, "sub-diplomatic" relationship with the Chinese People's Republic was firmly conveyed through the channel at Warsaw. The more the Kennedy administration probed for contacts and negotiations the more Peking recoiled.

Despite the persistent and vituperative rebuffs from Peking, Washington continued the effort in the Ambassadorial Talks during Ambassador Beam's last meetings in 1961 to suggest and urge more contacts. Ambassador Cabot kept on trying during 1962 and 1963. The press reported, for instance, that at the 118th meeting on August 7, 1963, when the exchange on disarmament began, the Americans took the initiative once again on the issue of newsmen for three reasons: the news agencies wanted it, such an exchange could not hurt the "frigid" relations between both countries, and it would refute Communist propaganda.[1] Although Ambassador Cabot reportedly argued for negotiation of an agreement on establishing contacts, Ambassador Wang insisted on a prior American withdrawal from Taiwan.

On November 14, 1963, at the 120th meeting, Ambassador Cabot apparently made another vigorous and comprehensive attempt to communicate Washington's intentions not only on disarmament but on general contacts seeking actively to relax tensions in East Asia.[2] Peking's representatives were presumably informed that an exchange would be valuable not only in giving the American people a clearer idea of Chinese views but also in giving the Chinese people a clearer idea of American views. However, the United States government did not consider the issue of the exchange of newsmen a bargaining device but rather a means of promoting mutual understanding. Evidently, during many presentations of this item at the Ambassadorial Talks, the Americans rather conspicuously omitted references, in their prepared and spontaneous statements, to the constitutional and other qualifications on the waiver for visa applications. The Chinese Communist representatives could not fail to note this further relaxation of the American position which, in fact, amounted almost to an automatic procedure for granting visas to Chinese newsmen.

With President Kennedy's initial encouragement, State Department officials late in 1963 began to advocate such contacts publicly. In what would have been President Kennedy's major statement on a more flexible policy on China, Roger Hilsman, Assistant Secretary of State for Far Eastern Affairs, announced on December 13, 1963, that the United States was pursuing a "policy of the open door" toward China, and was "determined to keep the door open to the possibility of change in mainland China," and emphasized the persistent American efforts to arrange an exchange of correspondence.[3] Thereafter during 1964—the year of political transition in the United States and increased engagement in Vietnam—Washington apparently quietly continued to press Peking for contacts. Then, on February 26, 1965, the Deputy Assistant Secretary, Marshall Green, went somewhat further in indicating the efforts of Washington in seeking improved and expanded contacts with China. He cited the continuation of the Ambassadorial Talks at Warsaw, informal contacts with Chinese delegates at international gatherings, authorization for newsmen and other individual Americans to go to mainland China for humanitarian purposes or reasons of national interest, unhindered flow of mail to and from China, and the export of films to and from both countries.[4]

During 1965–66, Washington exhausted every conceivable avenue open to it to overcome Chinese Communist resistance to contacts. As tension over Vietnam mounted in 1965, the United States government gradually expanded its efforts at Warsaw to promote and improve contacts.

According to press reports, Washington made a new liberalized and unconditional proposal at the three-hour-long Warsaw meeting of December 15, 1965.[5] In his first encounter, Ambassador Gronouski reportedly informed Ambassador Wang that the United States would be willing to have newspapermen from the People's Republic of China come to the United States unilaterally and even without reciprocity. That is to say, Peking could send journalists, apparently as many as it wanted, to the United States without any requirement for an equivalent number of American journalists to enter China—or for any American reporters at all. Washington apparently urged Peking to act on this proposal in the interests of promoting mutual understanding and improving relations, the unresolved disputes between the two countries notwithstanding. This proposal was a radical departure from the American arguments in 1956 and 1957 over nonreciprocity for Chinese newsmen and constitutional requirements.* Presumably, Ambassador Gronouski also proposed a formal or informal agreement between Washington and Peking for a reciprocal exchange of newsmen and other contacts. According to press accounts Peking neither rejected nor accepted the revised offer at first. Then, on December 29, the State Department announced that it would validate passports of doctors, scientists, and other scholars who wished to go to Communist China—a liberalization of policy which presumably had been conveyed to Peking at the Ambassadorial meeting two weeks before.[6]

In two public speeches early in 1966, the Assistant Secretary of State for Far Eastern Affairs, William Bundy, summed up the cumulative efforts of the United States to open and expand bilateral contacts with the Chinese People's Republic. He wished to emphasize that the United States had had the longest and most direct dialogue of any major Western nation with Peking and would deal with Peking in international conferences, but that it was the government of the Chinese People's Republic which was rejecting all possibilities and proposals for expanded exchanges. As Mr. Bundy put it:

Many people do not realize that it is Communist China which has prevented any movement toward bilateral contacts. The United States over the past several years has tried to promote a variety of contacts, but the Chinese have kept the door tightly barred.[7]

* In 1965–66, the United States government was making virtually the same offer to the Chinese People's Republic as the latter had made in 1956, and which Washington had then rebuffed. At that time, it will be recalled, Peking repeatedly offered to receive American newsmen in China unconditionally and without reciprocity. But Washington rejected this proposal and Peking's draft of a simple, unqualified agreement on an exchange of newsmen on two grounds: first, all American prisoners illegally detained in China should first be released before American correspondents should venture there; and second, the visa application of each Chinese reporter would have to be examined for a possible but not certain waiver. And at first in 1956–57 Washington even insisted on refusing reciprocity to Chinese newsmen. Now, despite a few Americans still imprisoned in China, Washington was willing to grant passports to American journalists for travel to China, and open the door unrestrictedly to Chinese newspapermen.

As he enumerated the American efforts, the United States government had validated more than 80 passports for representatives of newspapers and other media of communication for travel to the Chinese People's Republic; had tried unsuccessfully to arrange with Peking for either a formal or informal—or even a nonreciprocal—exchange of newsmen; had authorized doctors and scientists in the fields of public health and medicine to go to the Chinese People's Republic; had recently approved the efforts of American scientific, scholarly, and educational institutions to arrange people-to-people exchanges with Chinese on the mainland; had encouraged the exchange of publications between universities and institutions in both countries; and encouraged mail to flow freely to and from the Chinese People's Republic. Washington had also not opposed limited trade with China, Mr. Bundy noted, but "every time the subject is seriously mentioned in this country, it is shot down immediately in Peking."

At the Ambassadorial meeting on March 16, 1966, Ambassador Gronouski apparently repeated his proposals of December 15, 1965, and pressed again for Peking's agreement on exchanges and contacts, presumably along lines Washington made public subsequently. He apparently informed Ambassador Wang of Washington's willingness to permit scholars and scientists from Communist China to visit the United States on invitation from American universities as well as Washington's willingness to have American scholars and scientists accept invitations to go to the Chinese People's Republic.[8]

If an "open door" to contacts with mainland China could not be found, the door to public discussion in the United States was opened in 1966. Washington officials and Americans in general began to emphasize the need for rational dealings and more contacts with the Chinese People's Republic. The Hearings before the Committee on Foreign Relations of the United States Senate on "United States Policy With Respect to Mainland China" produced endorsements as well as criticisms of American efforts to establish bilateral contacts. For the most part, the American specialists on China, who testified, supported the liberalization of exchanges between the two countries. The majority of them told the senators that lines of communication with Peking through the Ambassadorial Talks, by mutual exchanges of newsmen, scholars, scientists, doctors, and businessmen, and in international conferences, should be maintained, encouraged, and expanded to the greatest extent possible. On the other hand, a few professors questioned the new policy of "de-isolation" either on the logical grounds that no improvement in United States–Chinese relations could take place until the fundamental difference over Taiwan was settled, or on the basis that the initiative for such exchanges and bilateral contacts should come from Peking in actual deeds. These Hearings and another series in the House Foreign Affairs Committee initiated national exposure to the "China problem" and started general discussion within the United States.[9]

Vice President Humphrey dramatized the new interest in contacts and relations with mainland China when he suggested a policy of "containment without necessarily isolation" in a speech on March 13.[10] Noting the administration's recent decision to permit American scholars and other professionals to travel to the Chinese People's Republic, the Vice President commented that "this could be the beginning of a much better relationship." Cautioning against any sudden changes he said:

I am afraid that we are going to have to wait until the men of the Long March, of the Mao generation, are out of position of leadership. But in the meantime we ought to maintain, as best we can, a spirit of friendship toward the Chinese people, but recognizing what the regime is, and making that regime understand they cannot achieve their purposes by military power.

In commenting on these remarks of the Vice President, a *New York Times* report noted that the administration, prompted by a concern over the lack of official and unofficial channels of communication such as there had been with Moscow to ease confrontations and avoid miscalculations, had undertaken "considerable discussion and examination" in recent weeks regarding the long-range efforts to be made to explore the possibility of contacts with Peking's leaders. However, uncertain over the possible shift in future Peking foreign policies either toward more militancy or more moderation, the administration was also reported to prefer moving cautiously in encouraging Americans to travel to mainland China.

The Vice President's remarks made the China problem a major topic for questions at Secretary Rusk's news conference on March 25, 1966. He emphasized that the United States government had tried over a considerable period of time to find ways of improving relations with mainland China through discussions in Warsaw, the attendance of both Foreign Ministers at the Geneva Conference on Laos, and encouragement of "exchanges of newsmen, doctors, and scholars, and weather information and all sorts of things." But he, too, pointed out that the United States kept running up against the problem of Taiwan because the authorities in Peking always "indicate that there is no prospect for improved relations unless we are willing to surrender Taiwan." On the question of "de-isolation," Rusk made the following comments, adding to the Vice President's previous remarks:

But on the question of isolation again, the efforts that have been made to break through this isolation have not been availing. We have made a number of efforts since I have been in my present position with little or no response from the other side. A good deal of this isolation is self-imposed, and we see evidences of that almost every day. But perhaps this situation will change. I don't know what the next generation of Chinese leaders will look like. We have perhaps too little information on just who they will be and what their attitudes will be. But in the longer run, I cannot help but believe that all peoples and Governments will recognize that somehow peoples and Governments must find a way to live at peace with each other.[11]

In the meantime the Department of State had prepared, and the Secretary of State had presented, on March 16, before the Subcommittee on the Far East and the Pacific of the House Committee on Foreign Affairs, a general review and projection of United States policies and dealings with the Chinese People's Republic. This first comprehensive and authoritative statement of policy toward Communist China in many years was publicly issued in mid-April 1966. It contrasted sharply and significantly in tone and approach from the policy statements of John Foster Dulles in 1957 and 1958, which articulated those basic tenets of isolating and ostracizing Communist China in the expectation that it was a "passing" phenomenon with which there should be no contact aside from the restricted and expedient Ambassadorial Talks.

Whereas the earlier statements reflected Washington's emphasis on stalemate diplomacy, the 1966 statement envisaged a diplomacy aimed at seeking peaceful relations with the Chinese People's Republic while maintaining the same hard-line analysis of Peking's objectives of world revolution and hostility to the United States, and the need for a counterweight of real power to Chinese Communist pressures. Expressing a significant shift of tone and approach, the new statement set forth ten elements of future policy on China. It is reasonable to infer from press accounts that Ambassador Gronouski

conveyed all or part of this statement to Ambassador Wang in Warsaw.

The United States hoped for friendly relations with mainland
China.

We expect China to become some day a great world power. Communist
China is a major Asian power today. In the ordinary course of events, a
peaceful China would be expected to have close relations—political, cultural and economic—with the countries around its borders and with the
United States. It is no part of the policy of the United States to block the
peaceful attainment of these objectives.

Washington would welcome "an era of good relations" with Peking
if it abandoned force as an instrument of policy, and dispensed with
its violent strategy of world revolution. Washington would nevertheless have to remain determined to help allied nations threatened
by Peking, to assist and maintain the Republic of China, and to
prevent its expulsion from the United Nations. Peking's membership in the United Nations, on the other hand, would be opposed as
long as Peking's conditions for joining implied that it did not want
membership or were meant to destroy the United Nations. Nevertheless, the United States declaration of policy of 1966 continued to
reassure Peking that the United States did not want war with the
Chinese People's Republic, and believed that "there is no fatal
inevitability of war with Communist China." Washington wished to
avoid assuming the existence of an "unending and inevitable state of
hostility between ourselves and the rulers of mainland China."

Given all these reservations and considerations, the statement of
policy stressed the importance of contact and communication with
Peking and the Chinese People's Republic. Washington wished to
maintain its "direct diplomatic contacts" with Peking at Warsaw, to
sit down with Peking and other countries to discuss problems of
disarmament and nonproliferation of nuclear weapons, and to keep
American policies on Communist China up-to-date. The seventh
element of the 1966 statement placed the question of contacts comprehensively and authoritatively for the first time in the total context of China policy since Washington began its reversal in 1959:

. . . when it can be done without jeopardizing other U.S. interests, we
should continue to enlarge the possibilities for unofficial contacts between
Communist China and ourselves—contacts which may gradually assist in
altering Peking's picture of the United States.

In this connection, we have gradually expanded the categories of American citizens who may travel to Communist China. American libraries may freely purchase Chinese Communist publications. American citizens may send and receive mail from the mainland. We have in the past indicated that if the Chinese themselves were interested in purchasing grain we would consider such sales. We have indicated our willingness to allow Chinese Communist newspapermen to come to the United States. We are prepared to permit American universities to invite Chinese Communist scientists to visit their institutions.

We do not expect that for the time being the Chinese Communists will seize upon these avenues of contact or exchange. All the evidence suggests Peking wishes to remain isolated from the United States. But we believe it is in our interests that such channels be opened and kept open. We believe contact and communications are not incompatible with a firm policy of containment.[12]

At about the same time as the publication of this declaration of policy, Washington added another relaxation in its gradual effort to widen the proposals for broadening scientific and cultural contacts with the Chinese People's Republic.[13] The State Department disclosed on April 14 that several American universities had been notified that they could invite scientists and scholars from the Chinese People's Republic to come to the United States. The American academic community had long sought this change. The press statements and comments implied that the offer had been already conveyed to Peking via the Warsaw Talks but had not yet met with any favorable response.

Public discussion of bilateral contacts with the Chinese People's Republic continued actively into the summer in the United States. On June 8, Vice President Humphrey stated that the United States was pledged to widen contacts with Communist China in this effort "to build bridges, and to keep open the doors of communication to the Communist States of Asia and, in particular, Communist China." [14] A mid-June poll of American opinion indicated that a majority favored rapprochement between the United States and the Chinese People's Republic, supported exchanges of reporters, scholars and other specialists, favored a test-ban treaty with Communist China, and approved its admission to the United Nations, provided that the Chinese Nationalist government on Taiwan were allowed to stay in the organization.[15] Also in mid-June, the Majority Leader in the United States Senate, Senator Mansfield, urged that a meeting between Secretary of State Dean Rusk, and Peking's Foreign Minister, Chen Yi, be held to seek the ending of the war in Vietnam, self-determination for the South Vietnamese people, reunification of all Vietnam, the independence of all Southeast Asia, and the prompt withdrawal of all military forces. This was the first time in almost four years that the long-forgotten issue of a bilateral ministerial meeting had been revived. Senator Mansfield had not consulted the administration in advance, but the White House indicated that the President welcomed any constructive suggestion from Senator Mansfield and the Congress and would review this particular suggestion with the Secretary of State.[16]

In mid-July, after President Johnson had made a major speech urging reconciliation, contacts, and trade with Communist China, the administration was reported to have suggested that it might permit some trade with Communist China under certain circumstances although State Department officials emphasized that they had no active plan and expressed doubt that Peking would be interested. A State Department spokesmen reportedly said:

Our Government has under continuing review the question of how policies and procedures governing trade with Communist China might, under certain circumstances, be changed or adjusted to contribute to the interests of the United States and the peace of that area.[17]

In his speech on July 12 President Johnson enunciated the most significant and far-reaching policy of reconciliation with China. Stressing that lasting peace could never come to Asia while the Chinese people were isolated by their rulers from the outside world, the President favored a "free flow of ideas and people and goods" to open "closed minds and societies." He then stated:

For many years now the United States has attempted in vain to persuade the Chinese Communists to agree to an exchange of newsmen as one of the first steps to increased understanding between our people. . . .

More recently, we have taken steps to permit American scholars, experts in medicine and public health, and other specialists to travel to Communist China. . . . All of these initiatives . . . have been rejected by Communist China.[18]

But the President declared that he intended to persist in these efforts because, among other things, "cooperation, not hostility, is really the way of the future," even if "it may be long in coming." At his news conference of July 20, in answering a question as to whether his "conciliatory" attitude toward mainland China under certain conditions indicated a new move toward a two-China policy in the

United Nations or no change in policy on Peking's representation there, the President answered:

I feel that we should do everything we can to increase our exchanges, to understand other people better, to have our scientists and our business-men and our authors and our newspaper people exchange visits and ex-change viewpoints, and I would hope that as a result of tearing down these barriers that some day all people in this world would be willing to be guided by the principles of the Charter of the United Nations, that all peoples would want to cease aggression, and would try to live with peace and understanding with their neighbors.

So far as I am concerned, every day I am looking for new ways to understand the viewpoint of others. And I hope that at a not too distant date mainland China will be willing to open some of the barriers to these exchanges and be willing to perhaps come nearer to abiding by the prin-ciples laid down in the United Nations Charter.[19]

On September 5, President Johnson's case for dealing with the Chinese People's Republic went a step farther when he spoke in Lancaster, Ohio, about building "bridges of friendship" in Europe:

In Asia we have a similar hope, though tonight it is clouded by war and by bitterness. But still we look to the day when those on the mainland of China are ready to meet us half-way—are ready to devote their enormous talents and energy to improving the life of their people, when they are ready to take their place peacefully as one of the major powers of Asia and the world.[20]

It was unusual and significant for an American President to offer to meet the Chinese Communists "half-way." Then, in Honolulu, Manila, Bangkok, and Kuala Lumpur during his trip across the Pacific to East Asia in October-November 1966, President Johnson repeatedly stressed his policies of exchange and reconciliation with "Mainland China" to end isolation and replace suspicion with trust. He even conveyed this policy to the Congress in his address on the State of the Union of January 10, 1967.

Private American Efforts: In addition to the important efforts of two Presidents of the United States, and especially of President Johnson, to break the "travel barrier," many private American at-tempts have been made over the past few years to establish some mutual agreement on procedure for unofficial travel to and from both countries. As far as is known, none of these efforts has suc-ceeded, although it is difficult to compile a full and reliable account of such private, unofficial, or even "extra-official" efforts. The fol-lowing incomplete summary is meant to be illustrative and not comprehensive.[21]

There have been authorized and unauthorized visits of Americans to China on a sporadic basis, and several unsuccessful private invitations from persons on both sides. The only Americans who, until 1966, had entered the "forbidden country" with Washington's permission were a few relatives of the American prisoners in China; Americans employed by the United Nations who have accompanied certain missions to China; lawyers on special cases; and the writer, Edgar Snow, who is a special exception. Several unauthorized visits by American students, a few journalists, and two American women on separate occasions have apparently also taken place, but none has been of particular consequence in developing contacts. One unsuccessful American attempt was apparently made nearly ten years ago to arrange for American performing artists to go to China. American scientists have on several occasions received oral invitations from Chinese scientists but these invitations have failed to obtain official clearance either in Peking or in Washington.

One Chinese scientist who had studied in America, invited a former professor to come to China, presumably with the knowledge and approval of Peking authorities, but the effort failed. Even when arrangements were completed with Washington's blessing for an American ear specialist to go to China in 1964 to provide some special medical treatment, Peking, at the last minute, refused authorization. A few years ago, an American librarian suggested an informal meeting of librarians from both countries, but the Chinese response apparently expressed regret that the policy of the United States government—meaning Taiwan again—prevented acceptance, although the answer seemed to leave the door ajar for later consideration. The American suggestion of such a meeting in a third country was not answered.

Nevertheless, a few Americans and Chinese from the Chinese People's Republic have met and established informal contacts in other countries. For example, American and Chinese Communist scientists both participated in an international aeronautical conference in Belgium in 1958. A few American doctors and other scientists have met their Chinese counterparts in the Soviet Union and other Communist-controlled countries and have talked with them informally about professional subjects. American and Chinese scholars have participated in and met together informally at the so-called Pugwash meetings in Canada and in the Soviet Union over the past few years. As another example, a scientist from Communist

China spent an evening in the home of a Canadian scholar, discussing sociology with two American social scientists. Exchange and communication on these and other occasions in third countries between scientists and scholars have apparently been congenial and feasible only under informal auspices but not at official gatherings or formal meetings. The public proprieties have been carefully observed.

In addition to these unorganized and sporadic meetings at international conferences, some individuals in other countries have also tried to arrange for travel of Americans to mainland China and for meetings between Americans and citizens from the Chinese People's Republic. There are reports, for example, that two or three years ago several Japanese inquired in Peking as to whether some American senators and some American Sinologists could receive permission to visit China. Apparently, several of the top officials in Peking reacted negatively but did not reject the informal suggestion outright. In the spring of 1966, the Overseas Press Club in New York City announced that it was trying to contact Chinese newsmen in London directly and to attempt, via third parties, to invite Chinese reporters to come to the United States as guests of the Club, in the hope that Peking, in return, would let American reporters be invited to China. In July 1966, the Department of State approved the visit of Supreme Court Justice William O. Douglas to the People's Republic of China. Peking, however, did not issue him an invitation to come. A congressman who wanted to visit China also was unable to do so. Moreover, the organizers of an International Conference on High Energy Physics were equally unsuccessful when they invited, with Department of State approval, three physicists from the People's Republic of China to attend.[22] Likewise, the International Congress of Orientalists, held in Ann Arbor, Michigan in mid-1967, issued invitations to scholars in China to attend.

In contrast to the failure to arrange exchange of persons, the exchange of documentary materials has been successful. Many universities, libraries, scientific or academic associations, and scholars in the United States have asked for and received publications and exchanged correspondence with their opposite numbers in the Chinese People's Republic. Apparently a mutual desire and facility exists, officially and privately, for an empirical, impersonal, and "immaculate" contact on a specific basis in both directions. It has not become general or voluminous. For their part, the Chinese Communists have restricted the exchange to technical and scientific fields and apparently decreased the outflow of books and periodicals from Communist China in 1966–67. Undoubtedly, the "cultural revolution" inhibited private, as well as authorized contacts and exchanges with the United States.

Chinese Communist Reactions and Rejections

Peking has continually spurned these official and private American overtures for new contacts and better relations. Presumably, Peking has given official notifications of its rejections at Warsaw, since Peking has publicly scorned American efforts for reasons of basic policies, particularly those relative to Vietnam. Perhaps because Washington has intensively publicized its policy of widening bilateral contacts, Peking has extensively justified its rejections in press commentary and official statements in or out of the Warsaw Talks. Quite consistently, Peking has publicly rejected overtures from American officials without waiting for a meeting in Warsaw.

Two days after the initial American overture in the "open door" speech of December 13, 1963, Peking called it "nothing new" and scorned the new American stance, sarcastically saying that it was "hard for a wolf to hide its tail" and the Chinese people would not "welcome a thief." Two months later, in February 1964, Peking rejected the "open door" as "preposterous," "day-dreaming" and only showing a "pretense of flexibility." At the Ambassadorial meeting on September 15, 1965, it was reported that Ambassador Wang had again rejected Washington's proposal on an exchange of newsmen as long as the principal issue of Taiwan was not settled. On March 14, 1966, the official Chinese Communist newspaper rejected Vice President Humphrey's expressions of friendship and desire for contacts as the "kiss of Judas," which "disgusts the Chinese people." [23]

On March 29, 1966, Peking took public note of the various American diplomatic and public efforts to promote bilateral contacts between the two countries in an authoritative newspaper article published four days after Secretary Rusk's news conference outlining American efforts to promote exchanges, perhaps reflecting a statement delivered at the Warsaw meeting on March 16.[24] Peking declared that "these blasts of 'good will,' set off by Washington at a time when United States imperialism is working more energetically than ever to direct the spearhead of its aggression at China, are quite absurd and ridiculous." Recalling the "open door" speech of two years before, Peking stated that Secretary Rusk's theme of "flexibility" would be "of no earthly use." In Peking's version, Washington had recently "kicked up a rumpus over the interflow of people between the two countries . . . urged more than once that Chinese and American correspondents visit each other's country . . . and indicated that it would permit some American physicians, scientists and other scholars to visit China." However, this authoritative article pointed out that continued strained relations between the People's Republic of China and the United States had nothing to do with the fact that no American doctors had come to China to study medical and health conditions or that no Chinese newsmen had gone to the United States to report on the American way of life. On the contrary, according to Peking, the source of all the tension sprang from "the extremely hostile policy" of the United States government toward China and from the fact that the United States "is forcefully occupying China's province of Taiwan." Expressing the position evidently so often conveyed across the tables in the Ambassadorial Talks, Peking's public statement emphasized:

So long as the United States government does not change its hostile policy toward China and refuses to pull its armed forces out of Taiwan and the Taiwan Straits, the normalization of Sino-American relations is entirely out of the question and so is the solution of such concrete questions as exchange of visits between people of the two countries. But what is the attitude of the Johnson Administration to this question? Dean Rusk stated bluntly not long ago that the answer to the demand for U.S. evacuation of Taiwan is "No, we are not prepared to do so." This reveals that the steps the U.S. government proposes for an "improvement" of Sino-American relations are just so many petty actions announced with much fanfare to fool the public.

Peking went on to charge that "in feigning eagerness to 'improve' Sino-American relations," all such expressions as "a flexible policy, without 'isolation' and 'more contact' are only pretenses for intensifying the 'containment' of China." Referring to what it called the American military build-up around China, the eastward shift of global strategy and "escalation of aggressive war" in Vietnam, Peking charged that the United States was preparing for a "trial of strength with the Chinese people" and not the improvement of relations with the People's Republic of China.

The article then significantly drew a distinction "between United States imperialism and the American people," stating that there was a profound friendship between the two peoples, that the Chinese people fully understood the American people's desire for resuming contact, but the government in Peking would not allow "the United States ruling group to exploit this justified desire of the American people for its own sinister ends." Someday the two peoples would "smash the schemes of the U.S. reactionaries . . . and truly establish close contact to bring about a tremendous growth of the friendship between our two peoples." Thus, this officially-inspired position, despite its harshness and allegations, did tell people in Communist China for the first time that the United States had repeatedly proposed an exchange of newsmen and relaxed its travel and visa regulations.

On April 5, 1966, the Foreign Ministry in Peking issued a formal statement of general policy accusing the United States of planning war in Asia against China, and rejecting Washington's proposals to "improve Sino-American relations, and hints of goodwill." [25] Presumably much or all of this official statement had also been already conveyed in the Ambassadorial Talks—perhaps at the 129th meeting on March 16, 1966. Peking's statement warned Washington of the alleged 400th encroachment on Chinese territorial waters and air space. In stark contrast to Washington's emphasis in its policy statement on minimizing armed conflict, establishing contacts, and improving relations, Peking's statement of policy rejected these suggestions as "counter-revolutionary" and concluded:

So long as United States imperialism exists we of this generation must be prepared, and so should be the second and the third generations. The sharp antagonism and fierce struggle between revolutionary China on the one hand and United States imperialism, which is continuously extending its aggression and war on the other, is the inevitable result of historical development.

This struggle will go on throughout this historical era. One mouthpiece of United States imperialism has said that the United States would need 30 years to deal with China. We tell him plainly: "With great revolutionary spirit, the Chinese people are determined to struggle against United States imperialism for one, two or even 300 years until it is utterly defeated and the world revolution is completely victorious."

An era of fierce struggle—that was how Mao Tse-tung and Chou En-lai viewed relations with the United States eleven years after they had dramatically announced their willingness to sit down and negotiate with the American government in April 1955.

On April 17, Peking broadcast the Foreign Ministry's rejection of

President Johnson's offer to invite scholars and scientists to visit American universities. Calling it "nothing but a fraud," Peking charged that its aim was "to deceive the American people and world opinion and exploit the American people's friendly sentiments for China in the interest of its policy of hostility towards China." [26] Two days later on April 19, just after Washington's ten-point declaration of policy was made public by the House Foreign Affairs Subcommittee and published in *The New York Times*, Peking specifically and brusquely turned it down:

The ten elements are a mixture of hostility to China and deception. The real aim is to be hostile to and launch aggression against China and to contain and encircle it. All talks about "improving" relations and "avoidance" of a state of hostility are a sham.[27]

Then, on May 10, Peking broadcast a high-level statement of policy regarding the United States which Prime Minister Chou En-lai had actually made a month earlier. Without altering it to take account of Washington's new policy published on April 17, Chou warned that American troops would be "annihilated" if they invaded China even if nuclear weapons were used, but declared that the Chinese People's Republic would not take the initiative to provoke a war with the United States. Chou En-lai tied the Ambassadorial Talks exclusively and uncompromisingly to the dispute over Taiwan:

China has not sent any troops to Hawaii. It is the United States that has occupied China's territory of Taiwan province. Nevertheless, China has been making efforts in demanding, through negotiations, that the United States withdraw all its armed forces from Taiwan province and the Taiwan Straits, and she has held talks with the United States for more than 10 years, first in Geneva and then in Warsaw, on this question of principle, which admits of no concession whatsoever. All this serves as a very good proof.[28]

It is important for the history of American dealings with Peking to underline the words "no concession whatsoever." In short, American efforts to arrange agreements on bilateral contacts would not be discussed or negotiated until the knot of Taiwan had been cut.

Following all the high-level American statements from March to July on relations and contacts, Peking formally replied in two harsh uncompromising statements, after instantly brushing aside President Johnson's offer of reconciliation. At the conclusion of the noteworthy 11th Plenary Session of the Central Committee of the

Chinese Communist party held in Peking August 1–12—the first such session in four years—the basic policy toward the United States, apparently as determined by Mao Tse-tung and his colleagues, was laid down in the following militant terms:

The plenary session holds that U.S. imperialism is the most ferocious common enemy of the peoples of the whole world. In order to isolate U.S. imperialism to the maximum and deal blows to it, the broadest possible international united front must be established against U.S. imperialism and its lackeys. . . .

We must liberate Taiwan. We must heighten our vigilance a hundredfold and guard against surprise attacks from U.S. imperialism and its accomplices. Should they dare to impose war on us, the 700 million Chinese people under the leadership of Comrade Mao Tse-tung and the Communist party of China will certainly break the backs of the aggressors and wipe them out resolutely, thoroughly, totally and completely.[29]

This statement of Peking's ruling leadership was diametrically opposed to Washington's attitude, and ignored bilateral contacts. However, on September 7, after the 131st meeting of the two Ambassadors in Warsaw, Peking took the unusual step of instructing Ambassador Wang to call a press conference and read the full text of his main statement made to Ambassador Gronouski, denouncing United States policy in Vietnam and officially rejecting as "sheer wishful thinking" the new policies expressed by President Johnson and other officials of the United States government to seek reconciliation, contacts, and better relations with mainland China. Because of its importance and because it authentically documents the harsh Chinese Communist manner of expression at these secret Talks, Peking's statement should be read in its entirety.*

To sum up, Chinese Communist reactions have used a lot of sharp and vivid words to say "no" to American official and private overtures. President Kennedy's "open door" was the work of a "thief," President Johnson's gesture of conciliation a "fraud," the Vice President's expression of friendship a "kiss of Judas," and Secretary Rusk's ten-point policy a "sham." Peking labeled American proposals for contacts day-dreaming, preposterous, absurd, ridiculous, petty actions, out of the question and not worth a penny. This categorical repudiation was at least consistent with Peking's image of the United States as "the most ferocious common enemy" of the whole world. Indeed it might be noted also that Peking escalated its

* See Appendix E.

vocabulary of rejection as Washington intensified its expression of conciliation.

Continuation of the Ambassadorial Talks

Nevertheless, despite all the years of no agreements, Washington and Peking concurred on one thing—to continue their Ambassadorial Talks in Warsaw. The two Ambassadors agreed at the 131st meeting on September 7 to hold the next session on January 11, 1967. Peking even publicized that. Despite the total divergence over Vietnam, Taiwan, nuclear disarmament, and bilateral contacts, neither government wanted to break off this one diplomatic contact. Each declared in 1966 that it intended to maintain this channel, each for its own purposes.

In denying Moscow's insinuation of a deal with Washington on Vietnam,* Peking's rebuttal permitted the inference that the government of the People's Republic of China intended to continue talking with Washington and wanted the Russians to keep out. Peking would deal with the United States because it served China's national interests. The rebuttal implied that the "dragging on" of the Ambassadorial Talks for more than ten years would continue in line with the Marxist-Leninist principle according to which it is necessary to wage a "tit-for-tat struggle" in negotiations.

A month later, Minister of Foreign Affairs Chen Yi made some public remarks explicitly indicating that Peking wished the Ambassadorial Talks to continue as a matter of policy. Chen Yi was reported to have told a delegation of eight Conservative members of the Japanese Diet on September 6:

The fundamental policy of Chinese Communist diplomacy is to settle problems through talking. Otherwise, Peking would have cut off the discussions with the United States in Warsaw instead of carrying them on for more than 130 meetings. . . .

The United States does not reciprocate the Chinese attitude. The United States is destroying everything and wiping out the possibility of a settlement through talks by trying to affect a settlement by force. . . .

We do not think that the present bad relations between the United States and China will last permanently. If the relations between the United States and China continue to be aggravated, it will produce a serious effect on the world.

* See Chapter 10, section on Vietnam.

In terms of the somewhat obscure internal struggle inside China, the Foreign Minister's relatively restrained tone and straightforward emphasis on settling problems through talks was significant.[30] According to Japanese interpretations, the Foreign Minister was also reported to have declared that the United States should withdraw its troops from Vietnam as a first step toward better relations. Moreover, he left the impression that since there were many problems pending between Communist China and the United States, it could not be expected that they could all be solved "at a stroke." Perhaps this was a shift in Peking's attitude and strategy from those of 1961.* In December 1966 he reportedly spoke to a Brazilian lawyer about the Talks but minimized their usefulness because "nothing practical was achieved and the prospects are not bright." [31]

The Americans have made their desire and intention to continue the Ambassadorial Talks even more abundantly clear than Peking has. In May 1966, the Assistant Secretary of State for Far Eastern Affairs, William Bundy, stated:

> We do want to keep open channels of contact and communication for a time when the Chinese Communists may be more willing to respond. This, in part, is the reason for our desire to maintain our direct diplomatic contacts with the Chinese at Warsaw and for our expressed willingness to sit down and discuss the critical problems of disarmament with Peking.[32]

Regarding the comments of Foreign Minister Chen Yi on September 6, President Johnson replied to a question at his next press conference that he was hopeful because Peking believed it did not face military confrontation with the United States. Expressing the administration's intention to follow up Chen Yi's remarks with an exploration of any possibilities of improving relations with Peking, the President stated: "We do explore every possibility that we are aware of and encourage everything that we think has any potential." [33]

At the end of 1966, after eleven years of dealings and negotiations with each other despite their frozen deadlock and growing tension, Washington and Peking were still keeping up the diplomatic appearance and public image of their intention and willingness to continue this ambassadorial contact.[34] Washington and Peking were saying essentially the same thing, whatever the contrast in vocabu-

* See Chapter 9.

lary: neither intended to start war, and each desired contacts between the peoples of both countries, if only political obstacles did not stand in the way. Indeed, President Johnson significantly included a conciliatory reference in his Message on the State of the Union addressed to the Congress on January 10, 1967:

> We shall continue to hope for reconciliation between the people of mainland China and the world community—including working together in all the tasks of arms control, security, and progress on which the fate of the Chinese people, like their fellow men elsewhere, depends.
> We would be the first to welcome a China which decided to respect her neighbor's rights. We would be the first to applaud her were she to apply her great energies and intelligence to improving the welfare of her people. And we have no intention of trying to deny her legitimate needs for security and friendly relations with her neighboring countries.[35]

In 1967, China's so-called revolution with its struggle for leadership and political turmoil disrupted Peking's diplomacy, including the Ambassadorial Talks. Confusion at home prevented decisions abroad and deferred the Warsaw dialogue. In January the Chinese Communists requested the postponement of the 132nd meeting from the 11th to the 25th of the month and apparently continued their stalemate at that long meeting. The Ambassadors reportedly met for three hours, discussed several issues "frankly and seriously," and agreed not to hold the 133rd meeting until June 7, evidently at Peking's insistence on this interval, which was a longer period between Talks than the three months usually adopted during the past few years. Conversely, the United States government reportedly proposed that the next meeting be held sooner and the frequency of subsequent Talks accelerated. Ambassador Wang Kuo-chuan apparently rejected these suggestions.[36] Moreover, Washington evidently desired to broaden the scope of the discussions. Nevertheless, the Warsaw meeting in January did not reduce the stalemate or lead to any significant new developments. Nor did the meeting at Warsaw in June change the outlook in any important way. Apparently the Ambassadors had to schedule their next session for November 1967, the second long interval of several months during the so-called cultural revolution. During the first six months of 1967, whoever was in charge of diplomacy in Peking was neither disposed to cut the Warsaw line to Washington nor to modify the deadlock with the United States on Vietnam, or to consider new contacts between both countries, or other major issues. Amidst turmoil and tension, the *status quo* of stalemated diplomacy continued.

Nevertheless, it was particularly significant that the first year of China's amazing "cultural revolution" did not lead to Peking's denouncing or severing its only link with Washington. Collapse of the Warsaw Talks would not have been surprising in view of the Vietnamese war, the bitter Sino-Soviet dispute, and the xenophobic outbursts of the "cultural revolution." More significantly, the charges and countercharges of the contending personalities and groups inside China intimated that one of the many issues in the "cultural revolution" was the correct policy for the People's Republic of China to take toward the United States. While the so-called Maoist groups continued to argue for an intractable line, some of Mao's opponents apparently argued behind the scenes for a reduction of tensions between Washington and Peking and perhaps even for some sort of accommodation.[37] Relations with Washington must have become a touchy subject in the internal confrontation, although these intimations of different strategies toward the United States should not be overemphasized. The essential point is that during 1966–67 the men deciding foreign policies in Peking preferred to keep a channel open to Washington for future eventualities, despite the war in Vietnam, the continuing Maoist line of implacable hostility toward "U.S. imperialism," and the internal struggle of the Chinese Communists.

For its part, Washington in 1967 became reticent, even silent, regarding the "cultural revolution" and Sino-American relations, as compared to 1966. It was noticeable and perhaps significant that the President and high American officials did not continue reiterating their emphasis of 1966 on a policy of reconciliation. Mention of the existence and numbers of the Ambassadorial Talks, reference to the desirability of official and unofficial exchanges between the two countries, and official declarations of a more open-minded and pragmatic approach toward the People's Republic of China seemed to have been muted and deferred in Washington during 1967.

In this same careful vein, President Johnson, when asked at a news conference on May 18, 1967, whether resumption of the Ambassadorial Talks gave him hope that relations between the United States and the People's Republic of China would improve, replied that he knew "of nothing that would indicate any optimistic changes." Noting that Ambassador Gronouski had seen him that very morning to report on the Warsaw Talks, the President remarked that "we still have a long way to go" concerning improvement of relations with many other nations. It is noteworthy that the President specifically did not refer to Peking in his reply at this news conference.[38]

Obviously the convulsion in China and the conflicts in Southeast Asia curtailed and deferred any realistic projection of these American attitudes. Notwithstanding these difficulties, however, the Department of State authorized the Commerce Department, in a scarcely noticed announcement of April 1967, to license American pharmaceutical firms who wished to provide medicines and drugs to help reduce any widespread disease or epidemic in mainland China. Yet, Peking rejected this humanitarian gesture on the grounds that it was a baseless allegation since China could have no epidemics.[39]

The Sino-American contacts had entered a period of mutual waiting, although the Americans now wished to intensify the Talks while the Chinese held back. How long they would wait for a new chapter to begin and how frequently they would meet, only time would tell. In any event, the joint facility for diplomatic contact and possible negotiations fortunately remained intact during 1967 for whatever might evolve. If contact were maintained, respected, and strengthened, it could help ease tensions at the right time in the future. Thus, the story of the United States experience since 1953 in negotiating with Communist China continued in 1967 not optimistically, but not hopelessly either.

PART V

The Negotiations Appraised

PART I

The Negotiators Appraised

CHAPTER TWELVE

Format and Machinery

Begun with mistrust and carried on with cold antipathy, the 132 Ambassadorial Talks, the informal contacts, and the three encounters in international conferences are difficult to appraise. Our dealings with the Chinese People's Republic appear to have been futile, with only one negotiated but unfulfilled agreement and at least nineteen proposals rejected; yet, on balance, the Talks have been useful. A comprehensive assessment should examine several categories of results and consequences emerging from this peculiar diplomatic relationship: the form and machinery of the exchanges and the need for alterations to improve the "sub-diplomatic relationship" in the future are discussed in this chapter; the posture of diplomacy and the substance of the negotiations are the subject of the next chapter; and, finally, the differences between American and Chinese Communist styles of negotiation are dealt with in subsequent chapters.

Matters of form, procedure, location, and atmosphere often affect the substance of diplomacy. In the case of American dealings with Peking, the format and procedure of the Ambassadorial Talks have probably met the technical requirements of each government. The "subdiplomatic" arrangements, even with the shrill echo and cold image of Panmunjom, probably have been as effective as any machinery that could have been devised and maintained over the years since August 1955 for two antagonistic governments which have no other diplomatic relations or contact whatsoever. While the procedure has remained ritualistic, it has become familiar, even somewhat flexible, and workable for both parties. Each knows where it stands and how it should proceed in terms of form and machinery. Nothing is left to chance. For two such hostile and distant governments, systematic procedures have contributed distinct advantages which spasmodic and variable lines of communications do not provide. As in any effective conduct of diplomacy, an assurance of conveying and receiving messages, whether oral or written, from sources of authority is indispensable. Nevertheless, the time has come to reconsider the present constricted framework in order to suggest improvements.

Effectiveness of Existing Format

In historical or current perspectives, the contemporary method of contact between Washington and Peking is, of course, only a reflection and instrument of policy, for the Ambassadors in their Talks do not make policy. In the absence of regular diplomatic relations, they substitute abnormal means for normal diplomacy. Nevertheless, however unusual and paradoxical, the Ambassadorial Talks have become more effective than some commentators would concede. A few years ago, an author urged the opening of diplomatic relations between the United States and the People's Republic of China to do away with the "awkwardness" of the Ambassadorial Talks because "facilities for communicating directly with Communist China are now totally lacking." [1] Another commentator had earlier called them "behind the barn type negotiations." [2] While they certainly remain somewhat artificial, irregular, and hidden, they are no more secretive than much standard diplomacy and equally substantive. It was also an overstatement in 1966 to suggest that their value, context, and framework of discussion have been limited, even "extremely limited," in view of United States policies of nonrecognition, isolation and containment of China. [3] After all, even the constricted format of the Talks has permitted repeated presentation and discussion of a wide range of topics.

Whatever else may be said about this peculiar diplomatic instrument, the crucial fact is that the Washington-Peking contact has become a well-operating channel for the notification and explanation of intentions and positions. Lacking other means and engaged in serious conflicts which could lead to armed hostility, each party can communicate with the other on schedule or at any time the occasion requires. In efforts to prevent miscalculation and allay misunderstandings, the State Department and the Foreign Ministry can signal each other instantly and effectively, and without publicity if necessary. Indeed, Ambassador Gronouski, the fourth American representative at the Talks, has reported that they are not limited to polemics and one-sided statements. The meetings, he has said, provide a substantial amount of discussion with a "very useful exchange of views," allow a give and take of questions and answers, permit each side "to develop nuances of thought," and take place in a serious, business-like manner.[4] Thus, the President does have a means to conduct his foreign policy vis-à-vis the People's Republic of China on Vietnam, disarmament, informal relations, or any other subject. He can notify the Politburo in Peking any time he needs to. The policy-makers there can, and have, done the same.

This curious and paradoxical contact between Peking and Washington works at the technical level. It is essential for both sides because the real value of the Ambassadorial Talks—despite their limitations—lies obviously not in the concrete results, but in the frequent nuances of expression and argument. It would not be productive for two governments with so much at stake just to reiterate lengthy broadsides or press statements at Warsaw if there were not the value of this elusive feature of subtle changes in terminology of language and emphasis of voice. Needed perhaps more than anything else in the calling of diplomacy is the trained ear which can instantly detect a slight modulation of inflection, and the perceptive mind which can immediately sense a subtle shift in emphasis. This refinement is the unique feature of the Ambassadorial Talks. However sterile they may have been in producing agreed results, and whatever their consequences, the Warsaw communications provide a useful and perhaps essential "diplomatic radar" to note slight variations in Peking's or Washington's wavelength from meeting to meeting and crisis to crisis.

Perhaps it was for such reasons, as well as others, that the Secretary of State, in issuing the comprehensive U.S. statement regarding China on March 16, 1966, before a closed session of the Far East Subcommittee of the House Foreign Affairs Committee, put such positive stress on bilateral links with the People's Republic of China. One of the ten main elements in that revised policy is the following:

Eighth, we should keep open our direct diplomatic contacts with Peiping in Warsaw. While these meetings frequently provide merely an opportunity for a reiteration of known positions, they play a role in enabling each side to communicate information and attitudes in times of crisis. It is our hope that they might at some time become the channel for a more fruitful dialogue.[5]

Some have argued, nevertheless, that American recognition and exchange of embassies would assure fully adequate communications and improve facilities for negotiating. While this might theoretically be true, various circumstances would indicate that, on balance, a stronger case can be made for maintaining the existing machinery of "sub-diplomatic relations" with Peking, while improving its parts. Having become standardized and workable for contact, notification and negotiation, the Ambassadorial Talks now represent a normal means for Peking in particular, but for Washington as well, to handle an abnormal relationship. They suit not only the realities of our times, but also the peculiarities of fitting together such different negotiating styles.

The Ambassadorial Talks, whatever their faults and weaknesses, may have the virtue of providing an intensely revolutionary Sino-centric China and a vigorously dynamic world-oriented America with the necessary time and judicious distance to adjust to each other's divergent philosophy. While carefully handling their complicated relationship, Washington and Peking can be preparing for the time when full diplomatic relations will be relevant and feasible. Since they are not likely to be so for some time, formal relations can and should incubate out of gradual adjustment by negotiation and conciliation. To hurry the pace or recast the framework of this process might retard or suspend it indefinitely.

Limitations of the Existing Format

Nevertheless, one might emphasize that the form and machinery of the Ambassadorial Talks are adequate and satisfactory only for dealing with one major issue at a time or a few less important matters. It is doubtful that the format of the Talks would be efficient for negotiating a number of complex matters, some of policy nature and others of technical substance, on a regular or routine basis. Basic changes in the mechanics of dealing between both Ambassadors in Warsaw as well as a shift in location might have to be made. Moreover, Peking's concentration on Taiwan may, in Peking's view, disqualify the Ambassadorial Talks for any serious discussion on anything else. Peking might prefer to take up issues other than Taiwan in a different place or in a different format.

The lack of any informal social or personal contacts between the two Ambassadors in Warsaw and members of the embassy staffs is probably not a major handicap to the Ambassadorial Talks, given their rigid formalism and repetitive uniformity. It would help, of course, if the Ambassadors occasionally met informally, as other diplomatic representatives do, for relatively easy and noncommittal exchange or casual remarks. The two Ambassadors in Warsaw might even vary the considerable monotony of presentation and audition by occasional telephone conversations if they could speak a common language. But even that possible opening is closed. However, a somewhat more relaxed, informal, and productive contact apparently has developed between the individual members of each embassy who are responsible for the translation of the oral statements at the meetings into English and Chinese.

In the circumstances, the Peking leadership will probably insist on these limitations to continue "arm's length" diplomacy for some time, inasmuch as the format of the Ambassadorial Talks reflects a traditional Sinocentric framework and procedure to deter agreements and insulate foreign negotiators from the center of power and decision-making.[6]

Suggestions for Changes in the Ambassadorial Talks

Because of Chinese traditionalism and procedural rigidities, Washington should take the initiative to propose improved or remodeled machinery for the Talks if they are ever to provide "an opening through which, hopefully, light might one day penetrate . . . for a more fruitful dialogue," as Secretary Rusk remarked.[7] The "little window of diplomacy" will have to be widened and modernized in various ways to facilitate the emergence of new dimensions in Sino-American relations.

In the first place, the two Ambassadors could move from the Polish palace and meet by rotation in each other's embassy in Warsaw. This might be criticized as being virtually the same as diplomatic recognition but, in fact, it would be the same sort of arm's length diplomacy as has been practiced under Polish auspices. But it would then be independently bilateral. Even without such a reciprocal exchange of meetings, the staffs of both embassies could be expanded in composition and expertise and called together in each embassy on a reciprocal basis.

Another possible change for making dialogue more fruitful would be a shift in the site to some other country. For example, the Ambassadorial Talks could be returned to Geneva where both countries might station special Ambassadorial representatives and where they might return to their direct bilateral use of United Nations facilities.

A move out of the Polish palace and to another country would also enhance the bilateral character of the Ambassadorial Talks. In that case, the Americans and the Chinese would be dealing more directly and fully with each other. They would alternately arrange their own sessions and be in charge of their own meeting places without the necessity or the benefit of any go-between. Of course, such a change would forego the particular and perhaps peculiar benefits and by-products of third-party auspices. But if the brittleness and sharpness of Washington-Peking relations were ameliorated slightly, the need for a go-between would diminish.

Theoretically, it might be possible to diversify the arm's length contact even further, if unconventionally, by Peking and Washington allowing their Ambassadors to visit each other's capital for additional discussions related specifically and exclusively to the topics of the Ambassadorial Talks. While this may seem tantamount to an exchange of Ambassadors and diplomatic relations, it would fall short of that if both governments did not take the explicit steps necessary under normal diplomatic practice for such recognition and exchange. Without going that far, given the current state of relationship between the two governments, they might each see some advantage in having officials in their respective capitals able to talk directly with a roving ambassador of the other. A more radical alteration would be to create special Ambassadors, each to reside respectively in his capital, Washington or Peking, but to meet at appointed times in some mutually designated place, such as the United Nations headquarters in New York or Geneva. However, that arrangement would probably widen the separation, at least mechanically.

The most significant improvement in the format of the Talks would be to give more flexibility and scope to their substance. While a better format might produce a more fruitful dialogue if the meeting place and location were changed, more light would come through the opening if the meetings were more frequent and the procedures less ritualistic, if the Panmunjom format were abandoned, contacts were more casual, and exchanges unlimited on ideas and proposals concerning all aspects of Sino-American relations. Communications would certainly be improved if there could be an informal exchange of questions and answers, an exchange of documents, joint preparation of transcripts of the meetings, and consultations or even negotiations at the staff or specialist level. Improved machinery and diversified substance would make it easier for the divergent style of the Americans and the Chinese Communists to meet rather than elude each other. Moreover, it would help public understanding of this significant channel between Peking and Washington if they could ever agree to issue a joint communiqué after each meeting, outlining the subjects discussed.

Hopefully, the government of the United States will suggest some such alterations, even if several years pass before the present leaders and their successors in Peking accept them or take their own initiatives to improve communications with Washington. If that came about, perhaps Talks at the ministerial level could take place.

CHAPTER THIRTEEN

Appraisal of Results and Consequences

The first general task in assessing the Washington-Peking negotiations is to put them in their prime context of "posturing" or "imagistic" diplomacy.

The Posture of Diplomacy

The conduct of professional diplomacy, old and new, indulges—often sensibly and usefully, but sometimes pretentiously or foolishly—in what diplomats call "posturing" or "assuming a posture." *
Put another way, it means taking a public position to demonstrate an attitude, regardless of the real policy or opinion of the government. The public and the private stance may be identical, or they may differ; but governments, whether democratic or totalitarian, particularly in our age of public diplomacy and massive communications, must "strike attitudes" and take public positions. The negotiations between Washington and Peking have been no exception. Both governments—as unlike as they are—have "assumed postures" toward each other and particularly toward the Ambassadorial Talks, each in its own characteristic style. Yet, the consequence has been strikingly similar.

Both Peking and Washington have often used the contact in the Ambassadorial Talks to convey the suggestive and concrete image to the world of realistically acknowledging and dealing with the

---

* In his provocative study, *The Image*, Professor Kenneth Boulding emphasizes that symbolic images are important in international relations, and that, among other things, they serve to present and summarize "an extremely complex network of alternatives and situations . . . a whole value system, a whole attitude toward life and the universe." (Ann Arbor: University of Michigan Press, paperback, 1961), p. 110.

existence of the other, of seriously maintaining these contacts in good standing, and of seeking to improve relations and decrease tensions between them—or of picturing the other as doing just the reverse. While, on the one hand, both parties have continuously failed to accommodate themselves to the other on many important as well as minor issues, each side has kept up the appearance or illusion of significant contact with the other. Even the major dispute over Taiwan and the dangerous divergence over Vietnam did not altogether rub out this tendency toward favorable posturing in the Ambassadorial Talks.

Both Washington and Peking have engaged in this diplomacy of posture from time to time with varying intensity during the entire period of their negotiations and contacts since 1955. In 1955 and 1956 Chou En-lai used the image of "sitting down" for negotiations in the hope and even expectation of settling disputes and eliminating tensions. Peking then used the Talks and other news media to bring pressure on Washington, and gave the Chinese people and the world a fairly steady, if self-serving, running account of important developments in the Geneva Talks. Peking insisted it was doing everything it could to make the Talks a success and reduce tensions, while accusing the Americans of inaction. In that era of coexistence, Peking utilized the Talks to demonstrate its adherence to the Bandung spirit. By its diplomacy of posturing and image-making Peking perhaps calculated that it could turn the Talks into a springboard for arranging a ministerial conference between Chou En-lai and John Foster Dulles, an understanding on the trade embargo, the establishment of mutual contacts between both countries, and the resultant lessening of tension over Taiwan. Originally Peking committed itself quite far in its public expressions of hope and expectation that negotiations with the United States would bring about some of these significant and lasting benefits for the Chinese People's Republic.

By comparison, the original American public image of the Geneva Talks was small, strained, and insignificant. John Foster Dulles probably had no desire at that time to sit down anywhere with Chou En-lai, and would not even shake hands with him at Geneva. To Washington this was a reluctant contact made for reasons of expediency for limited and specific purposes. Dulles probably accepted the Talks more for reasons of imagistic and posturing diplomacy than from any desire or expectation on his part of being able to negotiate and conclude beneficial agreements. He wished, and was diplomatically pressed, to demonstrate to the United Nations, the allies of the United States, and the Afro-Asian governments that the United States could be reasonable. But, as part of the normal posturing of diplomacy, Dulles was particularly interested in probing Peking's intentions and reactions at these Talks. Influenced so emphatically by Dulles in those early years, the United States government was not willing to go beyond this combination of image-making and reconnoitering to project the appearance of reasonableness and expediency.

Then, in a shift of position during the Taiwan crisis of 1958, Peking played down the Talks and limited their prospects. Instead, the Chinese Communist leaders manipulated the crisis for internal image-making. Peking used the "aggressiveness" of the United States to create a "foreign devil" and to whip up popular emotions for the massive mobilization which Peking's monolithic system required to launch the "great leap forward" and the new system of communes. By contrast, the United States government did not particularly exploit its relations with Peking or the Ambassadorial Talks for domestic consumption during the Taiwan crisis. If anything, Washington stressed the perspective of diplomacy rather than force, while Dulles hinted at conceivable changes of positive significance in Sino-American relations. In that crisis and in the years since, the contacts with Peking were for Washington a timely opportunity to explore the possibilities for change.

By 1959, Chou En-lai and his colleagues evidently decided that significant and major changes beneficial to the Chinese People's Republic could not be negotiated with the Americans. Since 1960 Peking has been following the diplomacy of stalemate and has indulged primarily in futile imagistic diplomacy. Nevertheless, it is significant that it chose to pursue that policy rather than suspend the Talks altogether. In late 1963 Foreign Minister Chen Yi told visiting Australians that "we do not wish to break off the Warsaw Talks with the United States which have gone on eight years—some contact is better than none." At about the same time Chou En-lai himself told a press conference in Cairo that the Chinese People's Republic was continuing the Ambassadorial Talks and cited them especially to deal with a reporter's question as to why the Chinese People's Republic seemed to oppose "peaceful consultations" between East and West.[1] When Ambassador Wang Ping-nan left

Warsaw in 1964, after ten years of negotiations with the Americans, he took the unusual step of meeting the press to give a favorable image of these "advantageous" talks. He was polite about the United States and expressed the belief that the differences between the Chinese People's Republic and the United States would eventually be settled, although he regretted that the Ambassadorial Talks had not yet produced any results, which in his opinion was not the fault of his side. His successor, Ambassador Wang Kuo-chuan, told the press on the occasion of his first Talk at Warsaw that his government favored settling disputes peacefully with the United States.[2]

In June 1964 Foreign Minister Chen Yi declared that while he did not expect any improvement in relations with the United States after its elections, the Chinese People's Republic still was willing to improve and develop relations with all countries, including the United States. As for the Ambassadorial Talks, they had dealt mainly, he said, with the questions of settling Sino-American disputes through peaceful negotiations, including the issue of American withdrawal from Taiwan and the Taiwan Straits, and the resort to force. He claimed that his government had put forward the very simple proposal that the Chinese People's Republic and the United States agree to coexist peacefully according to the Five Principles * and, second, that the United States government guarantee to withdraw its armed forces from "China's Taiwan province" and the Straits of Taiwan.[3] Later that year Chou En-lai told four Filipino newsmen in Peking that "we have had rich experience in dealing with the United States," which has continued the "illogical state of affairs" of holding Talks with the Chinese People's Republic for nine years while refusing to recognize the "new China." Nevertheless, Chou En-lai repeated in October 1964 that the Chinese People's Republic was willing to coexist peacefully with the United States on the basis of the Five Principles.[4]

Even after American military operations were stepped up in Vietnam during early 1965, Chou En-lai was still willing to evoke the image of the Ambassadorial Talks. In March 1965 he told a correspondent for the *New Statesman* that they had been going on for ten years in 125 meetings. He explained the Ambassadorial Talks in the following vein:

* Respect for territorial integrity and sovereignty, nonaggression, noninterference in the internal affairs of other states, equality and mutual benefit, and peaceful coexistence.

Our Ambassador proposed an agreement on principle on two points to the American Ambassador. First of all on peaceful coexistence. Revisionists pretend that China is opposed to peaceful coexistence, the U.S. repeats this loudly and the Indian Government echoes it. Yet we have been proposing peaceful coexistence to the Americans for 10 years. But obviously peaceful coexistence must be based on certain principles and there is no question of establishing it without principle. To ask China to coexist peacefully with the U.S. while the latter maintains military bases around China and occupies the Chinese territory of Formosa—that is impossible.[5]

This illustrates the use of the Talks for public posturing—in this case to refute the Russians, Indians, and Americans. Since mid-1965, however, Peking has been rather reticent about its continuing contact with Washington and the Ambassadorial Talks. Peking's reactions to American and Soviet references to them in 1966 could only leave the impression that the Peking leadership would rather not have been reminded of the Talks and would have preferred little or no public posturing about them by anybody.

In contrast, American officials increasingly used the number, continuation and purposes of the Ambassadorial Talks to convey the appearance of maintaining at least a minimum reasonable relationship with Peking. On December 24, 1963, Secretary Rusk referred to the Talks and noted a few days later that for eight years Peking had rejected Washington's effort to negotiate a reciprocal renunciation of force. In a speech of March 1964, he wished to clear away the "myth" that the United States government had ignored the Chinese Communist regime when he declared: "We know it exists. We talk with it regularly through our respective Ambassadors to Warsaw. There have been 119 of these talks. And what the Peiping regime itself says to us is among the reasons why we continue to have very grave concerns about it."[6] In 1965 he referred several times in the same vein to the Warsaw Talks. He told a press conference in 1966 that the United States had tried for a long time to find "particular points" for improving relationships with mainland China, citing the 129 Ambassadorial Talks among other things. As he pictured it vividly: "We are prepared to sit down at the table and talk if someone is prepared to come to the table and talk with us. But thus far we have no one at the table. . . . We are prepared for informal, private, discreet, preliminary discussions. But the difficulty is that the other side keeps hanging up the phone."[7] That may have been overdoing the imagery somewhat because at about the same time he told a Congressional Committee that the "extensive conversations" with Peking were very important and served "useful purposes." [8] On February 12, 1966, the Assistant Secretary for Far Eastern Affairs, William P. Bundy, characterized the Talks as the "longest and most direct dialogue of any major Western nation with Communist China" . . . and

more of a dialogue than we could expect to have if we were ever to recognize Communist China. . . . And it is an opportunity to try directly to make them understand that we have no hostile designs on mainland China or its leaders but that we fully intend to maintain our commitments to defend our friends and allies against Communist aggression and that the United States seeks peace, freedom, and stability for the countries of Asia.[9]

These periodic references in Washington and Peking to the uses and number of the Ambassadorial Talks have served a useful purpose in the tense international situation of the past dozen years. Each reference has had the effect of assuring various governments of a willingness to maintain the slender thread of liaison. The Americans have been able to reassure their allies, many neutrals, and the United Nations, as well as public opinion in many parts of the world, that a diplomatic avenue—or back alley—always remained open to Peking. For their part, Chou En-lai and his colleagues have been able, when necessary, to demonstrate that a line of communication with the Americans remained workable. All of this has contributed to whatever has been rational in the cold war of the 1950s and 1960s.

The frequent citing by both Washington and Peking of the total number of meetings as well as their continuity is, of course, somewhat misleading. It should not convey the impression that mistrust has thereby decreased or that the usefulness of the channel is constant or cumulative. In fact, perhaps only some twenty-five of all the Ambassadorial Talks were actually significant in terms of specific results or tangible consequences, specifically, the few meetings on the Repatriation Agreement, the first five in Warsaw on the Taiwan crisis and a dozen or so covering Laos, Taiwan, nuclear disarmament, Vietnam, and bilateral contacts since 1961. All the rest—more than one hundred Talks, and the conferences at Panmunjom and Geneva as well—were an unproductive ritual for both governments. Therefore, it confuses the significance of these Talks and distorts any appraisal of the record merely to point to the total number held over a period of time.

For, unfortunately if unavoidably, the posturing about the Talks may have deepened and extended the mistrust between both governments. The "sitting down" may actually have brought about a "closing up." The manner of introducing, handling, and discussing several subjects in private and in public may have increased the suspicion and antipathy between Washington and Peking as the years have passed. For one thing, Washington often extensively explained its "public posture" on contacts and conciliation with the Chinese People's Republic in 1966. To the extent that this effort was directed primarily toward influencing American public opinion, it was imagistic, posturing diplomacy. However, the probability is that Washington in 1966 assumed that its public posture on contacts and Vietnam would facilitate its diplomatic efforts at Warsaw, although it apparently had the opposite effect on Peking, just as Peking's public posturing in 1955–57 about prisoners, nonforce, a ministerial meeting, and newsmen had a negative effect in Washington. It is interesting in this connection that in September 1966 the Soviet newspaper, *Izvestia*, reprinted a French newspaper comment that "each side's picture of the other is not at all what one would suppose it to be" in the sense that both Washington and Peking were depicting the other as opposing coexistence and favoring hostility.[10]

The Substance of Negotiations

To appraise the actual results of United States negotiations and contacts with Communist China since 1953 is more difficult. In a clash of irreconcilable ideologies and interests, the substance of these negotiations has resulted in a simultaneous interplay of four kinds of diplomacy: maneuver, transaction, stalemate, and elusion. Because each side has emphasized one or another at any one time, the history of the negotiations is confusing.

The negotiations have compiled a public record of some nineteen definite proposals rejected in the course of twelve years, plus numerous resubmissions of rejected or revised proposals. Over the years, Washington has reportedly turned down Peking's propositions for a radical change in Taiwan's status, holding a bilateral meeting of the foreign ministers, ending the American embargo and opening trade, exchanging newsmen, establishing cultural relations with the United States, agreeing on atom-free-zones in Asia and elsewhere, convening a world-wide or nuclear powers' conference on disarmament, issuing a bilateral pledge not to use nuclear weapons against each other, and negotiating United States withdrawal from Vietnam. For its part, Peking has reportedly rejected Washington's proposals for a joint renunciation of force in the area of Taiwan, the immediate return of all imprisoned Americans to implement the Repatriation Agreement, various arrangements for the "neutralization" of the offshore islands and the stabilization of the Taiwan Straits, adherence to the Test-Ban Treaty, participation in conferences on general disarmament, a reciprocal pledge on no-first-use of nuclear weapons concurrent with Peking's adherence to the Test-Ban Treaty, a reciprocal or unilateral exchange of newsmen, an ending of travel barriers between each country for scholars, scientists, doctors, businessmen, and others, arrangements for non-strategic trade and shipments of surplus food, and various proposals to de-escalate and negotiate the conflict in Vietnam.

Taiwan: To take up the subjects in order, the Ambassadorial Talks have centered around the dominating issue of Taiwan and the change in its sovereign status. The Talks did not come near to breaking the deadlock. Peking instituted them in 1955, maneuvered for three years, and then impounded them in a rigid stalemate with a view to negotiating the transfer of sovereignty and control over Taiwan. This was more than "posturing"; it was a concerted diplomatic effort, yet the issue in 1967 was further from resolution or accommodation that it was in 1955.

Neither Washington nor Peking has seriously used the diplomatic channel available to suggest proposals to the other regarding the question of Taiwan and the offshore islands. During 1955–57 Peking maneuvered vigorously in various ways to create a better atmosphere and to open the subject for a meeting between Chou En-lai and John Foster Dulles. Although it never was in the realm of possibility, Chou kept probing his adversary. Dulles engaged in a resourceful diplomacy of stalemate to prevent the issue from crossing the tables at Geneva or reaching the point of an exchange of views. The result was the deadlock over applying agreed terms on the renunciation of force, the exchange of newsmen, a Foreign Ministers' meeting and the American embargo.

In the Taiwan crisis of 1958 both sides engaged in a kind of one-sided, non-engaged maneuver, which has been called the "diplomacy of elusion." Neither was willing to touch the other's proposals or commit itself to probing the actual proposal suggested or implied at Warsaw or in public. Peking hinted at some sort of extended formula, first in principle and then in execution, for staging, perhaps over a long period of time, the change in the status of Taiwan.

Dulles, on the other hand, limited himself to specifics on the off-shore islands, leaving the larger "core" issues of "principle" either open for later discussion at a higher level, or impounded. It is not clear from the public record at any rate, what he might have done had Chou En-lai negotiated an acceptable transaction on the off-shore islands. Thus, another result of the long diplomatic contact was the failure in Peking to respond to these probes, at least on the edges of the Taiwan issue. Peking stuck to the core: Taiwan itself. Washington, accordingly, must have concluded that any negotiation of "other practical matters at issue" had become a dead letter in Peking. An opportunity was rejected. The Talks returned to stalemate.

The failure of negotiations at Geneva and Warsaw, particularly after their effects on the triangular relations among Peking, Washington and Moscow became evident, presumably has led Peking since 1959 to adhere rigidly to its diplomacy of stalemate. It has apparently not attempted to probe Washington's attitude toward any form of negotiation on anything. The one exception was Peking's proposal of 1964 for a joint announcement that both governments agree not to be the first to use atomic weapons.

Thus, with regard to the prime dispute of Taiwan between Washington and Peking there has been, and could have been, no movement or substantial result. Rather, in the context of the Taiwan issue the Talks may have had the consequence of pushing Washington and Peking further apart.

Peking has never indicated what concessions, *quid pro quo*, or "complementary" measures the Chinese People's Republic would take if the United States ever agreed in principle to withdraw its armed forces from Taiwan and the Taiwan Straits. Peking only introduced and reiterated in private and in public its general proposal on the principle of American acceptance of such withdrawal. Since a normal negotiation requires some complementary reciprocal action on the part of both parties, it is difficult to see where there could have been any place for real negotiation, even from Peking's viewpoint, over the issue of Taiwan. Perhaps, in Peking's fixed frame of reference, the transaction of some concession was to come in the timing and manner of such a withdrawal.

In 1955 Chou En-lai spoke of "ultimately eliminating" tension in the Taiwan area. How far into the future did he envisage the adverb "ultimately" to go? Did the Americans ever try to ask him or his Ambassador? Presumably not. In 1956 he suggested that a joint renunciation of force and continuation of "Sino-American talks" had to be "advantageous to both sides." Again, what did he mean? Apparently, the Talks never uncovered any substance. In the first ten Talks at Warsaw in September-November 1958, it might again be inferred from Peking's attitude that the *easing* of tension, meaning the American withdrawal over a period of time, could be negotiated instead of the *elimination* of tension—the immediate removal of all American forces from the Taiwan area. The diplomatic exchange did not broach the question. Presumably Washington could not question the time factor without adhering to the principle of withdrawal.

In Edgar Snow's interpretation there is a difference in Peking's matter of principle and suggestion on implementation. Peking has held Ambassadorial Talks for ten years, he reported in 1965, in order to recover Taiwan by "peaceful negotiations," and has "steadily insisted upon a legal solution to the Taiwan question and the problem of United States recognition of the Chinese revolution as the stable national power of China." The Chinese People's Republic has demanded, he indicated, that the United States recognize Peking's sovereignty over Taiwan and simultaneously agree "in principle to cease using armed force" to prevent China's national unification. Chou En-lai told him in 1960 and 1965 that "once these matters of principle were conceded, the timing and manner of United States armed withdrawal would be subject to negotiation." Chairman Mao, Prime Minister Chou, and Foreign Minister Chen Yi all insisted to him that to compromise with Washington on Taiwan was impossible as long as American "armed intervention" continued there. On the other hand, Taiwan was the only dispute in early 1965, according to Snow, which prevented normalization of United States-Chinese relations from Peking's standpoint. He reported that the Peking leadership then did not regard disputes with Washington affecting neighboring countries as part of their direct and national territorial quarrel with the United States. At that time, conflicting interests with Washington over Vietnam apparently would not have prevented restoration of United States-Chinese relations, he claimed.[11]

While this sounds somewhat plausible, it should be noted that any such negotiation on this basis would have been one-sided in Peking's favor. Washington would have conceded a major change in its policy of protecting Taiwan and supporting the Republic of China with nothing significant conceded by Peking, such as an agreement not to attack Taiwan with force, an understanding on the security of other countries in Asia, or adherence to the Test-Ban Treaty. From Washington's point of view there was nothing that was advantageous in Peking's explicit proposition of principle and vague suggestion for implementation.*

The long hours spent on exchanging drafts for a joint renunciation of force reduced the verbiage to one word in this implacable dispute between Peking and Washington: Taiwan. Here the negotiation brought the two matters of principle together—withdrawal from Taiwan and renunciation of force—but not for any mutual transaction. In fact, each principle was non-negotiable or unacceptable to each party. Peking would not give up its right to obtain Taiwan, by force if necessary. Washington would not give up its stand on the renunciation of force concerning Taiwan before negotiating anything else, much less Taiwan itself. Thus the major question of resort to force also foundered on the issue of Taiwan. The long negotiations in 1956 on the joint renunciation of force reduced the other points of disagreement and produced a form of agreement between the People's Republic of China and the United States of America with regard to avoiding force in their disputes, with the one prominent and totally disqualifying exception of Taiwan. If the diplomacy of stalemate were to become a diplomacy

* There is another amplification of this nebulous idea from non-Communist sources apparently sympathetic to Peking's viewpoint on Taiwan. Chang Hsin-hai, a former Chinese Nationalist diplomat living in the United States, has written about a detailed non-Communist version of a negotiated settlement of the Taiwan question which, according to him, was submitted to President Kennedy by General Li Tsung-jen, once second to Chiang Kai-shek before Li spent many years exiled in America prior to returning to Communist China in 1965. First, if Washington accepted the principle of the Chinese People's Republic's sovereignty over Taiwan, Peking would agree to any proposition for its transfer such as demilitarization, neutralization, and even a twenty-year "custodianship" of the United Nations. Second, Peking would then become the representative of China in the United Nations. Third, the United Nations, at Peking's request, would then be asked to supervise the neutralization of Taiwan and the establishment of a purely civilian Chinese administration on Taiwan. The personnel in the "Taiwan government" would continue their functions indefinitely. Finally, Taiwan would, eventually one gathers, revert to its status as a province of China. For the full account of this plan, see Chang Hsin-hai, *America and China: A New Approach to Asia* (New York: Simon and Schuster, 1966), pp. 259–263. In addition O. Edmund Clubb's article on "Sino-American Relations and the Future of Formosa" in the *Political Science Quarterly* of March 1965 contains later unconfirmed reports that some variation of the "autonomous Province under a 20-year plan" was discussed between Peking and Taipei.

of maneuver between Peking and Washington, and mutually satisfactory arrangements in principle or in detail worked out for Taiwan, then it would be a simple matter for agreement on the renunciation of force to be signed by both governments almost as it is now drafted.

Yet, the discussion over Taiwan and the display of restraint in United States-Communist China negotiations have probably helped to dampen the danger of miscalculated hostilities in the area of Taiwan. In 1955, 1958, and 1962, both governments and their representatives in the Talks were compelled, as well as enabled, to talk with each other about this grave issue. They may have been at an impasse but they were not in the dark. The Ambassadorial Talks have been an escape hatch for Washington, Peking, and Moscow to prevent the build-up of pressures. When the embroilment of all three governments over Taiwan seemed to verge on an outbreak of major war, the diplomatic facility of the Ambassadorial Talks enabled them to undertake both public and private diplomacy at least to arrive at a stalemate. Although the Talks set negative limits on the resort to war over Taiwan, they did not lead to any positive results or consequences regarding Taiwan. As Ambassador U. Alexis Johnson, the first American representative at the Ambassadorial Talks, pointed out in 1963—some six years after his last encounter at Geneva—Peking makes the issue of Taiwan a stumbling block on every other issue because the Chinese People's Republic must assert that it is the sole government of China and because it must reject any understanding with the United States or any other government which does not accept that assertion and which recognizes Taiwan as a separate entity. Accordingly, he pointed out, the communications in Geneva and Warsaw have "proven to be a very sterile channel for the most part."

However, in April 1966, an American newspaper reported from diplomatic sources in London that Washington had initiated a new effort at the 129th Warsaw meeting to see if the stalemate over Taiwan could be broken. Whether or not this press report was true, it at least reflected diplomatic indications that Washington was continuing to seek some way of probing the possibilities for negotiation. According to the report, Washington had told Peking through the Warsaw Talks that normalization of relations and the seating of Peking in the United Nations might be discussed. Thereupon, according to this unconfirmed and probably inaccurate report, the Chinese Communists rebuffed the American initiative and demanded

United States withdrawal from Vietnam and an agreement on world disarmament.[12]

Repatriation of Civilians: Over the years the issue of repatriation, which the Talks were supposed to have to settle at the outset, has bedeviled and beclouded subsequent negotiations and Washington-Peking relations. The United States government has reiterated over one hundred times that the initial negotiations and the Agreement on Repatriation never excluded Americans in jail or included Chinese in America who had been accused, sentenced, and jailed for common crimes. The Department of State and its diplomatic representatives have repeatedly sought to set that point straight. At Geneva and Warsaw the American Ambassadors, one after another, have urged unconditional compliance with the Agreement of September 10, 1955, providing for the speedy, expeditious and unconditional return of the remaining Americans. Yet in 1967, while 36 Americans had been released, 4 were still in Chinese jails: Bishop James Walsh, over seventy-five years old, Hugh Redmond, John Downey, and Richard Feitean, all charged and sentenced for espionage. Since 1960, despite persistent American attempts, both Ambassadors Wang at Warsaw have consistently refused to discuss the return of American prisoners, stating that major matters must be settled before "minor" issues can be resolved.

On their side, the Chinese Communists have apparently expressed the hope that Washington would find it possible to discuss the release and return of the Chinese prisoners in the United States. This presumably refers to those aliens of Chinese nationality residing in the United States who have been convicted of a civil or criminal offense. In 1955–56 the Communists wanted all Chinese in prison first to be released and then given the choice of going to China or remaining in the United States. The Chinese Communists have continually claimed that, despite promises relayed by third parties, the United States has constantly failed to release some Chinese prisoners, but this appears to be an inaccurate and misleading charge. As noted above, the United States agreed to release any prisoner who wished to go to Communist China. Further, Peking has expressed the hope that those Chinese residents who would like to rejoin their families would also be discussed. Since 1955, all such residents have been and are free to leave the United States. Peking has said that it has appealed to Washington for a list of Chinese residents who wish to be repatriated; however, there is no such list. Neither the United States government nor the Indian Embassy has received the names of any

Chinese who wish to go to mainland China. The Indian Embassy or the International Red Cross would have followed up all requests from any Chinese wishing to return to mainland China.

The Chinese Communists have repeatedly asked for a complete list of names and addresses of all of the several thousand alien Chinese still residing in the United States. Washington has refused to furnish such a list even if it existed, or were possible to compile, because Washington contends that to do so would bring pressure on these innocent people's relatives in China to force their return or to solicit funds and support. All of them migrated voluntarily to the United States, some many years prior to the Communist take-over and others as refugees from communism. All of them are free to leave the United States whenever they wish to do so. It is true that the Chinese Communists allow relatives to visit American prisoners once a year. For reciprocity, the United States offered to allow visits by the Indian Embassy to Chinese serving sentences in American jails, but the Chinese Communists refused to permit authorization and the prisoners were interviewed by the Red Cross instead.

As for Chinese nationals residing in America, the United States government has stated over and over that no Chinese resident in the United States who had shown a desire to go to Communist China was being prevented from doing so in 1955, nor at any time since. The United States government believes that it has meticulously and completely carried out all its commitments under the Agreed Announcement of September 10, 1955. By press, television, and radio it widely publicized the right of any Chinese to return to Communist China unhindered. In 1956 it placed notices containing the text of the Agreed Announcement in 33,000 post offices throughout the country. On several occasions it publicly called on anyone to come forward who knew of any Chinese who believed his departure was being obstructed. There has not been a single response to date. The Indian Embassy, as provided by the Agreed Announcement, was authorized to make representation on behalf of any such Chinese, but has never brought any case to Washington's attention of any Chinese being prevented by the United States from returning to Communist China. Even though not specifically covered by the Agreement, twenty-four Chinese prisoners in Federal jails were asked in 1956 if they wished to be freed to go to mainland China. Twenty-one preferred jail in America. Not only have all Chinese been free to leave this country, but since July 11, 1955, many hundreds have done so without being hindered in any way. The United

States government has no means of knowing the final destination of any of those who have departed. Of the total who have left, several hundreds are known to have returned directly to mainland China through Hong Kong by ship from the United States.

Why has this written Agreement, seemingly so simple and straightforward and the only one ever reached on a bilateral basis between the United States and the Chinese People's Republic, been such a subject of contention and dispute in the discussions? To judge by the available public information regarding the transaction, the language of the agreement, and many official American statements, one can only conclude that one of two things has happened: a major misunderstanding between Washington and Peking or a deliberate falsification and misrepresentation by Peking. This one short, simple, and specific agreement has raised more questions and doubts than it has settled. Did Peking deliberately try to deceive Washington? Did Peking later twist the Agreement to suit its own purposes for negotiating other matters with Washington?

It seems reasonable to conclude that Peking deliberately delayed the implementation of the agreement for several months and then several years. Peking could have released all of the Americans in jail whether under sentence or not in September 1955, as the Americans had intended the Agreement to mean, and fully expected would happen. They were apparently taken by surprise when the repatriation of all Americans did not immediately occur. One can only speculate that Peking dragged its feet for fear that this tenuous opening to Washington might be shut again after all the Americans were sent home forthwith. Yet if repatriation was handled this way out of the fear that Washington would no longer continue the contact at Geneva, let alone negotiate, withholding American prisoners probably had the consequence of deterring and discouraging Washington in 1955–57 from proceeding with any further negotiations on other initiatives from Peking. Its bargaining strategy backfired in a miscalculation or misunderstanding of American psychology. In passing, it should be noted that Peking perhaps would have been able to put much more pressure on Washington if it had elected to release the prisoners rather than withhold them. If Peking wanted to bring about negotiations at a higher level and periodic or continuous contact with Dulles to discuss Taiwan, the embargo, and diplomatic recognition, quick release of American prisoners would have been far more productive for Peking, even resulting in an exchange of newsmen. But refusal to implement a negotiated agreement and the attempt to make the Americans pay twice had just the opposite result. It infuriated American officials and made them doubt the feasibility of any further negotiations with the Chinese People's Republic.

When one considers that only a few American prisoners were involved in the Repatriation Agreement, it seems astonishing and incredible that Peking could have so misjudged American reaction and so embroiled Peking's negotiating objectives. Perhaps Peking's behavior reflected complete distrust of Washington and its action was a defensive move.

An equally plausible explanation for this contradiction at the start of Peking's initiative for "sitting down" and negotiating with the Americans was Peking's obsession for "equalitarian" and "symmetrical" treatment, motivated by the Marxist and revolutionary elements in the Maoist negotiating style. During the Ambassadorial discussions in August and September 1955, Peking put great emphasis on exactly reciprocal, comparable provisions for repatriation of Chinese civilians and prisoners in the United States to those for Americans in China, although the issue over the former was not the main point or even a real one in the over-all transaction. Nevertheless, Peking raised all sorts of difficulties for Ambassador Johnson and Washington on the issue of Chinese in America, changing demands and provisions one after another once the Americans agreed to them or remained adamant. Since this attitude may have led to an even deeper mistrust in Peking of the Americans, Peking probably concluded that the Americans would not turn over any Chinese in the United States to Peking's jurisdiction or for any form of repatriation. Consequently, according to this interpretation of Peking's obstructionist behavior on the issue of American prisoners, Peking immediately retaliated by deferring the release of Americans in China. The evidence for this correlation is the fact that, upon the announcement of the Repatriation Agreement of September 10, 1955, the Peking government and its press immediately began to accuse the American government of mistreating and "incarcerating thousands" of Chinese in the United States before the Agreement could be implemented in the United States. An inference could be drawn that Peking was accusing Washington of doing to the Chinese in the United States exactly what Peking had already planned to do to the Americans in China. This form of reverse projection is often encountered in dealing with the Communists of all nationalities. It amounts to denouncing the other side in order to make a useful smoke screen to conceal one's own action. However futile, the United States government did go to exceptional lengths to inform all Chinese in the United States that every Chinese had a right and opportunity to return to the People's Republic of China unhindered. This meticulous implementation of the Agreement on repatriation failed to convince Peking that Washington was not discriminating against the Chinese contrary to Peking's interpretation of the Agreement.

Exchange of Newsmen and Other Contacts: The same chasm of mistrust and antipathy emerged in this matter. The Chinese in 1956–57 negotiated vigorously to get an agreement or an informal arrangement for such contacts. Washington at first sternly rebuffed these initiatives, but then retreated to an offer of unilateral and nonreciprocal entry of a selected group of American newsmen into China. Since 1960, Peking has remained adamant against negotiating the issue at all, while Washington has tried every possible avenue to overcome Chinese Communist resistance. The net result of more than ten years of intermittent discussion, several proposals, and numerous repetitions of each side's views on the issue of newsmen and contacts is no contact. Washington was first too rigid and then too late. It could have handled this matter more effectively in the long run, although Peking's later attitude has blocked any agreement.

One important consequence of the negotiations is the complete reversal of the two sides in the Ambassadorial Talks on this issue. In 1956 when the Chinese Communists took the initiative regarding newsmen, the Americans immediately assumed the posture, and held to it for some time, that they could not discuss subsidiary matters until the major issue of American prisoners was satisfactorily settled and until there was agreement on the elimination of force, or its threatened use. Until 1960 the Chinese urged agreement on specific, individual subsidiary or "easier" issues, leaving the major differences of principle for later discussion and settlement, if possible. In 1959–60 both sides switched. The Americans began to argue that it would be practicable and desirable to resolve the issue of newsmen even without any settlement of basic issues. But in September 1960 Peking stated the position, which it has held ever since, that the basic issue of Taiwan must be settled before the Ambassadorial Talks could proceed to individual or "easier" items.

On the specifics of the issue of the newsmen there was also a complete reversal of attitudes. In 1956 and 1957 the Americans opposed any reciprocal exchange. Peking wanted it but was willing to invite only American reporters. Washington stipulated that the assignment of American correspondents going to China was to report on the conditions in Communist China and on the Americans held in prison there. This annoyed the Chinese Communists, who repeatedly rejected the idea of attaching any such stipulations or conditions for working journalists. As Chou En-lai put it, what they reported to the American people was their business, however unfavorable it might be from the Chinese viewpoint. But then in 1959 and 1960 the Americans dropped these stipulations for American newsmen and, in effect, for Chinese newsmen who might have valid visas for the United States. Where the Chinese had proposed a nonreciprocal and unconditional visit of American newsmen to China in 1956, the Americans were by now proposing an equal and reciprocal exchange of newsmen from both countries in 1960. Then Peking turned around and attached extensive political conditions to the exchange and reporting of newsmen coming from the United States to China. Finally in 1966 Washington even proposed unconditional and nonreciprocal entry of Chinese newsmen into the United States.

Despite the years of negotiation on this issue, the Talks did not produce agreement any more than did the discussions on Taiwan, civilian repatriation, or renunciation of force. Yet, the discussion on the exchange of newsmen has brought the drafting to the point where it would not be difficult for both sides to reach an agreement if there were a major change of policy in Peking to exchange newsmen. The onus for noncontact lay there by 1967.

In an appraisal of the failure, both Washington and Peking have blocked and missed opportunities for permitting and facilitating nonofficial contacts. The early American rejection of reciprocity, whatever its justification in Washington's viewpoint, apparently had considerable psychological effect in Peking. There, it was another case of unequal treatment by a Western power, another affront to Chinese dignity, another blow to Chinese pride and sensitivities. At least it could be played up as such in Chinese Communist statements. The American rejection and discrimination could serve as witness to the image of the "foreign devil" in Uncle Sam.

Since 1960 Peking has repeatedly rejected the opportunity to exchange newsmen in the same negative spirit as Washington initially did, although for different reasons. At any time since then newsmen of both countries could have been reporting news and writing stories about the other country. Scholars, scientists and representatives of many different groups could have been meeting in the

People's Republic of China or the United States of America if Peking had not kept the forbidden country closed in both directions. By 1967, Peking's wall of isolation seemed even more impermeable to Americans than the Great Wall of the Ancient Age had been to the barbarians of a different West. In sum, all the negotiations over contacts resulted in no contacts. But, in view of Peking's ideological position and image-casting concerning the United States, such contacts might have been futile anyway.

We can only speculate as to why Washington made such a strenuous effort in 1965–66 to arrange bilateral contacts and why Peking resisted these overtures with increasing intensity. For their part, the Americans genuinely felt that contacts of reporters, scholars, scientists, doctors, and other responsible persons would increase mutual understanding on the theory that contact does produce understanding—an argument Washington had used since 1959 for improving American relations with China. United States government officials may have intensified their diplomatic and public efforts to break down the travel barrier in order to offset the increased tensions with Peking, following the sharply increased military involvement of the United States in South and North Vietnam beginning in February 1965. There is an implicit assumption in the American statements that a conciliatory posture and a systematic program looking toward conciliation and contacts between people in the United States and mainland China would counterbalance Peking's anticipated vehement response over Vietnam.

American strategy may have just had the opposite effect, however. Peking probably had several reasons for rebuffing President Johnson and the United States government on these overtures. Peking had to adhere to its 1960 policy that no subsidiary issues could be discussed or negotiated until the United States agreed in principle to vacate Taiwan. While Peking's rigidity over rejecting contacts was totally the reverse of its efforts in 1955–57 to arrange such contacts, the Chinese negotiating position remained firmly consistent with the decision taken in 1959–60. Peking also appears to have decided that the overtures had to be rejected out of hand in the light of developments in Vietnam. Given its Maoist approach to negotiations with its "arch enemy," Peking has evidently not wanted to dilute its "clear stand" on "U.S. aggression" in Vietnam by responding to any American efforts on bilateral contacts. In fact, when seeing the two issues combined, Peking reacted in just the opposite way from Washington by separating them for increasingly hard treatment. Moreover, indulging in any such overtures probably would have seemed to Peking to weaken and compromise its accusations against the Soviet Union of "collusion" with the United States. In order to disprove Moscow's citation of the Talks for rebuttal, Peking could not begin talking with the Americans at Warsaw about exchanges of newsmen and other bilateral contacts. Again, the Sino-Soviet relationship complicated Washington-Peking dealings. In any event, the mounting struggle and convulsions of the so-called great proletarian cultural revolution inside China presumably was reason enough to keep Americans barred and Washington rebuffed on any kind of bilateral contacts. Distant diplomacy of stalemate and elusion evidently met Peking's particular needs better.

Shifting Positions and a Ministerial Conference: Viewed as a whole, the Ambassadorial Talks are divided into two distinct periods, with each party reversing its role—either as challenger or defender. In the period 1955–58, Peking conducted a vigorous and wide-ranging diplomatic exchange with Washington. Prime Minister Chou En-lai was the versatile challenger, Secretary of State John Foster Dulles the resourceful defender. In 1959 and 1960, each side shifted ground. The negotiations lost momentum and ceased as such, while the Americans probed and the Chinese parried. The meetings turned into a useful outlet for oral communication and notification.

The reversal of positions from the first phase to the second centered on the order of, and the approach to, negotiations: on the one hand, the unqualified acceptance by the other side of a single major principle before discussions could begin on minor matters; on the other hand, the alternative of unconditioned agreements on these lesser issues notwithstanding the lack, or even the possibility, of any accord on the major principle. In the first period Peking was "flexible" on principle and Washington was rigid. In the second period Washington eased on principle, while Peking hardened. In 1955–57 Peking vigorously pressed for several specific proposals "comparatively easy to settle," such as a Foreign Ministers' conference, or trade, without predicating them upon prior American acceptance of the basic principle of withdrawal from Taiwan. The Americans refused to go into any of the specifics before Peking agreed to the fundamental principle of renouncing the use of force in disputes between the two parties, and released all American prisoners. In the second period, Peking reversed itself by insisting that the Americans unconditionally accept the principle of total American withdrawal from the Taiwan area before Peking would discuss or negotiate any specific agreements on lesser matters which Washington now wished to discuss and settle without insisting on principle.

During the first years Peking determined the form, substance, and atmosphere of the Talks; Washington reacted for the most part. Peking launched the proposal to negotiate, initiated the agenda, and introduced most of the topics for discussion. After sixty meetings Chou En-lai noted he had proposed a "Far Eastern settlement," a Foreign Ministers' conference, mutual contacts of newsmen and cultural exchange, trade relations, and the lifting of the United Nations and United States embargoes. In addition to taking the Americans by surprise and keeping them on the defensive by sudden and unwarranted public disclosures, the Chinese People's Republic seems urgently and desperately to have wanted in those years to engage the United States government in important agreements and concessions, principally by cleverly securing an association at the highest level of authority and power in the American government in what would have amounted to virtual diplomatic recognition. Chou En-lai was aiming at Taiwan.

In the Taiwan crisis of 1958, Secretary of State John Foster Dulles, reversing his previous role of defender, took the initiative to press for the resumption of the Talks and displayed a vigorous, versatile combination of diplomacy and power in an unsuccessful effort to negotiate an outcome of substantial proportions. From his standpoint he bargained hard, seeking a dialogue, probing for openings, trying out new proposals, and intimating promising possibilities of wider negotiations. Although Chou En-lai introduced and pressed adamantly for his formal proposal of American withdrawal in principle from Taiwan, he defensively rejected or eluded Dulles' initiatives and inducements until the Talks stalemated and the crisis abated. Neither side has since shifted its role of challenger or defender.

Peking became increasingly defensive in 1959 and 1960 as the Sino-Soviet rift expanded. Then, at the 100th meeting in Warsaw in September 1960, Peking, in a complete reversal from its initial position in the Talks, demanded American withdrawal from the Taiwan area as the absolute precondition for discussion and agreement on any other matter at issue, and ever since has rigidly and dogmatically held to its absolute principle of Taiwan first in all dealings with Washington.

In complete contrast, and in a reversal of its role from defender to challenger, the Americans have since 1959 initiated and influenced the substance and atmosphere of the Talks and bilateral dealings. Starting cautiously and conservatively the Eisenhower administration, under the inspiration of Secretary of State Christian A. Herter, tried to reopen a negotiation on an exchange of newsmen. Washington no longer stood fast on its sole principle and progressively dropped its stipulations on the entry of newsmen.

The Kennedy administration, preoccupied with serious difficulties in Laos, Vietnam, Berlin and Cuba, and confronted with an obdurate Khrushchev, kept up the role of initiator and challenger in the Talks. Although President Kennedy did not expect concrete results at Warsaw, he felt deep concern about China. Puzzled by Peking's constant vilification of him but more troubled with China's nuclear proliferation than with China's propagandistic postures, President Kennedy began a vigorous effort in the Ambassadorial Talks to widen contact and negotiate a nuclear agreement. He did not succeed. The Chinese Communists called him a "smiling tiger," and discouraged his initiatives.

During 1964–67 President Johnson gradually unfolded a new policy of specific overtures and broad assurances towards the people of "mainland China." Like a musical crescendo, contact and reconciliation with China became a major theme in Presidential declarations, including the significant address on the State of the Union in January 1967. The United States government had completely reversed its position of 1956. Instead of rejecting a reciprocal exchange of newsmen and other unofficial contacts, Washington urged them again and again at Warsaw and in public, even to the point of suggesting unilateral entry of Chinese newsmen into the United States without Americans necessarily going to the Chinese People's Republic. In the mid-1960s, as tension mounted over Vietnam, the Johnson administration pressed Peking to lower its barriers to American journalists, scholars, scientists, doctors, and professional representatives—and even seeds. But refusing to accept what they had so eagerly proposed in 1956, the Chinese Communists sharply rebuffed the President, the Vice President, and all other American officials. Their various assurances and proposals for contact and conciliation were nothing but "sham," "tricks," or "conspiracies" to Peking.

By 1967 the only important matter on which Peking and Washington had not reversed themselves during a dozen years was continuation of their contact at Warsaw. Nor had they ever reversed themselves on the level of contact which each preferred in their bilateral dealings—ministerial, ambassadorial or technical. Because Peking would have always liked the first, which Washington continually repulsed, and because Peking would not stoop to the lower level that Washington occasionally preferred, the Talks remained at the ambassadorial level by implicit but separate action of each government.

Reversal of one side's role during any phase of the Talks might have led to a meeting between the Secretary of State of the United States and the Foreign Minister of the Chinese People's Republic. Washington could have facilitated a conference in 1955–57; Peking since 1958. In the former period Peking treated the ambassadorial level as an arrangements committee for a ministerial conference. Chou En-lai specifically wanted it on the agreed agenda, urged its negotiation after the initial Agreement on repatriation, and linked it apparently as "trade off" to any acquiescence by Peking to a joint renunciation of force. The ministerial level was a significant matter of proper form and equal status—a question of face as Westerners would call it—for the leaders in Peking, who, being sensitive to unequal treatment or subordinate place, viewed the ministerial level as the suitable rank for negotiation of major issues between the "New China" and the United States. During those years Peking frequently denounced the Ambassadorial Talks for their failure and pressed for an elevation to the ministerial level, as only there could "settlement" of issues take place. No doubt the world-wide political impact for Peking of such a concession from Washington, in addition to matters of form and status, motivated the Chinese Communist leaders.

However, Dulles balked and frustrated Chou on this matter at every turn—on the agenda, at Geneva, and in press conferences. Yet many officials in Washington assumed in 1955–56 that some success at the ambassadorial level would logically and correctly lead to a meeting between Chou En-lai and John Foster Dulles. President Eisenhower seemed open to the prospect, and Dulles himself did not completely close the door on that contingency. If Peking had instantly repatriated all American prisoners in September 1955, pressures on Eisenhower and Dulles for a meeting with Chou probably would have become irresistible. By not changing his small bait, Chou missed his big strike. However, as the initial aura of hope and trust quickly subsided, the American willingness to raise the level of dealings declined to the point, in July 1956, where Vice President Nixon categorically rejected any ministerial conference with Peking.

Since late 1958, United States officials have moderated their view, not foreclosing the option of ministerial discussions if the two Ambassadors make some headway. In the Taiwan crisis of 1958 Dulles reversed American opposition to a ministerial conference in an effort to provide an added inducement to negotiate important understandings regarding the whole offshore islands–Taiwan question. Chou En-lai now balked and frustrated Dulles. Ever since then a bilateral Foreign Ministers' meeting has ceased to be a serious possibility. Peking seldom mentioned it after shifting to its rigid position on Taiwan in 1960. However, Foreign Minister Chen Yi did reopen the possibility in 1962 in a public statement although Peking apparently did not formally propose a conference at the Warsaw Talks. President Kennedy's reaction to Chen Yi's suggestion was that the Ambassadorial Talks would suffice for the time being and, until they produced some substance, a Foreign Ministers' meeting would be unnecessary and inappropriate. After four years without any reference by either party to high-level talks, Senator Mike Mansfield, Senate Majority leader, suggested a ministerial meeting in 1966 to discuss Vietnam which the White House did not reject in principle nor immediately accept. Meanwhile, Peking has displayed far less interest in the ministerial level, while downgrading and deprecating the value of the Ambassadorial Talks since 1960. But ministerial-level talks remained an open option in 1967.

No one can say for sure what results or consequences a ministerial meeting would have produced, if any. The personalities on both sides were obviously antagonistic and incompatible. In any event, each government has periodically missed opportunities to see if the higher forum could have elicited significant exchanges, increased understanding, and reduced tensions somewhat. That the Foreign Ministers might have failed had they met is perhaps more obvious than the subtleties of their ever trying.

A Registrar for Communications

Despite the diplomacy of stalemate and elusion, American officials have publicly indicated that the United States would keep the Talks going "to help prevent policy miscalculations." The notifications at Warsaw in 1961 did facilitate the negotiation of the Geneva Agreement on Laos. More significantly, the American communication of restraint on Taiwan in 1962 may well have had a most important result. It obviously made the flash-point less critical and deflected a fast-erupting military crisis. Whether the exchange of positions over Vietnam will prevent miscalculation or engender misunderstanding in that supercharged situation remains to be seen. At least, Washington's attempt to define the meaning and limit the scope of United States policy there, unambiguously and comprehensively, is on the record, whatever its interpretation by Peking may be. And Peking's intentions and warnings regarding Vietnam are also hammered onto the same record. It seems reasonable to conclude that having the medium for exchange of views at Warsaw regarding Vietnam has helped each side to sketch out the rough parameters of what the other might or might not do. In view of the deadlocks in the Talks on all issues and the divergence between Washington and Peking concerning Vietnam, the nature of this exchange could only be general and inferential, not involving any explicit understandings or round-about deals. In assuming that their public statements and the Warsaw Talks allowed each side to draw its own conclusions, Washington and Peking may have unwittingly facilitated a tacit form of precarious coexistence in tension during 1965–67. In the volatile atmosphere concerning Vietnam, many felt that maintaining even this imprecise, limited, and uncertain extent of responsible restraint was decidedly preferable to outright hostilities between the United States and the People's Republic of China.

Meanwhile, much information and many viewpoints were also exchanged on arms control. Those discussions confirmed that Peking intended to proceed with its own nuclear development and to oppose the approach advocated by Washington and Moscow. Peking received a full exposition of American thinking and experience on the crucial issue of arms control and was unofficially brought into the Geneva Conference discussion—by proxy as it were—on the whole range of disarmament and arms control. The Talks performed an important function in this regard. The fact that Peking stipulated conditions in its proposals of 1963 and 1964 which Washington could not accept without considerable modification does not altogether nullify the value of this exchange. Moreover, Peking and Washington exchanged proposals on disarmament conferences, the Test-Ban Treaty, and no-first-use pledges. The Talks thus involved both governments at least in an initial bargaining or exploratory situation.

Finally, despite the impasses on such critical major issues as Taiwan, Vietnam, and arms control, the Ambassadorial Talks have had useful results in communicating information on a number of relatively minor problems—if indications in the press are reliable. For example, agreements have apparently been reached on the handling of Chinese seamen who have "jumped Communist ships," were picked up by American or other ships, and who wanted to be returned to the mainland. Indemnities for a few collisions at sea between American and Chinese Communist ships seem to have been arranged. The American side has submitted inquiries at Warsaw about Americans and other nationals who were missing at sea near mainland China, and perhaps picked up or washed ashore and found by Chinese Communist authorities. The Embassy of the Chinese People's Republic in Warsaw has referred these inquiries to Peking and replied according to the facts, or lack of them. Washington has also used the Warsaw channel to inform Peking about the course of United States space satellites which would or might pass over the Chinese mainland and possibly cause property damage or personal injury in the event of their falling on Chinese territory.

The Triangular Relationships

An appraisal of the results and consequences of United States dealings with Peking would be incomplete without an allusion to the Soviet shadow cast on them over the years. Certainly these dealings and the Ambassadorial Talks were involved in and had some effect on Sino-Soviet, Soviet-American, and Sino-American relations. We know that Moscow used its diplomatic influence directly and indirectly to bring about the Talks between Washington and Peking in 1955 and favored developing their bilateral contacts. As we have seen, the Taiwan crisis in 1958 involved Moscow in the Ambassadorial Talks, thus providing an escape hatch, but also complicating subsequent Sino-Soviet relations in view of the fact that Moscow apparently put more emphasis on diplomacy than on force.

However, in 1966 the Ambassadorial Talks became publicly embroiled in the bitter Sino-Soviet dispute. The Soviet government capitalized on the exchanges between Peking and Washington to make a debating point in order to refute Peking's charges of Soviet-American collusion." Moscow accused the Chinese Communist leaders of "duplicity" in making their charges, claiming that the Chinese themselves were trying to "collude" and develop relations with the United States in order to reach tacit agreements. Peking has vehemently denied Moscow's accusations and retaliated with more of its own.[13]

In early 1967 Moscow's embroilment of the Ambassadorial Talks in the bitter Sino-Soviet dispute disrupted this one connection between Washington and Peking. Oddly enough, in May 1967 a naturalized American correspondent of Egyptian ancestry, Simon Malley, reported his version of Peking's attitude concerning this complication after his interviews in Peking, allegedly the first granted to an American or European since the onset of the "cultural revolution." When he asked Chinese Communist officials there whether they intended to continue these Talks, they showed great sensitivity and annoyance. Apparently, they were disturbed and unhappy over Moscow's many efforts to discredit the Ambassadorial Talks and to use them as evidence for substantiating Moscow's charges of Peking's "collusion" with Washington. The Chinese Communist leadership evidently felt adamantly that there was no basis whatsoever to support such charges—as this book abundantly bears out—that there were any "deals," agreements on understandings between Washington and Peking at Warsaw or anywhere else on anything at all. But high Chinese officials reportedly were so incensed by the Soviet "fabrication" that Peking, according to Malley, was considering publishing the whole record of the Ambassadorial Talks and even suspending them altogether in order to disprove Soviet rumors. While the government in Peking valued the Warsaw Talks as a "channel" for telling the Americans "the conditions under which really fruitful talks could take place," Peking apparently felt compelled "to determine whether their limited usefulness outweighs the risks they involve in creating false impressions." [14] In other words, Peking had to weigh the advantages of keeping its "switchboard" open to Washington against the disadvantages of letting Moscow continue to exploit this contact in order to compromise Peking's doctrinal position.

Of course, these Maoist officials, ascribing all the truth to Peking's version and all the falsehood to Moscow's, also attacked Moscow for rumoring Peking's "collusion" with Washington over Vietnam.*

---

* Indicating the concern of the Chinese Communist leadership over this Soviet pressure, the April issue of the *Peking Review* carried the authoritative article of "commentary" criticizing Moscow's "clumsy slander" for "spreading anti-China rumours concerning the Vietnam question for some time," and for the "startling" "absurdity and crudeness" of these rumors. The article went on to say:

> What can be more preposterous than the story they concocted that China has reached a "tacit agreement" with the United States. Of course people the world over can only laugh at such idiocy. Everybody knows the stand

One leader of the so-called cultural revolution, Chen Po-ta, indicated to Simon Malley that anti-Maoist forces had favored a measure of collaboration with the Soviet Union and the United States during the Taiwan crisis of 1958, which apparently would have involved some form of "collusion" with both countries in Mao's view. Seemingly, it had emerged again in similar form concerning Vietnam. Accordingly, the Maoists put first priority in destroying this alleged Soviet-American "collusion" to "impose a sell-out compromise settlement in Vietnam." Thus, Peking's vehement charge against Moscow of "collusion" with the Americans concerning Vietnam, which reflected Mao's fundamentalist antipathy toward Soviet "revisionism" and United States "imperialism," was actually the root cause of the embroilment of the Ambassadorial Talks in the triangular relationship in 1966–67. If they were to be suspended in this context, they would be an unfortunate casualty of the Sino-Soviet clash and not primarily of other factors. Yet, the blame would lie in the first instance with Moscow for not ignoring Peking's charges and for embarrassing Peking by distorting the Ambassadorial Talks far beyond recognition of what little they had actually accomplished. By the same token, Peking, for whatever Mao's reasons of ideology or prejudice, was ultimately responsible for starting and pressing these empty but consequential reprisals over a dogmatic issue of a nonexistent "collusion."

Whatever the implicit conclusions—if any—Peking and Washington may have drawn from their exchanges at Warsaw regarding Taiwan, disarmament, Vietnam, and bilateral contacts, there is not the slightest hint in the public record of the Talks that there has been any tacit agreement or understanding whatsoever between the Chinese People's Republic and the United States since October 1955, on Vietnam or any other issue of substance. It would be unfortunate if Moscow's difficulties with Peking intruded upon the

---

of the Chinese people in aiding Vietnam to resist U.S. aggression and U.S. imperialism [and] is in no way confused about this either. It is no one else but the Soviet renegades themselves who have ganged up with the U.S. aggressors, who have reached a tacit agreement with them and who have openly and actively collaborated with them. The Soviet renegades rack their brains fabricating rumours to smear China. But they are only thieves crying "stop thief!" (*Peking Review*, No. 16, April 14, 1967, p. 18.)

The increasing references in the Peking press to Moscow's unfounded charges of Peking's "deals," "collusion," or "tacit agreements" with Washington tended to lend credence to Malley's own impressions in Peking, despite Peking's denial of official contact with him and repudiation of his purported interviews.

already intense and difficult relations of Washington and Peking. However, Moscow's public intervention and exploitation of the Ambassadorial Talks indicate that the Soviet government might have become anxious about the possibility of some increasing contact and rapprochement between the Americans and the Chinese Communists. Meanwhile, the Soviet government seemed to move toward a policy of "isolation with containment" of its "Red Chinese" neighbor.

Thus, another ironic reversal may have come about after a dozen years of these Talks in that Moscow has been moving toward contracting relations with Peking, at least with the Maoist group there, while Washington sought to expand contacts and promote conciliation with Peking. If there were one "tacit agreement" which would be desirable and advisable for both Peking and Washington to work out explicitly or implicitly, it would be not to allow the mutual difficulties and antagonisms between the Soviet Union and China to interfere with the dealings and relations between the United States and China. These should be developed according to the national interests of both.

*   *   *

An authoritative American recapitulation of United States contacts and negotiations with the People's Republic of China was made in the Secretary of State's statement of policy on March 16, 1966:

I think it is accurate to say that no other non-Communist nation has had such extensive conversations with the Peiping regime as we have had.* The problem is not lack of contact between Peiping and Washington. It is what, with contact, the Peiping regime itself says and does.

Although they have produced almost no tangible results, these conversations have served and still serve useful purposes. They permit us to clarify the numerous points of difference between us. They enable us to communicate in private during periods of crisis. They provide an opening through which, hopefully, light might one day penetrate. But the talks have, so far, given no evidence of a shift or easing in Peiping's hostility toward the United States and its bellicose doctrines of world revolution. Indeed the Chinese Communists have consistently demanded, privately as well as publicly, that we let them have Taiwan. And when we say that we will not abandon the 12 or 13 million people on Taiwan, against their will, they say that, until we change our minds about that, no

---

* *The New York Times* text of this statement of policy (April 17, 1966) uses the term "Peking" wherever the Department of State's statement uses the term "Peiping," as contained in *United States Policy Toward Asia*, Hearings Before the Subcommittee on the Far East and the Pacific of the Committee on Foreign Affairs, House of Representatives, 89th Congress, 2nd Session, pp. 523, 534.

improvement in relations is possible. Today we and Peiping are as far apart on matters of fundamental policy as we were 17 years ago.

From even the divergent Chinese Communist standpoint, Peking would seem to have agreed with this appraisal of the Secretary of State regarding the impasse over Taiwan. At about the same time, Prime Minister Chou En-lai said he did not see any results in his attempt over a period of ten years to get the United States out of Taiwan, and insisted on refusing any "concession whatsoever" while continuing the contact at Warsaw. In September 1966 Foreign Minister Chen Yi anticipated more talking despite "the present bad relations" between the two countries and the fact that the United States was "wiping out the possibility of a settlement through talks." Peking has given no sign of any modification in its negotiating position regarding any of the issues discussed. Expecting an inevitable and long-term struggle with the United States, Peking has adhered to its diplomacy of stalemate while Washington has shifted to a diplomacy of maneuver and a desire for negotiations.

Nevertheless, the record of notification and negotiation at Geneva and Warsaw indicates that a sense of credibility has been established by both sides. That is an important consequence. In this limited but significant sense, dealing with the Chinese Communists in the Ambassadorial Talks has not been a failure. Stripping away the dogma, invective, emotionalism, and the postures, both sides have apparently come to believe in the validity of the facts and the substance of intentions and policies orally sent across the tables. Dealing with the Chinese Communists may be disagreeable, but the experience shows that it is workable if correctly practiced and effectively institutionalized.

Moreover, it might be suggested that, in any case, this "frail little thread" * could not have had much chance to facilitate real negotiations on so many matters at once. It was too overloaded in private and too overseen in public. Perhaps it might have been wiser to have tried to increase the frequency of meetings in order to discuss only one issue at a time—which is still a possibility. In any event, the Ambassadorial Talks have produced a wide range of subject matter and in this sense have not been limited. The Talks began as negotiations to produce contacts with less tensions. They continue with only the original contact, with no negotiation, and with increased tension.

* Richard Starnes used this phrase in 1965 in the *New York World-Telegram and Sun* to describe the nature and procedure of the Talks.

CHAPTER FOURTEEN

Confrontation— Ideological, Historical and Emotional

No more divergent, arduous, and unpromising negotiating process could be found elsewhere in the world than between the man from Peking and the man from Washington. Across the table, the Chinese Communist negotiator sits cold and taut as a steel spring sternly unapproachable, suspicious, and impenetrable, a rigidly disciplined agent reading his lines with mechanical precision. He is able, persistent, imperturbable—and frustratingly predictable in style. Negotiation with him is an ordeal, for he makes it so. The American negotiator moves into another world when he sits down at this table. He cannot drop his guard or muffle his reaction. He must always harden his resistance and restrain his temper in the face of a steady volley of hostile epithets and extreme allegations. Yet he needs to be constantly alert for an opening. The rival styles across this table have fashioned a unique kind of "adversary" diplomacy which must be experienced to be understood.

These dealings with the People's Republic of China at Panmunjom, the Geneva Conferences, and the Ambassadorial Talks can provide some guidance on why and how the Chinese Communist leadership in Peking negotiates with the United States. These findings are, of course, based on the circumstances and developments of the past fifteen years and the particular conditioning and outlook of Mao Tse-tung and his elderly colleagues in Peking. Yet, even when power passes on, the interplay of Sinocentric and "Marxist-Maoist" residues will still shape the way their successors will conduct contacts and negotiations with Americans. A fundamental change in power and ideology might, of course, alter this basic combination abruptly. However, whatever happens in post-Mao Peking—gradual

338

evolution or another revolution—the Chinese style of negotiating will be hard to cope with, probably for a long time to come.

Before concluding the story of United States dealings with Communist China, this chapter will, accordingly, touch on the complex and fascinating subject of the interacting roles of the Chinese Communist negotiator as bargainer, organization man, Sinocentric nationalist, and Marxist-Leninist-Maoist ideologue. The summary of this interplay briefly emphasizes the unique emotional intensity of Sino-American relations, illuminates the divergent negotiating styles of Peking and Washington, identifies the main determinants of Chinese Communist negotiating behavior, and establishes some guidelines for our effective handling of negotiations with them.

To keynote the two basic features of Peking's diplomacy—uniqueness and antipathy—let us preface this appraisal with an interpretation by an American diplomat who dealt with the Chinese Communists at close-range and another by a Chinese educator who worked with them in Peking. In 1963, O. Edmund Clubb wrote:

> In the field of foreign relations the Chinese mind becomes less elusive, but it remains governed by drives that give the country's foreign policy characteristics all its own. Some are dangerous to its neighbors, others so unrelated to Occidental values as to lie beyond the horizon of our expectations, falling, as the agricultural communes, in the category of the "irrational." But that is only because Chinese ratiocination is different from our own.
>
> . . . A new situation has arisen in China, in terms of foreign affairs even as of domestic affairs. After nearly forty years of division, China is again unified. Viewed against the lessons of history, the fact points up two salient elements of pertinence here: China unified, and thus politically strong, has always been expansionist; and Chinese ethnocentrism, embodied in the traditional feeling of cultural superiority to "barbarians" (all non-Chinese), from the time of the Boxer Rebellion onward has regularly required at least one foreign "enemy." [1]

In 1960 Chow Ching-Wen, after serving several years on the Administration Council of the Chinese People's Republic in Peking, which apparently gave him first-hand participation in and familiarity with Peking's foreign policy until 1957,* wrote after his defection and exile:

> Actually, there is nothing mysterious or hard to understand about Communist diplomacy. But in approaching the subject, we must put aside all

---

* Apparently he was a leader of the non-Communist party, the China Democratic League, which "cooperated" with the Communist Party after its takeover in 1949.

preconceived notions, and start with a completely open and objective mind. Unless we do this, we are likely to find ourselves playing into Communist hands, and there will be much guesswork and inaccuracy.

I call Communist diplomacy "fox and wolf diplomacy," and I think it is a pretty accurate description, for it is cunning like a fox and has the rapacity of a wolf. This makes for an insidious combination which is highly dangerous to the West.[2]

The Chinese Communist leadership expressed its general idea of diplomacy in its secret statement of 1961 to military cadres: "The world is like a chessboard, and one careless step will cause the loss of the whole game." Mixing metaphors, Peking has described this world contest as a "ping-pong game in which the People's Republic of China should win the championship and at all costs avoid second place."

The Organization Man

When he bargains, the Chinese Communist negotiator executes foreign policy somewhat, but not altogether, differently from his American counterpart. This is due to Peking's different organizational framework. Peking organizes its diplomacy in a particularly Chinese way and scrutinizes its diplomats closely and sternly. While the American negotiator is usually nonpolitical, the Chinese Communist diplomat is a long-standing, faithful member of the Chinese Communist Party. He is also a government official, but since the Party dictates State positions, his duty is to carry out the Party lines strictly according to its norms and rules, which represent "the interests of the Chinese people." Moreover, he also speaks for the "international proletarian movement"—as Marxist "Maoism" interprets it.

The control of the Party has been total and pervasive throughout every level of the Chinese Communist government, including the Ministry of Foreign Affairs and its embassies.[3] As for other governing agencies, Party determination of the staffing and the conduct of the Ministry of Foreign Affairs have been exercised by Party members designated by a special group under the Central Committee headed by Mao. Diplomats, like other members, have been selected more for their ideological reliability and virtue than for professional and technical ability.* With Party loyalty as the touchstone, the

* However, Donald Klein has detected a tendency to shift the emphasis from political reliability to diplomatic competence for Peking's diplomatic personnel sent to non-Communist countries. See his "Peking's Evolving Ministry of Foreign Affairs" in *The China Quarterly*, No. 4, October–December, 1960, pp. 28–39.

tests for selection and advancement are unquestioning zeal, automatic responsiveness, instant obedience, and personal subordination. Assignment to important responsibilities overseas has depended on ideological conformity in terms of Marxist-Leninist principles and Maoist thought, although the normal rules relative to seniority and personal relationships also exist.

For what it is worth, a young Chinese diplomat, who defected in 1964, has reported that

Party loyalty—not experience, knowledge or skill—is the requirement for advancement or for appointment to a high position. Mao Tse-tung trusts only old party comrades who "ate their belts" with him during the days of the Long March in 1934–35, or who fought by his side when he drove Chiang Kai-shek out of mainland China. That is why the 30 Red Chinese ambassadors abroad are all military men, with no training in diplomacy and no language other than their own. Most of them were with Mao on the Long March.[4]

These were the Party men whom the Americans encountered in negotiations, at least until the cultural revolution attacked the Party itself.

At Panmunjom, Huang Hua, later Ambassador to the United Arab Republic, had long been a member of the Party before he came to the other side of the table. Both Ambassadors Wang had had long apprenticeship in the Chinese Communist Party before participating in the Ambassadorial Talks. Ambassador Wang Ping-nan had been a high Party official with access to the Politburo, Chou En-lai, and Mao Tse-tung. Ambassador Wang Kuo-chuan, before his transfer to diplomatic service in 1957, had served as a "political commissar" in the Chinese Communist Army and had held several important Party posts, attending Communist Party meetings as a representative from "peasant organizations." He had also been a provincial governor, and had written about the "struggle against bureaucratism," which suggests that he may be more "red" than "expert" in the Maoist definition and not too much concerned with acquiring diplomatic polish. As Ambassador Gronouski has described him in Warsaw: "He is a very articulate man who gives the impression of hewing very closely to his instructions. He is also quite formal, perhaps in keeping with Chinese traditions or custom." [5]

Besides mirroring Party orders, Chinese Communist behavior in the Talks has been indeed typically Chinese in many respects. Traditional Chinese diplomatic practice has tended to insulate Chinese policy-makers from the negotiating situation and the negotiators.

Unlike the West (including Russia), those holding ultimate authority in China have not been parties to negotiations. The role of the decision-maker has been kept much more distinct from the role of the negotiator than has been the case in the West.* The Chinese Communists appear to have continued this traditional practice by separating the formulators of policy and its executors inside the Party into two different groups—each with certain power and competence concerning foreign relations. Traditionally and currently, as Ambassador Gronouski has indicated, the Chinese negotiator himself has little leeway in his actions or relationships. He is rigidly patterned by top authorities in Peking with just enough delegated authority to make limited decisions on technical points but none on major matters. The small group at the top in Peking retains the discretion and authority to make changes. Washington's practice, on the other hand, has been to delegate some initiative and discretion to its negotiators. The contrast between the Chinese separation of policy-maker from negotiator and the greater American reliance on negotiators was made clear by Ambassador Wang Kuo-chuan when he minimized the importance of Ambassador Cabot's departure and his replacement by Ambassador Gronouski in 1965: "We do not attach much importance to the change of American representatives. In our view, what is important is American policy and its actions in pursuing that policy." [6] However, Washington does attach considerable importance to the role of its diplomatic representatives. Unlike the Chinese, American policy-makers and negotiators are entirely nonpolitical in diplomatic dealings, less differentiated between each other in the negotiating process, and closely associated organizationally and personally. An American negotiator may, and often does, draft his own instructions, receives the Presidential mandate to proceed at his own discretion within broad terms of reference, and goes out to conduct the negotiations on his own authority.

Peking's pattern of separation and dichotomy can have two opposite consequences which complicate negotiations. On the one hand, the Chinese Communist negotiator may be expected predictably to stick to the letter of his instructions meeting after meeting, cliché after cliché, with no flexibility whatever. But, on the other

---

* When the first prototype of a Foreign Ministry—the Tsungli' Yamen—was set up in 1861, it was kept "remote" from the Grand Council over which the Emperor presided in making policy and writing the decisions. See Masataka Banno, *China and the West 1858–1861* (Cambridge: The Harvard University Press, 1964), p. 226.

hand, without the slightest indication of a contradictory shift, he may suddenly read out a new position, dictated by the flexible policy-makers in Peking, totally different from what he had been saying all along. The American negotiator has to be prepared for such sudden reversals or innovations, which, in the course of normal diplomacy, usually follow extensive probing and discussion.

In addition to this pattern of alternating rigidity and sudden change, any negotiation with the Chinese Communists must always take into account that Chinese negotiators, as a rule, assemble a collection of facts to support their ideological correlation of forces. Apparently Peking obtains objective information to conduct "a continuing calculation of the world balance of power"—in Communist terms, for the Chinese Communist leaders think in world terms. The organization in Peking keeps its negotiator accurately informed and precisely instructed. However, whatever the facts may be, a unique combination of tradition, history, ideology and personality determines their behavior and policy.

The Sinocentric-Maoist Negotiator

The Chinese Communist negotiator thinks, behaves, bargains and communicates in distinctive ways. The Maoist from Peking consciously and instinctively plays his role with a Sinocentric historical heritage. As Mr. Clubb, after his first-hand experience with the Chinese Communists, has observed:

In China, a "Chineseness" composed of historic influence and past grievances has combined with Marxism-Leninism and modern aspirations and national cares to reinforce certain highly personal policy decisions; but in Washington this Chinese complex has been viewed narrowly and simplistically.[7]

It is possible to single out of the Chinese Communist negotiating style several elements of this traditional "Chineseness," such as a world view of China's centrality, the practice of "distant diplomacy," sensitivity to unequal or nonreciprocal treatment, and the revolutionary experience. Moreover, Chinese tradition and history combine with "Marxist-Maoism" to produce a unique Chinese sense of time and an intensely emotional quality in their relations with the Americans.

On a more intangible plane than the bargaining tactics or organizational patterns of the Chinese Communists—but highly significant—is the persistence of the old Sinocentric, "nationalistic" view of the world which strongly reinforces and intensifies the new "Marxist-Maoism." This continuity of traditional Chinese values and assumptions partly determines the different "institutional vocabulary" used by Chinese Communist policy-makers and negotiators in playing the "great game" with the United States and the Soviet Union, as Professor Mancall has suggested.[8] Traditional Chinese policy was premised upon the basic conceptions of an hierarchical, not egalitarian, world order of states. The position of China was central in such an order; there were no competing systems and no balance of power. Thus, there was nothing to negotiate between "unequals." The rites of submission rather than the rules of litigation regulated China's foreign relations, especially under the Manchu dynasty during 1644–1911.

In brief, the legacy of the "Central Kingdom" emphasizes China's major role in world politics today as in the former East Asian hierarchical arrangements where China was the central authority over its widespread, long-standing "tributary system." Moreover, Chinese have long conceived an ideal single world order, with China providing the moral leadership and civilizing influence. For over 2,000 years this concept was expressed in the vocabulary of the Ta Tung, the "Great Peace." Now the international proletarian movement apparently represents Mao's version of this particularly Chinese concept. Charles Taylor, a Canadian journalist resident in Peking during 1964–65, has also caught this Sinocentric-Communist duality:

On the one hand the Chinese leaders are dedicated Communists who made their revolution with little outside help and who seem to believe sincerely that Mao has reworked Marx and Lenin to provide an inevitable revolutionary pattern for the world. On the other hand they are also Chinese with understandable nationalistic ambitions, traditional notions of cultural and racial superiority, and a determination to revive the glories of the Middle Kingdom when all the known world acknowledged China's sway.[9]

Professor John Fairbank has emphasized that resurgent Chinese nationalism will reinforce the traditional "deeply ingrained attitude" of viewing diplomacy and negotiation as a way of playing foreign powers against each other to reflect and enhance China's role.[10] Peking's attachment to "principled policies" and demand for unconditional acquiescence to them before negotiations hark back to China's age-old style of diplomacy, which treated all non-Chinese as inferior "barbarians" and dispensed with any concept or practice of foreign relations between equally sovereign nations or within an international system of states. Nor has Chinese statecraft arbitrarily divided negotiating and fighting into separate and alternating strategies, as the West has done, but instead has used them as parallel and complementary options reinforcing each other simultaneously to induce an adversary to submit. Chinese Communist behavior in Korea, the Taiwan Straits, Laos, Vietnam and the Ambassadorial Talks has thus echoed one ancient Chinese saying, that "a policy of peace and friendship is a temporary measure of expedience; war and defense is the real policy to pursue." [11] Perhaps, even unconsciously motivated by historical perspective, Peking has challenged the two world powers, Washington and Moscow, to negotiate on Peking's terms while waiting indefinitely for a unilaterally acceptable outcome. The Western egalitarian system in international relations with its non-hierarchical accommodation under Washington's leadership, and a Soviet commonwealth of Communist states with their hierarchical arrangements under Moscow's primacy, both contradict the Sinocentric concept of China's role and status.

As one Western writer put it: "The Chinese view of the world has not fundamentally changed: it has been adjusted to take account of the modern world, but only so far as to permit China to occupy, still, the central place in the picture." [12] Indeed, a French visitor to the Chinese People's Republic, the journalist Robert Guillain, saw in the resurgence of Chinese nationalism and rejection of the uncongenial outside world—Communist and non-Communist—"a return to China . . . the end of a long adventure in which China attempted to flee from herself and find her happiness in those lessons taught by the outside world." [13]

Accordingly, the Chinese Communists have returned to the traditional Chinese practice of "arms-length diplomacy," keeping foreign envoys at a distance, which reflects China's traditional concept of a hierarchy of unequal states and "barbarian" rulers, culturally inferior to the "Central Kingdom." * A glimpse of history shows the

---

* The Chinese characters used for various kinds of "barbarians" denote different kinds of animals such as dogs or sheep. This use of animalistic symbols for non-Chinese came up in the political talks at Panmunjom when the Chinese negotiator insulted Ambassador Dean with an unusually rude Chinese proverb which literally meant that "having eaten mutton, your entire body stinks." The insult was probably intended to show a haughty contempt for

parallelism of old and new in this persistence in maintaining the Sinocentric tradition. During the nineteenth century, the advent of the Europeans and Americans created a political enigma and diplomatic crisis for the Imperial Court and Peking because these foreigners were completely different from any other "barbarians" who had come knocking at the doors of China for two millennia or more. The "Central Kingdom" did not suffer inferiors or outsiders, and either demanded tributory obeisance or quarantined them until they converted. In 1844, a high Manchu official warned against overstepping the bounds and having personal relations with these new "barbarian envoys." [14] The Westerners were powerful and dangerous and peculiar because they demanded regular, direct, and permanent access to the supreme level—the Emperor himself. The Manchu Court and the Chinese Mandarins set up a buffer system in Canton, China, to quarantine Western representatives and keep them from visiting Peking, residing there, or seeking audiences with the Emperor and his highest advisers. But the Westerners finally overturned this "distant diplomacy." Just about one hundred years before the Ambassadorial Talks began, American, British and other Western representatives insisted on permanent residence and regular access by treaty. The British and French even fought a winning war with the Chinese, partly over this critical issue. [15]

This history is relevant because it has a significant parallel today in China, as well as in the Ambassadorial Talks with the Americans. Chinese have not forgotten the abrupt change in the traditional practice of putting off foreigners and the violent intrusion of an alien system of diplomatic intercourse which prematurely forced the Ch'ing Dynasty and the proud Mandarins to "Westernize" and modernize the handling of foreign relations.* Since 1949 Peking has

---

the U.N. negotiators and put them in their "subordinate" places. Ambassador Dean immediately replied that "the mention of lamb chops made him hungry" and reminded him that since it was long past the lunch hour, it was time to recess. See Robert B. Ekvall, *Faithful Echo* (New York: Twayne Publishers, 1960), p. 82.

* The following concluding paragraph from *China's Entrance into the Family of Nations* by Immanuel C. Y. Hsü (Cambridge: Harvard University Press, 1960), is relevant to an understanding of the continuity in the Chinese view of the world:

"But it was only through necessity, not free choice, that China had entered the world community. The old dream of universal empire, the glory of being the Middle Kingdom in East Asia, and the prestige of the tributary system still lingered in the Chinese mind, and their residual effects were clearly discernible. The nostalgia for the past generated a burning hope and even a

tried to "Sinicize" its procedures and institutions for handling foreigners and foreign affairs. As a case in point, the Chinese Communists in the Ambassadorial Talks in Europe reverted in some respects
to the old "Canton System" of keeping the Westerners segregated,
isolated, and far from the policy-makers in Peking.

Charles Taylor has commented in detail on this particular case of
the continuity of Chinese conduct.[16] On the basis of his experience
in China during 1964–65 he reported the "strange hermetic life" of
foreign residents in Peking which kept them "at arms-length," isolated from the government and the people. He found Chinese Communist dealings with foreigners reminiscent of the "arrogance" and
"cultural and racial superiority" implied in both the concept of the
world revolving around Peking and the treatment of "barbarians"
before 1861 in the Canton System. To him, the attitude of the Chinese toward foreigners had hardly changed, while Peking's methods
of handling them were "strikingly similar to those of previous
dynasties." As in Canton just a century ago, diplomats, embassies,
journalists and many other foreign residents were again being con-
gregated and segregated in the "remote and splendid isolation" of a
special compound outside Peking. Moreover, according to Mr. Taylor, the foreign diplomat was also intellectually and functionally
walled out by Chinese officials, who showed no interest in his ideas or
his country and rebuffed the "give-and-take" of contemporary diplomacy because, however hard the foreign diplomat might try,
"there is no question of any meaningful discussion or dialogue."
While this picture of "arms-length diplomacy" may be somewhat
overdrawn, it seems to reflect the general pattern today. Mr. Taylor concluded that "the function of the foreign envoy has changed
little in Chinese eyes. . . . the parallels to the treatment of Lord
Macartney (1795) and his successors are so numerous that they indicate a deep psychological response to the foreigner that has altered

---

strong conviction that some day China would again become strong and re-
assert her rightful place under the sun. If universal Confucianism could not
attain such an objective, perhaps some other system could. A century of trial
and error, and decades of groping in the dark led to the discovery that international communism, which envisages an ultimate universal classless society,
might be the new vehicle for the fulfillment of the old dream. With the rise
of Communist China as the most powerful nation in East Asia, with its growing influence in northern Korea, northern Vietnam and other peripheral states,
and with the constant flow of peace delegations to Peking from East European
and Asian states, one wonders whether the universal state and the tributary
system of the past have not been revived in a modern form."

very little." He also noted, as others have, that Peking's diplomats abroad keep to themselves, strictly segregated and uncommunicative. All in all, he left the Chinese People's Republic apparently impressed with "the vast indifference of China toward the foreigner." Ambassadors in Peking apparently seldom even see, let alone deal with, the policy-making authorities, for relations with embassies are deliberately kept to a relatively low technical level.

In the light of Peking's "arms-length" diplomacy, American officials are probably correct in claiming that Washington has higher-level and more direct access to authorities in Peking from the distance of Warsaw than it would have from the proximity of an embassy in Peking. Presumably the American policy-makers have in fact been communicating, even if distantly, with Peking's policy-makers. The remoteness of the Warsaw Talks in the Polish palace are but another variation of Peking's return to China. Peking's style and pattern of distant diplomacy have become the reverse of Washington's "close diplomacy"—two opposite traditions at work. Perhaps the long, unhappy pitfalls and undoings of perplexing foreign exposure have caused Peking to withdraw.

Understandably in the light of China's modern history, American negotiators—no matter how far from Peking—can expect the Chinese Communists to be unusually nationalistic in vehemently insisting on equal and reciprocal treatment for China, at almost any cost. A century of humiliation at the hands of the Western powers, including Russia, has made the proud "Central Country" unusually sensitive to slighting and disrespectful treatment.

Peking may dispense with the negotiations altogether, as it apparently did in the case of the Test-Ban Treaty when it felt ignored and mistreated by Moscow and Washington. Some interesting Chinese Communist and American indications coincidentally substantiate Peking's feeling of exclusion and rejection in the negotiation of that significant Treaty, and suggest that Peking might not have opposed the tripartite negotiation and even might have adhered to the Treaty if it had been properly consulted, equally treated, and not ignored.* Perhaps this infers too much. We can only speculate what

* Miss Myra Roper reports hearing Chen Yi tell a visiting Australian group in late 1963 that signing the Treaty "could have easily been delayed until China had been consulted but the USSR has been as guilty as the United States of big-power chauvinism." Myra Roper, *China—The Surprising Country* (Garden City, New York: Doubleday and Co., 1966), p. 114. High Peking officials in Moscow at the time of the negotiations apparently were never

might have happened if President Kennedy's administration had taken the initiative much earlier with Peking to undertake a serious, full-fledged exchange on the Treaty and grasp the "nuclear nettle," Moscow's treatment of Peking notwithstanding.

The Chinese Communists will certainly demand "absolutely" equal consideration in any situation. At the Geneva Talks in 1955, they insisted upon a completely symmetrical agreement for China and the United States in the negotiations on the repatriation of civilians. After the agreement was announced, the Chinese proceeded to protest over the alleged non-repatriation of Chinese in the United States, in prison and outside prison, as strongly as the Americans were denouncing the forced retention of Americans in China. The negotiations over newsmen foundered on the issue of equal and reciprocal exchange. Whatever their private official views in 1956 and 1957, the Americans insisted on a unilateral and nonreciprocal program, perhaps knowing that Peking would turn it down and thereby relieve Washington of any mutual exchange of newsmen. If this was the pyschological gambit of the Americans, it worked. Peking refused the nonreciprocal proposition, and denounced the Americans for suggesting the "absolutely unacceptable." Peking likewise reacted furiously when, in early 1958 during the nine-month hiatus in the Talks, Washington proposed that its First Secretary from the Embassy in London maintain liaison with Peking's Ambassador in Warsaw. Again that was "absolutely impermissible." *

Reflecting China's ancient pride and modern agony, Communist

---

consulted or notified by Soviet authorities. Whether Peking would have signed the treaty or not remains moot. Nevertheless, Kennedy's biographers corroborate the point about Peking's exclusion by Moscow. Theodore Sorensen reports that President Kennedy vainly hoped that Moscow would exert some pressure on Peking to sign, but Moscow would not or could not. He reportedly regarded China's isolation as a "major gain and the Soviets may also have been similarly motivated." Theodore C. Sorensen, *Kennedy* (New York: Bantam Books, 1966), p. 829. Arthur Schlesinger Jr. also reports that Moscow's coexistence policy with the United States may have been a move to isolate Communist China within the "communist civil war." He reports that when W. Averell Harriman, the American negotiator of the Treaty, asked Chairman Khrushchev in Moscow if he could "deliver China," Khrushchev replied, "That's your problem." Arthur M. Schlesinger, Jr. *A Thousand Days: John F. Kennedy in the White House* (Boston: Houghton Mifflin Co., 1965), pp. 908, 914.

* It is characteristic of the Chinese Communist preoccupation with precedence that they often arrive at the conference table before the Americans, to receive them so to speak, and leave ahead of the Americans.

China's revolutionary experience has also made its nationalistic foreign policy seem as aggrieved as it has been aggressive in negotiations with the United States. The combined impact of Sinocentric tradition and a successful revolutionary experience—both full of absolutes and intensities—has conditioned Peking's foreign-policy-makers in dealing with the Western powers, the Socialist camp, and the underdeveloped countries, as A. M. Halpern has observed.[17] We must always remember that we have been dealing with revolutionaries—aging of course, but fanatic zealots whose emotional and intellectual bases for beliefs and actions have remained unchanged since their youth. Their unlimited ambitions, with China's lingering humiliations and undeveloped strength, have ended in frustration when simultaneously confronted with outside obstacles like American power, Soviet opposition and Asian nationalism. In the American experience with the Chinese, their revolutionary but Sinocentric diplomacy has made normal negotiations a contradiction in terms. Ambassador Panikkar, an Indian diplomat who has dealt with this form of diplomacy, has observed:

The sense of universalism inherent in a great revolution is basically contradictory to national interests and therefore is incompatible with international usages. From this fact flow the anomalies and contradictions of revolutionary foreign policy.[18]

In the light of China's position, therefore—both traditionally and currently—it seems utterly incongruous and contradictory that Peking is willing to maintain even minimal contact with the United States.

The Divergence in the Sense of Time

Aged in different histories and cultures, the negotiating styles of the Americans and Chinese Communists operate on utterly different conceptions of time. The Americans hurry, while the Chinese Communists wait. They contemplate historical cycles; the Americans watch the clock. The man from Washington thus consumes time; the man from Peking uses it. The Maoist negotiating style spans time but does not measure it the way Americans do, because the Maoist sense of invincibility is timeless—the Chinese believe the struggle over "imperialism" will extend through a long period of history before achieving victory.

Speaking in terms of "epochs" and "eras," Chinese Communist statements and writings repeat the catch phrases "victory of socialism" and "doom of imperialism." Both are inevitable but will unavoidably have to take place over a long cyclical process reminiscent of traditional Chinese thinking. As Peking put it in 1964:

. . . Socialist society covers a very long historical period. . . . A very long period of time is needed to decide who will win in the struggle between socialism and capitalism. Several decades will not do it. Success requires anywhere from one to several centuries.[19]

In 1966 one of Peking's official declarations, it will be remembered, spoke of this as the "historical era" of struggle with the United States.[20]

The Chinese Communist negotiator thus indulges in his frustrating treatment of "imperialist" representatives because Marxist-Maoism reinforces his Chinese sense of timelessness and history. He operates in a traditional Chinese framework of time, which was always conceived as an accumulation of eras, epochs, and seasons "ordered into a number of definite, closed, discontinuous, and unrelated cycles emanating, like space, from a center." [21] Being Chinese and Marxist-Leninist simultaneously, the Chinese Communist negotiator implicitly believes that time and victory are on his side.* While the historical process may be nudged along, it does not need to be hurried, should that be disadvantageous. Success in bargaining, whether for a piece of goods or the enemy's defeat, will come more easily if no sense of haste or concern is shown. Viewing negotiations in extended periods of time, Chinese Communist negotiators give the impression that they can wait forever, if necessary, for they appear to think that they, not we, have the monopoly on the future. An early American analysis of the Maoist conception of time put it this way:

The first and most important of Mao's premises is that he and those who think like him have a monopoly on patience. This monopoly is comfortably cushioned moreover, by the flexibility built into Mao's doctrine of the inevitability of victory. . . . Indeed, it is the faith of the Communists in Southeast Asia in their monopoly on patience that has made Mao's the ubiquitous gospel it is. . . . The second premise, perhaps a corollary of the first, is that the anti-Communists front is committed to quick victory, and therefore cannot, and will not, underwrite a long-drawn-out war.[22]

In operating in this framework, patience, durability and imperturbability have epitomized Chinese Communist negotiators. Coupled with their sense of time and propensity for patience is their complete discipline in painstaking planning for any negotiation, no mat-

---

* Captured North Vietnamese documents of 1966, seen by the author, claim that Peking was urging Hanoi to play for time and fight on indefinitely until China's nuclear and conventional power totally defeated the United States.

ter how trivial the detail or implausible the purpose. They leave nothing to chance. They come with a paper and a reference for everything.

What Ambassador Arthur Dean, the first civilian negotiator with the Chinese Communists, said in 1953 after leaving Panmunjom still holds true about Peking's sense of time:

Communists are in no hurry. They have no timetable. They think time is on their side and that Americans, being optimistic, friendly, truthful, constructive and inclined to believe and hope for the best, will become discouraged.

They believe that at a long-drawn-out conference the American negotiators will be forced by American public opinion to give in, in order to have a successful conference. Impatience mounts as no progress is reported. People ask: "What progress did you make today?" The Communists know this and burn bonfires under the American negotiators and utter rude, insulting, arrogant demands that the American negotiators stop their unconstructive stalling tactics.[23]

Ten years later, in 1963, Ambassador U. Alexis Johnson, the first American representative at the Ambassadorial Talks, similarly described his long first-hand experience in dealing with Peking:

During the almost 4 years that I was negotiating with the Chinese Communists at Geneva, between 1954 and 1958, what I found most annoying and frustrating was their supreme self-confidence that they need make no concessions of any kind and that if they just waited long enough we would be forced to make all the concessions to them.[24]

The Chinese Communists know that the American representative is being pressed by his government or public opinion to produce a quick agreement. Thus, the Chinese Communist negotiator always has the advantage unless the Americans are able to play the same kind of endless game, and stop watching the clock. If the American can keep his negotiating situation flexible and even timeless, so that he, too, is not under pressure from the home office to agree, he can "outsit and outfile" his adversary. This is easier than it sounds because the Chinese Communist negotiators usually are not interested in gaining immediate advantages and making concessions for short-term gains.

The Emotional Syndrome

Time and history have generated an intense emotionalism in Sino-American relations. This unique and bizarre factor in world politics has already been fully recorded and interpreted by Tang Tsou,

Harold Isaacs, and A. T. Steele.[25] It is sufficient for our purposes to note that this syndrome of sharp images and fierce drives has largely conditioned the atmosphere, machinery, results, and consequences of dealings between Washington and Peking. Their emotional association resembles a brittle courtship, features reversible or identical "mirror-images," and indulges in extremes. Yet a strange attraction between them has preserved a lingering liaison, though adding to their mutual obsession. As in a difficult courtship, neither can fully come to terms nor totally dispense with the other.

Indeed, resemblance to a courtship or marriage is often noted. For example, an Asian diplomat in Panmunjom observed to the author in 1954 that the Americans and the Chinese Communists talked obsessively about each other and talked to him only about the other like embittered, unrequited lovers, as he put it, who would not speak to each other yet who could not break off. Looking farther back, Mr. Steele in his book referred to the post-Pearl Harbor "marriage after an over-long engagement," a "shot-gun marriage" in a happy union during this "Sino-American honeymoon" of "dreamy unreality."[26] In the summer of 1966 C. L. Sulzberger of *The New York Times* illustrated the continuity of this peculiar Sino-American complex of alternating attraction and repulsion when he reported that: "The other day a European diplomat conceded that the United States-China relationship was a love-hate affair, and that therefore one couldn't exclude the possibility the two might fall in love again."[27] Visitors to Peking during the tense years of 1965–66 noted the serious interest and realistic questioning of some Chinese Communist officials concerning trends and conditions in the United States. However, this intense "love-hate" syndrome has hindered past Washington-Peking dealings. It will discourage the prospects for future contacts and reconciliation unless we recognize it and cope with its repercussions.

While an analysis of emotional factors in foreign relations is difficult and dangerous because it can be so subjective, many Chinese and American observers have commented on the "love-hate" theme in the Chinese-American encounter. Professor John Fairbank has emphasized that the Chinese revolutionists "labor under serious emotional problems themselves and have a warped understanding of the outside world."[28] A former Chinese Nationalist diplomat expressed this experience from a Chinese standpoint before the Vietnamese crisis:

I am afraid the Chinese question has already drifted from a rational to an emotional sphere of response, and our first duty would seem to be to bring it back to where reason may again freely operate. The American people cannot forget the bitterness of the Korean War. It continues to rankle, and that is quite understandable. The Chinese on the mainland, on the other hand, are exasperated beyond measure by America's constant interference with what they deem China's domestic affairs and by its imperialist or aggressive attitude towards matters which are specifically Chinese. The two standpoints are at opposite poles to one another. There is no common ground for even the rudiments of reconciliation. . . .

The animosity between the United States and Communist China has been intense and will remain intense as long as the United States pursues its present policy. Unless something is done to reduce this tension, the situation can lead to consequences which neither side desires. Already both sides no longer think or act in a completely rational manner. Their responses have become emotional in nature, and that is where the danger lies. Of course, it is quite natural for Americans to think that they can do no wrong, and that the fault is all on the Communist Chinese side. But the Communist Chinese feel that they are entirely right in their views. They insist that the question of Taiwan is a purely domestic one and that there should be no external interference of any sort. . . .

Today unfortunately in that extensive and populous country there is being fostered a hatred for the United States. That is also a fact. But there is no reason to believe that this is a permanent fixation. We have witnessed a number of emotional somersaults on a national scale within recent years. Friends have become enemies, and enemies friends, and these changes have come about in very short periods of time. Must the 650 million people of China therefore continue to be antagonistic to the United States, especially as we must always bear in mind that in the past they have been on the best of terms? [29]

Harold Isaacs, an American scholar who has made a special study of this phenomenon, has described the emotional reaction to China from an American standpoint:

The screen through which Americans have seen Chinese has been more opaque than most. According to the light shining through it at any given time, the Chinese were either the most wonderfully remarkable people on earth or else they were, in their great faceless sub-human mass, its most fearful monsters. Depending on the political or emotional requirements at any moment in time, we could and did see them both ways. We do still. . . .

Our emotions about the Chinese have fluctuated between sympathy and revulsion, parental benevolence and parental anger, affection and hostility, love and a fear close to hate. Across the whole 200 years of our associations with the Chinese, such paired views have persisted, moving in and out of the center of people's minds, never wholly displacing each other, always coexisting, each ready to respond to the fresh call of circumstance, always new, yet instantly garbed in all the words and pictures of a rich lore, made substantial and unique in each historic instance by the reality of recurring experience.[30]

Sir Winston Churchill was amazed during the Second World War by what he called "the extraordinary significance of China in American minds, even at the top, strangely out of proportion." [31] Another European told Mr. A. T. Steele that

I was born in Europe . . . and therefore have no complex or sacred cow fixation about China. Here in the United States there is an emotional aura on China which I do not share. Americans feel a responsibility for China which they do not feel for other countries. This attitude started with the missionaries. I can only explain it on a basis of missionary activity. I don't know how much impact the missionaries made on China, but they certainly made an impact on the United States.[32]

Since the establishment of the Chinese People's Republic in 1949, when Mao Tse-tung categorically opted for "leaning to one side" and rejected normal contacts with the United States, widespread frustration and strong animosity have obviously dominated dealings between America and Communist China. Feelings, prejudices and images, all deeply embedded in the minds and emotions of Chinese and Americans, have created a "super-charged" atmosphere surrounding the negotiations. The American journalist, Robert Elegant, has summed up these reciprocal feelings in this context:

. . . Just as China feels herself misused by the West, the United States feels that China under the Communists is repaying a century of devoted friendship with abuse and threats. Both attitudes have a basis in reality, and both also rest upon a large measure of self-deception. But those antagonistic Chinese and American attitudes have themselves become realities in the sense that they determine the actions of two governments. The American emotion is so powerful that the United States tends to behave elsewhere in Asia in accordance with what it hopes will happen in China.[33]

This emotional syndrome and lingering liaison doubly affects the dealings of Washington and Peking through the fluctuations of opposite symptoms and the reflections of identical images.

The "love-hate" syndrome has seldom been symmetrical on both sides. The Sino-American relationship reflected bias, illusion, prejudice, wishful thinking, uncritical admiration, and hysterical criticism before 1949. Most Americans have felt fondly about China, assuming that the transplantation of democracy, Christianity, and capitalism would automatically facilitate compatible dealings. Mao and the Chinese Communist Party shattered the illusion and substituted a specter. They immediately turned on Americans in China, injuring the Vice Consul in Shanghai, imprisoning the Consul and four of his staff in Mukden, confiscating consular property in Peking, and mistreating the American Ambassador in Nanking. Instead of negotiating, or at least leaving that option open, Peking instantly mounted a venomous campaign of ridicule and hostility toward the United States. On the other hand, in 1949–50 Washington was weighing the pros and cons of whether to negotiate with and recognize the new government in Peking, if it proved reasonable.

However, the Chinese Communists never let that possibility even materialize before June 1950. They either deliberately prevented any such approach from the United States or recklessly missed a unique opportunity for an accommodation. The Korean War then produced identical mirror images of enmity and outrage which have not yet disappeared. The Americans and Chinese went overboard in their mutual hate affair, for understandable reasons. The Panmunjom negotiations were harsh and brittle, but again the Americans turned back to a moderate, negotiating mood, at least in their view, while Peking kept up its verbal belligerence and truculence across the table and on its radio. When in 1955 Peking switched to its grand "sit-down diplomacy" with Washington, Chou En-lai muted his tone of hostility and moved to probing and bargaining for agreements. Dulles then was inflexible and kept his guard up, losing an opportunity to establish unofficial bilateral contacts. The complete reversal after 1960 has already been described at length; the mirror images remained almost identically hostile until 1966 when Washington again cooled down its emotional vocabulary and made its series of overtures. It is significant—and rather ironic—that since the Talks started in 1955, American opinion, whatever the syndrome and image, has consistently and steadfastly opted for communication and contact with Communist China.[34] Nevertheless, the emotional relationship has remained asymmetrical, and the mirror images similar.

Foreigners who visited the Chinese People's Republic during 1964–66 came out with two interesting observations: the virulent anti-American campaign and the love-hate emotions of both Americans and Chinese toward each other. In what Mark Gayn, another Canadian journalist, has aptly called "a vast new culture of hatred," travelers to mainland China have described the constant, gigantic, and all-pervasive effort to portray the United States government and American officials in the worst possible light as "aggressors," "bandits" and "reactionaries," from President Kennedy and President Johnson on down. Chinese Communist bookstores, radio programs, and newspapers have been crowded with anti-American propaganda. School children have been taught to write essays on American "crimes," while Chinese Communist dance and theatre portray the same themes. Kindergarten children have even been reported singing about their determination to shoot down American planes! It was not difficult for the Chinese Communist government to get millions of China's huge population involved in this campaign of anti-Americanism.

To judge by accounts of personal meetings with Mao Tse-tung over the past decades, this campaign stems from his long-standing, unchanging, implacable hatred of the United States as the leader of the "imperialist camp." While Chinese officials and Chinese negotiators feel and reflect his anti-Americanism, it should also be pointed out that Mao and his colleagues have used it for political purposes at home, unrelated to negotiations with Washington. In the words of one foreign visitor to the Chinese People's Republic,

Beyond any doubt, Mao Tse-tung, Lin Piao and all the other leaders genuinely regard the United States as a deadly opponent, with whom no compromise is either possible or desirable. But, at the same time, the recurring waves of anti-American propaganda are an effective political device, enabling the leaders to maintain that climate of tension in which sacrifices can be demanded and obtained.[35]

Charles Taylor has reported what it is like to be in one of these organized anti-American demonstrations and also concluded that they have great importance on the domestic scene. Nevertheless, he stressed the necessity of realizing that this virulent opposition to the United States and the Soviet Union was generally and genuinely popular. If that image were to take hold in China—and he thought it would—there will be a new Chinese generation bred in this "orgy of anti-American hatred and hostility" unlike anything the American people and their diplomats have dealt with for over a century.

Accordingly, this intense phenomenon of the "mirror image" vitally affects relations and negotiations between the two governments as well as between the two peoples. An Australian journalist and educator, Myra Roper, who visited Communist China in 1958, 1963, and 1966, concluded her book with an essay on "the mirror image" in the relations between the two countries. She found that officials and people in each country were accusing the other government of the same thing: aggression, hostility, malicious propaganda and official falsification.[36] The people of each country were good; it was the government which was bad and needed changing. As Taylor put it: "In a very real sense official American outlooks are a reverse image of the Chinese contention that 'We love the great American people; it is only the narrow American ruling class that we hate and oppose'." [37]

To break through the love-hate syndrome in the Sino-American heritage and to change the images, American negotiators and Americans in general need to recognize and accept the fact that most Chinese want to obliterate China's historical weakness, regain its strength, and win at least a rightful if not the predominant place for China in the world. As has already been noted, the wellsprings of China's centrality and greatness run deep in the Chinese mind, whether Communist or not. Dealings with China, therefore, ignore these images and emotions at their peril. As C. P. Fitzgerald has warned:

. . . Failure to realize this aspect of China's policy is the weakness of Western current thinking. Obsessed with the belief that communist states are somehow fundamentally different from others—not merely in social and economic organization, but in the mental processes of their leaders— many Western observers and policy makers seem quite unable to see their mirror image in their Chinese rivals.[38]

Even the Ambassadorial Talks reflect this mirror image of charge and countercharge of aggression versus peaceful intentions.

The American negotiator needs to bear in mind that, to his Chinese Communist opposite number, he constitutes a unique combination of offensive symbols. He represents the American epicenter of world power, ringing China with military strength and countervailing China's return to the status of a great nation in the forefront if no longer the center of the world. He expresses American leadership of a new, world-oriented culture of technology and cosmopolitanism, subordinating China's unbroken tradition of cultural predominance and displacing the contemporary ideology of Maoist fundamentalism. The American diplomat personifies its "archenemy," due for certain extinction after implacable struggle. He typifies the century-old "foreign devil," propagated massively by the Chinese Communist Party to control the population of China. The American negotiator also stands for China's real and imagined inequities, humiliations, and misfortunes inherited from the century of acquisitive Western intrusion and worldwide predominance. In dealing with the United States government, "U. S. imperialism" serves Peking as the target, and anti-Americanism as the weapon. American policy-makers and negotiators need to weigh the reality and intensity of this emotional syndrome accurately.

It may be hard for Americans to take this Chinese Communist attitude seriously, but we should have learned our lesson. We often failed to in the past, and once it cost us dearly in lives, efforts, and prestige. In the Korean War the United States miscalculated the "force of ideology in shaping the policies of the Chinese Communists" and misjudged the "intensity of their thrust and hostility toward the United States," as Professor Tang Tsou has so correctly pointed out. The author's own experience in Washington in the fall of 1950 corroborates Professor Tang Tsou's version of this appalling case of American underestimation of the Chinese Communists:

It failed to gauge their willingness to take well-calculated risks to achieve political gains while warding off serious dangers, a trait which had been planted by their ideology, strengthened by their revolutionary experience, and which had become deeply imbedded in their mentality.[39]

The complex emotional heritage of Sino-American relations should warn us that many years and much effort will be needed to overcome this unfortunate hang-over of history so intensely reflected by these mirror images in both countries. Meanwhile, the passion and intensity of antipathy towards Americans and Westerners have had much to do with the evolution of Mao's thought and the ideology of Marxist-Maoism which he bred and then spread throughout contemporary China to the point where every Chinese in 1967 supposedly was carrying and reading "The Thought of Mao Tse-tung."

Marxist-Maoist Ideologue

A Chinese Communist negotiator is an ideologist more than anything else. In his dealings with Americans, this makes him a formidable adversary because his version of negotiation thus becomes so different from, and even incompatible with, the American. Ideology molds and controls the Party man. The principles of Marxism-Leninism and the "Thought of Mao Tse-tung" arm him with a complete strategy, or "Tao," for negotiations with the United States.

"Marxist-Leninist-Maoist ideological orthodoxy" can be conveniently labelled "Marxist-Maoism." [40] Here, in Mao's own pictures, is an expression of this strategy, often repeated in Peking's declarations and indoctrination:

Make trouble, fail, make trouble again, fail again . . . till their doom; that is the logic of the imperialists and all reactionaries the world over in dealing with the people's cause, and they will never go against this logic. This is a Marxist law. When we say "imperialism is ferocious," we mean that its nature will never change, that the imperialists will never lay down their butcher knives, that they will never become Buddhas till their doom.[41]

In the context of Peking's protracted time cycle, Mao's words contain the three essential elements for dealing with Washington: the unchangeability of "Marxist laws," the total enmity towards the United States, and the tactic of temporary coexistence with limited negotiations.

The "immutable" Maoist theory of contradictions and practice of struggle determine the world outlook, objectives, and tactics of Chinese Communist negotiating style. According to Mao, the process of development of everything exists in and by contradictions between opposites, which in all but a few exceptions move inevitably toward a new beginning "in a never ending series of dualities." In his words: "Contradiction and struggle are universal, absolute, but the methods of solving them, that is, the forms of struggle differ according to the nature of the contradiction." [42] Mao has made the notion of constant and desirable struggle towards a goal the core of his life and thought since he became a Communist in the early 1920s. This ideology of contradiction and struggle molds and dictates the automatic response of the Communist state of mind in the Central Committee or at the negotiating table. In Mao's own oft-quoted words, repeated in Peking again in October 1966:

The socialist system will eventually replace the capitalist system; this is an objective law independent of man's will. However much the reactionaries try to hold back the wheel of history, sooner or later revolution will take place and will inevitably triumph.[43]

Accordingly, all the world is divided into two parts, or two camps, in the doctrine according to Mao. And never the twain shall meet when the split involves "imperialism" and socialism.

The beginning and the end of our story of United States dealings with Communist China illustrate this Maoist dialectic view of the world. In Ambassador Johnson's original meeting with the Chinese Communists in Geneva, he arranged the chairs more or less in a circle just so as to avoid the dialectic division into two sides and facilitate a more informal give-and-take than had obtained at Panmunjom. But when their turn came to arrange the next meeting, the Chinese Communists placed the chairs so that the opposing sides again confronted each other across a divide. The Panmunjom bisection and stalemate has lasted ever since. A decade later, in September 1965, Foreign Minister Chen Yi concluded a remarkable news conference, after violently attacking the United States, by telling the world that it had to choose between "two alternatives": the reimposition of colonial shackles under United States imperialism or the waging of "resolute struggles" to defeat United States imperialism. Chou En-lai's declaration in 1966 ended our story in the same dichotomy.[44]

Despite the availability of much factual information, the Chinese Communist leaders must fit every development into the Leninist-Maoist mold. Despite their collection of facts, they seem to make little if any logical deductions from what others would call the criteria of objective analysis and empirical observation of the real world. In the American phrase, they know all the answers. Because of their discipline and dogma, the Chinese Communist representative believes in his infallibility. The American negotiator, accordingly, can expect his Chinese Communist opposite number to adhere rigidly to a whole set of doctrinal preconceptions and ideological behavior patterns.

Although many contradictions can be reconciled, the struggle between the two camps is the cardinal exception in the dogma. It excludes any lasting compromise, doctrinal acceptance, or basic reconciliation and accommodation. The Chinese Communist Party definitively stated the Maoist doctrine of international contradictions during the Sino-Soviet ideological dispute in the summer of 1963 when Peking listed the contradiction between the "socialist" camp and the "imperialist" camp first in the contemporary world scene. The struggle between two fundamentally different social systems —socialism and capitalism—was conceived *a priori* to be "very sharp." Peaceful "all round" negotiation and lasting coexistence with the United States were out of the question.

It should never be extended to apply to the relations between oppressed and oppressor nations, between oppressed and oppressor countries or between oppressed and oppressor classes, and never be described as the main content of the transition from capitalism to socialism, still less should it be asserted that peaceful co-existence is mankind's road to socialism. The reason is that it is one thing to practise peaceful co-existence between countries with different social systems. It is absolutely impermissible and impossible for countries practising peaceful co-existence to touch even a hair of each other's social system.

. . . The class struggle, the struggle for national liberation and the transition from capitalism to socialism in various countries are quite another thing. They are all bitter, life-and-death revolutionary struggles which aim at changing the social system. Peaceful co-existence cannot replace the revolutionary struggles of the people. The transition from capitalism to socialism in any country can only be brought about through the proletarian revolution and the dictatorship of the proletariat in that country.

In the application of the policy of peaceful co-existence, struggles between the socialist and imperialist countries are unavoidable in the political, economic and ideological spheres, and it is absolutely impossible to have "all-round-cooperation." [45]

Since struggle, antagonism and contradiction must have a specific opposite, Maoism has singled out the United States, particularly since 1960, as the "enemy" of socialism and Communist China. This is the cardinal thesis, always expressed in violent terms. For example, the Chinese Communist party stated in another letter to the Soviet party during their polemics of 1963 that "the United States imperialists are the wildest militarists of modern times, the wildest plotters of a new world war and the most ferocious enemy of world peace." [46] In March 1966 the Chinese Communist party again accused the Soviet Union of aligning itself with "United States imperialism, the main enemy of the people of the world," while the party's Central Committee officially declared in August that "U.S. imperialism is the most ferocious common enemy of the peoples of the whole world." [47] In November, disregarding President Johnson's appeals for better relations, Chou En-lai repeated this label.[48] This Maoist image of the United States has been well summed up by Professor Franz Schurmann:

. . . Given China's revolutionary status and role in the world, the Chinese Communists regard the enmity between the United States and China as fundamental. This does not mean that they believe a major war between these two countries is necessarily in the offing. Following their own experiences which gave them victory only after decades of struggle, they see this enmity lasting for years and decades. Periods of peace and even collaboration between the two countries are conceivable, comparable to their united front with the Kuomintang between 1936 and 1946.

But peace and collaboration cannot change the fundamental nature of the relationship.[49]

The man from Peking evidently negotiates in the conviction that the United States government and "United States imperialism" constitute the unchanging enemy of the People's Republic of China to be beaten in negotiations, and destroyed in fact.

With this ideology, Maoist diplomacy and negotiating style completely express Mao's political philosophy stated in his simple, notorious phrase that "political power comes out of the barrel of a gun." Glorifying martial virtues and military tactics, the Sinocentric, Maoist and revolutionary diplomat considers negotiation, at least with Americans, an eventual death struggle for the adversary and not a joint benefit for both parties. He has no feeling for his American adversary nor any interest in his case. He indulges in the language of invective and exhausts the vocabulary of the extreme.* Such negotiation resembles a classical military campaign and a conventional military maneuver.

The goal is total defeat of the adversary by complete victory. The mission of revolutionary diplomacy is unremitting, implacable effort by diplomatic guerrilla warfare to secure this ultimate triumph no matter how long stalemate and capitulation may take. Tactically, this kind of negotiator tries to outflank his opponent, demoralize and weaken him by every conceivable means at every possible point, take over his strategic position, separate him from allies, leave him no exit, and give him no quarter. Such militant and militaristic diplomacy makes short shrift of mutual confidence, truthful exchange, or fair dealing. Capitulation for the adversary replaces compromise in the revolutionary diplomacy, which views an adversary's concession as a step toward his inevitable defeat rather than a way of accommodation toward a mutual settlement. Where adjustments by bargaining and compromise to reach a durable understanding are scorned, extremes instead of middle points are prized.

Mao's martial ideology is difficult and even impossible to deal with

---

* His vocabulary can include any or all of the following words to attack the American position: absurd, audacious, fantastic, ridiculous, deceitful, dishonest, distorted, shameful, insincere, intolerable, invidious, impertinent, mendacious, malicious, rapacious, slanderous, preposterous, lecherous, scandalous, vicious, stupid, nonsensical, treacherous, perfidious, etc., through the thesaurus. In the Ambassadorial Talks, Peking's Ambassador has labeled serious American proposals as a "trick," "conspiracy," "fraud," "swindle," and "sham."

not only because of the uncompromising thesis of struggle and doom, but also because of his rigid and unchanging beliefs. Biographers or observers of Mao Tse-tung over the past decades concur on the static quality of his opinions and attitudes. He has remained "the prisoner of his own history," according to Robert Payne in his biography of Mao.[50] Mark Gayn, who has interviewed Mao, described this key factor for understanding the lack of ideological change or dialogue in Communist China:

. . . This unchanged doctrinal approach is an essential fact in any new assessment of Mao Tse-tung. It is as if time had stood still for him and his companions, and they were still totally isolated from all reality except that of their own limited domain.[51]

In short, the United States government and the American negotiator are dealing with a closed mind in which conceptual thinking and logical analysis have not developed or matured for over a generation. The world has changed but Maoist ideology has enclosed China within a new ideological wall. It is designed to keep out change and to preserve the pristine state of mind shaped by Mao in his early days. Maoist ideology thus insulates Chinese negotiators from understanding the rapidly evolving modern world while it reinforces their ability to repeat the doctrine endlessly in dealings and negotiations with the United States.

Peking's Dualistic Concept of Negotiations

If China's aging and revolutionary ideologists view the United States government so belligerently and absolutely, how can they possibly negotiate with Washington on anything? Is it not a total contradiction in terms for Peking to treat with "the main enemy of the people," or negotiate for "peaceful negotiations" with this "ferocious" adversary as Peking tried to do in the 1955–56 exchanges over renunciation of force? Peking's theory and practice of negotiating with the United States have indeed seemed contradictory, and this is part of the problem of having to reconcile ideology and national interest.

Peking's policy-makers and negotiators, as in the case of all governments, have had to handle both these determinants. Even for such ideologically and historically minded men as the revolutionary leaders of Communist China, these components of foreign policy are full of variables and vagaries. The leaders have shown a considerable capacity in operating practically and flexibly without becoming totally trapped in the dogmas and rigidities of either Maoist ideology or national interest. A. M. Halpern, an authority on Communist China's foreign policy, is inclined to believe that Peking does tend to formulate its actions in foreign policy in terms of a long-range judgment "of how they will contribute to the complete liquidation of imperialism." With long-range objectives in mind, the Chinese Communists tend to emphasize the potential long-term development of situations much more than current relationships. Moreover, they appear to favor courses of action which will realize maximum long-range gains even at the expense of losing or deferring immediate advantages. In a word, the Peking policy-makers are "mini-max" operators. Accordingly, they deal with the United States on both a minimum basis of gaining some tactical immediate advantage at the same time that they seek the maximum long-range objective of major concessions from Washington.

An illustration of this dualistic concept of negotiations and "mini-max" treatment of the United States appeared in the secret work bulletins issued to the Chinese army in 1961, referred to earlier. Prepared and circulated only for Chinese with a relatively high level of education and sophistication, these instructions are cited here to show this differentiated treatment:

We should have no illusions about imperialism. With regard to the disarmament problem, if some agreement should be made in the morning, it may be broken in the evening. We Chinese people have to fall back on our own experience. . . .

The present situation is to stand firm against the United States and maintain peaceful coexistence with many other countries. . . .

At present, there is a note in international affairs sounding a call to mediate between China and the United States and to act as a bridge between China and the United States. Both Japan and England wanted to do some work by bridging the relations between China and the United States. We have no objection to this, provided they build the bridge. After the bridge is built, who will take the first step to cross it? Will the United States come first? Or shall we go first? The United States must withdraw from Taiwan so that we shall meet at the center of the bridge, and neither one will have an advantage over the other. . . .

The policy of our country towards the United States must also be different from that of the Soviet Union. But this difference will not hinder the transition from Socialism to Communism or the overall opposition to imperialism. At present both China and the Soviet Union are fundamentally unanimous in their attitude toward problems like Kennedy, disarmament, Laos, Cuba and the Congo. The Moscow statement regarded American imperialism as the world's most wicked enemy, admitted that the national capitalist class has two faces, agreed that there can be no true peace before Socialism is realized in the world, *took cognizance of the possibility of negotiating with the West though we must be pugnacious in disposition and not be paralyzed in our will to fight,* and recognized that the fraternal parties must consult on an equal footing with each other. . . .[52] (italics added)

Indeed, a long series of public Chinese Communist statements made over many years likewise have implied this qualified kind of coexistence, which theoretically is, of course, unconditional. The explanation for this lies in the Maoist differentiation of two different sorts of coexistence and negotiation. Among various Socialist governments and peoples the resolution of basic contradictions and the reaching of "all-around agreements" are desirable and necessary. This is strategic or general negotiation and coexistence in the Maoist sense. On the other hand, coexistence and negotiation with the United States and other "imperialistic and reactionary forces" are purely tactical, only possible in a limited, highly qualified sense. They are exclusively tactical and expedient stratagems in the long-range strategy of bringing about the inevitable extinction and disappearance of United States "imperialism." Peking's statements must be interpreted in the total context of Marxist-Maoist ideology in order to avoid confusion over seemingly contradictory semantics. For example, a Chinese Communist leader can declare that antagonism toward the imperialists is a "life-and-death matter" because there can be no "live and let live or actual co-existence and friendly cooperation." But, on the other hand, Peking has defined its expedient tactical diplomacy toward the "imperialists" with the following mixture of clarity and ambiguity:

It is necessary for the socialist countries to engage in negotiations of one kind or another with the imperialist countries. It is possible to reach certain agreements through negotiation by relying on the correct policies of the socialist countries and on the pressure of the people of all countries. But necessary compromises between socialist countries and the imperialist countries do not require the oppressed peoples and nations to follow suit and compromise with imperialism and its lackeys. No one should ever demand in the name of peaceful co-existence that the oppressed peoples and nations should give up their revolutionary struggles.

Negotiation is one form of struggle against imperialism. Necessary compromises can be made in negotiations, so long as the principle of upholding the fundamental interests of the people is observed. But if one regards negotiations as the main means, or even the sole means, of striving for peaceful co-existence and does not scruple to sell out the fundamental interests of the people in order to seek compromises with imperialism, that is not peaceful co-existence but capitulationist co-existence. And it will only result in endangering world peace.[53]

The typically ambiguous Communist "code words" used for the initiated—such as "correct policies," "pressure of the people," "revolutionary struggles," "fundamental interests of the people," and "world peace" are, in fact, the key to an understanding of what Maoist negotiators really mean and are helpful in dealing with them. These key words, signifying the fixed, absolute double strategy of destroying "imperialism" by struggle and diplomacy, prohibit "all-round" negotiations but sanction "necessary compromises" by "certain agreements." Fortunately, Mao Tse-tung has described his dualistic concept of negotiations in the simpler, but not entirely self-evident, metaphor of "tit-for-tatism," which also reflects Chinese traditional style:

How to give "tit for tat" depends on the situation. Sometimes not going to negotiations is tit-for-tat, and sometimes going to negotiations is also tit-for-tat . . . if they start fighting, we fight back, fight to win peace. Peace will not come unless we strike hard blows at the reactionaries who dare to attack the liberated areas.

The CPSU leaders assert that by advocating a tit-for-tat struggle, the CCP has rejected negotiations. This again is nonsense. We consistently maintain that those who refuse negotiations under all circumstances are definitely not Marxist-Leninists. The Chinese communists conducted negotiations with the Kuomintang many times during the revolutionary civil wars. They did not refuse to negotiate even on the eve of nation-wide liberation.

Whether the peace negotiations are overall or local, we should be prepared for such an eventuality. We should not refuse to enter into negotiations because we are afraid of trouble and want to avoid complications nor should we enter into negotiations with our minds in a haze. We should be firm in principle; we should also have all the flexibility permissible and necessary for carrying out our principles.[54]

When the Sino-American Ambassadorial Talks were publicized by Moscow in the summer of 1966, Peking rebutted Moscow by stating that its attitude toward the question of negotiation had always been consistent, for the Chinese Communist Party had "firmly adhered to the Marxist-Leninist principle that it is necessary to wage a tit-for-tat struggle . . . sometimes not going and sometimes going for negotiations . . ."[55]

In the general framework of unlimited struggle to win total victory over the United States and imperialism, Chinese Communist doctrine sanctions and practices limited negotiation and temporary coexistence to gain specific tactical targets:

1. To facilitate diplomatic undertakings which extract concessions from the "enemy," thus enhancing the position of the Chinese People's Republic and the socialist camp, while weakening and hastening the defeat of "imperialism."

2. To promote commercial, financial, technological and cultural exchange which will assist the internal development and international standing of the People's Republic of China.

3. To disengage from some situations which are embarrassing or untenable for Peking because of the counteractions or initiatives of Washington and other Western governments.

4. To promote dissension among the "imperialists" or weaken their flank by negotiating arrangements with the allies of the United States or other countries in Asia, Africa, Latin America, and even Europe.

Peking has negotiated with all of these considerations in mind at the Geneva Conferences and in the Ambassadorial Talks. But it should be stressed that limited negotiations with the United States and "imperialists" rule out the possibility of seeking or concluding any general "all-round" settlement of over-all issues which would lessen the struggle and lead toward lasting reconciliation and peaceful relations. As long as the Chinese Communists adhere strictly and fanatically to Maoist ideology at home and abroad, there can be no détente or secure settlement with Peking. Any limited negotiation or temporary coexistence is part of the struggle and not any evidence of favorable attitude or change in posture.

For example, an agreement on a general settlement in Southeast Asia would only mean that Peking had found such an agreement tactically expedient; it would not mean any real accommodation of mutual interests with the United States in Southeast Asia. Nor could it be taken as a binding commitment to renounce the use of "proletarian forces" to support and expand the revolutionary struggle there. It is hardly likely that the present leadership of Communist China would agree in practice or in theory to negotiate and enforce an agreement which would prevent Peking from engaging in all-out support for "national liberation movements" and the expansion of Communist subversion and seizure of power for the ultimate triumph of "socialism" in the "countryside" of the whole world.

On the other hand, Peking would negotiate with Washington for a general settlement providing the withdrawal of American armed forces and influence from Taiwan and East Asia in general. But it is doubtful that in exchange Peking would agree to any meaningful nonagression pledge regarding other countries in East Asia and the Pacific. Any such negotiation and settlement with the United States would be viewed in Peking primarily as a tactical retreat by Washington and a net gain for Peking in the unlimited struggle, and not as a beginning of a new period of good relations with the Americans. The Chinese Communist secret documents acquired in 1961 have revealed that Peking's secret strategy for dealing with the United States then envisioned a single total negotiation, all on Peking's terms:

It is better to maintain a frozen relationship between China and the United States, with a continued impasse for many years. If this problem is to be settled, we want to do so all at once; that is, the United States must withdraw its troops from Taiwan, recognize the new China and be ready to exchange newspaper reporters, etc. These should all be solved simultaneously. In this way we shall continue to raise high the banner of anti-imperialism, freely support the struggle for national independence of colonies and semicolonies, maintain the power to strengthen our political position and lift up our morale. At present our country is still keeping in touch with the United States, and the Warsaw negotiations are still in progress. Some people criticize us for being too stiff and unbending, but this is not correct criticism. Our country has already made many concessions such as giving entry permits to the American writer (Edgar) Snow and an American Negro scholar to visit China; we have further released more than 40 American criminals, but the United States has not made one concession. Up to the present time we can see no expression of relaxation concerning Sino-American relations or any sign of sincerity. This is why we say that the unbending attitude is found on the side of the United States, and not on the side of China. Of course, the far-reaching view of the relationship between the two countries is optimistic and some day this problem will arrive at a satisfactory solution.[56]

The Chinese Communist documents exchanged in the polemics with Moscow have publicly confirmed Peking's general line on its American strategy. As the Ambassadorial Talks have abundantly demonstrated, Taiwan is the only negotiation in which Peking is interested.

* * *

All these fundamental factors make up the Chinese negotiating style—the orders of the Party, the determinants of Chinese history, the cycles of time, the dictates of Marxist-Maoism, and the "mirror images" of mental bias and emotional prejudice. Of course they do not all confront the American negotiator equally at any one time. But they do comprise the total mix in dealing with the Chinese Communists. The man from Peking will play a different role, exhibit automatically hostile motivations, insist on a total approach, display dogmatic certainty, and convey a sense of timelessness. His negotiating style is designed not to facilitate the task of his opposite numbers, but to harass and exasperate them as much as possible. At a meeting or conference, he will try to prove that the Americans are deceitful and unreliable by not accepting Peking's proposition without question. If the Americans were "sincere," they would only have to sign on the dotted line and ask no questions. Badgering the Americans constantly, the Chinese negotiator tries to put them on the defensive in order to make them reply that they are indeed sincere and will, therefore, come to an agreement. Meanwhile, the Chinese government's total control of its own news media, which can orchestrate a conciliatory or a belligerent public reaction, and the Chinese-Maoist monopoly of time and certainty of triumph, which do not watch the clock, make the negotiating process all the more difficult for others.

In such a complex kind of "adversary" negotiations, Americans will certainly confront this totally divergent style of negotiations which will require a considerable change in the typical American way of comprehending and handling diplomatic transactions with the Chinese Communists. At this negotiating table, the man from Washington needs farsighted vision, nerves of steel and some nonchalance, in addition to stamina and patience, in order to be able to see beyond the inevitable struggle and the dialectic enmity to a rational bargaining process having some mutually acceptable rules of accommodation.

CHAPTER FIFTEEN

Adversary Negotiating with Peking

What motivates the Asian Communists and particularly the men from Peking to negotiate is an enigma. On the one hand, they can ignore major concessions and significant assurances as they did in 1958 during the Taiwan crisis and as they so conspicuously have during 1965–67 with regard to Vietnam. They even take the risk of incurring overwhelming retaliation from the United States as they apparently did in Korea and Taiwan, by engaging in hostilities outright. On the other hand, the Maoist regime has negotiated with the United States and kept up a form of diplomatic contact with Washington, and followed a strategy of restraint.

What is Peking's propensity to negotiate? Can a pattern of incentives be traced? How is Peking's reversal in dealing with Washington to be explained? Does some interaction of diplomacy and power override strictly ideological dictates to induce the Chinese to come to the table, whether to bargain or merely to preserve some semblance of contact?

Our experience in dealing with Peking strongly suggests that the "mix with the mostest" does promote a negotiating propensity and pattern. Diplomacy without force produces a farce, while force without diplomacy can leave a fiasco. Without both diplomacy and power, negotiation with Peking is unlikely or impossible. In each case that Washington informed Peking of the readiness of the United States to resort to the use of preponderant power, despite its strong preference for a diplomatic settlement, the Chinese Communists negotiated the outcome in a prudent accommodation: the Korean Armistice was finally put into effect in 1953; cease-fire agreements for Indochina were reached in 1954; the Taiwan Crisis was eased in 1958, the conference on Laos, opened in 1961, was completed in 1962. Unlike the style and process of Western litigation

371

and transaction, only a dynamic bargaining process of adversary negotiations which produces parallel advantages by offsetting mutual risks, gains, and losses will induce Peking to join a conference and transact an outcome.

The pattern of adversary negotiation with Peking includes formal and informal, explicit and tacit, bargaining processes. Some outcomes emerge only from a precise, organized transaction and formal written agreements. Others arise from intimations alone, inferred from statements or even changes in attitudes. In its particular negotiating pattern, Peking has put unusual emphasis on immutable ideology and non-negotiable principle compared with the conventional negotiating process which always requires the parties to indicate their fixed points or "ideological" minimum. The need to identify and analyze Peking's pattern of being in favor of negotiations but against haggling over principle requires a proper assessment of the relative weight attached at any one time to adherence to ideology and principled policies on the one hand, and tactical flexibility on the other. The American experience in dealing with Peking has shown that its policy-makers and negotiators have, in fact, merged theory and practice, Marxist ideology and national interest in their process of bargaining, communicating and maneuvering. However, this pattern is by no means clearly conceived or properly defined; it reveals a conglomeration of styles, tactics and objectives rather than a systematically devised scheme.* The Chinese Communists have given some evidence of pragmatism, too, but among the Communist nations the Maoist regime has tended least in the direction of moderating ideology in the pursuit of short-range objectives.

Historical and ideological contrasts and divergencies in styles of negotiation have inevitably created this special style and process of "adversary negotiation" between Peking and Washington, given Peking's dualistic concept of "allowed" or limited negotiation. What, when, and how to concede and bargain, or to elude in discussion, is the hard crux of any negotiating process and always a problem. For the men from Peking and Washington it becomes particularly acute. How can a concession be extended to or accepted from a sworn enemy? How can the American be expected to submit to ulti-

* This analysis of Peking's negotiating style and the Washington-Peking negotiations, in the context of the interplay of diplomacy and power, is based upon the useful discussions of intergovernmental negotiations contained in F. Charles Ikle, *How Nations Negotiate*, and Thomas Schelling, *The Strategy of Conflict*, cited.

matums, act "sincerely" and accept Peking's demands while being treated with belligerent, abusive, and uncompromising language in the Communist press and official speeches? And if the man from Peking intends to sit out the Talks for years, will he ever come halfway to bargain for concessions or will he wait for a future, more auspicious time? Should concessions be so much as spelled out, given the impossibility of negotiating, and then kept alive by endless reiteration? Indeed, where is the room for surprise, maneuver and the so-called give-and-take of modern diplomacy in dealings between Washington and Peking?

In short, how can these negotiators conciliate the irreconcilable? One answer, and perhaps the only one, lies in capitalizing on Peking's version of expedient negotiations in limited coexistence. The American can emphasize the pragmatic and leave the ideological to the future. For reasons of national interest and to avoid abstract ideological confrontations, both parties can theoretically offer and transact concessions and compromises within this limited frame of reference if they both play the risky and difficult rules of the same game in what might appropriately be called "adversary negotiations."

Adversary Diplomacy, Peking Style

The differences, not the similarities, between negotiating with friends and negotiating with enemies are the significant elements in the adversary negotiating process of the Chinese Communists. Peking's style is quite the reverse of ours. In the context of Western civilization, American negotiators tend to think in terms of "good will" and "bona fide" negotiations. Although deliberate deception has not been entirely absent from the conventional style of Western negotiating, its thrust is toward the shared notions and values of mutual trust, good faith, reciprocal respect, and common interests. The Western negotiating process tends to encourage fair dealing, accurate statements, courteous behavior, and conciliatory practices. It assumes, and is designed to facilitate, a mutual desire for a common outcome by the accommodation of some mutual conflict and by the development of a common understanding. In this type of negotiation, compromise is prized as a good thing in itself, and the full and faithful performance of a negotiated contract is revered with "immutable sanctity."

Adversary negotiations, however, are based on reverse notions —mistrust, suspicion, the utter lack of any good faith, and the intent to upset and not accommodate "the other side," even to widening rather than adjusting a basic conflict. In fact, the adversary negotiating process can sanction a breach of contract and usually scorns reciprocal compromises. As Thomas Schelling has reminded us, this style of negotiating is as old as mankind:

. . . The ancients exchanged hostages, drank wine from the same glass to demonstrate the absence of poison, met in public places to inhibit the massacre of one by the other, and even deliberately exchanged spies to facilitate transmittal of authentic information. It seems likely that a well-developed theory of strategy could throw light on the efficacy of some of those old devices, suggest the circumstances to which they apply, and discover modern equivalents that, though offensive to our taste, may be desperately needed in the regulation of conflict.[1]

The Chinese Communists have only brought this up to date with their own unique variations. Inasmuch as the standard Western approach to a mutual negotiating process for a shared outcome is impractical, we need to formulate a new understanding and strategy to cope with Peking's adversary negotiations.

The Chinese Communist adversary style can indeed be "foxy" and "wolfish" in treating with the "imperialist" negotiator as a carefully-defined expedient or a well-timed temporary retreat. According to Mao Tse-tung:

"First to go back and then get a better run for a bigger leap forward" is precisely Leninism. Marxism-Leninism does not allow concessions to be regarded as something purely negative. . . . Our concessions, withdrawal, turning to the defensive or suspending action, whether in dealing with allies or enemies, would always be regarded as part of the entire revolutionary policy, as an indispensable link in the general revolutionary line, a segment in a curvilinear movement.[2]

The line and the movement have a single objective: total and final victory. The Chinese negotiators and policy-makers do not seem to consider cooperative negotiations and concessions as valid bargaining devices to find a common ground for genuine and lasting agreement, or for seeking a compromise of principles in order to conclude a basic agreement. For example, the Agreement on prisoners in 1955 was a short-term tactical link in the long-range design to surround Taiwan, while the refusal after 1960 to make any more such tactical or expedient agreements on newsmen or bilateral contacts undoubtedly reflected Peking's changed estimate of the limited value of short-term gains. As our experience has shown, the Chinese Communists have not negotiated or signed agreements, whether on prisoners, renunciation of force, the offshore islands, disarmament or Vietnam, which precluded Peking from ever reaching the top of the mountain, i.e., total victory, to paraphrase Lenin.

Dogmatically and fanatically, the Chinese Maoist negotiator appears to assume that the American negotiator is similarly motivated in viewing China as the adversary to be beaten, destroyed, and never appeased. Thus, in the typical Chinese Communist martial and adversary outlook, neither representative is seen as regarding the other as a negotiator on equal and acceptable terms. Nor is the other side a "party to negotiations" in a normal framework on a *bona fide* basis, as Westerners put it. Only hostile motives and irrevocable goals determine the strategy and techniques of both sides according to Peking's views.

In any such contest of categorical extremes and ideological ultimates, if the ground rules are not modified by both parties, concessions will never be made by either side. The United States negotiator will get nowhere with unilateral expressions of good will, sincere intentions, and conciliatory assurances. His honest efforts to achieve "a negotiated settlement" in good faith will seem fraudulent and deceitful to the Peking negotiator, who is preconditioned to consider American overtures and genuine compromises inconsistent with imperative struggle and inevitable defeat of the United States government. He takes for granted from incessant indoctrination that any concession or conciliatory gesture by Washington is nothing but sham and evidence of weakness. In such mortal combat, the United States could not conceivably and voluntarily yield any advantage except by force. An American concession in Peking's usual view would only be a "trick" or "conspiracy" on Washington's part to weaken and overturn Peking.

To make the normal cooperative negotiating process more rational and a concession more credible, the American negotiator often appeals to the law of nations, the standard principles of international negotiations or the general ethic and comity of interstate relations. None of them works in adversary negotiation with Peking. Unfortunately, no shared basis of international equity or relationship exists in negotiations with the Chinese Communists. Instead, the man from Peking applies the "immutable sanctity" of the "morality" of Marxist-Maoism, which justifies all expedients and concessions necessary to bring about the eventual destruction of the non-Communist system and the establishment of a world classless society at the final stage of communism. According to this fundamental premise, the negotiation or execution of any form of diplomatic agreement with the United States or other non-Communist governments is not a contract or obligation which needs to be fulfilled fully or faithfully under any "bourgeois" law of equity. A revolutionary ethic is Peking's only guide. That is non-negotiable. No amount of empirical argumentation, marshalling of data, and bargaining concessions has yet moderated the irreconcilable difference between Peking's style and ours.

Communist China typifies a new kind of state, organized and motivated by a revolutionary ethic thoroughly incompatible with the existing structure of international law and relations. It struggles to attain unbridled freedom of action for the implementation of doctrines which can no longer be exposed to objective scrutiny and evaluation. If it accepts restraint, it does so from political and tactical considerations alone and not from any sense of legal obligation under international law. International law does not even receive its lip-service.[3]

Two totally different versions of the facts and two utterly opposite standards of truth are opposed across the negotiating table. Mistrust and suspicion becloud any gesture of accommodation.

Consequently, the Chinese Communist negotiator easily and subtly applies a double standard of Marxist-Maoist morality. This is more than the technique of negotiating the same issue twice. Whatever promotes the interests of the People's Republic of China or the "international proletarian movement"—that is, the Communist Party—is correct and necessary. What promotes "imperialism" or capitalism is wrong. Thus, it was normal and logical for Peking to hold Americans in prison despite the Joint Agreement, while denouncing Washington for detaining Chinese in the United States despite American efforts to satisfy Peking's demands. It was right for Peking to reject American approaches on disarmament and the Test-Ban Teaty while proceeding to manufacture nuclear weapons. Yet it was entirely wrong for "United States imperialism" to have any atomic bombs at all. Peking blandly denounced the United States for violations of the Geneva Agreements of 1954 and 1962 regarding Vietnam, but concealed its own (from Washington's viewpoint) flagrant violations of both. It is wholly permissible for Peking to send ultimatums to Washington, as in 1956 on an arrangement in two months for a bilateral ministerial conference, or in 1958 for an answer in fifteen days to resume the Talks, but it is wholly unacceptable for Washington to reject them or to make similar demands.

The Chinese Communist style of adversary negotiations closely correlates the timing and other phases of the "struggle with the enemy." With the negotiation just one part, and usually a small part, of a grand strategy, expedient concessions and tactical trading cannot be hurried or fragmented in Peking's protracted time frame. As far as the problems of timing and bargaining are concerned:

> . . . Perhaps one of the clearest measures of the influence of underlying attitudes is the Chinese method of calculation of the relative values of immediate and distant-future advantages. The Chinese are less inclined to accept immediate advantages at the potential cost of future disadvantages and more inclined to make present sacrifices in the hope of future gains than are most countries. Furthermore, the Chinese apparently see this kind of calculus as applicable in situations where others do not.[4]

Moreover, all aspects of the negotiation are linked together in the light of the total world situation in which current and future internal and international developments, both in the Chinese People's Republic and in the United States, as well as elsewhere, are taken into consideration with comprehensive doctrinal analysis which sometimes seems unrealistic when these developments appear to have little association with the subjects under negotiation. In particular, developments within the Communist world can have a more important bearing on negotiations with the United States than a direct encounter over Taiwan or trade, for example. This aspect of totality in dealing with the Chinese Communists helps to explain the shift from a negotiating stance in Warsaw to the diplomacy of stalemate in 1959 when the Sino-Soviet split began to becloud Washington-Peking negotiations. The bitter break between Peking and Moscow may do more than that in the future.

The American negotiator is often at a disadvantage in negotiating with the Chinese Communists not only because of their divergent sense of time but also because of the totality of their approach on the nature and timing of concessions. The customary style of the United States government and the American negotiator is to negotiate on one subject at a time. It is easier for the pragmatic American mind to deal with an individual subject on its merits, separated from the endless complex of international relations. Where the Marxist-

Maoist is timeless and total, the American tends to be instant and particular. Unfortunately, however, in an ironic twist, negotiating with the Chinese Communists becomes increasingly complex because they assume that the "imperialists" likewise follow a total, long-term strategy and a correlation of effort within the "imperialist camp." The Chinese Communist, who adheres faithfully to his special process of analysis, cannot easily envisage the contingency that his opposite number might act quite differently. Nor can he accept the reality or appraise the implication of such contrary behavior. And equally unfortunate is the "deviant" readiness of the American to make concessions in bargaining, for this has not yet helped to modify the molded mind of the Chinese Communist negotiator.

Of course, American negotiators, in making concessions, must also make a correlation in a total context of diplomatic relations. Concerning critical issues such as Taiwan, disarmament, Vietnam, and bilateral contacts, Washington always has to consider potential reactions in Taipei and calculate possible effects on other Asian governments and its European allies. If some of their responses are likely to be too unfavorable, the Americans have to hold back. Nevertheless, the circumstantial evidence indicates that Washington is conducting its part in the Ambassadorial Talks primarily on a unilateral basis without drawing on any "general diplomatic strategy." Washington has looked upon its contact and negotiation with Peking as its own private dialogue and not as a diplomatic chorus for many parts in a world-wide strategy of a "common camp." Nor indeed is it part of any triangular relationship involving the Peking-Moscow rupture or some imagined Moscow-Washington "collusion."

On the other hand, Peking appears to have followed a completely correlated strategy. Peking, in the 1960s, has challenged Washington to leave the Asian continent, Moscow to forfeit Communist leadership, the "underdeveloped" world to follow the Maoist model and the Chinese people to adopt a strident anti-American fanaticism in preparation for some forthcoming cataclysm—domestic or foreign. The combined impact of these several challenges on the Ambassadorial Talks has been to reduce the opportunity of negotiating any concessions to virtually nothing.

It is not surprising, then, that the characteristic feature of adversary negotiations with the Chinese Communists has been their manipulation of the agenda to place their opposites in an unfavorable trading position and to fix the substance of negotiations by the way an item is phrased or listed on the agenda. This is more than a hard bargaining technique; it is designed to get two concessions from the American negotiators for the price of one agreement. The Chinese Communists used this technique in the Panmunjom meetings and again, as noted earlier, during the Ambassadorial Talks.

American negotiators should be particularly wary of agendas which can represent this potential danger. Arguments over a "prejudicial" versus a "neutral" agenda are usually misunderstood by the public. American negotiators are frequently criticized because they will not concede what seems to be a trivial or technical point of sequence or semantics in the agenda. But the whole outcome of the negotiation may be at stake and the entire issue won or lost in the initial process of battling over a "neutral" agenda. Chinese Communist negotiators are tough, adroit, and persistent in that stage. Ambassador Arthur Dean, a veteran of negotiations with Peking, has precisely made this point: "The battle for the agenda is fundamental to Communist negotiators, because they believe they can humilate the other side and win or lose a conference in this first battle. . . . Quite often, they are correct." [5] Only if the Americans stand firm and insist on an equitable compromise will the Chinese Communists come to an agreement. At this initial stage, they know they can bring public pressure to bear on the Americans, and, therefore, they will try to build the real issue which they wish to win into a "prejudicial" agenda. If their agenda is accepted, they can assume that their issue is no longer in dispute.

In 1955, they apparently wanted the agenda of the Ambassadorial Talks specifically to include discussions for arranging a Foreign Ministers' conference and ending the American embargo. If Washington had accepted some such agenda in the belief that these two items were merely topical headings, the Americans would have discovered that from the Chinese point of view Washington had already conceded the principle of the ministerial meeting and the lifting of the embargo. Only the details of definition and arrangements would have been left to discuss and negotiate. The issue of "withdrawal from Taiwan in principle" would have been a similar case. Perhaps the American reaction to the agenda has become somewhat "gunshy" because of several disagreeable experiences such as these. Nevertheless, it remains true that American negotiators should be on their guard concerning the agenda, the manipulation of the negotiating atmosphere, and the exploitation of the press.

Perhaps our experience in negotiating with the Chinese Communists and taking their own public and private definitions of negotiations at face value portray too sharp and critical a picture of their "adversary" style. Indeed, we might well focus on their own more moderate versions of dealing with us. For example, Chou En-lai in 1956 said that the negotiations should be advantageous for both sides and not for just one side, although, as we have seen, he never explained what he meant by "advantageous." [6] Then Peking's Bulletin of 1961 spoke of "a bridge between China and the United States" to which Peking did not object, provided others built the bridge, and apparently if the United States took the first step to cross it by withdrawing from Taiwan "so that we shall meet at the center of the bridge, and neither one will have an advantage over the other." [7] Accordingly, it can be suggested that an American strategy for adapting adversary negotiations with Peking can use this idea of the bridge for mutual advantage as a logical point of departure for formulating and conducting adversary negotiations within the restricted framework of limited coexistence by expedient diplomacy. American dealings with Peking support the basic theorem in this case that adversary negotiations as defined and described above consist of three different but related methods or processes: convergent bargaining, elusive communicating, and tacit maneuvering. The various phases and divergent proposals covered in the Ambassadorial Talks have involved each of these processes.

Convergent Bargaining

In at least two cases—the issues of prisoners and renunciation of force—Washington and Peking have practiced what might be called convergent bargaining, or what Professor Schelling calls "pure bargaining." In brief, each party was strongly interested in obtaining a mutual outcome from their negotiating process. Both parties introduced several offsetting items for bargaining and gave a relative or an absolute weight to each in making a concession in order to keep the process moving or in refusing to concede on a basic point. Peking and Washington in these two cases were each willing to make a commitment to the other and to keep it. This convergent bargaining found explicit common interests in holding the negotiation, co-ordinating the bargaining and the drafting, and ensuring an outcome by formal agreement. Moreover, both parties indulged in the usual negotiating practices of suggesting inducements and making warnings to open the bargaining process, continue the atmosphere necessary for compromise and concession, and to facilitate the outcome.

Indeed, the issue of the prisoners provides a good illustration of Peking's way of practicing convergent bargaining. Peking correctly calculated that it could use this bait to hook a reluctant Washington into the Talks, as Chou Ching-wen has reported.* It is certain that Dulles would not otherwise have agreed to participate. But Washington then frustrated Peking by insisting on an agreement and refusing to make unnecessary concessions in the absence of an agreement. Peking recognized that it had to drop its series of demands and accept the essence of the American draft—on the condition that terminology provided equal and reciprocal treatment for the Chinese People's Republic—if it wanted the Talks maintained at all. In their initial encounter in 1955, Peking built up tension in the Taiwan Straits to add pressures on Washington to continue the Talks at Geneva. Both Peking and Washington used the device of warning against stalling and threatening the possibility of breaking off the Talks in order to keep them going in August–September 1955.

Following the Agreement, Peking apparently assumed that it could use all of these negotiating devices to bargain for the subsequent outcomes of a ministerial meeting with John Foster Dulles, the negotiation of an end to the American trade embargo, and the arrangement of cultural contacts between the two countries. Here, the Chinese Communist overplay of warning and failure to implement the Agreement made Washington in 1955–56 less interested in such negotiated outcomes though wishing to negotiate an agreement on the renunciation of force if it were possible to converge the interests and policies of both governments on this general topic. Chou En-lai, deferring his other specific objectives, shrewdly bargained with Dulles over the latter's proposal for an agreed renunciation of force. Both governments were interested, for different reasons, in getting

* He reports hearing Chou En-lai say, "We have attacked America bluntly several times, and every time the attack was effective. Through the Korean War, we forced her to attend the Panmunjom Truce Conference; out of the battle of Dienbienphu, there came the Geneva Conference and peace for Indo-China; the internment of American civilians compelled her to agree to a conference at the Ambassadorial level." Cited, p. 287.

that outcome by a convergent negotiating process. The Chinese Communist negotiators skillfully referred to the United Nations Charter, peaceful negotiations and a subsequent ministerial conference which Dulles and the United States government could not completely sidestep, though they tried. In this case the negotiators from Washington and Peking transacted an almost complete but meaningless agreement on the renunciation of the use of force, owing to their deadlock over Taiwan.

Elusive Communicating

This diplomacy of elusion characterizes most of the bilateral dealings between Washington and Peking since their one agreement was concluded in 1955. Elusive communicating is less than convergent bargaining but more than tacit maneuvering. Each party maintains contact and communication with the other, but at least one of them avoids engaging in any commitment, does not desire a negotiated outcome, and will not bargain, make concessions or even agree to the desirability of an agreement. That party wants stalemate. This process of elusive communicating is a unilateral, uncoordinated operation on each side. Each party avoids and eludes the other's negotiating tactics of warnings, inducements and public pressures. Commitments and advantages are extended in this form of adversary negotiations by one party with the expectation of the probability that they will be ignored by the other. Each adheres strictly to its own proposal and process of negotiation. In short, the two tracks in this form of elusive communicating never meet or converge. They may be parallel or totally unconnected. The subject of bilateral contacts, the Taiwan crisis of 1958, and nuclear disarmament are illustrative cases of this typical form of negotiating between Peking and Washington.

In 1956, the Chinese Communist bargainers skillfully shifted the negotiating initiative to journalistic and cultural contacts, which naturally provoked favorable reaction from many Americans, particularly news managers. Washington froze initially, resorting to various stratagems and disclaimers elusively to sidestep Peking's initiative, on the ground that "principle" ought to be settled first. Chou En-lai then used the pressure of American public opinion to induce Dulles to negotiate a joint agreement on newsmen. Holding the bargaining initiative, Peking kept Washington under pressure by hinting that the few remaining American prisoners could be released in exchange for Washington's agreement on newsmen. Washington called it "blackmail," eluding Peking's proposals. Then Washington felt itself under enough pressure to have to validate passports for a selected pool of newsmen to go to China. But Dulles prohibited Chinese Communist newsmen from entering the United States. That explicit and public refusal of reciprocity, after Peking had proposed a short formal agreement to permit an equal and reciprocal exchange of newsmen, ended the possibility of any convergent bargaining for an agreed outcome on that issue. In this case the bargaining tactics of both parties contributed to the failure of the negotiation.

In the 1958 Taiwan crisis, Dulles' diplomacy of proposals, inducements, and hints did not generate any convergent negotiating. Not wanting an outcome of American-initiated concessions or innovations, Chou En-lai and Ambassador Wang evidently avoided all the American proposals for a cease-fire and demilitarization of the offshore islands, urged the military withdrawal of the United States, which the Americans avoided, and called off Peking's military action unilaterally outside the negotiating room. Since then the terms of trade have been too far apart to permit effective bargaining, despite the resourceful efforts on the part of the United States. No convergent negotiating has occurred on bilateral contacts or anything else. The Chinese negotiators have eluded or rebuffed every American effort to arrange or negotiate an understanding on nuclear matters, and have offered only the one specific transaction of a joint pledge on no-first-use of nuclear weapons. Washington also eluded all of Peking's proposals on disarmament, at first refusing to consider the joint pledge, but then countering by trading off its joining that pledge for Peking's adhering to the Test-Ban Treaty. Peking negotiators have so far refused to consider—let alone bargain —on these general terms.

Tacit Maneuvering

As in the diplomacy of elusion, in tacit maneuvering both adversaries wish to keep in contact but expect no negotiated outcome. However, they do implicitly correlate or coordinate their communications and tactics to produce implicit or explicit consequences. Bluff, indirection and ambiguity characterize tacit bargaining. Warnings and even threats also enter this process where the incentive is to influence the other party to take certain unilateral but related actions. This is more of a "stalking" than "talking" process. Any communication and exchange of views is obviously not complete but a certain common interest in a tacitly-arrived-at result does exist and is mutually recognized. It is risky because of its uncertainty. Each side is maneuvering to find the limits and probability of the other side's intentions and possible actions. It is an intricate process of trying to establish the sum of the individual and joint maneuvers and probable actions of both parties in the dispute. Keeping the channel open is the basic requirement for tacit maneuvering. It also needs a shared sense of the spectrum of desirable and undesirable reactions in terms of actual commitment to potential retaliation or potential adjustment. The latter contingency is the essential factor in tacit maneuvering because it can leave the way open to facilitate other phases of adversary negotiations.

As has been described in detail in this book, Washington and Peking both maneuvered in this sense during the Taiwan crisis when diplomacy and force were used together in different ways by both governments. In fact, Washington's explicit warnings of retaliation if Peking went beyond certain limits in the offshore islands or toward Taiwan perhaps induced the Chinese Communists to call off their military operation and avoid any convergent negotiation or elusive communicating tacitly to bring about a *de facto* cessation of hostilities and a diminution of the high tension.

Washington and Peking have been tacitly probing each other over the high stakes of crisis control and confrontation in Southeast Asia and Vietnam since 1961. Exchange of signals in the Ambassadorial Talks brought about their compromise over Laos in 1961 and 1962. More significantly, during 1965–67, Washington and Peking each unilaterally and tacitly maneuvered around the question of Vietnam without approaching any agreement whatsoever. Like wary antagonists they have been stalking each other to keep the other "at bay," which is not really "collusion" at all.

Contradictions in Process

However, this combination of elusive communicating and tacit maneuvering on mutual contacts, disarmament, Vietnam, and Taiwan suggests that misunderstanding may have increased as the scope of the Talks has widened. Peking vigorously circumvented or rebuffed all the conciliatory gestures of President Kennedy and President Johnson, although both spoke of China sometimes in unconciliatory, uncompromising language while, in fact, seeking an open door. When President Johnson tried to open contacts and improve relations ostensibly because of Vietnam, Peking demanded that the United States withdraw from Asia altogether. Washington sought nuclear disarmament; Peking followed the nuclear road. When Washington stressed conciliation, Peking accentuated the spirit of conflict. One can only conclude on the basis of circumstantial evidence that the negotiating process used in the Ambassadorial Talks was unable to reduce the divergence and bridge the gap with mutual advantages.

The question might then be asked whether or not Washington's negotiating tactics with Peking might not have had the reverse consequences from what American officials apparently expected. United States assurances of respect for Peking's security along its southern frontiers and its pledge not to invade North Vietnam and destroy its regime, presented at Warsaw and confirmed in public presumably to moderate Peking's uncompromising attitude and to facilitate moving the Vietnam crisis to the conference room, may have actually delayed or prevented any such negotiations. Perhaps American assurances emboldened Peking toward intransigence rather then moderation. The more the American Ambassador in Warsaw stressed the assurances, the more the Chinese Communists seemed to have denounced American policies in Vietnam and rejected peace talks. This is not to say that Washington's efforts at Warsaw to avoid miscalculation in the military sphere were inconsequential; they were not. Rather, it is to suggest that the assurances might have had the by-product of inducing Peking and Hanoi to reinforce their elusive communicating and rejection of any convergent bargaining rather than encouraging them to join a negotiation to transact a cease-fire agreement and a mutually advantageous settlement, although Communist policies really prevented that.

Likewise, Washington's simultaneous overtures in private and in public for contacts and conciliation may have solidified Peking's private repudiation of convergent bargaining and its public rigidity against negotiating with "U.S. imperialism." Evidently, American efforts toward an extension of bilateral contacts stage by stage engendered increasingly harsh and adamant refusals until finally Peking denounced them in the Warsaw Talks and for the public record. It would seem that on this topic there remained nothing more to say and no option left open by late 1966. Moreover, it might be suggested by some that the extension of overtures for contacts made simultaneously with the expansion of military operations in Vietnam might have indeed induced a reaction in Peking of exasperation, suspicion, and incredulity which, in turn, further rigidified postures and increased misunderstanding on both sides. To Peking, American actions in Vietnam contradicted Washington's overtures for improved relations and a more flexible policy toward China. In this context nuclear disarmament seemed unfeasible to Peking. In addition, Washington's support for Taiwan blocked Peking's primary goal and made the latter think that Taiwan was an obsession with Washington. Also, Washington's offers and overtures on nuclear control, Vietnam and contacts in the Ambassadorial Talks in 1966 coincided with an internal power struggle, the proletarian "cultural revolution," and the so-called Red Guard movement. From Peking's standpoint, 1966 was a bad time to shift the diplomacy of stalemate and elusion back to one of maneuver on these vital and complex issues.

Under these circumstances and in view of the long impasse over diplomatic nonrecognition and Taiwan, it might have been more realistic if Washington had underplayed or withheld its efforts on contacts, limited its tacit maneuvering in the Talks concerning Vietnam and sought convergent bargaining on disarmament instead. Perhaps an American effort to conduct an extensive private exploration of the various facets of arms control and international conferences —beyond what apparently actually took place in Warsaw—might have produced different consequences if at the same time blanket security assurances on Vietnam had not been emphasized and bilateral contacts not pressed, at least in public. Serious negotiations are seldom conducted through the press. Of course, it must be emphasized that American officials are always subject to the force of public opinion while Chinese Communist leaders evidently never have to face that limitation on their power. With growing criticism of its China policy and increasing private interest in bilateral contacts with mainland China, Washington may have felt itself under intensifying pressures at home and abroad to get some diplomatic movement going at Warsaw and take a more flexible position in public. While this may have seemed like imagistic, "posturing" diplomacy, a careful reading of Washington's public record does leave the convincing impression that President Johnson and his administration were indeed quite sincere in desiring to converge the bargaining to produce concrete results and specific agreements on bilateral contacts in order to allay tensions and for other purposes. Peking evidently doubted the sincerity and rejected the approach for reasons already outlined.

The American Response

Coping with Peking's ideological and revolutionary style of adversary negotiations is never easy or simple. However, a combination of techniques will help American negotiators avoid pitfalls and widen margins, thereby encouraging a Chinese propensity to negotiate when Peking inclines toward some outcome. The key to inducing such an inclination lies in the proper combination at any one time of the application of diplomacy and power. The relative degree and sequence of each makes the best "mix." Both are necessary. But too much or too little of one can make an inefficient mixture for bringing about negotiations and transacting an agreement.

The pressure of too much military power to challenge the Communists can backfire if it results in a loss of face, an attack on their pride or patriotism, or the appearance of capitulation and compromise under undue pressures. Accordingly, a power play will not necessarily engender the opening of negotiations or the making of concessions. Experience seems to show that a maximum dependence on power and diplomacy should not be used simultaneously. It is the sequence of varying degrees of each that seems to have the most telling effect in adversary negotiating with Peking. Moreover, if the mixture ignores the peculiar and somewhat ambiguous role of "principled policy" of the Communist approach to negotiating with the United States or the West—that is, questions of prestige, honor, reciprocal treatment, and some "moral" issue as Maoist-Marxism has defined morality—then even an efficient combination of diplomacy and power will not lead to the opening or conclusion of negotiations. But, assuming that the correct mixture is made on a case-by-case basis, the best technique is to suggest a range of options and limits in multiple choices. The fundamental tactic in responding to Peking's adversary negotiating is to complicate and diversify its decision-making process by both establishing the limits of Peking's use of its diplomacy and power and suggesting variable options of both advantages and disadvantages. The result is the dynamic bargaining process.

If and when Peking enters a true negotiating process, the initial stages will be difficult and intricate for American policy-makers, American negotiators, and particularly American public opinion. As our experience since Panmunjom has demonstrated, the Chinese Communists will use this initial period to harass and put the Americans off balance to the greatest extent possible. They will try to manufacture the image of an artificial deadlock to make the Americans seem the intransigent party, or assume the posture of readiness for settlement to make it seem easy for the Americans to get on with negotiations. The Chinese Communist negotiators have either been publicly strident and hostile, making a succession of serious charges and recriminations against the United States, or just the opposite, suddenly appearing moderate, friendly, and conciliatory about seeking mutual satisfaction. Whichever tack the Chinese Communists follow, the American response should not tend toward overcompensation or premature compromise. To overcome Peking's hostility, Americans may lean over backward to be more moderate, hopeful and conciliatory, often suggesting ways out of the initial deadlock even before negotiations have begun. It is at this stage that techniques for identifying and setting the terms of the negotiations are crucial. Just before the opening of a negotiation and during the discussion of the suggestions for transaction, the Americans must perfect the technique of standing firm on the agenda and keeping the diplomatic initiative. The Chinese Communists will try to use all sorts of possible pressures, unexpected maneuvers, and changes in pace or tone to frighten or wear down the American negotiators. This is the time for them to remain cool and steadfast, responding in a low key.

In moving from the opening skirmishes to the stage of transaction, the problems and techniques of substance replace those of form and image. A straightforward and uncomplicated style seems to serve best in any actual adversary process with the Chinese Communists. Abstract principles and vague generalities should be avoided in proposals or explanations. In particular, a conventional device often used in Western litigation or diplomacy of suggesting and concluding "an agreement in principle" first and deferring for later bargaining the disagreeable "details"—which usually form the crux of the negotiation—should not be used in negotiating with Peking. Rather, concrete propositions should be advanced, but only one at a time. Their explanation and presentation can be spelled out in closely related detail. But it is important that the terminology in both English and Chinese should be kept as precise and clear as possible. However, the Western style of negotiating by presenting or explaining the same point from various angles or by a series of examples or analogies in an effort to bring about understanding or agreement can also be confusing and inefficient when dealing with Chinese Communist negotiators. They look upon a variety of possible approaches and refinements as "tricks" rather than *bona fide* bargaining and conciliation in an effort to reach a compromise.

Making a concession or adjustment is the trickiest technique of all in adversary negotiating. If a move toward compromise is made too emphatically or too soon, the Chinese Communist negotiators will look upon it as a sign of weakness and defeat. They will be even less inclined to show any interest in any such American proposal, nor will they then advance a version of their own. How and when to move from what is bargainable to what is not negotiable, to the bedrock of minimum demand, is never easy. Americans tend to put too much material between what can be conceded away and what cannot be given up under any circumstances than do the Communists, who usually enter a negotiation with stiff terms and stick to them.

The essential technique for the Americans is to submit only clear, specific, and self-enforcing compromises which are reciprocal. They must have built into them their own precise *quid pro quo* containing the Chinese Communist concession in return. Whenever the American negotiator offers a concession, he should see to it that he will receive one of comparable value in exchange before the deal is closed. In this process, he needs to know that he can always stand indefinitely on his minimum terms, and that any commitments or warnings made by his government for the carrying-out of the agreement or concerning the consequences of the negotiation's failure will be certain. Only such a guarantee of his bargaining position will create the credibility of his proposals, concessions, and rock-bottom terms. But, if general principles should be avoided and specific propositions advanced, the American response should also seek comprehensive treatment of the issue. This means leaving nothing to chance and taking extra pains to visualize every conceivable aspect of the potential agreement, which should be transacted as precisely and completely as possible within a reasonable amount of time, even if the negotiations have to be prolonged despite Chinese Communist pressures for conclusion or termination and the even greater pressures from American sources for bringing delayed negotiations to an end.

It is at this point that meticulous care in the use of the two languages is crucial. Chinese and English often do not have exact equivalents. Sometimes the English word is understood and acceptable to both sides while neither can find and agree on the Chinese equivalent, or vice versa. In every case, the American negotiator needs to pay particular attention to the nuances of the Chinese language and search for the nearest Chinese equivalent to the English on which both sides can transact an agreement. Such meticulous care in interpretation and translation will not only facilitate more reliable communication and prevent unnecessary recrimination in the future, but will also reinforce the credibility of American intentions and proposals. Obviously, the transactional stage of adversary negotiating is an exacting, extensive process.

But if the negotiation does not seem to the Chinese Communists to be producing the result which they desire, their additional pressures or threats of imminent breakup will again test the American mettle. The Chinese Communist negotiators will begin to impugn American motives, charge bad faith, harp on one subject of attack and bring up more and more extraneous issues. They will threaten to end the discussions and accuse the Americans of total insincerity. During such breakoff maneuvers, as well as during the initial stages when invective and violent language and combative tactics characterize the Chinese Communist negotiating style, the American negotiating technique should be to remain silent and to wait.

CHAPTER SIXTEEN

A Look at the Future

A new long-range strategy on our part might someday begin to moderate the method and ideology of Chinese Communist negotiators. By never taking our eyes off our goal and remaining at the table, so to speak, we might confound Maoist infallibility. Cool objective persistence might wear down the cardinal thesis of struggle and contradictions, and blur the image of irrevocable "enmity." Our convergent negotiations might even encourage the Chinese to relate their notion of China's centrality to the reality of a rapidly emerging world community based on permanent coexistence rather than protracted struggle. For the long run, the American negotiator can come to personify a reasonable duality of cooperative competitiveness in contrast to the Maoist duality of antagonisms, so obsolete in the contemporary world of speed, change, and interdependence. Indeed, the American style could demonstrate that the theory of doom is doomed itself.

As long as the man across the table is a Maoist or neo-Maoist practicing some form of Chinese Communist adversary negotiations, an American negotiator must "sit tight and talk straight" knowing that for a long time there will be no result. His main consolation will be the satisfaction of at least communicating accurately for better understanding, and, at best, the faith that the future will bring changes. Meanwhile, in facing this arduous, complex, and long-suffering ordeal of "adversary" negotiations with the Chinese Communists, the best course for an American negotiator is not to spend his main time trying to figure out what is at the back of a Chinese negotiator's mind, but to focus his greatest efforts on making sure that his Chinese counterpart is left in no doubt as to what is in the American's mind for the present and for the future, too. His credibility and reliability, whatever else he may stand for in Peking, will significantly enhance the validity and viability of Sino-American contacts and negotiations for the future, however China may evolve. To ensure even greater credibility and reliability, the American people and the United States government should develop new attitudes, approaches, and policies in order to cope effectively in the years ahead with Chinese affairs that include mainland China, Taiwan, Hong Kong, and the overseas Chinese.

The essential new approach is to reduce the emotional intensity of the love-hate syndrome in Sino-American relations and to become more objective and realistic about Chinese matters. We should try to keep "cool" in our attitudes and reactions regarding Chinese affairs. We should understand China's agony of humiliation and hunger for a respected rightful place in the world, and be prepared to provide this whenever it chooses to forego its hostility and apply the provisions of the United Nations Charter. We can recognize China's legitimate security interests, while joining in resistance against Maoist or post-Maoist tendencies to dominate Asian developments. We will continue to appreciate China's magnificent culture and learning. We can sympathize with China's unusually complex problems of modernization and change. Above all, we need to be objective, scholarly, cool-headed, and unsentimental in our dealings.

Our second new approach should be to stress understanding before contact. Just as Manchu China was quite unprepared, lacking sufficient knowledge or understanding of the West, when nineteenth-century Europe and America made such an impact, Americans in the next decade of the twentieth century may have dangerously insufficient understanding of the evolving history and contemporary outlook of the Chinese on the mainland. If contacts are eventually renewed with a radically changed, nuclear-armed, and unified post-Mao China, we may likewise be quite unprepared as a nation. In the light of our mirror images and unfortunate past associations, it would seem wiser for us, at least, to get ourselves emotionally and intellectually ready to resume contacts before we undertake them. It would be as wise as it might be novel for American journalists, scientists, businessmen, and others to engage in extensive study of Chinese culture, history, and development before visiting China once again.

A new strategy of dealing with the China problem in terms of prior objectivity and knowledge could include six parts: (1) emphasizing but improving the adversary diplomacy of the Ambassadorial Talks in scope, frequency, staffing procedures and representation, including periodic ministerial meetings; (2) organizing China studies and *ad hoc* preparatory committees in various professions to establish a national state of perceptive readiness for instituting exchanges and contacts with the Chinese People's Republic at the auspicious time; (3) limiting American contacts initially to impersonal exchanges of things, rather than persons, by mail-order arrangements through the staffs of the Ambassadorial Talks or a new joint secretarial setup in Hong Kong or conceivably Shanghai; (4) encouraging international conferences and contacts in third countries with mainland China's association and American private or official participation whenever feasible; (5) keeping our short- and long-range policies and approaches toward China geared to our national interest in Sino-American relations, thus avoiding pressure from the Soviet Union or other countries to align our China policy with the Soviet interests in the triangular relationship or generally with other major factors in world developments; and (6) maintaining a balanced, well-rounded perspective on all related aspects of the single, over-all Chinese question including the mainland Chinese, the Taiwanese, Hong Kong and the overseas Chinese.

First, the United States should seek to strengthen and improve the sub-diplomatic system of the Ambassadorial Talks to provide a manageable and flexible format of modified adversary negotiations. Then wider and more formal relations, including meetings of the two foreign ministers, could develop as contacts and exchanges in specific lines between both countries begin to build up a solid practical base, while the emotional intensity and widespread prejudice and ignorance in Sino-American relations hopefully decrease.

The whole experience of United States dealings with Communist China suggests that we should not change the form and machinery of our relationship too soon or too much. The Ambassadorial Talks have done better for the United States in dealing with the Chinese People's Republic than established diplomatic intercourse has for most other countries. At least for a while, the system of "sub-diplomatic relations" provided by the Talks at Warsaw should remain the exclusive diplomatic contact on a regular schedule between the United States and the Chinese People's Republic. With this novel system of arms-length diplomacy in working order, it would be better on our part, at least, not to press for formal recognition and normal diplomatic relations until a suitable stage is eventually reached where the leaders and people in both countries have overcome their historical antagonisms and prepared themselves for the renewal of contact so that they can deal with each other less emotionally and more objectively.

With this available "bridge" for diplomatic exchange kept in good or improved working order, and given mutual acceptance of the three forms of feasible adversary negotiation, Washington could seek to transact a broad range of options with Peking where bilateral interests might eventually converge even within the neo-Maoist context of expedient dealings and limited co-existence. Americans could thus envision a wide series of major off-setting commitments, inducements, risks, and advantages by dealings with Peking over a long period of time. In this perspective of a real negotiating rather than imagistic or elusive diplomacy, five options of diplomatic encounter, among others, might become possible for exploration in the Ambassadorial Talks: a bilateral accord or an Asian-Pacific treaty to deal with nuclear protection, anti-ballistic weapons, and nuclear nonproliferation, in addition to redeployment of conventional forces and defensive alliances; a guaranteed and satisfactory settlement for Southeast Asia; the proper and acceptable evolution of the status of the offshore islands and the Taiwan Straits area; the evolution of triangular relations among Peking, Washington, and Moscow in terms of the bilateral interests of the Chinese People's Republic and the United States to safeguard and maintain the integrity, viability, and utility of their joint dealings; and the transaction of nonstrategic trade and assistance for China's development. Arrangements for bilateral contacts could be geared to the necessities and realities of these issues. They are theoretically—and perhaps idealistically—only illustrative of some of the principal factors which future wide-ranging discussions and negotiations could tackle, rather than elude, in a spirit of converging accommodation —if a new psychological atmosphere were ever to prevail over the current vicious circle in which the basic challenges of ideology and of national interests overshadow everything else. Each issue suggested for transaction is complex. They all clearly involve other nations—and the United Nations.

Yet the United States possesses substantial negotiating resources to break that vicious circle. Whether and how Peking would respond to such far-reaching, almost "all-round" diplomacy with

Washington, or whether it would even allow the Ambassadorial Talks to be engaged in sounding out such subjects on a bilateral basis before a unilateral settlement of the Taiwan issue on Peking's terms is made, remains to be explored. If Peking did consent, it still would remain debatable whether the machinery in Warsaw would be sufficient to handle such broad-gauged negotiations without even more substantial modifications than already suggested in this book. Perhaps different and better channels would then be needed.

Second, private and public American institutions and interested American citizens could now begin to organize preparatory studies and ad hoc *groups along professional lines in anticipation of eventual renewal of contacts with mainland China in order to build in advance a solid-base understanding of China's heritage and contemporary developments.* For this whole new strategy we need to formulate a few hypotheses on the timing, type and scope of such contacts to form the operational basis for a state of readiness on the part of American intellectual, business, and cultural leaders, and American opinion broadly speaking, to undertake renewal of contacts whenever Peking lifts the barriers.

As a world community emerges with the growing desire to bring mainland China into constructive association, Peking increasingly withdraws within itself. But this self-induced isolationism may not last, barring chaotic conditions. China's central location, increasing changes, and growing needs will probably generate tendencies in a post-Mao China to seek rational and effective modernization to become "better fed than red," so to speak. China's next sets of leaders, if united, probably will reject maximum self-isolation and self-containment and expand cultural, economic, and intellectual contacts in an unfolding association from the minimum to the general. Barring disunity in some new configuration of "warring states" over the next decade, this evolution will move slowly, not abruptly, through several stages. Post-Maoist China, initially at least, may keep the country closed to the West and Westerners. China's political evolution and vast internal needs will, nevertheless, encourage and require a gradual and controlled renewal of trade, contacts, and many exchanges with Asian and European countries and associations. Asian leaders will increasingly seek out and receive reciprocal contacts with China. However, Chinese Communist authorities will at first prohibit or limit direct personal contacts and exchanges with America and American organizations, whereas an exchange of things as distinct from persons will slowly expand. Meanwhile, Chinese representatives from the Chinese People's Republic will increasingly attend international conferences and private or official meetings of advantage and benefit to China. Chinese and Americans will be able to meet and talk informally in third countries at such meetings. In all events the restoration of a relationship between the United States and the Chinese People's Republic in the post-Mao period will be slow, difficult and minimal for a while.

This speculative look at the future of China's possible peaceful internationalization, if new Chinese leaders unitedly minimize ideological struggle, avoid civil wars, reject foreign intervention, and forego hermetic isolation, suggests that the United States might be last as well as least on the list of China's foreign associations, except in the unlikely event of a complete ideological reversal. Therefore, in view of the reciprocal love-hate syndrome, a deferment in this contact would be beneficial for the time being. It should help to build a strong bridge based on objective understanding. At least it would give Americans much-needed time, if they have the interest, to set their priorities systematically in order before agitating for contacts with the Chinese People's Republic. The first priority is for American leadership to learn about Chinese affairs and past Sino-American relations as quickly as possible in order to have some understanding of how to go about preparing the United States for dealing perceptively and effectively with post-Mao China. We need first to look at ourselves through Chinese eyes to see the American "scratches" on the Chinese mind and heart. The second priority would be to intensify and expand Chinese studies and preparatory groups in many American professional fields. The third priority would be to reach a national state of perceptive readiness to deal with Chinese from the mainland, whether indirectly at first in other countries or directly in a gradual resumption of exchange and contact. An emerging state of readiness could also enable us to react quickly but sensibly, should a radical shift in attitude suddenly occur in China favoring relations with Americans and the United States government, unlikely as that possibility may have seemed in 1966–67.

The preparatory programs for developing and maintaining the impetus toward any such state of readiness would have to be diverse, broad-based, and national in scope. A well-integrated preparatory program could include many segments, for example, the systematic translation of Chinese writings of historical and contemporary fiction and non-fiction to give us some *authentically Chinese* interpretation of their traditional values and social patterns, ignorance of which has severely handicapped our dealings with them (and with all Asians as well); the organized dissemination of balanced material on all aspects of the Chinese question primarily by educational media; the improvement in our journalistic skills for reporting on and interpreting Chinese affairs accurately to the American public; the holding of more public and private seminars and conferences throughout the United States of experienced persons who have dealt with the Chinese or studied Chinese affairs professionally; the publication of short authoritative policy pamphlets to identify, analyze, and judge the issues, opportunities, and prospects regarding specific developments affecting Sino-American relations; and strengthening the abilities of American, Asian and European educational institutions to expand teaching, research, and publication of studies and to produce more scholars on China.

For implementation, informal, *ad hoc* preparatory groups of experts from the American universities, businesses, foundations, voluntary organizations, the government, and private life should be formed in a number of disciplines or professions such as archaeology, the arts and architecture, aviation, communications media and computer analysis, comparative linguistic studies, cultural anthropology, economic and technological modernization, education, journalism, jurisprudence and the law, medicine and public health, political and social development, and science in general. The purpose of each group would be to study the "state of the art" in China and identify or fill in gaps in our knowledge with a view to preparing and maintaining an inventory of interested American volunteers, perceptive and competent to handle the resumption of commodity exchanges, personal contacts, and reciprocal visits or residence on a professional basis in each of the above fields. In preparation, priority should be given to the production and dissemination of translated and other materials on Chinese affairs, and to a comparative structural and functional analysis of Chinese and English, two such very different languages, so that Americans and Chinese could learn to communicate with each other on a sound basis of systematic linguistic equivalence and so that both languages could be more easily taught and learned on a large-scale basis in each other's country. A second priority would be to identify those particular American biases, prejudices, and assumptions in our value systems which differ so much from the Chinese and which complicate Sino-American contacts and dealings.

Third, the United States initially should undertake only imper-sonal exchanges with Communist China on a case-by-case basis be-fore seeking widespread personal or generalized contacts within each country. It might be preferable for the United States, instead of stressing extensive exchange of people as Washington did in 1965-66, to seek to arrange for trade and technical exchanges in specific nonstrategic items as the first step in renewing contact with Communist China. This would postpone having Americans in China and Chinese from the mainland in the United States. At the start an exchange of books and goods rather than persons could be arranged at the Warsaw Talks. Each Embassy there could then maintain the staff necessary to process the requests for books, periodicals, and other published material, which would continue to be handled by regular, normal mail facilities. Other tangible exchanges might be handled by a new office or joint secretariat in Hong Kong, or con-ceivably in Shanghai, operating out of the United States Consulate General in Hong Kong in conjunction with the Embassy in Warsaw —or wherever the Ambassadorial Talks are maintained. Technical materials, samples of machinery, blueprints and designs, packages of seeds * and other stocks could be processed for transfer and trans-shipment in Hong Kong or Shanghai. Trade in nonstrategic items, when the embargoed list is amended, would be handled by normal trade channels. Direct contacts between American and Chinese Communist representatives would obviously be preferable to third-party agents for all the servicing and financing of the arrangements and the handling of the goods. Thus, reciprocal visits and residence in each country would be limited to a few designated professional representatives of news agencies, business firms, etc., on a restricted basis of specific need. Widespread and general travel of Americans to the mainland and Chinese to the United States would thereby be minimal for a few years.

Fourth, the United States should encourage the maximum prac-tical extent of international and third-party contacts with China to provide China's leadership with multiple options in their policies and

---

* During the Ambassadorial meeting at Warsaw on September 7, 1966, the United States government proposed an exchange of seeds, according to a report in *The New York Times* of December 2, 1966.

foreign relations. Of course, barring unavoidable or miscalculated hostilities, internal strife, or China's total reversion to a self-imposed isolation, our limited contacts with Peking will hopefully amount to one of a growing number of third-party approaches to China—at least non-Soviet and non-Communist—in which the United States might be able to participate. At best, our link with Peking for several years to come will perform a minor role in an international diplomatic process of gradually inducing Peking to participate in a multitude of other bilateral, multilateral, and United Nations activities which we might seek to join. These third-party contacts might serve us better than our own efforts for bilateral contacts, even if the latter were to develop sometime during the next twenty years. In fact, if independent Asian governments worked out common approaches to China, and regional security systems and development plans that included China, as Professor Lucian Pye has suggested,[1] they could substantially help reintegrate China into a modern and workable international system and reshape Peking's ideology. Its dogma, paranoia and other delusions will alter only from within China by Chinese action sometime after, perhaps long after, the "catalytic cracking process" of de-isolation and renewed worldwide associations have convinced Peking leaders that they cannot recast international relations to suit China's image. The Chinese are pragmatic. Even the Communists among them can be expected to shift with the inevitable change of irresistible circumstances. An American policy of seeking contact and negotiation with Peking—despite rebuffs—will encourage and facilitate the entire world-wide effort toward the moderation of China's world views, the stabilization of its global relations, and its articulation into the international community.

Many Asian and European governments as well as the Canadian government, and nonofficial organizations, which have been exchanging contacts and trade with the Chinese People's Republic, already possess the facilities or have the opportunities to organize conferences or contacts including persons and representatives from mainland China. The American strategy might be quite openly able to take advantage of such lines of development whenever appropriate. American specialists, participating in such third-party affairs, could seek out their Chinese counterparts on a personal and informal basis for conversation and any subsequent feasible exchange.

Fifth, the United States government and the American people

should, as much as possible, keep Sino-American affairs disentangled
and unengaged from the Washington-Moscow and Peking-Moscow
sides of the triangular relationship. Moscow has naturally become
concerned about what it has come to characterize as "Maotse-
tungism" with its "anti-Sovietism" and "anti-Marxism-Leninism."
Accordingly, in its own interests Moscow will conceivably try to
discourage contacts and negotiations between Washington and
Peking and seek to prejudice Americans against the regime of Mao
Tse-tung as it evolved in the mid-1960s, as though we needed any
such prompting. Barring major military provocations against Soviet
territory or the "externalization" of revolution inside China, American reactions should not automatically take a stand favoring either
Moscow or Peking in their bitter conflict, thus compromising direct
Washington-Peking dealings. Indeed, who knows when leaders in
Peking and Moscow might renew contact and reach an understanding on a joint struggle against "imperialists"? The Sino-American association should proceed, as far as we are concerned, according to
our own calculation of how Sino-American relations should be
developed to serve our national interests. If Moscow prefers not to
have the United States "de-isolate" China and not to have the Peking government talk with Washington just when the Soviet government and many Communist parties are seeking to isolate Peking,
or at least Mao Tse-tung and "his entourage," Washington should
adhere to its policy of contact and conciliation with modified containment. We should not be deflected from seeking a convergence
rather than collision with mainland China. In view of long-standing
Chinese feelings about the Russians, in addition to Sinocentric attitudes toward Westerners and Western humiliations of China, the
United States must be particularly alert and sensitive about its part
in the triangular relationship.

Sixth, with a deepened perception and a long time-frame, we
Americans need to develop and keep a balanced perspective on all
aspects of the Chinese question which, in essence, is how to deal
with the Chinese people living in mainland China, on Taiwan, Hong
Kong, and in Southeast Asia. Phrased in the broadest terms, we need
first to meet the crucial challenge of successfully bringing about
the articulation of the whole Chinese people with a peaceful, orderly
world structure. In that most perplexing task, Sino-American negotiations could be helpful if both governments someday actively
conduct them convergently. Meanwhile, Mao's "cultural revolu-

tion"—one of the most significant developments of our time—has plundered his regime's store of prestige around the world; the loss may not matter to some current Chinese leaders, but it may matter much more to China's future leaders and younger people if it robs them of the time, knowledge and experience for catching up with the rapid transformation of modern society. We may see the Chinese people falling farther and farther behind the rapid advances in agriculture, education, communications, industry, and much non-nuclear technology. An increasing conceptual and technological lag would surely generate massive pressures and critical dangers. If and when a pragmatic Chinese leadership emerges, peaceful re-entry into the world community to uphold China's legitimate interests and to find resources for China's desperate needs will confront the Chinese and the rest of us with a rude awakening and a hard adjustment. For this, knowledge of the current "state of the art" in the technologies and professions would be particularly necessary to indicate what technological and conceptual gaps and other changes may be developing between China and the rapidly advancing nations of the world. Then we could better measure the dimensions of Chinese requirements at the time when the hoped for, if prickly, process of China's articulation with the world occurred. It might even be possible for some discussion and data on these technological and scientific fields to be exchanged confidentially in future meetings of the Ambassadorial Talks.

A balanced perspective would also enable us to deal with that other complex problem which has constantly bedeviled Washington–Peking negotiations: the ultimate relationship between the people on Taiwan and the mainland. Whether the relation is separate sovereignties, some provisional formula of dual representation in the United Nations, a federated autonomy, or some other arrangement, it must be left to future Chinese leaders to work out peacefully together. This, in turn, would strengthen an American policy of encouraging the local assimilation of Chinese in Southeast Asia. Clearly, cool restraint and long perspective on the part of Americans will be indispensable for dealing with these and other aspects of the whole Chinese question because the Chinese will probably be hypersensitive and resistant, the Russians suspicious and antagonistic, and Asians fearful and divided. In a world of violence, misery and conflict, American contacts and negotiations with new men in Peking could become a major factor in successfully bringing the

Chinese into a stable community of Asian states all adhering to the United Nations Charter.

In sum, such a six-point program would help to stabilize United States dealings with Peking and bring about real coexistence and substantive negotiations in the future. For that objective, it is essential for world peace, Asian stability, and international associations that Sino-American relations find a viable, even if limited, foundation of rationality and convergence. Americans need a vision of a world goal, a strategy for its attainment, and disciplined minds to persevere. Above all else, we will have to alter our traditional behavior and customary expectations. It will take a stern and steely temper for Americans to abide with the Chinese question for a long time, to discard the all-or-nothing approach with its absolute requirement of total victory or complete defeat, and await the far-off prospects of intricate, often confusing, moves of bargaining, communicating, and maneuvering between the adversaries from Peking and Washington.

To look at the reverse contingency: if Peking, despite our efforts and persuasion, nevertheless indefinitely suspends or breaks off the Ambassadorial Talks, closing the door to any further contact with the United States, we have no alternative but to defer to the time when some renewal of communications with China becomes feasible again. We cannot prevent any such termination of contacts if Peking remains adamant, nor should we show undue concern or make unwise concessions to seek immediate resumption of the Talks. In this contingency, we must prepare ourselves not for a long sit-in, but for an indefinite wait.

A final question for the future remains to be answered: Is all this effort and preparation worth it? Is there any point even in maintaining or trying to expand the contact with such an adversary if results are so meager, tactics so combative, procedures so arduous, and styles of approach and outlook so divergent? Despite the long-suffered frustrations and dismal record for both sides, several fundamental considerations suggest an affirmative answer. For one thing, the credibility, regularity and viability, which have been cumulatively experienced in the Ambassadorial Talks despite setbacks and impasses, have created a diplomatic momentum and a negotiating precedent which should be carefully preserved, for they would be difficult or even impossible to recreate if contacts were broken. Moreover, the need for an avenue of peaceful coexistence, the evolution of political change in China, the important impact of China in the world, and the uniqueness of the Sino-American association strengthen the desirability of keeping open, and enlarging "the little window of diplomacy."

Coexistence is the first necessity and prime consideration. Responsible diplomacy must keep the channel clear to cross the gap between adversaries, particularly nuclear ones, whose interests clash in such dangerous proximity. However meager their past worth and no matter how bleak their future prospects, the Ambassadorial Talks and general conferences with the People's Republic of China should continue to contribute something to the maintenance of an honorable if fragile peace. In the volatile situation in Southeast Asia, a precarious stalemate is at least better than a total breakdown in communications. The credible notification of intentions and the subtle exchange of nuances based on objective and perceptive understanding can do away with miscalculation and pave a firm footing for new initiatives on constructive issues.

Moreover, China itself will change. That is the second basic consideration. Only through an open window can one hope to reach an opening mind some day. The Marxist-Maoist division of the world into rigid alternatives and the revolutionary conduct of adversary negotiations for total capitulation rather than measured accommodation will not stay fixed and unalterable forever. Many new pressures and changing situations will soon come to bear on China. New leaders and younger generations may act differently than Mao's group does. Of course, in post-Mao China some Sinocentric and even Maoist residues, along with nationalism, will continue to champion legitimate national interests, while responding—in Chinese fashion, to be sure—to new tendencies in the world. A long-range policy of flexible diplomacy toward China will be able to take advantage of the new and unexpected. The machinery should be kept there for listening, probing, and proposing when the time comes.

Whatever we do, we cannot escape the vital factor of China's significant impact on global affairs. The dynamic Chinese people, soon to reach a population of one billion, heir to a magnificent culture, occupying the massive core of Eurasia, pressing upon the frontiers of Soviet Russia, Southern Asia, and the Western Pacific, and possessing industrial and nuclear potential, will profoundly affect the world's future. As an American newspaper remarked after Peking's third nuclear explosion: "No nation can be allowed to roam the world as a lone wolf with hatred in its heart and hydrogen bombs at its command." [2] This is especially true for an alien China in an interdependent world. Until China's international relations are "de-Sinicized," and developed within the framework of some sort of world order, the United States will have to continue to provide the primary strategic restraint on China's ambition for external power and hegemony. In this politico-military context, as the exchange on Vietnam at Warsaw demonstrates, it is essential to maintain a line of communication from Washington to Peking under any conditions, no matter how unconvincing the exchange or infrequent the contact. As Professor Fairbank has emphasized: "Contact and negotiations, far from being an either-or alternative to fighting, are essential to balance our continued military presence and keep it within a larger political framework." [3] This might be simply called the "close-door-open door" policy. While we try to contact Peking, we also have to contain it until we can converge diplomatically on some mutually satisfactory basis, jointly acknowledging China's rightful role in the world and the world's place for China. But we face a long, uncomfortable and unpromising prospect for some time to come before China's articulation with the world is reached.

With a compulsion for rage, fury, and revolutionary drama, the tendency of some Chinese Communists to distort world realities could develop into serious danger for world peace if wrongly handled, because the "hazards of semantic confusion and emotional self-deception" are great in dealing with the Chinese Communists and even greater than they have been with the Soviets.[4] Peking's leaders today, and those to come, can cause fatal harm if they press the wrong option to the extreme. Incredible as it may seem, some of them may still dream of transforming the world into a Maoist version of China's old image of the "Great Peace." Some Maoists may even be fantastically conceiving of a nuclear Pearl Harbor somewhere. At least some may persist in taking on both the Soviet Union and the United States, or pitting one against the other in a global Armageddon or a Chinese civil cataclysm. In any case, the Maoists and their successors can continue succoring revolutionary insurgents and proxy parties in Asia and other breeding grounds of unrest. At least, if unopposed, they may try to stamp out the emergence of a modern "revisionist," "bourgeois" society in China which would otherwise, and perhaps anyway, overtake and reshape Maoist Marxism. Or, in final desperation, some Chinese leaders might even try to force the long-suffering Chinese people to imprison themselves again in a neo-Maoist "Great Within," as Manchu China virtually isolated itself from contact with outside "barbarians," although, again, such arcane, anachronistic domestic containment would, in our interrelated world, build up huge, irresistible internal pressures for food, education, technology and modernization. These various options for Peking are only possibilities, yet the savage consequences of any one of them could be overwhelming if allowed to have full play without any external influence from regular contact and new approaches toward moderation and change. Conversion by association is the most hopeful long-run policy to deflate compulsions and self-deceptions in Peking after Mao Tse-tung.

We must make every possible effort to remain in touch with the Chinese and, if possible, bring about some minimal convergence of outlook. Only if they moderate their Sinocentric revolutionary Maoist view of the world—and such a vital change can come only from the Chinese, not us—can we cope with China and reach a stage for practical negotiations. Only if we lower our tempers, correct our images, and fix our sights by modifying our own outlook in the direction of convergence beyond containment can we ever help them close the gap. That will be difficult at best and perhaps unlikely for a long time. Hence, the little window of diplomacy, no matter how narrowly opened, must continue to provide the world with one alternative to the "lone wolf" with hydrogen bombs. It could be an alternative with substantial perspective and considerable consequence for global coexistence and world politics.

Indeed, a final consideration concerning the question of continuing the contact with Peking lies not only in its important expediency and validity but also in its very uniqueness. Of course, Peking could sever the contact any day and stop the Ambassadorial Talks. But, notwithstanding all the scars, there seems to be an unremovable adhesiveness in the relationship of America and China. It is *sui generis*, something exceptional and unique in contemporary diplomacy. A century of contacts has bequeathed a legacy of deep emotions to both sides, and they are now hard put to undo their mutual obsessions and unravel their inimical connections. Chinese hostility, resentment and anti-Americanism may reflect the historical hangover of humiliation. Yet, in order to manufacture a convenient "foreign devil" indispensable to the monolithic state of Marx-Lenin-Mao, Peking deliberately distorts and ignores the decent aspects of

America's long involvement with China. Likewise, American anger and hostility toward China have reflected real American emotional reactions since Korea, unresponsive to deep feelings and concerns on the mainland.

Now, however, even if leaders in Peking continue to challenge America all over the world with a litany of hate out of tune with world evolution as we see it, the time has come for us to deal with them henceforth to reduce this emotional intensity and increase objective understanding. We can challenge new Chinese generations with our very different articles of faith and with our own revolutionary perspective for the future. The posture, substance, and machinery of our contacts and negotiations with the People's Republic of China can serve not only to lower specific flashpoints, but also to relieve the traumas within the obsession of the hate-love syndrome.

American forbearance, patience, and perspective will be necessary as Sino-American relations mark time; they may someday be the measure of the maturing of the peculiarly ingrained association of the two countries. Initial prudence and subtle reserve in the method and tempo of our diplomatic contacts with revolutionary China might gradually lead a Sinocentric Peking and world-oriented Washington, not to any easy or rapid solution of their many political divergencies—for that is a naïve expectation—but to a reliable, rational, long-term regulation of their diplomatic intercourse which is essential for the future evolution of negotiations and accommodation in one world.

Appendices

APPENDIX A

Biographical Sketches of Principal Negotiators in the Ambassadorial Talks *

Chou En-lai (1898–   )

The leading Chinese Communist diplomat for many years, Chou En-lai was minister of foreign affairs of the Central People's Government at Peking from 1949 to 1958 and has remained Peking's chief foreign affairs expert.

Unlike many other leaders of the Chinese Communist party, Chou En-lai's origins were urban; his family background was scholar-official rather than peasant. A Communist party member since the early 1920s and a major figure in the party leadership for almost as long, Chou has for many years been noted in China for his competence, versatility, and unusual durability. He was prominent as negotiator with the Chinese Nationalists and with American representatives, notably General George C. Marshall, in the 1944–46 period when the United States attempted to mediate in the Chinese civil war. Since 1949, Chou has served as premier of the government and head of the massive civil bureaucracy that administers Communist China. Chou En-lai has had far more experience outside China than any other senior Communist leader at Peking. He made his debut in international conference diplomacy at the Geneva Conference in 1954 and scored a notable personal triumph when he appeared as an apostle of reason and goodwill at the First Asian-African Conference at Bandung, Indonesia, in the spring of 1955. Since that time, Chou En-lai has logged more air miles than any other single Asian diplomat; visited many capitals on all continents except Western Europe, Latin America, and North America; spent more time in Africa than any other ranking

* The author is indebted to Mr. Howard Boorman and Mr. Donald Klein for this information.

world statesman; and survived his diplomatic duel with his redoubtable American adversary John Foster Dulles. Forty years after he was first elected to the Political Bureau of the Chinese Communist party, Chou retains his senior ranking in the top command around Mao Tse-tung in 1967. Energetic, shrewd, and urbane, Chou En-lai is essentially the consummate political man, a disciplined individual who has spent his entire adult life working to extend Communist authority within China and to increase Chinese Communist influence in the world arena. The American journalist Edgar Snow has recorded a clear pen portrait of Chou, together with a detailed record of his 1960 views on Sino-American relations, in *The Other Side of the River: Red China Today* (1962).

Chen Yi (1901–   )

A member of the Political Bureau of the Chinese Communist party since 1956, Chen Yi followed Chou En-lai as foreign minister at Peking in February 1958.

One of the group of student patriots who went to France after the First World War, Chen joined the Communist party after his return to China and soon forsook student life for political action in the mid-1920s. Although he had no formal military training, he gained practical experience in the Chinese hinterland and rose to become one of the top Communist generals in China during the 1930s and 1940s. He made his mark directing Communist units behind the Japanese lines in east China and confirmed his abilities during the civil war against the Nationalists after 1946. Chen exercised general command of the Communist armies committed in the massive battle of Hsuchow in the winter of 1948, which led to a crushing defeat for Chiang Kai-shek's forces and opened the way for the Communist drive on Nanking and the rich lower Yangtze valley. Assigned as mayor of the turbulent metropolis of Shanghai during the early years after the Communist victory in China, Chen Yi moved to Peking in 1954 and succeeded to the post of foreign minister four years later. Although he had had no diplomatic or negotiating experience, Chen Yi became increasingly prominent during the 1960s as an articulator of Peking's views on current foreign policy issues, mixing joviality, vituperation, and moderation of statement in a manner well designed to confound the calculations of Western diplomats unattuned to Chinese Communist political styles. Chen Yi's career in the Chinese Communist movement was constructed on the foundation of his record as an imaginative and vigorous combat commander, and he has remained one of the small group of experienced military officers with direct political influence at the top level of the Chinese Communist party. Chen Yi is known to possess a quick and incisive intelligence, as well as a notable ability at composing poetry in the classical Chinese manner.

Wang Ping-nan (1907–   )

A veteran Communist and associate of Chou En-lai, Wang Ping-nan represented the Chinese Communists from 1955 until 1964 in the Ambassadorial Talks conducted with United States representatives at both Geneva and Warsaw.

After receiving his early education in China and Japan, Wang spent several years during the early 1930s in Berlin, where he studied, observed European life, and encountered political radicalism. After his return to China, Wang Ping-nan became known to Western diplomats and journalists during the 1940s, when he was assigned as an assistant to Chou En-lai in the Chinese Communist liaison mission at Chungking, and later at Nanking. Following the Communist victory and the establishment of the Central People's Government in 1949, Wang served for several years as director of the general office, or executive officer, of the ministry of foreign affairs. In 1954 he accompanied Chou En-lai to the Geneva Conference, where Wang was secretary general of the Chinese Communist delegation. The following year, he was named Chinese Ambassador to Poland, and he began to serve concurrently as his government's spokesman in ambassadorial-level talks with United States government representatives. Through nine years of arduous, though inconclusive, exchanges, Wang Ping-nan established a solid record as an astute and disciplined professional diplomat. He was recalled to Peking in 1964 and assigned as a vice minister of foreign affairs. Wang's German former wife, Anna von Kleist, has recorded some aspects of her life in China in a volume published in Germany under the title *Ich kämpfte für Mao* (*I Struggle for Mao*).

Wang Kuo-chuan (dates unknown)

Wang Kuo-ch'uan served as Communist China's representative in the Ambassadorial Talks with the United States at Warsaw after the departure of Wang Ping-nan in the spring of 1964.

While his predecessor had spent several years in Europe and had had negotiating experience extending back to the 1930s, Wang Kuo-chuan had no formal apprenticeship in the diplomatic profession. A virtually unknown figure when the Chinese Communists gained national authority in China, he held only provincial-level positions for several years after 1950: secretary of the Communist party committee, and later governor of Jehol province at the fringe of Inner Mongolia. In June 1957, Wang soared to his first diplomatic post: Chinese ambassador to the German Democratic Republic. After seven years in East Berlin, Wang Kuo-chuan was re-assigned to Poland in 1964 as Wang Ping-nan's successor.

U. Alexis Johnson (1908–)

Highest-ranking career officer in the Department of State since his appointment as Deputy Under Secretary of State for Political Affairs in 1961, U. Alexis Johnson has been a Foreign Service Officer since 1935, after waiting out the Depression years following postgraduate study at Georgetown University.

Assigned to Tokyo as Ambassador in 1966, Mr. Johnson has had long and intimate acquaintance with the Far East. His first post was in Tokyo as a language officer, and he subsequently served in different capacities in the area—as vice consul in Seoul, Tientsin, and Mukden and as consul and then consul general in Yokohama until 1950. He was Director of the Office of Northeastern Asian Affairs in the Department in 1951, and Deputy Assistant Secretary of State for Far Eastern Affairs until 1953. He was Ambassador to Thailand from 1958 to 1961, and he served as General Maxwell Taylor's deputy in Saigon in 1964–65.

During the period of his ambassadorship to Czechoslovakia in 1955–58, Mr. Johnson used his extraordinary negotiating skills in the arduous, though unproductive, ambassadorial-level talks with Wang Ping-nan, the representative of the Communist Chinese government, whom he had met the year before in an informal capacity in Geneva.

Jacob D. Beam (1908–)

A Princetonian by birth and education, Jacob D. Beam has served in Geneva, Berlin, London, and Djakarta, and as chief of the Central European Division in the Department of State. He was acting head of the United States Mission in Moscow during 1952–53 and was later named minister-counsellor.

He was Ambassador to Poland during 1957–61, during which time he served as the United States representative at the Ambassadorial Talks with the Communist Chinese, succeeding U. Alexis Johnson. In 1962 he became Assistant Director of the International Relations Bureau of the United States Arms Control and Disarmament Agency, and in May 1966 was appointed Ambassador to Czechoslovakia.

John Moors Cabot (1901–)

A Foreign Service Officer since 1926, Ambassador Cabot has had widely varied experience but has concentrated mainly on Latin America and the Communist-bloc countries.

While chargé d'affaires in Belgrade during 1946–47, he foresaw the possibility of a split with Moscow and pointed to the opportunities to be seen as a result of such a break. He was in Shanghai as consul general during the time of the Communist take-over in 1948–49. Following Ambassador Beam's transfer to a post in the U.S. Arms Control and Disarmament Agency in Washington, in 1962, he was appointed Ambassador to Poland and served in that capacity until 1965 and continued the talks with the Chinese Communist representative.

John A. Gronouski (1919–   )

Ambassador Gronouski began his career in the academic world, serving on the faculties of the University of Maine and Wayne State University, simultaneously pursuing a professional career with various tax organizations. Subsequently, he was appointed Commissioner of Taxation of the State of Wisconsin, a post he held until 1963 when he was appointed Postmaster General of the United States. In 1965 he was named Ambassador to Poland, and also serves as the United States representative at the ambassadorial-level Sino-American talks.

APPENDIX B

September 10, 1955
Agreement on Exchange of Civilians

The Ambassadors of the United States of America and the People's Republic of China have agreed to announce measures which their respective governments have adopted concerning the return of civilians to their respective countries.

With respect to Chinese in the United States, Ambassador U. Alexis Johnson, on behalf of the United States, has informed Ambassador Wang Ping-nan that:

1. The United States recognizes that Chinese in the United States who desire to return to the People's Republic of China are entitled to do so and declares that it has adopted and will further adopt appropriate measures so that they can expeditiously exercise their right to return.

2. The Government of the Republic of India will be invited to assist in the return to the People's Republic of China of those who desire to do so as follows:

A. If any Chinese in the United States believes that contrary to the declared policy of the United States he is encountering obstruction in departure, he may so inform the Embassy of the Republic of India in the United States and request it to make representations on his behalf to the United States Government. If desired by the People's Republic of China, the Government of the Republic of India may also investigate the facts in any such case.

B. If any Chinese in the United States who desires to return to the People's Republic of China has difficulty in paying his return expenses, the Government of the Republic of India may render him financial assistance needed to permit his return.

3. The United States Government will give wide publicity to the foregoing arrangements and the Embassy of the Republic of India in the United States may also do so.

With respect to Americans in the People's Republic of China, Ambassador Wang Ping-nan, on behalf of the People's Republic of China, has informed Ambassador U. Alexis Johnson that:

1. The People's Republic of China recognizes that Americans in the

412

People's Republic of China who desire to return to the United States are entitled to do so, and declares that it has adopted and will further adopt appropriate measures so that they can expeditiously exercise their right to return.

2. The Government of the United Kingdom will be invited to assist in the return to the United States of those Americans who desire to do so as follows:

A. If any American in the People's Republic of China believes that contrary to the declared policy of the People's Republic of China he is encountering obstruction in departure, he may so inform the Office of the Chargé d'Affaires of the United Kingdom in the People's Republic of China and request it to make representations on his behalf to the Government of the People's Republic of China. If desired by the United States, the Government of the United Kingdom may also investigate the facts in any such case.

B. If any American in the People's Republic of China who desires to return to the United States has difficulty in paying his return expenses, the Government of the United Kingdom may render him financial assistance needed to permit his return.

3. The Government of the People's Republic of China will give wide publicity to the foregoing arrangements and the Office of the Chargé d'Affaires of the United Kingdom in the People's Republic of China may also do so.

APPENDIX C

Renunciation of Force

1. *United States Statement and Proposal on Renunciation of Force, October 8, 1955*

One of the practical matters for discussion between us is that each of us should renounce the use of force to achieve our policies when they conflict. The United States and the PRC [People's Republic of China] confront each other with policies which are in certain respects incompatible. This fact need not, however, mean armed conflict, and the most important single thing we can do is first of all to be sure that it will not lead to armed conflict.

Then and only then can other matters causing tension between the parties in the Taiwan area and the Far East be hopefully discussed.

It is not suggested that either of us should renounce any policy objectives which we consider we are legitimately entitled to achieve, but only that we renounce the use of force to implement these policies.

Neither of us wants to negotiate under the threat of force. The free discussion of differences, and their fair and equitable solution, become impossible under the overhanging threat that force may be resorted to when one party does not agree with the other.

The United States as a member of the United Nations has agreed to refrain in its international relations from the threat or use of force. This has been its policy for many years and is its guiding principle of conduct in the Far East, as throughout the world.

The use of force to achieve national objectives does not accord with accepted standards of conduct under international law.

The Covenant of the League of Nations, the Kellogg-Briand Treaties, and the Charter of the United Nations reflect the universal view of the civilized community of nations that the use of force as an instrument of national policy violates international law, constitutes a threat to international peace, and prejudices the interests of the entire world community.

There are in the world today many situations which tempt those who have force to use it to achieve what they believe to be legitimate policy objectives. Many countries are abnormally divided or contain what some consider to be abnormal intrusions. Nevertheless, the responsible governments of the world have in each of these cases renounced the use of force to achieve what they believe to be legitimate and even urgent goals.

It is an essential foundation and preliminary to the success of the dis-

414

cussions under Item 2 that it first be made clear that the parties to these discussions renounce the use of force to make the policies of either prevail over those of the other. That particularly applies to the Taiwan area.

The acceptance of this principle does not involve third parties, or the justice or injustice of conflicting claims. It only involves recognizing and agreeing to abide by accepted standards of international conduct.

We ask, therefore, as a first matter for discussion under Item 2, a declaration that your side will not resort to the use of force in the Taiwan area except defensively. The United States would be prepared to make a corresponding declaration. These declarations will make it appropriate for us to pass on to the discussion of other matters with a better hope of coming to constructive conclusions.

2. *Chinese Communist Draft Declaration on Renunciation of Force, October 27, 1955*

1. Ambassador Wang Ping-nan on behalf of the Government of the People's Republic of China and Ambassador U. Alexis Johnson on behalf of the Government of the United States of America jointly declare that,

2. In accordance with Article 2, Paragraph 3, of the Charter of the United Nations, "All members shall settle their international disputes by peaceful means in such a manner that international peace and security, and justice, are not endangered"; and

3. In accordance with Article 2, Paragraph 4 of the Charter of the United Nations, "All members shall refrain in their international relations from the threat or use of force against the territorial integrity or political independence of any state, or in any other manner inconsistent with the purposes of the United Nations";

4. The People's Republic of China and the United States of America agree that they should settle disputes between their two countries by peaceful means without resorting to the threat or use of force.

5. In order to realize their common desire, the People's Republic of China and the United States of America decide to hold a conference of Foreign Ministers to settle through negotiations the question of relaxing and eliminating the tension in Taiwan area.

3. *United States Draft Declaration on Renunciation of Force, November 10, 1955*

1. The Ambassador of the United States of America and the Ambassador of the People's Republic of China during the course of the discussions of practical matters at issue have expressed the determination that the differences between the two sides shall not lead to armed conflict.

2. They recognize that the use of force to achieve national objectives does not accord with the principles and purposes of the United Nations Charter or with generally accepted standards of international conduct.

3. They furthermore recognize that the renunciation of the threat or use of force is essential to the just settlement of disputes or situations which might lead to a breach of the peace.

4. Therefore, without prejudice to the pursuit by each side of its policies by peaceful means they have agreed to announce the following declarations:

5. Ambassador Wang Ping-nan informed Ambassador U. Alexis Johnson that:

6. In general, and with particular reference to the Taiwan area, the People's Republic of China renounces the use of force, except in individual and collective self-defense.

7. Ambassador U. Alexis Johnson informed Ambassador Wang Ping-nan that:

8. In general, and with particular reference to the Taiwan area, the United States renounces the use of force, except in individual and collective self-defense.

4. *Chinese Communist Draft Counterproposal for an Agreed Announcement, December 1, 1955*

1. Ambassador Wang Ping-nan, on behalf of the Government of the People's Republic of China, and Ambassador Alexis Johnson, on behalf of the Government of the United States of America, agree to announce:

2. The People's Republic of China and the United States of America are determined that they should settle disputes between their two countries through peaceful negotiations without resorting to the threat or use of force;

3. The two Ambassadors should continue their talks to seek practical and feasible means for the realization of this common desire.

5. *United States Revision of Chinese Communist December 1 Counterproposal, January 12, 1956*

1. Ambassador Wang Ping-nan, on behalf of the Government of the People's Republic of China, and Ambassador U. Alexis Johnson, on behalf of the Government of the United States of America, agree to announce:

2. The People's Republic of China and the United States of America are determined that they will settle disputes between them through peaceful means and that, without prejudice to the inherent right of indi-

vidual and collective self-defense, they will not resort to the threat or use of force in the Taiwan area or elsewhere.

3. The two Ambassadors should continue their talks to seek practical and feasible means for the realization of this common desire.

6. *United States Draft Proposal for Announcement of April 19, 1956*

1. Ambassador U. Alexis Johnson, on behalf of the Government of the United States of America, and Ambassador Wang Ping-nan, on behalf of the Government of the People's Republic of China, agree, without prejudice to the pursuit by each side of its policies by peaceful means or its inherent right of individual or collective self-defense, to announce:

2. The United States of America and the People's Republic of China are determined that they should settle disputes between their two countries through peaceful negotiations without resorting to the threat or use of force in the Taiwan area or elsewhere.

3. The two Ambassadors should continue their talks to seek practical and feasible means for the realization of this common desire.

7. *Chinese Communist Draft Counterproposal for an Agreed Announcement, May 11, 1956*

1. Ambassador Wang Ping-nan, on behalf on the Government of the People's Republic of China, and Ambassador U. Alexis Johnson, on behalf of the Government of the United States of America, agree, without prejudice to the principles of mutual respect for territorial integrity and sovereignty and non-interference in each other's internal affairs, to announce:

2. The People's Republic of China and the United States of America are determined that they should settle disputes between their two countries in the Taiwan area through peaceful negotiations without resorting to the threat or use of force against each other;

3. The two ambassadors should continue their talks to seek and to ascertain within two months practical and feasible means for the realization of this common desire, including the holding of a Sino-American conference of the foreign ministers, and to make specific arrangements.

*Prime Minister Chou En-lai's Letter
of August 2, 1963, to President Kennedy
and to All Heads of State,
Proposing General and Complete Disarmament*

Your Excellency,

The Chinese Government issued on July 31, 1963, a statement proposing a conference of the government heads of all countries of the world to discuss the question of complete, thorough, total and resolute prohibition and destruction of nuclear weapons. The text of the proposal reads as follows:

The Government of the People's Republic of China hereby proposes the following:

(1) All countries in the world, both nuclear and non-nuclear, solemnly declare that they will prohibit and destroy nuclear weapons completely, thoroughly, totally and resolutely. Concretely speaking, they will not use nuclear weapons, nor export, nor import, nor manufacture, nor test, nor stockpile them; and they will destroy all the existing nuclear weapons and their means of delivery in the world, and disband all the existing establishments for the research, testing and manufacture of nuclear weapons in the world.

(2) In order to fulfill the above undertakings step by step, the following measures shall be adopted first:

a. Dismantle all military bases, including nuclear bases, on foreign soil, and withdraw from abroad all nuclear weapons and their means of delivery.

b. Establish a nuclear weapon-free zone of the Asian and Pacific region, including the United States, the Soviet Union, China and Japan; a nuclear weapon-free zone of Central Europe; a nuclear weapon-free zone of Africa; and a nuclear weapon-free zone of Latin America. The countries possessing nuclear weapons shall undertake due obligations with regard to each of the nuclear weapon-free zones.

c. Refrain from exporting and importing in any form nuclear weapons and technical data for their manufacture.

d. Cease all nuclear tests, including underground nuclear tests.

(3) A conference of the government heads of all the countries of the

418

world shall be convened to discuss the question of the complete prohibition and thorough destruction of nuclear weapons and the question of taking the above-mentioned four measures in order to realize step by step the complete prohibition and thorough destruction of nuclear weapons.

In view of the urgent desire of the people of the world for the removal of the threat of nuclear war and for the safeguarding of the peace and security of the world, the Chinese Government earnestly hopes that its proposal will receive the favourable consideration and positive response of the Government of your country.

Please accept the assurances of my highest consideration.

CHOU EN-LAI
*Premier of the State Council of
the People's Republic of China*

August 2, 1963

APPENDIX E

Full Text of Ambassador Wang Kuo-chuan's
Main Statement at the 131st Meeting
of the Sino-American Talks, Rejecting American
Proposals on Vietnam and Bilateral Relations

I

Mr. Ambassador, today I would like first of all to speak on the question of Sino-U.S. relations.

(1) Throughout the past seventeen years the U.S. Government has all along pursued a policy of hostility and aggression with respect to China. This policy has met with the strongest condemnation by the Chinese people and the people of the world and has gone completely bankrupt. However, unreconciled to its failure, the U.S. Government is employing its counter-revolutionary dual tactics in every possible way in order to cover up its criminal acts of hostility against the Chinese people.

Of late, one U.S. official after another has indicated a wish for "reconciliation," "building a bridge" and entering into "peaceful cooperation" with China. The U.S. Government thinks that the Chinese people and the people of the world will be hoodwinked by these high-sounding words it has uttered. This is sheer wishful thinking. Armed with Mao Tse-tung's thought, the 700 million Chinese people neither fear intimidation by the United States nor believe in its lies. The ironclad facts in the past seventeen years, and particularly in the recent period, prove that the U.S. Government's talk about "easing" Sino-U.S. relations is not worth a penny.

(2) The U.S. Government's military provocation and war threats against China have not only never stopped, they have become more and more unbridled. Since the last meeting, U.S. military aircraft and warships have again intruded into China's airspace and territorial waters on many occasions. Against this, the Chinese Ministry of Foreign Affairs has served the 403rd-411th serious warnings on the U.S. Government. In the meantime, U.S. military aircraft have repeatedly harassed and attacked Chinese merchant ships and fishing boats on the high seas. On May 28, U.S. military aircraft wildly attacked Chinese fishing boats engaged in fishing in the high seas fishing area of the Bac Bo Gulf, killing and

420

wounding as many as 21 Chinese fishermen. On August 29, U.S. military aircraft flagrantly attacked small Chinese cargo ships sailing along a normal route in the western part of the Bac Bo Gulf, sinking one Chinese cargo ship and damaging another and killing nine Chinese crew members and wounding seven. The Chinese Ministry of National Defence has made the strongest protest against the U.S. Government on this. The great Chinese people are not to be trifled with. The debts of blood incurred by the U.S. Government must be cleared and repaid. I am now instructed once again to address the most serious warning and the strongest protest to you and through you to the U.S. Government against its above-mentioned military provocations against China.

The U.S. Government is still occupying Chinese Territory, the province of Taiwan, by armed force and has increasingly turned it into a colony and military base. Not long ago, U.S. Secretary of State Dean Rusk personally went to Taiwan for secret talks with the Chiang Kai-shek gang to hatch criminal plots against the Chinese people. It was at this juncture that the Chiang Kai-shek gang clamored for "counter-attack on the mainland." The forcible occupation of the Chinese province of Taiwan by the U.S. Government absolutely cannot be tolerated by the Chinese people. The recent scheming activities of U.S. Secretary of State Dean Rusk in Taiwan have further aroused the boundless indignation of the Chinese people. I am now instructed to reaffirm that the Chinese people are determined to liberate Taiwan and that the U.S. Government must withdraw all its armed forces from Taiwan and the Taiwan Straits.

The U.S. Government's invasion and occupation of Taiwan not only cannot be tolerated by the liberated Chinese people but also can under no circumstances be tolerated by their compatriots in the Chinese territory of Taiwan still under U.S. occupation. Taiwan is an inalienable part of Chinese territory.The strong desire of our compatriots in Taiwan to return to the embrace of their motherland is certain to be attained and can never be repressed. The U.S. Government's attempt to employ the small handful of Chiang Kai-shek's gang to prevent our compatriots in Taiwan from realizing their aspirations is doomed to ignominious failure.

For a long time, the U.S. Government has set up military bases around China and rigged up military blocs. Furthermore, it is now energetically tightening its military encirclement of China. Recently, it summoned some of its vassals in Asia and the Pacific region, including the Chiang Kai-shek gang, for a meeting in Seoul, in an attempt to organize a new military alliance directed against China. Immediately afterwards, it collaborated with the Soviet revisionist leading clique and Japanese militarism in plotting a new "Holy Alliance" against communism, against the people, against revolution and against China. The U.S. Government's attempt to encircle China is futile. The Chinese people who hold high the banner of opposition to U.S. imperialism will never be encircled. It is definitely not China, but the United States, which has been besieged ring upon ring by the people of the whole world. The Chinese people are confident that together with the oppressed peoples and nations of Asia, Africa, Latin America and the rest of the world, they can thoroughly smash any scheme of the U.S. Government for aggression, and are determined to do so.

The U.S. Government's clamor for the establishment of a military encirclement of China is by no means a new trick. Didn't Japanese militarism formerly give much publicity to the "Greater East Asia Co-prosperity Sphere" and play the trick of making "Asians fight Asians"? The U.S. Government's machination is merely something it has picked up from the garbage heap of Japanese militarism. The purpose of the U.S. Government in all this is to oppose China and at the same time to subject the entire Asian people to aggression and enslavement. The people of China and Asia will never be duped by you.

(3) What the U.S. Government has done to China irrefutably proves that the U.S. Government does not have the slightest sincerity about easing Sino-U.S. relations. On the contrary, it is carrying out its policies of hostility and aggression against China with redoubled efforts, shifting the centre of gravity of its global strategy eastward and regarding the Chinese people as its main enemy.

Twenty years ago, Chairman Mao Tse-tung, the great leader of the Chinese people, put forward his brilliant thesis that imperialism and all reactionaries are paper tigers. We would like to take this opportunity to warn the U.S. Government: The Chinese people have already had trials of strength with you and we know full well what you are capable of. We have made preparations. Should you dare to impose a war on the Chinese people, we will surely take you on and keep you company to the end.

Mr. Ambassador, the affairs of any country in the world should be managed by its people themselves. Asian affairs should be managed by the Asian people themselves and definitely not by the United States. U.S. aggression against Asia can only arouse the broad and resolute resistance of the Asian people. In coming to Asia to perform its so-called duty, the United States will only run against a brick wall and have itself badly battered. It is now high time that the U.S. Government should realize this point. The U.S. aggressors must get out of Taiwan and the Taiwan Straits. They must get out of Asia.

II

Mr. Ambassador, I would now like to make some comments on the U.S. Government's expansion of its war of aggression against Vietnam.

(1) Make trouble, fail, make trouble again, fail again...till their doom; that is the logic of the imperialists and all reactionaries the world over in dealing with the people's cause. The U.S. Government will never go against this logic in its actions in Vietnam.

Since the last meeting, the U.S. Government has flagrantly extended its bombing of the Democratic Republic of Vietnam to Hanoi, the capital of Vietnam, and Haiphong, its important harbor, carrying out the most despicable and most shameless war blackmail against the Democratic Republic of Vietnam and pushing its war of aggression against Vietnam to a new and still graver stage. At the same time, the U.S. Government has increased the number of its aggressor troops in southern Vietnam to over 300,000 and with increasing vigour pursued its scorched earth policy of "burn all, kill all, destroy all" against the south Vietnamese people. Furthermore, the U.S. Government has instigated its south Vietnamese puppets, the Thai reactionaries and the Laotian Rightists to make military provocations against Cambodia and launch frantic attacks on the liberated areas of Laos in its attempt to spread the flames of war to the whole of Indo-China.

The U.S. Government has done its utmost to make trouble in Vietnam, but all it gains or can gain is the most disgraceful failure. U.S. pirate planes have been dealt head-on blows over northern Vietnam by the heroic Vietnamese people. The U.S. aggressor troops have been badly beaten in southern Vietnam. The U.S. aggressors have suffered defeats at the hands of the Vietnamese people and are foredoomed to failure in Vietnam.

It is a pity that the U.S. Government has failed to draw the lessons and become a bit cleverer. Like a gambler, the more it loses, the more desperate and reckless it becomes. All indications show that the U.S. Government is speeding up recruitment and preparing to increase its aggressor troops in Vietnam to 400,000, 500,000 or even 750,000. In a word, it is still trying to save itself from defeat by means of war expansion.

But history has always proved merciless to the aggressor. The more the U.S. Government expands the war, the more disastrous will be its defeat. Each time the U.S. Government suffers a defeat, it escalates the war; and each time it escalates the war, it suffers a correspondingly heavier defeat. The U.S. Government has been inescapably caught in a vicious circle in Vietnam.

(2) In order to maintain their rule and carry out expansion abroad, reactionary ruling classes have always resorted to the dual tactics of butcher-like suppression and priest-like deception. This is exactly what the U.S. Government has been doing in Vietnam.

Each time the U.S. Government throws a faggot into the flames of war in Vietnam, it always follows this up with a prayer for peace. Recently, while widening the war the U.S. Government has spread another smokescreen of "peace talks" with the collaboration of the Soviet revisionist leading clique and reactionaries in various countries. They plead energetically for "de-escalation" of the Vietnam war. They loudly advocate a settlement of the Vietnam question on the basis of the Geneva agreements.

The heroic and long-tested Vietnamese people are neither to be cowed nor to be duped. However glibly the U.S. Government talks and however actively the Soviet revisionist leading clique lends you its supporting voice, the Vietnamese people will never believe that a treaty on paper alone will make U.S. imperialism lay down its butcher's knife and suddenly become a Buddha or behave a little better. They have exposed the U.S. peace talk swindles one after another.

As everyone knows, escalation or de-escalation, the U.S. war against Vietnam is a war of aggression. The crux of the Vietnam question at present is absolutely not the gradual de-escalation of the war, but the immediate and complete withdrawal of the U.S. aggressors from southern Vietnam. The U.S. Government can never succeed in its scheme of "forcing peace talks through bombing." As everyone knows, the Geneva agreements were torn to shreds by the U.S. Government long ago. The attempt to use the Geneva agreements to tie the hands of the people of Vietnam, China and the whole world will never succeed.

The U.S. Government's peace talks swindle has already been discredited, and is bound to be thoroughly discredited. The U.S. Government will never be able to obtain at the conference table what it has failed to obtain on the battlefield. By playing its counterrevolutionary dual tactics, the U.S. Government absolutely cannot deceive the Vietnamese people and the people of the world; on the contrary, it will only further reveal its sinister features before the whole world.

(3) The Vietnamese people's struggle against U.S. aggression and for national salvation is a just one; it has won the firm support of the people throughout the world and is sure to be victorious. The Vietnamese people's war is an iron bastion which it is impossible, and absolutely impossible, for any force on earth to smash.

On July 17, President Ho Chi Minh of the Democratic Republic of Vietnam issued an Appeal in which he solemnly declared: "Johnson and his clique should realize this: They may bring in 500,000 troops, one million or even more to step up the war of aggression in south Vietnam. They may use thousands of aircraft for intensified attacks against north Vietnam. But never will they be able to break the iron will of the heroic Vietnamese people to fight against U.S. aggression, for national salvation. . . . The war may still last 5, 10, 20 years or longer. Hanoi, Haiphong and other cities, and enterprises may be destroyed, but the Vietnamese people will not be intimidated! Nothing is more precious than independence and freedom." This sublime and heroic declaration of President

Ho Chi Minh's is the most powerful answer to the U.S. imperialist policy of war blackmail.

The Chinese people most warmly and most resolutely support the Appeal of President Ho Chi Minh of the Democratic Republic of Vietnam and firmly support the Vietnamese people in carrying the fight through to the end until not a single American soldier remains on the sacred soil of Vietnam and final victory is won in the war of resistance against U.S. aggression and for national salvation. The Chinese Government has time and again solemnly stated that U.S. imperialist aggression against Vietnam is aggression against China. The 700 million Chinese people provide powerful backing for the Vietnamese people. The vast expanse of China's territory is the reliable rear area of the Vietnamese people. In order to support the Vietnamese people in winning thorough victory in the war of resistance against U.S. aggression, the Chinese people are ready to undertake maximum national sacrifices.

The Chinese people mean what they say. If you underestimate the strong determination of the Chinese people to support the Vietnamese people in carrying the fight through to the end and if you underestimate the actions which the Chinese people will take to this end, then you will be committing a grave historical blunder and will find it too late to repent.

Notes

Chapter 1

1. *The New York Times*, July 11, 1956.
2. Same, April 22, 1964.
3. *U.S. News and World Report*, Vol. LXI, No. 1, July 4, 1966.
4. *The New York Times*, March 2, 1961.

Chapter 2

1. *The New York Times*, December 11, 1953.
2. Same.
3. Same, December 13, 1953.
4. Same.
5. Same, January 12, 1954.
6. Same.
7. Dwight D. Eisenhower, *Mandate for Change, 1953–1956* (New York: Doubleday and Company, 1963), p. 353.
8. Anthony Eden, *Full Circle* (Boston: Houghton Mifflin Company, 1960), p. 98.
9. Same, p. 99.
10. Edgar Snow, *The Other Side of the River* (New York: Random House, 1961), pp. 94–95.
11. Eden, cited, pp. 130, 136–137.
12. *The New York Times*, May 27, 1954.
13. Same, May 30, 1954.
14. *Department of State Bulletin*, Vol. XXX, No. 782, June 21, 1954, p. 950.
15. *The New York Times*, August 12, 1954.
16. *Department of State Bulletin*, Vol. XXXII, No. 814, January 31, 1955, p. 191.
17. *The New York Times*, January 29, 1955.
18. *Department of State Bulletin*, Vol. XXXII, No. 816, February 14, 1955, p. 253.
19. *The New York Times*, February 5, 1955.
20. Same, March 1, 1955.
21. *The New York Times*, March 1, 1966.
22. *Department of State Bulletin*, Vol. XXXII, No. 825, April 18, 1955, p. 643.
23. *People's China*, No. 10, May 16, 1955, Supplement; *The New York Times*, April 24, 1955.
24. *Department of State Bulletin*, Vol. XXXII, No. 827, May 2, 1955, p. 738.

25. *The New York Times,* April 24, 1955.
26. Same, April 26, 1955.
27. Same.
28. Paul E. Zinner, ed., *Documents on American Foreign Relations, 1955* (New York: Harper, for the Council on Foreign Relations, 1956), p. 310.
29. *The New York Times,* April 28, 1955.
30. *People's China,* No. 12, June 16, 1955, Supplement, p. 6.
31. *The New York Times,* May 31, 1955.
32. Same, June 11, 1955.
33. Same, May 31, 1955.
34. Same, June 29, 1955.
35. Same, July 22, 1955.
36. Same, July 23, 1955.
37. Eden, cited, p. 343.
38. Same, p. 345.
39. Zinner, cited, p. 312.
40. Same, p. 311.
41. *Department of State Bulletin,* Vol. XXXIII, No. 841, August 8, 1955, pp. 219–220.
42. Same, pp. 220–221.
43. Same.
44. *The New York Times,* August 2, 1955.
45. See Karl Lott Rankin, *China Assignment* (Seattle: University of Washington Press, 1964), pp. 246–253.
46. *The New York Times,* July 25, 1955, and July 27, 1955.
47. Same, July 28, 1955.
48. *People's China,* No. 16, August 16, 1955, pp. 3–8.
49. *The New York Times,* August 2, 1955.
50. *Department of State Bulletin,* Vol. XXXIII, No. 842, August 15, 1955, pp. 260–262.
51. Same, p. 262.
52. Rankin, cited.

Chapter 3

1. Robert B. Ekvall, *The Faithful Echo* (New York: Twayne Publishers, 1960), p. 87.
2. *The New York Times,* August 1, 1955.
3. *The New York Herald Tribune,* August 3, 1955.
4. Same, August 5, 1955.
5. *The New York Times,* August 5, 1955.
6. Ekvall, cited, p. 88.
7. *Department of State Bulletin,* Vol. XXXIII, No. 844, August 29, 1955, pp. 341–342.
8. *The New York Herald Tribune,* August 20, 1955.
9. Letter of October 6, 1961, to Edgar Snow from Joseph A. Yager, quoted in full in Edgar Snow, *The Other Side of the River* (New York: Random House, 1962), pp. 753–755.

10. *The New York Times*, September 13, 1955.
11. *Department of State Bulletin*, Vol. XXXIII, No. 848, September 26, 1955, p. 492.
12. Same, p. 489.
13. Same.
14. *The New York Times*, September 16, 1955.
15. *People's China*, No. 18, September 16, 1955, pp. 40–41.
16. *The New York Times*, September 20, 1955.
17. Same, September 21, 1955.
18. *Department of State Bulletin*, Vol. XXXIII, No. 851, October 17, 1955, p. 606.
19. *The New York Times*, October 4, 1955.
20. Same, October 9, 1955.
21. Same, October 15, 1955.
22. *People's China*, No. 21, November 1, 1955, p. 41.
23. *Department of State Bulletin*, Vol. XXXIII, No. 853, October 31, 1955, pp. 689–690.
24. Same, No. 860, December 19, 1955, p. 1008.
25. *New China News Agency*, December 15, 1955.
26. *Department of State Bulletin*, Vol. XXXIII, No. 861, December 26, 1955, pp. 1049–1050.
27. *The New York Times*, January 7, 1956.
28. *Department of State Bulletin*, Vol. XXXIV, No. 865, January 23, 1956, p. 125.
29. See full text in *The New York Times*, January 19, 1956.
30. *Department of State Bulletin*, Vol. XXXIV, No. 866, January 30, 1956, p. 166.
31. *People's China*, No. 3, February 1, 1956, Supplement.
32. Same, No. 4, February 16, 1956, Supplement, p. 7.
33. Two examples are in Same, No. 3, February 1, 1956, and No. 8, April 16, 1956.
34. *The New York Times*, March 5, 1956, and March 7, 1956; and *Department of State Bulletin*, Vol. XXXIV, No. 873, March 19, 1956, p. 451.
35. *People's China*, No. 7, April 1, 1956, p. 19.
36. *The New York Herald Tribune*, May 25, 1956.
37. *The New York Times*, June 3, 1956, and June 5, 1956.
38. Department of State *Bulletin*, Vol. XXXVI, No. 921, February 18, 1957, pp. 261–263.
39. *Department of State Bulletin*, Vol. XXXIV, No. 887, June 25, 1956, p. 1070.
40. *People's China*, No. 16, August 16, 1956, pp. 11–15.
41. *Department of State Bulletin*, Vol. XXXV, No. 902, October 8, 1956, p. 553.
42. *The New York Times*, December 10, 1956.
43. *The New York Herald Tribune*, December 31, 1956.
44. *The New York Times*, January 26, 1957.
45. Same, January 20, 1957.
46. Same, January 30, 1957.
47. Same, February 2, 1957.
48. Same, February 6, 1957.

49. Same, February 15, 1957.
50. Same, February 7, 1957.
51. San Francisco speech of June 28, 1957, in *Department of State Bulletin,* Vol. XXXVII, No. 942, July 15, 1957, pp. 91–95.
52. Same, No. 949, September 2, 1959, p. 390.
53. Same, No. 965, December 23, 1957, p. 1000.
54. *Peking Review,* No. 8, April 22, 1958, p. 6.
55. *The New York Times,* November 6, 1958.
56. Snow, cited, pp. 89–91.
57. *The New York Times,* March 6, 1961.
58. *The New York Times,* January 29, 1964.

Chapter 4

1. See *The New York Times,* February 17, 1955, and March 19, 1955; Paul E. Zinner, ed., *Documents on American Foreign Relations, 1955* (New York: Harper, for the Council on Foreign Relations, 1956), pp. 309–310; Department of State *Bulletin,* Vol. XXXIII, No. 842, August 15, 1955, pp. 260–262.
2. *The New York Times,* November 8, 1955.
3. Same, November 9, 1955.
4. Same, November 11, 1955.
5. Same, January 19, 1956, and *People's China,* No. 3, February 1, 1956, Supplement.
6. *The New York Times,* January 7, 1956.
7. Same, January 19, 1956.
8. *Department of State Bulletin,* Vol. XXXIV, No. 866, January 30, 1956, p. 165.
9. Same, pp. 165–166.
10. Same, No. 867, February 6, 1956, pp. 195, 198.
11. *People's China,* No. 3, February 1, 1956, Supplement.
12. *The New York Times,* March 5, 1956.
13. *Department of State Bulletin,* Vol. XXXIV, No. 873, March 19, 1956, p. 451.
14. *People's China,* No. 4, February 16, 1956, Supplement, pp. 1–16.
15. Same, No. 5, March 1, 1956, p. 44.
16. *Department of State Bulletin,* Vol. XXXIV, No. 887, June 25, 1956, p. 1070.
17. *The New York Times,* June 13, 1956.
18. Same.
19. Same, June 2, 1956.
20. Same.
21. Same, June 13, 1956.
22. *Department of State Bulletin,* Vol. XXXIV, No. 887, June 25, 1956, pp. 1070–1071.
23. Same.
24. Same, Vol. XXXV, No. 894, August 13, 1956, p. 278.
25. *People's China,* No. 14, July 16, 1956, Supplement, p. 11.
26. Same, Supplement, p. 12.
27. Same, No. 19, October 1, 1956, Supplement, p. 48.

28. Same, No. 16, August 16, 1956, p. 13.
29. Same, No. 20, October 16, 1956, p. 39.
30. Karl Rankin, *China Assignment* (Seattle: University of Washington Press, 1964), p. 251.
31. Same, p. 250.
32. *Department of State Bulletin*, Vol. XXXVII, No. 942, July 15, 1957, p. 92.
33. Edgar Snow, *The Other Side of the River* (New York: Random House, 1961), p. 91.

Chapter 5

1. *The New York Times*, August 7, 1956.
2. *Department of State Bulletin*, Vol. XXXV, No. 895, August 20, 1956, pp. 313–314.
3. *The New York Times*, August 8, 9, and 20, 1956.
4. *The New York Times*, August 8, and 9, 1956.
5. Same, August 12, 1956.
6. Same, August 21, 1956.
7. Same, August 24, 1956.
8. Same.
9. Same, September 1, 1956.
10. *Department of State Bulletin*, Vol. XXXV, No. 902, October 8, 1956, p. 553.
11. *New China News Agency*, statement of September 21, 1956, quoted in *The New York Times*, September 22, 1958.
12. Same, October 16, 1956.
13. *Department of State Bulletin*, Vol. XXXV, No. 906, November 5, 1956, p. 718.
14. *The New York Times*, November 28, 1956.
15. Same, December 10, 1956.
16. Same, December 25, 1956.
17. Same, December 27, 1956.
18. *Department of State Bulletin*, Vol. XXXVI, No. 916, January 14, 1957, p. 54.
19. *The New York Times*, January 30, 1957.
20. *Department of State Bulletin*, Vol. XXXVI, No. 922, February 25, 1957, pp. 301, 305.
21. *The New York Times*, February 21, 1957.
22. *The New York Times*, February 15, 1957.
23. *Department of State Bulletin*, Vol. XXXVI, No. 930, April 22, 1957, pp. 665–666.
24. Same, p. 646.
25. Same, No. 933, May 13, 1957, p. 769.
26. Same, No. 936, June 3, 1957, p. 897.
27. *The New York Times*, July 19, 1957.
28. Same, August 10, 1957, and *Department of State Bulletin*, Vol. XXXVII, No. 949, September 2, 1957, pp. 392–393.
29. *The New York Times*, August 13, 1957.

30. *Department of State Bulletin*, Vol. XXXVII, No. 950, September 9, 1957, pp. 420–421.
31. Same, No. 950, July 15, 1957, p. 95.
32. Same, No. 951, September 16, 1957, p. 460.
33. Same, pp. 461–462.
34. *The New York Times*, September 2, 1957.
35. *The New York Herald Tribune*, September 5, 1957.
36. *The Christian Science Monitor*, September 5, 1957.
37. *The New York Herald Tribune*, September 9, 1957.
38. *The New York Times*, August 26, 1957.
39. Same, September 8, 1957.
40. Same, September 13, 1957.
41. Same.
42. Same, September 15, 1957, and September 17, 1957.
43. Same, September 28, 1957.
44. *Department of State Bulletin*, Vol. XXXVII, No. 965, December 23, 1957, pp. 999–1000.
45. *The New York Times*, December 13, 1957.

Chapter 6

1. *Peking Review*, Vol. I, No. 19, July 8, 1958, pp. 21–22.
2. *The New York Times*, July 3, 1958, and July 16, 1958.
3. Same, September 14, 1958, for the full text of the State Department statement on the Ambassadorial Talks.
4. *Peking Review*, No. 24, August 12, 1958, pp. 6–7.
5. *The New York Times*, August 12, 1958.
6. *Department of State Bulletin*, Vol. XXXIX, No. 1002, September 8, 1958, pp. 385–390.
7. *Peking Review*, No. 25, August 19, 1958, pp. 6–11.
8. Donald S. Zagoria, *The Sino-Soviet Conflict, 1956–61* (Princeton: Princeton University Press, 1962), p. 210.
9. Dwight D. Eisenhower, *Waging Peace: 1956–61* (New York: Doubleday, 1965), Chapter XII, pp. 292–304, reveals some of the President's thoughts and actions in the Formosa Crisis.
10. Same, Appendix O, pp. 691–693.
11. Same, p. 296.
12. John R. Thomas, "Soviet Behavior in the Quemoy Crisis of 1958," *Orbis*, Vol. VI, No. 1, Spring 1962, p. 41.
13. *The New York Times*, August 28, 1958.
14. Same, August 29, 1958.
15. *The Current Digest of the Soviet Press*, Vol. X, No. 35, October 8, 1958, pp. 16–17.
16. *The New York Times*, September 5, 1958.
17. *The Current Digest of the Soviet Press*, Vol. X, No. 36, October 15, 1958, p. 9.
18. *Department of State Bulletin*, Vol. XXXIX, No. 1004, September 22, 1958, pp. 445–446.

19. *The New York Times,* September 5, 1958.
20. Same, September 6, 1958.
21. *Peking Review,* No. 28, September 9, 1958, pp. 15-16.
22. Same, p. 16.
23. *Department of State Bulletin,* Vol. XXXIX, No. 1004, September 22, 1958, pp. 446-447.
24. Paul E. Zinner, ed., *Documents on American Foreign Relations, 1958* (New York: Harper, for the Council on Foreign Relations, 1959), pp. 443-452.
25. Soviet radio broadcast of September 9, 1958, quoted in Thomas, cited, p. 45.
26. *The New York Times,* September 9, 1958.
27. *Peking Review,* No. 29, September 16, 1958, p. 4.
28. *Department of State Bulletin,* Vol. XXXIX, No. 1005, September 29, 1958, pp. 488, 492.
29. Same, pp. 483-484.
30. Same, p. 499.
31. *The New York Times,* September 13, 1958.
32. Same, September 14, 1958.

Chapter 7

1. *Department of State Bulletin,* Vol. XXXIX, No. 1009, November 3, 1958, p. 682; *The New York Times,* September 16, 1958, September 18, 1958; *Peking Review,* Vol. I, No. 30, September 23, 1958, pp. 7-9.
2. *Peking Review,* Vol. I, No. 30, September 23, 1958, pp. 7-9.
3. *The New York Times,* September 19, 1958.
4. *Department of State Bulletin,* Vol. XXXIX, No. 1006, October 6, 1958, p. 526; *The New York Times,* September 20, 1958.
5. *The New York Times,* September 20, 1958.
6. Same, September 21, 1958.
7. *Peking Review,* Vol. I, No. 32, October 7, 1958, p. 4; and Vol. I, No. 33, October 14, 1958, p. 4.
8. *Department of State Bulletin,* Vol. XXXIX, No. 1006, October 6, 1958, pp. 530-531.
9. Secretary of the Air Force on September 27th announced that the United States was prepared to use nuclear weapons in the defense of Quemoy. *The New York Times,* September 28, 1958.
10. *Peking Review,* Vol. I, No. 30, September 23, 1958, pp. 5, 6.
11. *The New York Times,* September 21, 1958.
12. Same.
13. Same, September 23, 24, 26, 1958; *Peking Review,* Vol. I, No. 31, September 30, 1958, p. 26.
14. *The New York Times,* September 25, 1958.
15. *Department of State Bulletin,* Vol. XXXIX, No. 1007, October 13, 1958, pp. 561-66; *The New York Times,* September 26, 1958.
16. *Washington Post,* September 26, 1958; *The New York Times,* September 28, 1958.

17. *The New York Times,* September 27, 1958.
18. Same, September 30, 1958.
19. Same, September 29, 1958.
20. Same, October 1, 1958.
21. *Department of State Bulletin,* Vol. XXXIX, No. 1009, October 27, 1958, p. 653.
22. *The New York Times,* October 11, 1958.
23. *Department of State Bulletin,* Vol. XXXIX, No. 1008, October 20, 1958, pp. 597–604.
24. *Peking Review,* Vol. I, No. 32, October 7, 1958, pp. 10–11.
25. *Current Digest of the Soviet Press,* Vol. X, No. 40, November 12, 1958, p. 18.
26. *The New York Times,* October 5, 1958.
27. *Peking Review,* Vol. I, No. 32, October 7, 1958, p. 1.
28. *The New York Times,* October 8, and 9, 1958; *Peking Review,* Vol. I, No. 30, October 14, 1958, pp. 9, 10.
29. *The New York Times,* October 10, 1958.
30. Same, October 11, 1958.
31. Same, October 14, 1958.
32. *Department of State Bulletin,* Vol. XXXIX, No. 1010, November 3, 1958, pp. 685–686.
33. *The New York Times,* October 15 and 16, 1958.
34. Same, November 2, 1958.

Chapter 8

1. *Department of State Bulletin,* Vol. XXXIX, No. 1014, December 1, 1958, p. 878.
2. Same, Vol. XXXIX, No. 1015, December 8, 1958, p. 902.
3. Same, Vol. XXXIX, No. 1017, December 22, 1958, p. 991–992.
4. Same, Vol. XL, No. 1024, February 9, 1959, p. 185.
5. Same, Vol. XL, No. 1025, February 16, 1959, p. 222.
6. Same, Vol. XL, No. 1029, March 16, 1959, p. 376.
7. Same, Vol. XL, No. 1032, April 6, 1959, p. 477.
8. For this personal sketch of Dulles' attitude and reaction during the Taiwan crisis, see Andrew Berding, *Dulles on Diplomacy* (Princeton: Van Nostrand, 1965), p. 61. Berding was Assistant Secretary of State for Public Affairs and in daily contact with Dulles during the crisis and its aftermath. Not many studies and biographies of John Foster Dulles so far published pay sufficient attention to the Taiwan crisis or give nearly enough credit to his effective diplomacy and strategy. See also Richard Goold-Adams, *The Time of Power: A Reappraisal of John Foster Dulles* (London: Weidenfeld and Nicolson, 1962); John R. Beal, *John Foster Dulles, 1888–1959* (New York: Harper, 1959); Roscoe Drummond, *The Duel at the Brink* (Garden City, New York: Doubleday, 1960). *John Foster Dulles: The Last Year,* by Eleanor Lansing Dulles (New York: Harcourt, Brace and World, 1963), is the only biographical study to give some analysis

to Dulles' negotiating ideas and tactics in this crisis. (See pages 169–184.)

9. *Peking Review*, Vol. II, No. 16, April 21, 1959, p. 27.

10. V. P. Dutt, *China's Foreign Policy, 1958–62* (Bombay: Asia Publishing House, 1964), p. 40.

11. Edgar Snow, cited, p. 634.

12. All of the following studies highlight the sequence of Soviet moves in conjunction with the Ambassadorial Talks: Donald S. Zagoria, *The Sino-Soviet Conflict—1956–1961* (Princeton: Princeton University Press, 1962); O. Edmund Clubb, *Twentieth Century China* (New York: Columbia University Press, 1964); David Floyd, *Mao Against Khrushchev* (New York: Frederick A. Praeger, 1964); Tibor Mende, *China and Her Shadow* (New York: Coward-McCann, 1962); Alice Langley Hsieh, *Communist China's Strategy in the Nuclear Era* (Englewood Cliffs, New Jersey: Prentice-Hall, Inc., 1962); Morton H. Halperin, *China and the Bomb* (New York: Frederick A. Praeger, 1965); William E. Griffith, *The Sino-Soviet Rift* (Cambridge, Mass.: The M.I.T. Press, 1964); Alexander Dallin, *Diversity in International Communism* (New York: Columbia University Press, 1963); Harry Schwartz, *Tsars, Mandarins and Commissars* (Philadelphia: Lippincott, 1964); John R. Thomas, "Soviet Behavior in the Quemoy Crisis of 1958," *Orbis*, Vol. VI, No. 1; Tang Tsou, *The Embroilment over Quemoy: Mao, Chiang and Dulles* (Salt Lake City: University of Utah Press, 1959); Klaus Mehnert, *Peking and Moscow* (New York: Putnam, 1963); G. F. Hudson, Richard Lowenthal, and Roderick MacFarquhar, *The Sino-Soviet Dispute* (New York: Frederick A. Praeger, 1961); Robert Elegant, *The Center of the World* (Garden City, New York: Doubleday, 1964); Tang Tsou, "Mao Tse-tung and Peaceful Coexistence," *Orbis*, Vol. VIII, No. 1, Spring 1964; John R. Thomas, "Sino-Soviet Relations After Khrushchev and Mao," *Orbis*, Vol. VII, No. 3, Fall 1963; O. Edmund Clubb, "Sino-American Relations and the Future of Formosa," *Political Science Quarterly*, March 1965.

13. *Peking Review*, Vol. VI, No. 36, September 6, 1963, p. 13.

14. *Soviet News*, No. 4896, September 23, 1963, p. 162.

15. Thomas, cited.

16. Zagoria, cited, p. 217; Thomas, cited, p. 41.

17. *Peking Review*, Vol. VI, No. 36, September 6, 1963, p. 13.

18. *Department of State Bulletin*, Vol. XLI, No. 1045, July 6, 1959, p. 9.

Chapter 9

1. *Department of State Bulletin*, Vol. XL, No. 1037, May 11, 1959, pp. 673–674.

2. *The New York Times*, May 20, 1959.

3. *London Times*, May 19, 1959.

4. *The New York Times*, May 20, 1959.

5. *Department of State Bulletin*, Vol. XLI, No. 1066, November 30, 1959, p. 787.

6. *Current Digest of the Soviet Press*, Vol. XI, No. 39, October 28, 1959, pp. 21, 22.

7. *Peking Review*, Vol. VI, No. 36, September 6, 1963, p. 13.

8. Zagoria, cited, p. 279.

9. *Peking Review*, Vol. VI, No. 36, September 6, 1963, p. 13.

10. *Documents on American Foreign Relations*, edited by Paul E. Zinner (New York: Harper, Inc., for the Council on Foreign Relations, 1960), pp. 442–447.

11. Floyd, cited, p. 265.

12. *The New York Times*, March 23, 1960.

13. Floyd, cited, p. 269.

14. *The New York Times*, May 3, 1960.

15. *The New York Times*, June 6, 1960.

16. *Department of State Bulletin*, Vol. XLIII, No. 1109, September 26, 1960, pp. 497–498.

17. *Peking Review*, Vol. III, No. 24, June 14, 1960, p. 13; Floyd, cited, p. 275. Klaus Mehnert, *Peking and Moscow* (New York: G.P. Putnam's Sons, 1963), p. 435; Floyd, cited, p. 281.

18. Snow, cited, p. 281.

19. Same, pp. 91–92.

20. Dutt, cited, p. 25.

21. *Department of State Bulletin*, Vol. XLIII, No. 1109, September 26, 1960, pp. 497–499.

22. Same.

23. Same, pp. 471–472; *The New York Times*, September 9, 1960.

24. *The New York Times*, September 14, 1960, p. 11.

25. Zagoria, cited, pp. 357–358; Floyd, cited, pp. 287–288.

26. G.F. Hudson, Richard Lowenthal, and Roderick MacFarquhar, eds., *The Sino-Soviet Dispute* (New York: Praeger, 1961), p. 161 and p. 222.

27. *Peking Review*, Vol. IV, No. 4, January 27, 1961, p. 7.

28. Tang Tsou and Morton H. Halperin, "Mao Tse-tung's Revolutionary Strategy and Peking's International Behavior," *The American Political Science Review*, Vol. LIX, March 1965, pp. 80–99. I am much indebted to this article for the use of the "Work Correspondence." They have since been translated in full and issued by the Hoover Institution at Stanford. See *The Politics of the Chinese Red Army: A Translation of the Bulletin of Activities of the People's Liberation Army*, edited by J. Chester Chang (Stanford, California: The Hoover Institution on War, Revolution and Peace, 1966).

29. *Public Papers of the Presidents of the United States: John F. Kennedy, 1961*, p. 15.

30. Same, p. 38.

31. *The New York Times*, March 6, 1961.

32. *The New York Times*, March 9, 1961.

33. *Public Papers of the Presidents of the United States: John F. Kennedy, 1961*, p. 159.

34. *Department of State Bulletin*, Vol. XLIV, No. 1135.

35. *The New York Times*, March 14, 1961; Klaus Mehnert, cited, p. 425.

36. *Public Papers of the Presidents of the United States: John F. Kennedy, 1961*, p. 436.

37. Same.

Chapter 10

1. Theodore C. Sorenson, *Kennedy* (New York: Harper & Row, 1965), p. 642.
2. *Public Papers of the Presidents of the United States: John F. Kennedy, 1961*, p. 658.
3. *The New York Times,* June 27, 1962; Sorensen, cited, p. 747.
4. *Public Papers of the Presidents of the United States: John F. Kennedy, 1962*, p. 509.
5. *The New York Times,* September 21, 1962.
6. *Public Papers of the Presidents of the United States: John F. Kennedy, 1962*, p. 850-851.
7. Same, p. 887.
8. Same, pp. 898, 900.
9. Same, 1963, p. 93.
10. Same, pp. 507-508.
11. Same, p. 604.
12. Same, p. 614.
13. Same, p. 616.
14. *Peking Review,* Vol. VI, No. 33, August 16, 1963, p. 15.
15. Same, Vol. VI, No. 32, August 9, 1963, pp. 11, 13.
16. Same, pp. 34-35.
17. Same, Vol. VI, No. 33, August 16, 1963, p. 12.
18. Same, Vol. VI, No. 36, September 6, 1963, and No. 37, September 13, 1963.
19. *The New York Times,* August 8, 1963.
20. Same, September 12, 1963.
21. *Public Papers of the Presidents of the United States: John F. Kennedy, 1963*, pp. 845-846.
22. Morton H. Halperin, *China and the Bomb* (New York: Praeger, 1965), p. 92. For text of Peking's statement on its nuclear test see *The New York Times,* October 17, 1964.
23. *The New York Times,* October 19, 1964.
24. Same, October 24, 1964.
25. Same, November 26, and December 31, 1964.
26. *Peking Review,* Vol. VII, No. 44, October 30, 1964, pp. 6, 7; No. 48, November 27, 1964.
27. *Department of State Bulletin,* Vol. LII, No. 1344, March 29, 1965, pp. 451-452.
28. Same, Vol. LIV, No. 1392, February 28, 1966, p. 316.
29. *The New York Times,* May 10, 1966.
30. *Peking Review,* Vol. IX, No. 21, May 20, 1966, p. 17.
31. *The New York Times,* May 12, 1966.
32. *Department of State Bulletin,* Vol. LIV, No. 1406, June 6, 1966, pp. 884-885.
33. *The New York Times,* June 3, 1966.
34. *Washington Post,* June 4, 1966.
35. *Peking Review,* Vol. IX, No. 26, June 24, 1966, pp. 27, 28.
36. Same, No. 8, February 19, 1965, pp. 5-6; and No. 9, February 26, 1965, pp. 4, 11-12.
37. *The New York Times,* February 25, 1965; *Department of State Bulletin,* Vol. LII, No. 1342, March 15, 1965, p. 364.
38. *The New York Times,* April 22, 1965; *Peking Review,* Vol. VIII, No. 1, April 23, 1965; No. 17, April 23, 1965; and No. 76, pp. 14-16.

39. *The New York Times*, July 1, 1965.
40. Same, September 16, 1965; *Washington Post*, September 15, 1966.
41. *Newsweek*, November 29, 1965.
42. *The New York Times*, December 16, 1966; *Peking Review*, Vol. IX, No. 4, January 21, 1966.
43. *Washington Post* and *The New York Times*, March 17, 1966.
44. *The New York Times*, June 3, 1966, and June 22, 1966; *The Baltimore Sun*, June 30, 1966.
45. *U.S. News and World Report*, July 4, 1966.
46. *Peking Review*, No. 33, August 12, 1966, p. 31; see also the *Washington Post* and *The New York Times* of July 29, 1966, for American press accounts of this Sino-Soviet exchange regarding the Ambassadorial Talks.
47. *The New York Times*, November 28, 1966; English translation of the full text of this editorial was made available by the Soviet Mission to the United Nations.
48. *Washington Post*, December 21, 1966; also the Russian text of this article in the *Literary Gazette* available to the author.
49. *The Peking Review*, No. 7, February 10, 1967, p. 30–31.
50. *The New York Times*, January 26, 1967.

Chapter 11

1. *The New York Times*, August 8, 1963.
2. Same.
3. *The New York Times*, December 14, 1963.
4. *Department of State Bulletin*, Vol. LII, No. 1344, March 29, 1965, pp. 449–453.
5. *The New York Times*, December 16, 1965, and February 15, 1966.
6. *Department of State Bulletin*, Vol. LIV, No. 1386, January 17, 1966, p. 90.
7. Same, Vol. LIV, No. 1392, February 28, 1966, p. 317.
8. *The New York Times*, March 17, 1966, and April 15, 1966.
9. *United States Policy With Respect to Mainland China*, Hearings Before the Committee on Foreign Relations, United States Senate, 89th Congress, 2nd Session, March 8–30, 1966; and *United States Policy Toward Asia*, Hearings Before the Subcommittee on the Far East and the Pacific of the Committee on Foreign Affairs, House of Representatives, 89th Congress, 2nd Session, January 25–February 3, 1966.
10. *The New York Times*, March 14, 1966.
11. *Department of State Bulletin*, Vol. LIV, No. 1398, April 11, 1966.
12. Same, Vol. LIV, No. 1401, May 2, 1966, pp. 686–695.
13. *The New York Times*, April 15, 1966.
14. Same, June 9, 1966.
15. *The New York Post*, June 27, 1966.
16. *The New York Times*, June 17, 1966.
17. Same, July 15, 1966.
18. Same, July 13, 1966.
19. Same, July 21, 1966.
20. *Weekly Compilation of Presidential Documents*, Monday, September 12, 1966, p. 1234.
21. The author has collected this information on unofficial and private efforts to break the "travel barrier" from interviews with many private American sources who wish to remain unidentified.

22. *The New York Times*, July 22, and August 12, 1966.
23. Same, December 15, 1963, February 20, 1964, March 15, 1966.
24. *Peking Review*, No. 14, April 1, 1966; *Washington Post*, March 30, 1966; *The New York Times*, March 30, 1966.
25. *Peking Review*, No. 15, April 8, 1966, p. 69.
26. *The New York Times*, April 17, 1966.
27. *New York Herald Tribune*, April 19, 1966.
28. *Peking Review*, No. 20, May 13, 1966, p. 5; *The New York Times*, May 10, 1966.
29. *The New York Times*, August 14, 1966.
30. *The New York Times*, September 7, 8, 27, 1966; See also Franz Schurmann's "What is Happening in China," in *The New York Review*, October 20, 1966.
31. *The New York Times*, December 11, 1966.
32. *Department of State for the Press*, No. 106, May 7, 1966.
33. *The New York Times*, September 9, 1966.
34. *Washington Post*, September 9, 1966; *The New York Times*, September 8, 1966.
35. *Department of State Bulletin*, Vol. LVI, No. 1440, January 30, 1967, p. 162.
36. *The New York Times*, January 17, 1967; *The Washington Post*, January 20, 1967; *The New York Times*, January 20, and 26, 1967.
37. See A. Doak Barnett, *China After Mao* (Princeton: Princeton University Press, 1967), p. 66.
38. *The New York Times*, May 19, 1967.
39. Same, April 21, and 30, 1967.

Chapter 12

1. Robert P. Newman, *Recognition of Communist China?* (New York: Macmillan, 1961), p. 130.
2. Ernest A. Gross, "Some Illusions of our Asian Policy," *Far Eastern Survey*, Vol. XXVI, December 1957.
3. *U.S. Policy with Respect to Mainland China*, Hearings Before the Committee on Foreign Relations, U.S. Senate, 89th Congress, 2nd Session, March 8–30, 1966, p. 72.
4. *The New York Times*, May 12, 1966.
5. *United States Policy Toward Asia*, Hearings Before the Subcommittee on the Far East and the Pacific of the Committee on Foreign Affairs, House of Representatives, 89th Congress, 2nd Session, p. 534.
6. Mark Mancall, "The Persistence of Tradition in Chinese Foreign Policy," *The Annals of the American Academy of Political and Social Science*, Vol. 349, September 1963; Immanuel C. Y. Hsu, *China's Entrance into the Family of Nations: The Diplomatic Phase, 1858–1880* (Cambridge: Harvard University Press, 1960); Masataka Banno, *China and the West, 1858–1861: The Origins of the Tsungli Yamen* (Cambridge: Harvard University Press, 1964).
7. *The New York Times*, April 17, 1966.

Chapter 13

1. Myra Roper, *China—The Surprising Country* (New York: Doubleday and Co., 1966), p. 116; *Peking Review*, Vol. VI, No. 52, December 27, 1963, p. 14.

2. *The New York Times*, April 9, 1964; same, July 30, 1964.

3. *Peking Review*, Vol. VII, No. 27, July 3, 1964, p. 8.

4. *The New York Times*, Oct. 29, 1964.

5. *New Statesman*, Vol. LXIX, No. 1776, March 26, 1965, p. 477. The entire text of the interview with Chou En-lai is in Appendix E of K. S. Karol's *China, The Other Communism* (New York: Hill and Wang, 1967), pp. 448-453.

6. *Department of State Bulletin*, Vol. L, No. 1290, March 16, 1964, p. 395.

7. Same, Vol. LIV, No. 1398, April 11, 1966, p. 565.

8. *United States Policy Toward Asia*, Hearings before the Subcommittee on the Far East and the Pacific of the Committee on Foreign Affairs, House of Representatives, 89th Congress, 2nd Session, p. 526.

9. *Department of State Bulletin*, Vol. LIV, No. 1392, February 28, 1966, pp. 315-316.

10. *The Current Digest of the Soviet Press*, Vol. XVIII, No. 38, October 12, 1966, p. 8

11. *Washington Post*, April 30, 1965.

12. *St. Louis Globe-Democrat*, April 14, 1966.

13. *The New York Times*, November 28, 1966; *Peking Review*, No. 47, November 18, 1966, "Another Deal Between the Two Nuclear Overlords, The United States and the Soviet Union."

14. *The Chicago Daily News* and the *Daily Times* (Mamaroneck, New York), of May 16, and 18, 1967, carried articles of Simon Malley, a correspondent for various Asian and African newspapers at the United Nations. (It should be noted that the Chinese Foreign Ministry in Peking officially denied that any Chinese leaders received Mr. Malley, which he, in turn, has refuted. *The New York Times* and the *Washington Post*, May 17, 1967. Malley, according to the *Post*, was the first American newsman admitted to mainland China since Edgar Snow's visit in early 1965, but Peking apparently allowed his visit by the somewhat irregular procedure of issuing him a "detachable entry permit" rather than by stamping a visa on his United States passport. In any case, Mr. Malley informally confirmed his reports on Peking's attitudes toward the Ambassadorial Talks in a telephone conversation with the author on May 19, 1967.)

Chapter 14

1. O. Edmund Clubb, *20th Century China* (New York: Columbia University Press, 1964), pp. 413-414, 423.

2. Chow Ching-wen, *Ten Years of Storm* (New York: Holt, Rinehart and Winston, 1960), pp. 274-275.

3. *Staffing Procedures and Problems in Communist China: A Study Submitted by the Subcommittee on National Security Staffing and Operations to the Committee on Government Operations*, U.S. Senate, 88th Congress, 1st Session (Washington: U.S. Government Printing Office, 1963).

Donald W. Klein, "Peking's Evolving Ministry of Foreign Affairs," *The China Quarterly*, No. 4, October-December 1960, pp. 28-39.

John W. Lewis, *Leadership in Communist China* (Ithaca, N.Y.: Cornell University Press, 1963), pp. 191-203.

Conrad Brandt, Benjamin Schwartz and John K. Fairbank, *A Documentary History of Chinese Communism* (Cambridge: Harvard University Press, 1962), pp. 318-343.

4. Tung Chi-Ping as told to Quentin Reynolds, "Red China," *Look* Magazine, Vol. 28, No. 24, December 1, 1964, p. 25.
5. *U.S. News and World Report*, July 4, 1966.
6. *The New York Times*, September 16, 1965.
7. O. Edmund Clubb, "Sino-American Relations," *Diplomat* Magazine, Vol. XVII, No. 196, September 1966, p. 67.
8. Mark Mancall, cited, p. 16.
9. Charles Taylor, *Reporter in Red China* (New York: Random House, 1966), p. 79.
10. John K. Fairbank, *The United States and China* (Cambridge: Harvard University Press, rev. ed., 1958), p. 316.
11. Masataka Banno, *China and the West, 1858–1861* (Cambridge: Harvard University Press, 1964), p. 221.
12. C. P. Fitzgerald, *The Chinese View of their Place in the World* (London: Oxford University Press, 1964), p. 71.
13. Robert Guillain, *When China Wakes* (New York: Walker and Company, 1965), p. 183.
14. Ssu-Yu Teng and John K. Fairbank, *China's Response to the West* (Cambridge: Harvard University Press, 1954), pp. 37–42.
15. Masataka Banno, cited.
16. Taylor, cited, pp. 50–67, 204.
17. A. M. Halpern, ed., *Policies Toward China* (New York: McGraw-Hill, for the Council on Foreign Relations, 1965).
18. K. M. Panikkar, *The Principles and Practice of Diplomacy* (Bombay: Asia Publishing House, 1956), p. 99.
19. *Peking Review*, Vol. VII, No. 28, July 10, 1964.
20. Same, No. 15, April 8, 1966, p. 69.
21. Amaury de Riencourt, *The Soul of China* (New York: Harper and Row, 1965), p. 79; Derk Bodde, "Harmony and Conflict in Chinese Philosophy," in Arthur F. Wright, ed., *Studies in Chinese Thought* (Chicago: University of Chicago Press, 1953), pp. 27–36.
22. H. Arthur Steiner, "Mainsprings of Chinese Communist Foreign Policy," *American Journal of International Law*, Vol. 44, No. 1, January 1950, p. 99.
23. *The New York Times*, December 22, 1953.
24. *Department of State Bulletin*, Vol. XLVIII, No. 1235, February 25, 1963, p. 277.
25. Tang Tsou, *America's Failure in China, 1941–1950* (Chicago: University of Chicago Press, 1963); Harold Isaacs, *Scratches on Our Minds* (New York: The John Day Co., 1958); A. T. Steele, *The American People and China* (New York: McGraw-Hill Book Company, for the Council on Foreign Relations, 1966).
26. A. T. Steele, cited, p. 22.
27. *The New York Times*, July 17, 1966.
28. John K. Fairbank, "New Thinking About China," *China: The People's Middle Kingdom and the U.S.A.* (Cambridge: Harvard University Press, 1967), p. 102.
29. Chang Hsin-Hai, *America and China: A New Approach to Asia* (New York: Simon and Schuster, 1965), pp. 237–238, 246–247, 258.
30. Harold R. Isaacs, "Old Myths and New Realities," *Diplomat* Magazine, Vol. XVII, No. 196, pp. 43.
31. Winston Churchill, *The Second World War, Vol. 4: The Hinge of Fate* (Boston: Houghton Mifflin Co., 1950), p. 133.
32. A. T. Steele, cited, pp. 53–54.

33. Robert S. Elegant, *The Center of the World* (Garden City, N.Y.: Doubleday and Co., Inc., 1964), p. 371.
34. A. T. Steele, cited, pp. 94–103, 229–236.
35. Mark Gayn, "To Mao We Are the Prime Enemy," *The New York Times Magazine*, October 24, 1965, p. 182; Arthur A. Cohen in *The Communism of Mao Tse-tung* (Chicago: University of Chicago Press, Phoenix Edition, 1966), pp. 200–202, outlines Mao's convictions and policies of enmity and hatred toward the United States.
36. Myra Roper, *China—The Surprising Country* (Garden City: Doubleday and Co., Inc. 1966), pp. 223–240.
37. Charles Taylor, cited, p. 81. See Hans Koningsberger's *Love and Hate in China* (New York: The New American Library, Signet Books, 1966), p. 78, 83; also see Hugo Portisch *Red China Today* (New York: Fawcett World Library, 1967), p. 337–338.
38. C. P. Fitzgerald, "Chinese Foreign Policy," Ruth Adams, ed., in *Contemporary China* (New York: Pantheon Books, 1966), p. 24.
39. Tang Tsou, cited, p. 579.
40. John K. Fairbank, *The United States and China*, cited, p. 309.
    For a detailed analysis, the reader is referred to Franz Schurmann's *Ideology and Organization in Communist China* (Berkeley: University of California Press, 1966); Harold C. Hinton's *Communist China in World Politics* (Boston: Houghton, Mifflin Co., 1966); Robert S. Elegant's *The Center of the World*, cited; A. Doak Barnett's *Communist China and Asia* (New York: Harper, for Council on Foreign Relations, 1960); and R.G. Boyd's *Communist China's Foreign Policy* (New York: Praeger, 1962).
41. Mao Tse-tung, *Selected Works, Vol. V* (New York: International Publishers, 1962), p. 428.
42. John W. Lewis, *Major Doctrines of Communist China* (New York: W. W. Norton & Co.), p. 89.
43. *Peking Review*, Vol. IX, No. 44, October 28, 1966, p. 7.
44. Same, Vol. VIII, No. 41, October 8, 1965, p. 14.
45. William E. Griffith, *The Sino-Soviet Rift* (Cambridge: The M.I.T. Press, 1964), pp. 275–276.
46. Same, p. 481.
47. *The New York Times*, March 24, 1966, and August 14, 1966.
48. *Peking Review*, Vol. IX, No. 47, November 18, 1966.
49. Franz Schurmann, *Ideology and Organization in Communist China* (Berkeley: University of California Press, 1966), p. 44.
50. Robert Payne, *Portrait of a Revolutionary: Mao Tse-tung* (New York: Abelard-Schuman, rev. ed., 1961), p. 277. Cohen, cited, describes Mao's thought as tedious, unoriginal, childish, and platitudinous.
51. Mark Gayn, "Peking Has a Yenan Complex," *The New York Times Magazine*, January 30, 1966. See also Mark Gayn, "Mao Tse-tung Reassessed," a working paper for the China Conference (Chicago, February 8–12, 1966), in Franz Schurmann and Orville Schell, eds., *Communist China: Revolutionary Reconstruction and International Confrontation, 1949 to the Present* (New York: Random House, Vintage Books, 1967), p. 92–108.
52. J. Chester Chang, ed., *The Politics of the Chinese Red Army* (Stanford: The Hoover Institution on War, Revolution and Peace, 1966), pp. 480–2.
53. William E. Griffith, cited, pp. 276, 386.
54. Same, pp. 488–489.
55. *Peking Review*, Vol. IX, No. 35, August 26, 1966.
56. J. Chester Chang, cited, p. 486.

Chapter 15

1. Thomas C. Schelling, *The Strategy of Conflict* (Cambridge: Harvard University Press, 1960).
2. Mao Tse-tung, *Selected Works*, cited.
3. E. L. Katzenbach, Jr., and Hanrahan, G. Z., "The Revolutionary Strategy of Mao Tse-tung," reprint from *Political Science Quarterly*, September 1955.
4. A. M. Halpern, "The Influence of Revolutionary Experience on Communist China's Foreign Outlook," in Werner Klatt, ed., *The Chinese Model* (Hong Kong: Hong Kong University Press, 1965), p. 152.
5. Arthur H. Dean, "What It's Like to Negotiate with the Chinese," *The New York Times Magazine*, October 30, 1966.
6. *People's China*, No. 14, July 16, 1956, Supplement, p. 12.
7. J. Chester Chang, cited, p. 481.

Chapter 16

1. See Lucian W. Pye, "China in Context," *Foreign Affairs*, Vol. 45, No. 2, January 1967, pp. 229–245.
2. Quoted from the *Milwaukee Journal* in *The New York Times*, May 15, 1966, p. E 15.
3. John K. Fairbank, "New Thinking About China," in his *China: The People's Middle Kingdom and the U.S.A.* (Cambridge: Harvard University Press, 1967), p. 101.
4. W. A. C. Adie, "Some Chinese Attitudes," *International Affairs*, April 1966, p. 243.

Index

[Note: *Unless otherwise specified, the adjective "Chinese" applies to the Chinese Communists.*]

457

PUBLICATIONS

FOREIGN AFFAIRS (quarterly), edited by Hamilton Fish Armstrong.

THE UNITED STATES IN WORLD AFFAIRS (annual). Volumes for 1931, 1932 and 1933, by Walter Lippman and William O. Scroggs; for 1934–1935, 1936, 1937, 1938, 1939 and 1940, by Whitney H. Shepardson and William O. Scroggs; for 1945–1947, 1947–1948 and 1948–1949, by John C. Campbell; for 1949, 1950, 1951, 1952, 1953 and 1954, by Richard P. Stebbins; for 1955, by Hollis W. Barber; for 1956, 1957, 1958, 1959, 1960, 1961, 1962 and 1963, by Richard P. Stebbins; for 1964, by Jules Davids; for 1965 and 1966 by Richard P. Stebbins.

DOCUMENTS ON AMERICAN FOREIGN RELATIONS (annual). Volume for 1952 edited by Clarence W. Baier and Richard P. Stebbins; for 1953 and 1954 edited by Peter V. Curl; for 1955, 1956, 1957, 1958 and 1959 edited by Paul E. Zinner; for 1960, 1961, 1962 and 1963 edited by Richard P. Stebbins; for 1964 by Jules Davids; for 1965 and 1966 by Richard P. Stebbins.

POLITICAL HANDBOOK AND ATLAS OF THE WORLD (annual), edited by Walter H. Mallory.

FROM ATLANTIC TO PACIFIC: A New Interocean Canal, by Immanuel J. Klette (1967).

AFRICAN ECONOMIC DEVELOPMENT (Revised Edition), by William A. Hance (1967).

TITO'S SEPARATE ROAD: America and Yugoslavia in World Politics, by John C. Campbell (1967).

U.S. TRADE POLICY: New Legislation for the Next Round, by John W. Evan (1967).

TRADE LIBERALIZATION AMONG INDUSTRIAL COUNTRIES: Objectives and Alternatives, by Bela Balassa (1967).

THE CHINESE PEOPLE'S LIBERATION ARMY, by Brig. General Samuel B. Griffith II U.S.M.C. (ret.) (1967).

THE ARTILLERY OF THE PRESS: Its Influence on American Foreign Policy, by James Reston (1967).

ATLANTIC ECONOMIC COOPERATION: The Case of the O.E.C.D., by Henry G. Aubrey (1967).

TRADE, AID AND DEVELOPMENT: The Rich and Poor Nations, by John Pincus (1967).

BETWEEN TWO WORLDS: Policy, Press and Public Opinion on Asian-American Relations, by John Hohenberg (1967).

THE CONFLICTED RELATIONSHIP: The West and the Transformation of Asia, Africa and Latin America, by Theodore Geiger (1966).

THE ATLANTIC IDEA AND ITS EUROPEAN RIVALS, by H. van B. Cleveland (1966).

EUROPEAN UNIFICATION IN THE SIXTIES: From the Veto to the Crisis, by Miriam Camps (1966).

THE UNITED STATES AND CHINA IN WORLD AFFAIRS, by Robert Blum, edited by A. Doak Barnett (1966).

THE FUTURE OF THE OVERSEAS CHINESE IN SOUTHEAST ASIA, by Lea A. Williams (1966).

THE CONSCIENCE OF THE RICH NATIONS: The Development Assistance Committee and the Common Aid Effort, by Seymour J. Rubin (1966).

ATLANTIC AGRICULTURAL UNITY: Is it Possible?, by John O. Coppock (1966).

TEST BAN AND DISARMAMENT: The Path of Negotiation, by Arthur H. Dean (1966).

COMMUNIST CHINA'S ECONOMIC GROWTH AND FOREIGN TRADE, by Alexander Eckstein (1966).

POLICIES TOWARD CHINA: Views from Six Continents, edited by A. M. Halpern (1966).

THE AMERICAN PEOPLE AND CHINA, by A. T. Steele (1966).

INTERNATIONAL POLITICAL COMMUNICATION, by W. Phillips Davison (1965).

MONETARY REFORM FOR THE WORLD ECONOMY, by Robert V. Roosa (1965).

AFRICAN BATTLELINE: American Policy Choices in Southern Africa, by Waldemar A. Nielsen (1965).

NATO IN TRANSITION: The Future of the Atlantic Alliance, by Timothy W. Stanley (1965).

ALTERNATIVE TO PARTITION: For a Broader Conception of America's Role in Europe, by Zbigniew Brzezinski (1965).

THE TROUBLED PARTNERSHIP: A Re-Appraisal of the Atlantic Alliance, by Henry A. Kissinger (1965).

REMNANTS OF EMPIRE: The United Nations and the End of Colonialism, by David W. Wainhouse (1965).

THE EUROPEAN COMMUNITY AND AMERICAN TRADE: A Study in Atlantic Economics and Policy, by Randall Hinshaw (1964).

THE FOURTH DIMENSION OF FOREIGN POLICY: Educational and Cultural Affairs, by Phillip H. Coombs (1964).

AMERICAN AGENCIES INTERESTED IN INTERNATIONAL AFFAIRS (Fifth Edition), compiled by Donald Wasson (1964).

JAPAN AND THE UNITED STATES IN WORLD TRADE, by Warren S. Hunsberger (1964).

FOREIGN AFFAIRS BIBLIOGRAPHY, 1952–1962, by Henry L. Roberts (1964).

THE DOLLAR IN WORLD AFFAIRS: An Essay in International Financial Policy, by Henry G. Aubrey (1964).

ON DEALING WITH THE COMMUNIST WORLD, by George F. Kennan (1964).

FOREIGN AID AND FOREIGN POLICY, by Edward S. Mason (1964).

THE SCIENTIFIC REVOLUTION AND WORLD POLITICS, by Caryl P. Haskins (1964).

AFRICA: A Foreign Affairs Reader, edited by Philip W. Quigg (1964).

THE PHILIPPINES AND THE UNITED STATES: Problems of Partnership, by George E. Taylor (1964).

SOUTHEAST ASIA IN UNITED STATES POLICY, by Russell H. Fifield (1963).

UNESCO: ASSESSMENT AND PROMISE, by George N. Shuster (1963).

THE PEACEFUL ATOM IN FOREIGN POLICY, by Arnold Kramish (1963).

THE ARABS AND THE WORLD: Nasser's Arab Nationalist Policy, by Charles D. Cremeans (1963).

TOWARD AN ATLANTIC COMMUNITY, by Christian A. Herter (1963).

THE SOVIET UNION, 1922–1962: A Foreign Affairs Reader, edited by Philip E. Mosley (1963).

THE POLITICS OF FOREIGN AID: American Experience in Southeast Asia, by John D. Montgomery (1962).

SPEARHEADS OF DEMOCRACY: Labor in the Developing Countries, by George C. Lodge (1962).

LATIN AMERICA: Diplomacy and Reality, by Adolf A. Berle (1962).

THE ORGANIZATION OF AMERICAN STATES AND THE HEMISPHERE CRISIS, by John C. Dreier (1962).

THE UNITED NATIONS: Structure for Peace, by Ernest A. Gross (1962).

THE LONG POLAR WATCH: Canada and the Defense of North America, by Melvin Conant (1962).

ARMS AND POLITICS IN LATIN AMERICA (Revised Edition), by Edwin Lieuwen (1961).

THE FUTURE OF UNDERDEVELOPED COUNTRIES: Political Implications of Economic Development (Revised Edition), by Eugene Staley (1961).

SPAIN AND DEFENSE OF THE WEST: Ally and Liability, by Arthur P. Whitaker (1961).

SOCIAL CHANGE IN LATIN AMERICA TODAY: Its Implications for United States Policy, by Richard N. Adams, John P. Gillin, Allan R. Holmberg, Oscar Lewis, Richard W. Patch, and Charles W. Wagley (1961).

FOREIGN POLICY: THE NEXT PHASE: The 1960s (Revised Edition), by Thomas K. Finletter (1960).

DEFENSE OF THE MIDDLE EAST: Problems of American Policy (Revised Edition), by John C. Campbell (1960).

COMMUNIST CHINA AND ASIA: Challenge to American Policy, by A. Doak Barnett (1960).

FRANCE, TROUBLED ALLY: De Gaulle's Heritage and Prospects, by Edgar S. Furniss, Jr. (1960).

THE SCHUMAN PLAN: A Study in Economic Cooperation 1950–1959, by William Diebold, Jr. (1959).

SOVIET ECONOMIC AID: The New Aid and Trade Policy in Underdeveloped Countries, by Joseph S. Berliner (1958).

NATO AND THE FUTURE OF EUROPE, by Ben T. Moore (1958).

INDIA AND AMERICA: A Study of Their Relations, by Phillips Talbot and S. L. Poplai (1958).

NUCLEAR WEAPONS AND FOREIGN POLICY, by Henry A. Kissinger (1957).

MOSCOW-PEKING AXIS: Strength and Strains, by Howard L. Boorman, Alexander Eckstein, Philip E. Mosely, and Benjamin Schwartz (1957).

RUSSIA AND AMERICA: Dangers and Prospects, by Henry L. Roberts (1956).